Fragments of Our Time

Fragments of Our Time

MEMOIRS OF A DIPLOMAT

Martin J. Hillenbrand

The University of Georgia Press · *Athens & London*

Published by the University of Georgia Press
Athens, Georgia 30602
© 1998 by Martin J. Hillenbrand
Designed by Walton Harris
Set in 10 on 13 pt. Sabon by G & S Typesetters, Inc.
Printed and bound by Braun-Brumfield, Inc.

The paper in this book meets the guidelines for
permanence and durability of the Committee on
Production Guidelines for Book Longevity of the
Council on Library Resources.

Printed in the United States of America
02 01 00 99 98   C   5 4 3 2 1

Library of Congress Cataloging in Publication Data

Hillenbrand, Martin Joseph, 1915–
Fragments of our time : memoirs of a diplomat /
Martin J. Hillenbrand.
p.   cm.
Includes bibliographical references (p.
and index.
ISBN 0-8203-2016-1 (alk. paper)
1. Hillenbrand, Martin Joseph, 1915–
2. Ambassadors—United States—Biography.
3. Diplomats—United States—Biography.
4. United States—Foreign relations—20th
century.   I. Title.
E748.H57A3   1998
327.73′092—dc21   98-3853

British Library Cataloging in Publication Data available

For my wife, Faith,
and children, Ruth, David and John

Contents

Preface

· ·

Why does one write memoirs? It could be because in the course of a long life one has had many interesting experiences that seem to deserve description and preservation. Or it could be that one has been in a position to observe and even to participate in important decisions and events that have shaped the history of our time. Or it could be partly an ego trip, a somewhat overblown feeling that what one has done must necessarily be of interest to others. I suppose there is a little of all three motives in my case, perhaps in most cases. In any event, I finally undertook this project about which I had thought much but from which I have always been diverted by more immediate and presumably more urgent tasks, and other writings.

Unlike some writers of memoirs, I do not pretend to have apparent total recall of my childhood and teens but only of bits and pieces. I shall pass over my first twenty years or so, lightly drawing on them only when seemingly relevant to what came later. When one looks back over more than a half century of adult life and tries to reconstruct the main events in which one has participated, the past can appear more kaleidoscopic than coherent. Fortunately, I have kept a journal during much of my many years as an official, more or less faithfully, and I have not hesitated to refer to it when necessary to refresh my memory. On the whole my recollections of main events and personalities are reasonably clear and, I believe, accurate.

As an American Foreign Service officer beginning in 1939, I have been stationed sequentially in Switzerland, Washington, Burma, India, Washington, Mozambique, Germany, Washington after a year at Harvard for postdoctoral studies in economics, Paris, Berlin, Washington, Germany, Hungary, Washington, and again Germany. Among the senior positions I have held were U.S. political adviser in West Berlin; director of the Office of German Affairs in the Department of State as well as deputy director and then director of the Berlin Task Force; minister and deputy chief of mission in Bonn; ambassador to Hungary; assistant secretary of state for European affairs; and finally ambassador to the Federal Republic of Germany. I have been fortunate from the beginning (without regard to the old Chinese curse "May you live in interesting times") to have been in countries and cities when interesting and frequently historically significant things were happening there. This luck, wedded to a curious and inquisitive mind, has prompted what I hope are more than random reflections on the course of history in our troubled century and at least some of the men, great or less great, who have contributed to the making of that history. The philosophy that I have developed and honed through a lifetime of observation and participation will, I trust, emerge as my account proceeds.

Important as it may be, I have never thought that the politics of a country is all that need concern the practicing diplomat. Interest in the principal cultural and intellectual currents, and of course economic trends, within one's country and region of assignment is an essential ingredient of the kind of comprehensive understanding and appreciation without which any approach is likely to be both narrow and unbalanced. Overspecialization at the cost of distorted perspective is bad for the practicing diplomat despite all the latter-day injunctions that we have against the generalists. Area and linguistic specialization by all means but within a broad framework of understanding! How could I argue otherwise. After five years in Asia and Africa, I have since 1946, whether in Washington or abroad, been essentially involved in the affairs of Europe.

Even after retirement from the Foreign Service at the end of 1976, I spent more than 5½ years in Paris as director general of the Atlantic Institute for International Affairs—an international research organization— and since returning to the United States in 1982 have served at the University of Georgia as Dean Rusk Professor of International Relations, for seven years as director of the Center for Global Policy Studies and since 1987 as codirector of the Center for East-West Trade Policy (now the Center for International Trade and Security).

Given this background of diplomacy, research, and teaching, there is a story to tell. There is no ghost writer or collaborator. It will not be the first book I have written, and commitments to supply chapters to other collected works on various topics have provided constant distraction. The time had come, I felt, to concentrate on memoirs that make at least some contribution to understanding the era through which my generation has lived. A country of special fascination for me as paradigmatic (a word academics love to use) of so many good and bad things in our century has been Germany. A number of postwar assignments there beginning in 1946, several tours in Washington with responsibility for German affairs, and a strong continuing interest in a troublesome but gifted people and culture may, I hope, ensure against the superficiality of the casual observer.

An inevitable concomitant of memoirs is a seemingly excessive use of the first person singular. Given the nature of the genus and the fact that it purports to be a personal record, I see no escaping this necessary evil. At least it makes for declarative sentences in the active voice; it also avoids the need for circumlocutions like "It is believed that."

For the statistically minded, I have served as a diplomat under seven presidents and nine secretaries of state. Some I have come to know reasonably well. The interplay of people and events, of decision making and ineluctable external causation that constitutes the historical process, is fraught with both personal tragedy and achievement. Things never quite work out as we would wish. Chance, unforeseen interventions, the unpredictable behavior of others, and the sheer momentum of onrushing events can sweep aside the best-laid calculations. Sometimes when our leaders achieve a desired result, the gain is hollow or sets an unexpected and negative chain of causation in motion. Overshadowing everything is the essentially ephemeral nature of all that people can do. They can construct buildings that endure for centuries, but policies tend to pass with those who conceived them, or they are redefined into their opposites. Yet within all this flux, certain individuals and the principles they espoused do show enduring qualities. To comprehend the paradox of the abiding amid the transient is the task of both the philosopher and the historian. The experience of our century can provide rich material in this context for the questing mind.

It is impossible to thank everyone by name who over the years has made some contribution, either by word or deed, to these memoirs. My wife, Faith, and children, Ruth, David, and John, have been a constant source of encouragement. Many Foreign Service colleagues whose friendship and collaboration I have shared have made a unique contribution. Finally, graduate assistants like Liam Anderson, Cassady Craft, Scott Elder, and Seema Gahlaut provided needed help, while masters of the word processor like Peggy Bales, Jennifer Sherrock, Trey Taylor, and Ashley Bell made a reasonably error-free final manuscript possible.

Fragments of Our Time

1

On Growing Up

. . . .

       As already said, I am not one of those autobiographical writers who claim almost complete recall of their childhood years. This chapter about growing into manhood will therefore be mercifully brief. I was born in Youngstown, Ohio, on August 1, 1915—an event that set no bells ringing. Ohio is a splendid heartland state, but my connection with it until college proved fragmentary. My parents quickly took me (at the age of three months) to Chicago, which, allowing for some considerable traveling during preschool years, became my hometown. This early move has sometimes created an identification problem for those introducing me as a speaker; they are never sure whether to label me an Ohioan or a Chicagoan. In terms of time spent in each place, I am clearly the latter. A construction superintendent specializing in by-product coke ovens (an integral part of the classical steel mill complex), my father went from job to job, and place to place, for the Koppers Company of Pittsburgh. Given the huge steel complex in South Chicago, Hammond, and Gary along the lake shore, which demanded ever more coke ovens, Chicago seemed a logical place eventually to settle the family. I do recall, however, accompanying my father and living in such scattered places as Allentown, Baltimore, Birmingham (Alabama), and Germany before definitely settling in Chicago to enter grammar school—all of this early movement perhaps an omen of the peregrinating existence I was to lead as a diplomat.

       I cannot postulate an unhappy childhood as an excuse for later defects of character or performance. My parents were loving, and we lived in reasonably good circumstances. If I had any complaint, it was that my father was absent too much on construction jobs outside the Chicago area. Despite its reputation as the center of gangsterism, the stalking ground of Al Capone and the locus of the St. Valentine's Day Massacre, the Windy City provided a good environment during the 1920s for many of us in which to grow up. Our home was in a mixed middle-class neighborhood on the northwest side, part Irish, part German, and part Jewish, but the city still contained many pure ethnic neighborhoods, appropriately named, for example, Little Italy or Bavarian Heaven. Chicago was alive with a mixture of economic optimism, artistic creativity, great musical performances, and dynamic, if sometimes rough, journalism. It could also be a cruel city for those who were unable to compete and, as the Great Depression demonstrated, no more qualified than any other to cope with the human needs and displacements of that tragic era.

I developed an early attachment to competitive team sports, playing football, basketball, and baseball—an interest that has continued throughout life, if only as a spectator and connoisseur of relevant statistics. It has been one way an itinerant diplomat has avoided losing his roots. The American predilection for compiling batting averages, earned-run statistics, and data on yards gained and punted, baskets scored, and assists made has undoubtedly helped to keep a good memory for figures finely tuned. I have never had much use for the kind of intellectual snobbishness that scorns this sort of thing, nor for the self-constructed ivory towers that separate the intellectually pretentious from most Americans.

My participation in sports came with a price. Football brought a badly broken leg and basketball a serious streptococcus infection from a skinned knee that put me in the hospital and almost resulted in the amputation of my right leg. Other, more minor injuries were a matter of course. While I am sometimes bemused by the character-building claims of coaches and boosters of athletic involvement, particularly in our era of runaway professionalism, I would not want to deny that, even at my level of competence, it did contribute something valuable to my life. It was a simpler era, of course, when one did not have to be built like a modern-day Goliath to play football or basketball. Strangely enough, many years later, my good friend Dr. Wolfgang Stresemann, for an extended period intendant (general manager) of the Berlin Philharmonic Orchestra, who had spent the Hitler period in the United States, shared an interest with me in the American national game, and we engaged in what, I trust, was much knowledgeable talk.

I went through my period of weltschmerz fairly early. The mystery of the great urban complex that was Chicago evoked both wonder and pity. I can recall many lonely evenings spent on the clay hills along the Chicago Canal that provided a panoramic view over the northern part of the city (one could still walk about freely at night without fear of getting mugged). As I saw the many lights below me, I would reflect on the drama, the joys, the hopes, and the tragedies of the thousands of individual lives that those lights represented. In this mood of poetic and generalized empathy, I would slowly walk home. I was a great walker, and the sidewalks of Chicago provided an inexhaustible panorama of interesting things to observe.

Religious difficulties were a part of my troubled mood. At a particularly agitated time, by happy chance I came across Jacques Chevalier's biography of Blaise Pascal. This was my introduction to the life and thought of that stupendous seventeenth-century French genius, mathematician, physicist, inventor, philosopher, literary stylist, religious activist, and mystic. Reading his *Pensées* (at that time still in translation), I found his eloquent arguments more persuasive than those of any other writer. The profound logic of his wager has remained with me throughout the years, the necessity for making life choices between vastly disparate options in their ultimate consequences. Whenever I have needed intellectual refreshment, I have returned to the *Pensées* as an inexhaustible resource. Other writings that impressed me were the essays of G. K. Chesterton and Paul Claudel's lengthy and moving play *The Satin Slipper*. But as a teenager I was reading voraciously in a number of fields, and I became a well-known habitué of several branches of the Chicago Public Library. If they did not have what I wanted, there was always the main downtown library on Michigan Avenue or the Newberry Library off Chicago Avenue. I also read a great deal of poetry and wrote some that has mercifully been spared the world.

Despite all this Sturm und Drang, I had on the whole a reasonably active and happy adolescence. Apart from sports, scouting provided a major outlet. I found a good friend in Eddy Bobalek, of Slovak lineage, later to become professor of chemistry at the University of Maine and a respected scientist. Together we went swimming in Lake Michigan, took long walks, attended ball games at Cubs' Park, and, above all, collaborated in acquiring merit badges. I can remember our frantic quest of bugs, cyanide jars in hand, as we wandered through the woods. Our objective was the Insect Life merit badge, one of the most difficult in the panoply of available merit badges. We chased green bugs, gray bugs, black bugs, slimy bugs, and stinging bugs—all to acquire the requisite number of species. Our greatest triumph of the day was to catch a relatively rare beetle. Occasionally a bug would bite, but finally, after days of unbroken effort, we had popped enough insects of assorted varieties into our cyanide jars to complete the required two collections. We acquired the twenty-one merit badges necessary to become Eagle Scouts and proudly received our Eagle medals at a citywide court of honor. We continued qualifying for merit badges. It was almost like a disease. When I stopped, I had accumulated some sixty, as I recall.

Being a Boy Scout was a salutary experience. Not only did I learn a great deal about nature and the outdoors, but such awakened interests as astronomy have remained with me through adulthood. The climax of a scouting year was the two summer weeks spent at one of the Chicago Council camps in Michigan. I went regularly to Camp Daniel Beard on Crystal Lake, a dwindling body of clear water in a large crater. The last few years I served as leader of the group from Troop 855 and became an assistant scoutmaster. There was always a good mixture of Indian lore with the regular swimming, canoeing, and camping. The highest honor was to be inducted into the Order of the Arrow after undergoing a day and night of special testing, proving one's resourcefulness in a minor way, as a young Indian brave might have had to do. I came through with reasonable aplomb and proudly joined the Order of the Arrow.

"Kid stuff," one might say with some justice, yet the values and skills we Scouts absorbed were good values and skills. Although I have long since lost any active connection with scouting, I have little patience with those who condemn the movement that I knew because of its links with the establishment, of its alleged obsoleteness in the post-1960s era, or even because its founder, Sir Robert Baden-Powell, was a product of British imperialism. Nor, in my experience, were the Scout leaders with whom I had anything to do little more than a bunch of poorly disguised pedophiles or homosexuals, as has sometimes been alleged.

Can one look back, even with understanding and sympathy, at the foibles and concerns of youth and still not laugh? Great simplifications as well as broad emotions master the thinking of the young of each generation, but that need not mean that the concerns of youth are necessarily tainted or irrelevant. The quests for certainty in truth, for ideals, and for knowledge, however devoid of deep experience, remain worthy objectives throughout life, and it is the more mundane distractions that consume our adult lives that represent an imperfection. Most of us are burdened by the pressures of daily living, and few would claim the right to criticize with Wordsworth, "The world is too much with us; late and soon, getting and spending, we lay waste our powers." Despite all the surging problems of teenagers, their happiness is that they can only have a dim awareness of the tragic dimensions of life—the inevitable disillusionments that time will bring, the frustrated ambitions, the dashed hopes, the failed promise.

When the time came to go away to college, I had to leave Chicago and all that it had meant to me behind. I had won a four-year full scholarship to the University of Dayton, a medium-sized Catholic college in the state of my birth, and decided to accept it. I was not sorry I had made that choice. My years at the University of Dayton turned out to be years of growth. I had good teachers and bad teachers, more of the former than the latter. I learned how better to organize my thoughts and my writing, to give them greater precision and clarity. As editor of both the school paper and the literary magazine, I had no choice but to grind out both editorials and longer essays on a regular basis. Philosophy, history, political science, economics, and Latin had the most appeal to me as subjects, and an indulgent administration allowed me to take practically as many courses as I wanted. The result was that, at the end of three years, I had enough credits to graduate with a major in both philosophy and history. It had been a wild period of intense activity and the amassing of knowledge. In the computerized course scheduling that characterizes the mega-universities of today, such a program would have been impossible, and I am eternally grateful to Father Walter Tredtin, S.M., president of the University of Dayton, and the other top administrators and professors for their flexibility and generosity.

By the spring of 1937, I was ready to move on to graduate school. A fellowship from Columbia University determined where I would go. But first there would be a summer of work at the Ford plant in Dearborn, Michigan. One way of preventing my deterioration into a pure academic grind, I had discovered, was to obtain summer jobs—admittedly with the help of my father—at locations where he happened to be doing a construction project. These were never sinecures but involved hard, sometimes backbreaking work, and always, I found, they provided valuable experience and insights into the problems and thinking of the nonacademic world.

During the summer of 1935, I had worked in the chemistry laboratory of the Massachusetts Gas Company in Everett, Massachusetts. My task was to determine the ash and volatile matter content of the various types of coking coal used to produce gas and other by-products. I had had chemistry in high school, and it did not take me long to learn the relatively simple routines of analysis required to perform satisfactorily. I quickly noted that young Harvard- and MIT-trained chemists were working by my side doing essentially the same thing. It also did not take me long to decide that I did not want to be a chemical engineer, a career my father had recommended. The United States was, of course, still deep in depression, and professional jobs remained scarce. My unhappy colleagues, frustrated by routine work and lack of opportunity for advancement, or even to use their skills in a more meaningful way, spent a great deal of time expressing their discontents, which merely confirmed my negative resolve. I hope at least some of them went on to better things. For me the prospect of going back to Dayton in a few months made life more tolerable.

During the summer of 1936, I worked as a brick stocker on a coke oven construction job in Camden, New Jersey. Stocking silica bricks for coke ovens required a certain level of skill. There were many different shapes, and they had to be put in the right order, on top of each other, so that impatient bricklayers could take them off precisely as required. It was hard and sweaty work under a shed where the temperature frequently went over one hundred degrees Fahrenheit. We drank gallons of water and ate many salt tablets each day. About Camden of 1936 I have little good to say, except that Philadelphia was just across the Delaware River. One small claim to fame appeared on a plaque in the Hotel Hamilton saying Enrico Caruso had stayed there while making records at the RCA-Victor recording studios in Camden, and the smell of cooking tomatoes in the Campbell soup factory seemed ever present. On weekends I would dutifully cross the bridge to Philadelphia to visit the art museum, to go to a movie, or on Sundays to attend the Philadelphia Symphony concerts in the Robin Hood Dell. A great experience I remember was to hear Paul Whiteman conduct the full orchestra in his arrangement of Gershwin's "Rhapsody in Blue."

My summer of 1937, at the Ford Motor Company plant in Dearborn, Michigan, provided still another kind of experience. Fortunately, I was not on the main assembly line, but I could see what a dehumanizing, mind-shattering routine it represented for those committed to a lifetime of labor "on the line." Burnout was a luxury the average Ford worker could not afford, and yet the prospect of no real improvement in the daily routine inevitably cast a pall over his assessment of the future. Charlie Chaplin's portrayal of an assembly line in his film *Modern Times* may have been a caricature, but it caught the mind-numbing aspect of repetitive motion as both farce and tragedy. My own job was not particularly inspiring. I found that one way to fight boredom was to memorize long poems and to shout them out to myself as I worked, unnoticed by anyone else because of the surrounding din. Writing this in the 1990s, I can only acknowledge the ironical fact that, with automation and robotics, conditions of work in car-manufacturing plants have greatly improved, but at the cost of many thousands of jobs at relatively high but no longer competitive rates of pay.

Thus I spent roughly nine months of my life, over three summers, working in environments unknown to most diplomats and scholars, most of the time doing hard physical labor. I do not regret the experience. It brought me closer to the lives of average working Americans, their problems, their anxieties, and their despairs, than I could ever have come without those summer jobs, as oppressive and wasteful as they sometimes seemed. At least I had the consolation of knowing that it was only for brief interludes; most of the others could not escape during the best years of their lives.

Graduate Studies at Columbia University

My entry into graduate studies at Columbia University required no great adaptation on the part of a Chicagoan. One could still walk safely about the streets of Manhattan during day or night, and my quarters in John Jay Residence Hall were comfortable enough. New York in the fall of 1937 seemed an exciting place to be, with a dynamic cultural and political life. Columbia was undoubtedly a great university, and the Department of Public Law, in which I was enrolled, boasted a reputedly strong faculty. Some members were also outstanding teachers; a few had lapsed into cynical insouciance about bringing their materials up to date. One quickly learned who the good people were and chose courses accordingly. I had few real complaints and bit eagerly into new segments of knowledge.

I found such professors as Robert McIver, Schuyler Wallace, Thomas McMahon, Lindsay Rogers, and Philip Jessup (the last of the law faculty) stimulating and helpful. Early on, however, I did note a certain philosophical vacuity in their approach to government and society, although McIver undoubtedly had a fine speculative mind and a creative approach to political theory and sociology (both of which subjects he taught). This impression of theoretical shallowness in contemporary political science was to be reflected in both my M.A. thesis and later in my Ph.D. dissertation. With all the brashness of youth, I dared to attack the thinking of the great men, both in class and in what I wrote. On the whole, they took it in good grace and acknowledged that I had provided some "interesting perspectives." As I gradually came to appreciate, the more thoughtful of them personally felt the lack of a sound philosophical basis for the political ideals they advocated. The 1930s saw the heyday of the so-called legal realists in the law school, and I audited several courses to see what they had to offer. I concluded it was not very much, other than the rather obvious truism that the beliefs and convictions of judges influenced their decisions. The idea of some lawyers that the judicial process involved nothing more than a semiautomatic, almost machine-like, application of precedents, particularly in the field of constitutional law, seemed absurd on the face of it.

My first year at Columbia allowed me enough time to enjoy some of the nonacademic attractions of New York. I bought a season's ticket for the New York Philharmonic, then playing at Carnegie Hall. I also frequented the Metropolitan Opera, admittedly from the upper balcony, from where I had no trouble hearing the magnificent voices of Kirsten Flagstad and Lauritz Melchior doing the entire Ring tetralogy as well as *Tristan und Isolde*. Never again, even at Bayreuth many years later, did I enjoy Wagner as much as during that first youthful year in New York. I was aware, of course, that Wagner was Adolf Hitler's favorite composer and that his music contained a febrile quality not unrelated to the excesses of late German romanticism and the turbulence of twentieth-century artistic and political movements in the Weimar Republic.

I frequently visited the headquarters of the Catholic Worker movement in lower Manhattan and made friends among those associated with it. Although I could not agree with everything they advocated, I admired the quality of their dedication and the selflessness with which they gave help to all who needed it within the limits of their means. The discussion groups that met in the evenings provided intellectual stimulation and a perspective on events quite different than one got at Columbia University. Those on the periphery of the movement, like myself—many of them young academics or lawyers—helped where they could but shrank from the full commitment that more active participation would have required. Ironically enough, some of us enlisted as volunteer poll watchers on the West Side of Manhattan to ensure that too many Tammany supporters did not attempt to snatch electoral victory away from the crusading, but very Republican, district attorney Thomas Dewey. Dewey won, and we felt that our efforts to support the cause of public morality had been worthwhile.

The academic year 1937–38 passed quickly enough, and I qualified for an M.A. degree in June. My fellowship was renewed, and I looked forward to returning to Columbia in the fall. I decided not to work that summer but to devote the months to extensive reading. I had an ambitious plan for the next school year. I would complete the required course work for the Ph.D. but would also register for night classes at the downtown Fordham University Law School. I did not ask whether regulations forbade this, and no one ever raised the question. Since the law school was located in the Woolworth Building, this meant a good deal of riding back and forth on the New York subway system, but I figured that I could do my studying of the law on the subway while riding to and from classes. Actually, this worked pretty well, even though legal casebooks are heavy and I could not always get a seat. My earlier practice at carting library books home in Chicago served me in good stead. Somehow I managed and, considering the rather superficial study time allotted to the law, was content with an assortment of Bs and As at the end of the semester. Events, as we shall see, obviated the need to register at Fordham for the next term, a development I did not really regret. I found the strict casebook method endemic in American law schools stultifying and guaranteed to narrow the vision and ruin the prose style of young lawyers exposed exclusively to it.

At Columbia meanwhile, I took everything available and audited some courses for which I could not formally register. My professors must have regarded me with a mixture of bewilderment, irritation, and affection. I could be iconoclastic in discussing the idols of the academy but also show some dedication in the pursuit of knowledge. I came to respect some of them for their scholarship and humaneness. As is the case with most universities, Columbia was not without its intrigues, manipulations, and conspiracies. The virtues of academic life, I could observe, were often smothered by professorial ambitions and frustrations. "Rackademics," Lindsay Rogers used to call it.

Thus I was sailing along in my course work until the unexpected happened.

2   Entry into the Foreign Service:
Switzerland, the China-Burma-India Theater, Mozambique

. . . .

My entry into the Foreign Service was neither long pre-
meditated nor intensely dramatic. The study of diplomatic history and international law had obviously made me aware that such an organization
existed, but in the autumn of 1938 I took the three-day written examination with no formal preparation other than the courses I had had. I had
heard about so-called cram schools in the Washington area that provided
intensive preparation for eastern seaboard worthies and were supposed to
know what kind of information needed to be pumped into putatively re-
ceptive minds in order that they do well in the examination. The thought
never occurred to me to attend one.

In any event, I passed the examination and thought little more about it.
Early in 1939 I was hailed down to Washington for an oral examination
given to those applicants who had obtained the necessary grade in the
written examination. Here I met a group of my Foreign Service classmates-
to-be. Some were more nervous than others, and none of us really had any
idea what to expect. The examining panel chaired by Joseph Green was
rumored to be tough and particularly hard on those who tried to fake it. I
entered the examination room with some trepidation. I can recall that we
discussed medieval Latin poetry, my experience as a summer worker in
coke and auto plants, and some assorted problems in diplomacy. After a
brief wait, they told me I had passed and would in a relatively short time
be inducted into the Foreign Service and sent abroad.

So what to do? I could not complete my course work for the Ph.D. at
Columbia until the end of the spring semester, and I had good hopes of
being offered a teaching position in the Department of Public Law. Here
my principal professors, Lindsay Rogers, Schuyler Wallace, Robert Mc-
Iver, and James T. Shotwell, demonstrated commendable flexibility. They
agreed that I could take my oral examination for the doctorate before

completing the semester. With a few weeks' notice I passed it. Meanwhile, I had received orders from the State Department assigning me as vice consul to the American consulate general in Zurich, Switzerland. All such orders customarily ended with a monitory sentence: "This assignment is neither for your convenience nor pleasure." I was never quite certain what purpose such language served. Perhaps some erring diplomat had once tried to escape an assignment by implying that it was both inconvenient and unpleasant.

There was something slightly absurd about the whole process of my induction. I had really not intended to become a diplomat, and here I was shipping off to Switzerland with a presidential commission in my baggage. Anyway, it was supposed to be a sort of trial marriage, according to Professor Rogers. If I liked it after a year or so, well and good. If not, I could return to a teaching position at Columbia. Thus are personally fateful decisions sometimes made. We drift into them, one thing leading to another until we are committed, and the natural inertia of life confirms one in the tentative. I have often experienced the truth of the French proverb "C'est le provisoire qui dure" (It's the provisional that lasts). Any professional diplomat who ignores this rule in the search for permanent solutions does so at his or her peril.

Switzerland

After my arrival in Switzerland the advent of World War II obviously put everything in a different perspective. I could sense that dramatic events were in the offing that would change the political and economic world as we knew it and that life as a professor would not be the best way to observe or even participate in them. When I arrived in Zurich after a stormy ocean crossing to Le Havre, I was an inexperienced young man to be caught up quickly in the turmoil of the visa section to which the consul general assigned me. It was under enormous pressure from more than one hundred thousand Jewish visa applicants, most of whom had fled to Switzerland from Austria after the Anschluss of 1938. They provided a hard early lesson in the incongruities between the demands of humane morality and the constrictions of possibility created by bureaucratic rules and regulations. In a century of enormous atrocities, as well as two world wars, the limitations imposed by those rules and regulations could only seem an unacceptable burden to conscientious American officials in the face of overwhelming need. Our options, however, were limited, given the quota system for immigration to the United States. Bending a rule here to let a particularly heartbreaking case squeeze by meant that some other worthy and perhaps better qualified visa applicant would lose out. In 1939, of course, one could not predict, even in one's darkest moments, the monstrous scale of the Holocaust or the Gulag, or for that matter Pol Pot's Cambodia or Idi Amin's Uganda. Despite the language of *Mein Kampf* and the horrors of the Crystal Night (Kristallnacht) in Hitler's Germany, few in 1939 could anticipate the capacity of people for unrestrained evil that the next decade was to reveal.

Indeed, despite pressures on the consulate general, those prewar months in Switzerland seemed uneasily tranquil in an old bourgeois European sense—a way of life that World War II was to shatter forever, even for those countries that were not directly engulfed. When I compare the Switzerland of today with my memories of 1939, I find the old certainties gone. The country is still as beautiful as ever, the cities clean and now again well ordered, and the Swiss themselves more prosperous than ever. Yet the sense of permanence, stability, societal cohesion, and inevitable progress that deserted some countries during World War I, and others only after World War II, has not returned to provide a conceptual, if largely materialistic, basis for European bourgeois society.

A small group of young Foreign Service officers assigned to Zurich quickly banded together to enjoy the amenities of life in Switzerland. We went on bicycle trips; drove to Lucerne to hear Toscanini conduct at the Lucerne Music Festival; attended excellent productions in Zurich theaters, enriched by numerous refugee actors and actresses from Germany; and savored the excellent, if sometimes underrated, cuisine of Zurich's restaurants. Those months, both tranquil and harassed, now seem unreal to me after more than half a century. All of us knew it could not last, that an explosion in Europe that would radically affect the course of our own lives was inevitable. I suppose a more detached observer would have detected a certain feverishness in our trying to maximize experience in a period of intense foreboding. I made good friends, as I have along the way at other posts, but it is one of the tragedies of life in the Foreign Service that, with each transfer, one begins the process of losing touch. "Partir, c'est mourir un peu." Only if, by chance, one ends up again at some point at the same post can one renew old ties. Christmas-card friendship, while better than nothing at all, I suppose, is not enough. As Foreign Service officers drift apart, they not only make new friends but also acquire new interests as they move about in different parts of the world.

When war broke out in Europe, the Swiss sprang to protect their neutrality in the way they knew best: they mobilized. Every male citizen of that small but indomitable country was then and is still subject to compulsory military service. Virtually every Swiss home was the repository for the rifle or rifles of those still of military age. I can recall going down to the main railway station in Zurich on the day of general mobilization to watch the troops by the thousands bearing their rifles and other equipment boarding the numerous special trains. The organization and the spirit were impressive.

I left the station and walked the streets of Zurich into the late evening. The foreboding we had felt now became reality. Would Switzerland, the traditional neutral that had managed to stay out of World War I, be drawn into the new war? We knew after the war had ended, of course, that it would not be, but in 1939 there were no certainties. Although I had left Switzerland by the end of the calm that followed the Nazi-Soviet conquest of Poland (the so-called phony war), with the fall of France that sense of uncertainty about the survivability of Swiss neutrality could only have greatly increased. General Henry Guisan, the commander in chief of Swiss forces, immediately became a national figure, and his announcements reported on radio and in the press became a major source of news about Swiss intentions and determination to resist aggression. The strange false calm of the "phony war" created an atmosphere of indeterminacy; it could not endure, but at the same time no one could anticipate the military catastrophe for France and Britain that the spring of 1940 would bring. A fortuitous major contributor to Swiss morale was the Swiss National Exhibition (Landesaustellung) in Zurich during the summer and early autumn of 1939. Brilliantly conceived and organized, it showed Switzerland at its best in terms of history and solid economic achievement. I went many times that summer and could not help but think, as I viewed the exhibits, that it must make the numerous Swiss visitors, many in uniform, more determined to preserve the integrity of their country.

As we have had only recently confirmed, there was a darker side to Swiss behavior during the war. A degree of collaboration with the Nazis by Swiss bankers and some officials in providing shelter for German gold and other assets looted from Jews and conquered countries clearly seems to have taken place.

With the outbreak of war in Europe, the tension among our visa applicants mounted from day to day. Their mood constituted a sort of *Torschlusspanik* (panic caused by fear of the gate slamming shut)—a phenomenon we witnessed again in 1961, before the Berlin Wall was built, when refugees were streaming out of East Germany by the many thousands, in anticipation of restrictive action by the government of the German Democratic Republic. The daily lines in front of the consulate general grew ever longer, and those of us in the visa section felt under enormous pressure, dispensing new life or destroying hope. A suicide outside our office, shared with a Swiss bank, shook us: the dead man was a rejected visa applicant. We could not produce additional quota numbers out of thin air, and even otherwise qualified applicants had to remain in Switzerland until they were reached on the waiting list. Far and away the most difficult technical barrier for the majority of applicants was "the likely to become a public charge" clause of the U.S. immigration laws. Since only a few refugees from Austria had managed to get out with much money, most had to depend on affidavits of support from relatives or friends in the United States. We were under strict instructions to look beyond the individual affidavit, that is, whether the offer of support was credible in terms of income, blood relationship, or long-standing friendship. We had lists of Americans who, in pity, had executed far more affidavits of support than they could possibly honor. Although the consular officer had the ultimate power of decision as to whether a visa should be issued, it was also a harsh reality that at the American port of entry, Immigration and Naturalization officials of the U.S. Department of Justice had the ultimate power of decision as to whether they would permit entry. Any excessive kindness on our part in applying the rules or regulations would only lead to final rejection.

This was the bind I was in. The demands of conscience ran into seemingly insuperable bureaucratic barriers. The Swiss did not help, of course, by threatening to expel and, in a few cases at least, actually expelling refugees whose residence permits had expired. Every day brought new pressures and the need to steel oneself to say no or not yet, mixed with the daily pleasure of being able to hand issued immigration visas to happy applicants.

I can recall many poignant experiences. One of the saddest involved the little Jewish cellist who had played in a Vienna orchestra sponsored by the Socialist Party. His visa file was hopeless, totally lacking in anything to rebut the public charge clause, but he insisted on bringing his cello to my office to demonstrate how such a talented musician was bound to be able to support himself in the United States. He also hoped, I suppose, to soften the heart of a seemingly unsympathetic American consular officer. And so he played, screechingly out of practice and perhaps with minimum talent, as I listened. I thanked him when he had finished but had to say that being able to play a musical instrument would not suffice to get him past our immigration barriers.

My transfer in early fall from the visa section to the citizenship section of the consulate general (part of the training process) came as a great relief. I was troubled that I had not been able to do more to assuage the deep anxieties and needs of more refugees. I did not share the anti-Semitic sentiments of some of my colleagues but had to admit that, given the laws they were administering, they had tried to be reasonably fair, if not particularly forthcoming. No one who qualified was refused a visa for extraneous reasons. Looking back to those turbulent years with the knowledge we now have of what the Nazis did to the Jews of Europe, one can only deplore the absence of more sweeping measures to let in the homeless and dispossessed. Apart from the interventions of people like Mrs. Roosevelt in individual visa cases, there was little apparent realization in Washington of the moral factors and human stakes involved in the plight of the Jewish refugees.

My duties in the citizenship section gave me time to write some reports for Washington on economic, social, and political conditions in Switzerland. I remember doing one thirty-page essay on Swiss demographic trends, which led Consul General Frost in his efficiency report on my performance to remark that I seemed to be overly academic in my approach to the work of the Foreign Service. I was pleased to discover, when I returned to Washington, that the desk officer in the State Department responsible for Switzerland along with a few other countries had commented on the same report that here was an officer with a high degree of technical skill in population studies and that this should be noted for future reference in case of need.

Accurate and perceptive reporting has always been one of the essential skills of the effective diplomat, and young officers of my generation as well as later ones have been aware that good reporting is an excellent way to make both a name for oneself and a useful contribution to the conduct of foreign affairs. The country desks were the primary consumers in those days; now the entire Washington intelligence community, as well as the largely expanded number of operational officers, benefit. The evaluation system has always been defective. During the 1930s and 1940s I found, to my surprise, the rating of reports to be in the hands of a group of elderly women who had never served abroad and who were sequestered physically and organizationally in the Evaluations Branch of the department. They, I was glad to note, also thought highly of my Swiss population study, although I was never able to find out precisely why.

Washington

My remaining months in Switzerland went by quickly enough, and by February of 1940 I was back in Washington to attend the Foreign Service Officers Training School. This session was for the sixteen members of the class of 1939. We had all acquired some experience and, it was to be hoped, some wisdom from our less than a year abroad. Some of us were to go on to professional success; others were to fall by the wayside, a few rather quickly. But, as we assembled in the basement of the Old State Department building next to the White House, our ambitions were still high and our sense of the future vague.

There is not much to be said about a training school. We learned some things that would prove useful, including which of the Foreign Service officers who lectured to us were smart and articulate and which mediocre. Such judgments proved surprisingly accurate as predictions of their future success or failure as senior diplomats. The State Department was a much simpler organization in those days. The entire personnel of the department in Washington joined together for a group photograph on the Pennsylvania Avenue steps of the Old State building. The Foreign Service itself, abroad and at home, numbered scarcely eight hundred. Membership was clearly weighted in favor of the eastern establishment and the Ivy League, although efforts were already under way to diversify recruiting to other sections of the country. As a Chicagoan with a Columbia connection, I seemed to meet both criteria. One senior official described the department as "a pretty good club,"[1] and he was not far off the mark. Whether that kind of State Department and Foreign Service could meet the requirements of wartime and the postwar period was to be a continuing and perplexing question for an institution essentially geared to a less complicated world of diplomacy.

Our training class watched with horror as the German armies swept through France in the spring of 1940, and with some anxiety we received our next assignments at the end of the session. Mine was to Baghdad. The prospect did not fill me with great joy, and I fatalistically started my round of required preventive shots. It was a hot Washington summer, conditioned, I thought, to prepare me for the heat of the Middle East.

Before departure, however, I spent a month as night watch officer in Secretary of State Cordell Hull's office. This literally meant sitting up all night to read the cables and, if necessary, bring urgent matters to his attention. It proved to be a highly educational experience for a young officer; it was the closest to a secretariat job, a seemingly sure road in later times to rapid advancement in the Foreign Service, that I ever came. Even in wartime, life was much simpler in those days. Apart from the cryptographers who did the coding and decoding, I was the whole operating State Department during those early morning hours.

Secretary Hull spent part of that month in Havana at a conference of Western Hemisphere foreign ministers. A telephone call from him early in the morning, after a late-night session, provided firsthand evidence of the animosity between the secretary of state and his deputy, Undersecretary of State Sumner Welles. The secretary asked me to convey an urgent message from him to Welles, in effect requesting the latter to get in touch with President Roosevelt first thing in the morning, to ask his approval of the position Hull was taking in Havana. When I said I would call Welles before breakfast, the secretary responded, "Wake him now." I telephoned the impressive Welles mansion on Massachusetts Avenue (now the Cosmos Club) with some trepidation. The undersecretary did not know me from Adam, and he had the reputation of being a cold, aristocratic official with close personal ties to the president. An obviously irritated butler answered the phone. He was not about to wake up his employer, but I insisted. Finally, with an expression equivalent to "Let this be upon your head," he buzzed Mr. Welles. A deep angry voice came on. I tried to convey the secretary's message as accurately as I could. After a considerable and forbidding silence, the deep voice said, "That will be all." Our conversation—if one could call it that—thus terminated. There was no message for the secretary, and I never did find out how, and at what pace, Welles carried out Hull's request.

When I discussed the rather strained intermediary role I had played with an old hand in the secretary's office, he indicated that this was what one might have expected. Hull had a strong personal political position as a long-term Democratic congressman and senator from Tennessee but little clout with the White House, an attribute that Welles possessed in quantity. The two wasted no love on each other but had worked out a kind of armed truce that involved slicing out respective, nonoverlapping areas of responsibility. The secretary was happy with his dedication to the negotiation of liberal trade agreements, but it was the undersecretary who, in 1940 and subsequently, made trips to Europe on behalf of the president. Hull finally won out, however, when, in 1943, Roosevelt decided that Welles had to go and asked for his resignation.[2]

The China-Burma-India Theater

My involvement with Asia began with Baghdad, Iraq, as objective. As a bachelor, I had been considered a good choice for a post where the minister's wife had the reputation of being a terror with younger wives. I can recall the look of relief on training school director J. Klahr Huddle's face when, after my assignment to Baghdad had been announced at the end of the session of the Foreign Service Officers' Training Course, he asked me, just to make sure, whether I had any intention to get married before proceeding to my post, and I assured him I had no such immediate intention. It was relatively easy to handle personnel matters in that bureaucratically uncomplicated era.

I sailed from San Francisco in early September on the SS *President Polk* (which we quickly dubbed the "SS President Poke"). An old American President Line vessel—half passenger and half cargo—it set a leisurely course, calling at Honolulu, Yokohama, Shanghai, Manila, Singapore, Penang, and onward to points west. When we arrived in Manila, a telegram awaited me saying that my assignment to Baghdad was canceled and that I was to proceed to Rangoon, Burma, instead. That meant getting off the ship in Penang.

The State Department expected that the assorted group of Foreign Service officers aboard would be some forty to fifty days en route to their posts. In this era of jet planes and practically no passenger ships (which in any case can no longer be used by the Foreign Service), one looks back with great nostalgia at those leisurely ocean voyages one was fortunate enough to enjoy. Life seemed to stand still as one sailed some hundreds of miles a day and fell into the shipboard routine. The purser, or whoever was in charge of keeping the passengers entertained, would dream up various divertissements, only a few of which the Foreign Service officers on board found amusing. We formed a tightly knit little group with a proper mixture of senior officers and beginners. Each of us had a book of U.S. government drafts in our possession. In those relatively uncomplicated days, our travel orders had simply contained language telling us to "draw drafts and render accounts" at the end of each month until we arrived at post. This old-fashioned and trusting system was bound to vanish after the war in the face of the State Department's growing administrative bureaucracy. The story, possibly apocryphal, was that a venturesome and unscrupulous Foreign Service officer had vanished into the hinterland of China after drawing a draft for one hundred thousand dollars. This, it was alleged, persuaded the department of the need for tighter controls over disbursements.

Even with the war in Europe going badly and Britain embattled after the fall of France, we were a strangely detached and insulated group as we sailed westward over the boundless Pacific. The world as we knew it might be collapsing, but we were proceeding to our respective posts under official orders, and there was nothing we could do about impending catastrophe in Europe. The daily shipboard journal was a travesty: its main concerns were the schedule of activity for the day and the weekend college football scores, with an occasional intrusion of bulletins about the war far away. A typhoon off the coast of Japan injected a note of reality, but only for a few days. I can recall meals in the dining room with only a couple of hardy passengers present and soup bowls being flung wildly about with the excessive and groaning movements of the SS President Poke. Fortunately, I do not get seasick, something for which I am deeply grateful, but many of my companions were less lucky and therefore absent from the dining room—a room festooned with ropes, so that one could get from the entrance door to one's table without major catastrophe.

There would be a rush to the nearest hotel when we arrived at a port where an English-language newspaper might be available, but the results were usually disappointing. The war in Europe was far away, and press coverage was fragmentary at best. We could only speculate about what we thought was happening. What we lacked was the kind of factual information that the modern worldwide communication system now provides to the point of superfluity when the media focus on a country or development.

Our most colorful Foreign Service traveling companion was undoubtedly William Farrell. In his early thirties, he was a brilliant linguist, overweight, witty, with a great appetite for good food and drink. He already spoke fluent Arabic, Amharic, and every known Western European language. Shortly after our sailing from San Francisco, he announced that he planned to learn Russian on this voyage—his first excursion into the Slavic languages. He did not seem to spend much time studying, although every now and then he appeared with a book in his hand. By the time we reached Shanghai, he was able to carry on what seemed like a fluent conversation with the many White Russian bar girls who graced local nightclubs. Poor Bill! He was a classic example of the fact that linguistic brilliance does not always equate with stability, balance, and common sense. Some years later, after an unpleasant incident with the French ambassador's wife in Baghdad, he was called home for consultation and shortly thereafter resigned from the Foreign Service. He spent a few years at St. Elizabeth's Hospital in Washington and then went to live with a relative in New York City and supported himself by doing odd jobs of translating. We corresponded from time to time, and he called on me twice at the State Department. He was still interesting, able to provide appropriate proverbs in a dozen languages, but the spark was gone. He died in his early fifties of a heart attack.

After forty days en route, I disembarked at Penang in the Malay Peninsula. It had been for me a memorable voyage, my first exposure to Asia. I said goodbye to new friends with some sadness. They continued on to Calcutta, and we had only a few fortuitous contacts in later years. Now they are nearly all gone, part of my personal memory bank fading ever farther into the past.

My first task was to find transportation from Penang to Rangoon. A small coastal freighter carrying copra was scheduled to leave in three days, and the American consul made the necessary arrangements. He warned me to expect to find some copra beetles on board. Once we had sailed, I quickly learned that it was not a question of some but of many. The green beetles were all over the ship, in one's bunk, in one's drink, and in one's constant thoughts. The captain and the first mate were English, the crew Lascar. They took it all calmly, and when I asked the captain how he could stand it, he answered that it was just a matter of getting used to it. I never did, and I was a happy man when we docked in Rangoon.

My predecessor as vice consul, Leonard Parker, was standing on the quay to greet me. He seemed pathetically grateful that I had actually arrived, and planned to lose no time in leaving for Singapore and home. I was to get no breaking in. The only other official American in Rangoon was the venerable consul general, Austin C. Brady. A widower and a gentleman of the old school, he was serving at his last post before retirement. He seemed frail, almost liable to be blown away by the first gust of wind, but his mind was still sharp, and he wrote a literate, sometimes even elegant, prose. I was to be a frequent beneficiary of his kindness and affection.

Parker deposited me at the Strand Hotel—a typical grand hotel in British colonial style run by the seemingly inevitable Swiss manager. I quickly noted that all the waiters and attendants were Indians rather than Burmans. I was tired and looking forward to a beetleless night's sleep. To my surprise and irritation, someone awakened me by knocking on my door. It was 5:00 A.M. An Indian entered bearing a plate with banana on it and a filled cup. "Sahib, I bring you morning tea." I could not help but laugh at what I construed to be an early exposure to rigid British imperial practice.

When, some hours later, I turned up at the American consulate general, I noted again, as Brady introduced members of the staff, that they were all Anglo-Indians and the messengers Indians. Amin, an Indian Muslim, was the "fixer" of the office. I had already learned in Zurich that an indispensable member of any Foreign Service establishment is a local employee who has contacts with the bureaucracy, generally knows his way around town, and can get things done. I was to find Amin invaluable during the turbulent months ahead. His specific job was to help the vice consul in dealing with American vessels calling at Rangoon and to clear shipments of supplies through customs, but in any kind of emergency, he was the one on whom to call.

The absence of Burmans in both British and American firms and banks, in shops, and in restaurants was revelatory of a significant fact about Burma: the commercial and clerical life of Rangoon was essentially in the hands of nonindigenous ethnic groups. The large Indian and Anglo-Indian community was, of course, permanently settled in the major cities, but the Burmese people seemed to play little or no role in running the economy of their country. In the British-run Secretariat—the central governing apparatus in Rangoon—there were some Burmans, and the prime minister, Sir Paw Tun, was a Burman with a highly intelligent American wife. When one went into the villages or Burmese sections of the city, another fact became apparent. If Burmese society was not a matriarchy, it came close to it. Most of the work and clearly the selling of produce in local markets were handled by women. What the men did with their time was never entirely clear, but the standard stereotype was that they loafed, gambled, and in surprisingly large numbers killed each other (the murder rate in Burma, I was informed, was the highest in the world).

When it arrived, I did acquire a Burmese driver for my new Chevrolet. He was reasonably competent, although I caught him once siphoning gasoline out of the tank of the car. He pointed lamely to his cigarette lighter, but I noted that he had already taken enough fuel to keep that implement going for a year or two. He did have an obvious and inordinate hatred for Indians, a hatred that he shared with his compatriots. When I saw him plow into a group of Indians on the street, scattering them wildly in all directions but not striking anyone, my heart jumped. My remonstrances evoked only a big grin, and my subsequent efforts to say "Never again" were like preachments to the deaf. This deep-seated antagonism periodically erupted into riots leading to large-scale slaughter of innocent Tamil and Telugu coolies. On one such occasion during my stay in Rangoon, the dead numbered some thousands. One of the reasons for their hatred was the heavy indebtedness of many Burmans to moneylenders from South India of the Banya caste, but the emotional depths aroused seemed to be deeper and more broadly spread among the native Burmans than simply to those who were rebelling against the bondage of high interest rates. Although the term "running amok" is originally a Malay derivative, I could only think that it applied, at times equally, to the Burmese male.

My first impressions of Rangoon were hardly likely to evoke gratitude to the State Department for having sent me there. Despite some massive buildings in the imperial style occupied mainly by British firms and banks, the architecture of the city seemed overwhelmingly drab, crumbling, and a total hodgepodge. The streets and sidewalks were red with expectorated betel nut juice. Most Indians of lower castes seemed addicted to chewing the nut for such lift as it could give to a drab and labor-laden life. There were a few lovely things like the golden Shwe Dagon pagoda on the Royal Lake, but the sheer collective amount of misery, poverty, disease, filth, and stench was bound to overwhelm a newcomer who had never previously lived in an Asian city. I can recall my first Sunday in Rangoon, when I went by foot from the hotel to the Catholic cathedral for mass. At least twenty lepers were lined up in front of the church begging for alms and reaching out to grab the arms of passersby. The term "cultural shock" has since come into vogue. I suffered from it during those early days in Burma, as do most Americans who venture abroad into non-European parts of the world. One becomes hardened in time, however, to the open misery and disease that are part of daily life in Asia as part of a process of psychological detachment and insulation. There are few Mother Teresas who are willing to become a loving part of that misery. One heard many bad things about missionaries in Burma and India from businessmen and sometimes officials who, perhaps, suffer guilt feelings for their lack of charity. I had only admiration for those—and they were obviously not all—whose dedication to the poor and the suffering was genuine and continuing.

At the top of all this stood the British raj, essentially a few British ICS (Indian Civil Service) officials assigned on a permanent basis to Burma, supported by some British policemen (for a few years, George Orwell was one, as he related in his book *Burmese Days*), and a small military force. I quickly came to know the ICS people (it was, after all, a relatively limited official community) and found them generally intelligent and dedicated, though with a certain sad cynicism and feeling of foreboding about the future. Although they did not talk much of the white man's burden, their dedication did involve an assumption that no one could do the job of civil administration anywhere nearly as well.

An American exposed to British imperialism, even in its declining days, was likely to have ambivalent feelings. There was a certain residual, if somewhat tattered, majesty to the way of life official Britain had developed. Even if the mother country drew some wealth and sustenance from Burma and India, the recompense was an ordered administration and a system of justice seemingly better than any that could indigenously replace it. In those fading last years, partly owing to the gloom inspired by defeat in Europe, there was a febrile quality to the life of British colonials, whether officials, bankers, or businessmen. They sensed there could never be a return to the prewar glory days and that fundamental change would come, but before Pearl Harbor and what followed, they had no idea of how rapidly and decisively the empire would collapse.

Despite its good reputation, life at the Strand Hotel was depressing, and I decided early that I must find a house in which to live. By luck and the fine nose of Mrs. Heathcliffe, an Anglo-Indian real estate agent, I was soon ensconced in the top floor of a splendid colonial-style house on a peninsula jutting into the Victoria Lakes, about six miles from downtown Rangoon. I was able to buy essential furniture, all in flowered teak, through the agent and ordered some additional bookcases. All of this was destroyed by fire with the fall of Rangoon to the Japanese early in 1942. A prime asset of the house was a real porcelain bathtub, in contrast to the tin tubs used by most Europeans. There was no running water, of course. A water bearer (*pani wallah*) provided this with two five-gallon gasoline drums heated over an open fire out in the cookhouse. The drain was open, and the advice was to look each day to make sure a highly venomous krait had not found its way up the drain and was now resting in the bottom of the tub.

At the consulate general, I found that the arriving and departing American freighters provided a constant flow of problems. Many of them were bringing cargo for transportation by rail up to Lashio on the Chinese frontier for onward delivery by truck over the Burma Road to Kunming and Chungking. American seamen seemed to have a predilection for getting into trouble while in port. We had a reasonably effective arrangement with the local police to be tipped off as soon as a sailor ended up in jail. I came to know the Rangoon jail well as, accompanied usually by Amin, I would obtain the release of hapless and feckless seamen, usually considerably the worse for wear. Apart from jail, there were also the numerous dens of ill repute to which sailors were attracted. When a captain would report three of his crew missing on the day of sailing, Amin and I would make a hurried tour of likely places. Our batting average was not 1,000 percent, but we had a surprising amount of success in tracking down the errant. Finally, there was Maxim's, an enormous and rowdy nightclub popular with sailors and the city's demimonde. The chief bouncer was an American Indian, Chief Michael Thunderface, who had been stranded in Rangoon years before when the Wild West troupe of which he was a member went bankrupt. As a loyal American, he would let us know promptly when trouble was brewing involving Americans, and off to the rescue we would ride. All of this was, for me, a highly educational experience in the seamier side of life, an experience upon which I was able to build later in Calcutta, where for some months I also found myself in charge of the shipping section of the consulate general. I have since never been one to underestimate the depths to which human beings sometimes sink, just as I am also aware of the heights to which they are sometimes capable of rising.

I do not have any general reason for gratitude toward Standard Oil, in whatever form that group of companies may take, but I do owe a great debt to one particular Standard Oil employee. Bill Law came through Rangoon shortly after my arrival. We had dinner together, and he told me of the imminent arrival of an unusually pretty and vivacious Methodist missionary, Faith Stewart. My antennae vibrated, and I made sure that when she called at the consulate general to register, as all missionaries were instructed to do, I would be there to receive her and to provide such beneficent advice as I could. Bill's description had, if anything, been an understatement. Faith and I had a dinner date a few days afterward, and the following June we were married in Rangoon—the best thing that ever could have happened to a young Foreign Service officer.

Our courtship was not without drama, as well as ripening love. Faith was to study Telugu (a South Indian language) for a year or so before beginning her work with the Telugu-speaking Indians in the Rangoon area. She never got beyond her language studies before resigning to marry me, but in typically generous fashion she was soon involved in good works. My private car (there were no official cars in those days) hauled many a sick Indian off to the hospital. We also found time in the evening to enjoy the dining pleasures of Rangoon's restaurants, such as they were, and to admire the moonlight, with the golden Shwe Dagon pagoda glimmering across the Royal Lake to provide a magnificent and aesthetic setting for mutual exchanges of endearments. Now, after more than fifty years of married life, I realize all the more how lucky I was.

For occasional amusement we would go to the Silver Grill, Rangoon's premier nightclub. Here some senior British officials danced their way into the night, somewhat too frenetically, I thought, as if they were anticipating a speedy end to all this forced gaiety. We quickly noted that the entertainment consisted mainly of revolving groups of Hungarian dancing girls—a phenomenon fairly typical of Asia before the war. I was never able to obtain a satisfactory explanation for the Hungarian comparative advantage in this export field.

The passage of the first American lend-lease legislation in early 1941 set in motion a chain of causation and launched a debate that was significantly to affect the respective roles of Burma, India, and China in the war to come. The China-Burma-India theater (CBI), as it came to be known, was to be a source of bitter strategic contestation both within the U.S. government and between Britain and the United States. The underlying official American assumption in 1941, even before Pearl Harbor, was that the government of Chiang Kai-shek in Chungking had an indispensable part to play in resisting Japanese aggression in Asia and that the Burma Road connecting Lashio at the Burmese border with Kunming and Chungking, hewn out of sheer mountainside by thousands of Chinese coolies, could provide a practical, if sometimes precarious, way of supplying the Chungking government with needed supplies. Whether the actual amount of cargo that the road could carry warranted such an evaluation was at least a debatable question, but no one could deny the symbolic importance that it assumed in both Chinese and American eyes.

The sheer audacity of the Burma Road, as described in the Western press, inevitably attracted the more venturesome correspondents who passed through Rangoon either on their way in or out. I would try to ascertain what they knew that might be of interest to the U.S. government, or to provide such advice and guidance as they requested. There were a few celebrities, among them Ernest Hemingway and his third but not last wife, Martha Gellhorn. They were on their honeymoon and arrived in Rangoon in early May 1941, having come down the road from Kunming to Lashio and then on to Rangoon. I saw them a number of times, usually in the bar or dining room of the Strand Hotel. My impressions were mixed. The famous author obviously had a high regard for himself, but he could be amusing and friendly. I do not recall any minted words worthy of preservation for posterity, but Hemingway did assert bragging rights for having invented the Bloody Mary in a Hong Kong bar. There have been other claimants for this contribution to human welfare around the world, and I know of no living authority who could adjudicate between them.

The Flying Tigers Come to Burma

Even before the lend-lease legislation was on the books, the Chinese government had pressed Washington for some five hundred to one thousand aircraft and a large loan. The planes were not available, as Claire L. Chennault (a former U.S. Army Air Force officer and then a colonel in the Chinese air force) also discovered, when he persuaded his employers to ask for a large number of heavy and medium bombers to be operated by American crews. The idea of an American-manned Chinese Air Force caught on in Washington, and soon a front organization, Chinese Defense Supplies, Inc., was created. President Roosevelt released military pilots to join the American Volunteer Group (AVG), the members of which soon became known as the Flying Tigers. Some one hundred P-40 fighter planes became available by taking them from the total allocated to the British.

I can recall the June 1941 arrival in Burma of the first group of American volunteers. They seemed to have that combination of bravado and fatalism that characterizes so many fighter pilots. In Burma, of course, they would be operating in a completely alien, if somewhat exotic, environment. I quickly came to know most of them and saw that maintenance of morale would not be easy. Colonel Chennault provided effective leadership and made sure that pilots assigned to up-country air bases at Toungoo and Magwe were also able to spend some time in Rangoon. Problems with weaker individuals inevitably developed. Liquor was plentiful, but on the whole the group maintained its cohesion and fighting spirit—a spirit that was to be sorely tested in the months after Pearl Harbor.

Another American objective that was to play a continuing role during the next few years was the equipment and training of ultimately thirty

Chinese divisions (the equivalent of about ten American divisions) that were to engage the Japanese in central China and prevent any offensive to the south. The American Military Mission to China came into being in the early fall of 1941, its Rangoon office headed by Colonel Frank Merrill (later of Merrill's Marauders fame). Frank and I became good friends; his task was an enormous one: to keep the flow of supplies unloaded on heavily congested Rangoon docks moving out of the city and ultimately over the Burma Road into China.

Whether this vision of a large Chinese force, honed by American training into a formidable fighting army against the Japanese, ever made much sense is an open question. Certainly, it never became a reality, despite the efforts of a talented group of American Chinese-speaking officers, both in China and eventually in Assam. A constant strategic tug-of-war was inevitable between their mission, which General Joseph W. Stilwell took over in March, and that of Colonel (later General) Chennault, with its emphasis on air power as the determining strategic factor against the Japanese in China. Both approaches, it was to become clear, contained a large dose of illusion, but then the planning and conduct of war have generally done so. I was, of course, caught up in all this, as the only active State Department official on the spot in Burma (Mr. Brady faded pretty much from the scene in the hubbub of late 1941). I tried to stay out of the internecine quarrels and to be as helpful as I could to both the protagonists of land and air. I could not but wonder at times whether either approach really added up to a coherent and well-thought-out strategy.

With the Japanese attack on Pearl Harbor, what had been tentative and problematic suddenly became real. My British friends of military age were quickly called up to become part of Burma's defense force. No one could guess, of course, what a series of military disasters would befall Britain and America in Asia within just a few months.

Reinforcements for me arrived in the shape of a new consul general, Lester L. Schnare, and two seasoned Foreign Service officers, Bob Streeper and Bob Buell. The two latter came up from Penang and Singapore. The three did not particularly like one another, I soon discovered, and I found myself, the most junior of the four, frequently in an intermediary role. The problem became even more complicated when it was decided that Faith and I should move into town from the Victoria Lakes. We did not, however, join the others in the large house formerly occupied by the Japanese consul general, confiscated after Pearl Harbor by the British and turned over to us. These were all dedicated professionals, and yet such vital issues as the sharing of a small supply of canned shad roe and a premium brand of scotch became sources of controversy. Under different circumstances, it might have been amusing in a cynical sort of way. I am ever amazed at the ability of intelligent men and women to act foolishly. The strains were heavy, of course, particularly when the bombing of Rangoon started, and our work had to be done under physically difficult circumstances, including encoding messages in a slit trench bomb shelter.

I began keeping a journal on a regular basis only after I arrived in India, but rereading the notes that I jotted down in Burma, I find that a sense of terrible inadequacy emerged about British military capability and effort in the face of determined and well-led Japanese armies. The first year of the war in Asia brought a series of unmitigated defeats for both Britain and the United States (the French in Indo-China were already effectively out of contention, having been conquered by the Nazis in Europe). There was no way an American vice consul sitting in Rangoon could be aware of the details of British strategic thinking about the defense of Asia, but what I did learn about it could not make me think of it as other than fundamentally flawed. It did not require unusual perspicacity to see the huge gap between assumptions and reality, between requirements and availabilities. In colonial Burma we seemed to be living in a land of illusion and, for the more realistic, of forlorn hope or outright despair.

Well-researched books written by Louis Allen and Raymond Callahan have ably described the disastrous military strategy and campaigns that led to the fall of Burma.[3] As is so often the case in a troubled period of defeat and regression, even though followed by eventual victory, the allocation of blame and credit became endlessly disputed. There was a British and American version of what happened in Burma; no one, however, could really argue with General Stilwell's pithy summary: "I claim we got a hell of a beating."[4] Whether giving a higher priority to Asia, which meant withdrawing troops and supplies from the Middle Eastern theater, would have made any decisive difference in 1941–42 is doubtful. Japanese momentum was enormous and was at least halted before it could move effectively into India.

In Rangoon we may not have had much of the big picture, but the constant flow of bad war news from points south and from the Philippines provided no reassurance. Moreover, Japanese bombers began to visit the city as a harbinger of worse to come. The one bright spot in the enveloping gloom was to be the performance of the Flying Tigers. With the first Japanese air raid, the American-manned P-40s began to take a heavy toll of bombers and Zero fighters. Bombs dropped on the city causing inevitable panic among the Indian and Burmese population, but in a period of universal defeat, even apparent temporary victory in the air helped boost our morale. Rangoon quickly took on the appearance of a ghost town. At least 90 percent of the population had vanished into the rice paddies and jungle, including all of the Indian servants and our Burmese driver.

The Anglo-Indian staff of the consulate general, for the most part, hung bravely on. Having lost all its staff, Barnett's Cold Storage (the principal source of imported food) simply locked up tight. A sole English custodian opened up for recognized customers, to let them help themselves free of charge from the freezers. The unloading of ships practically stopped for lack of dockworkers. Air raid shelters were nonexistent, so we simply dug ditches in our front or backyards and piled into them when air raid warnings sounded.

My notes reflect great personal anger at British ineffectiveness in those early months of the war. The fall of Singapore was an obvious fiasco for British arms and tactics. The Burma Rifles, which included some of my friends who had been called up, were literally cut to pieces on the Moulmein front and at the Sittang River. I can recall the pathetic return to Rangoon of the tattered remnants of one battalion led by a solitary wounded bagpiper and two drummers. It was clear that Rangoon would soon fall, and with it the supply port for the Burma Road to China.

While the fighting was going on to the east, we were engaged in the daily battle of operating in a dismantled economy and a depopulated city. The buildings were there, but nearly all of the people were gone. We knew that sooner or later the end would come, but in the interim our task was to report back to Washington what was happening in Burma, even though, as we knew realistically, our preoccupations on the spot were unlikely to be at the top of Washington's concerns. Frank Merrill became the main American source of information about the war in Burma, and since the consulate general possessed the only sensitive cryptographic equipment, our now enhanced staff spent a considerable amount of time encoding his messages with the very cumbersome and eye-deadening strip system (long since replaced). The American Volunteer Group continued to shoot down Japanese bombers with some losses of its own, but many bombs also fell on Rangoon and its suburbs. One of these landed near our former residence on the Victoria Lakes and set it on fire. My library and all the furniture in the house were destroyed. Small matter! There was no way I could have gotten them out of the country anyway. More serious was the permanent disappearance, during this frenetic period, of my partially completed Ph.D. dissertation, on which I had worked in Switzerland, Washington, and Burma.

An unpleasant feature of the daily and nightly bombing attack was the report that those Japanese crew members who managed to bail out would come down with machine guns in their hands or strapped to their legs, firing away. The few British security forces left in the city could be heard shooting at parachuting Japanese. The thought occurred to me during bombing raids that it would be decidedly unpleasant if such a crewman happened to land on top of or near our slit trench. Fortunately, we never saw one coming down except at a distance. Bombs landed nearby on many occasions but did no real damage to our house.

The Sunderland Flying Boats of the British Overseas Airways Corporation continued to call at Rangoon from Calcutta, landing on the river, and a few hardy captains brought their vessels in and out of port. This, we knew, would soon end. One of our tasks was to evacuate as many of the American missionaries as we could, either by air or sea, and by the middle of January, we had succeeded in doing this, except for those who opted to remain up-country. The time to get Faith to Calcutta came. She had been driving for the volunteer St. John's Ambulance Corps but finally (and reluctantly) left on one of the last Flying Boats to come to Rangoon.

Our consular group fatalistically saw the end approaching. There was not much more we could do in a deserted Rangoon about to fall. Fortunately, we had a few jeeps available and plenty of gasoline. In early March, we departed the city for points north, to be followed by Merrill and other members of the American Military Mission to China. There were reports, accurate enough, that the Japanese had already cut off the main road north to Prome, so we took a more circuitous route, heading for the summer capital of Maymyo in the Shan Hills, to which the British governor general, Sir Reginald Dorman-Smith, and his government had retreated.

Driving through Rangoon during those last days was an eerie experience. Buildings burned on all sides, but no one attempted to put out the fires. Hopelessness was in the air, but there were few living beings to share that feeling. There would be occasional explosions as demolition squads did their work. These included a few members of the Military Mission to China, who desperately attempted to destroy equipment that had been destined to go over the Burma Road into China. It is difficult to recapture the psychological mood of defeat, retreat, and military collapse of more than fifty years ago. We were obviously depressed and yet in a strange, contradictory sense elated that the Rangoon phase was over and that the time had come to escape from a soon-to-be-captured city.

Although strafed a number of times by Japanese fighters, forcing us into ditches along the side of the road, our small contingent finally reached Maymyo intact. Jumping into a ditch in Burma is not a simple physical move—a highly venomous snake might be present to keep one company. There is not much to say about the Maymyo interlude. It had a clear air of improvisation and impermanence. A summer capital in the Shan Hills, it featured the usual Government House, British clubs, and villas—one of which our consular group occupied. It required more confidence than I possessed to think that the Chinese Fifth Army interposed between Maymyo and the Japanese to the South would be able to hold the line very long. One could hope, of course, that Japanese forward momentum would subside for a time because of logistic problems.

We American Foreign Service officers really did not have much we could do effectively. I would call occasionally on the governor general to see what he knew, which was generally not much. We still had the only secure American cryptographic system in Burma, but the usual consular services were not much in demand, so we largely sat there contracting amoebic dysentery from the delicious but contaminated Maymyo strawberries.

One still, quiet day in early April, I was ensconced reading in the main hall of the local hotel, with openings on three sides to large verandas. Suddenly, a medium-sized dog dashed in, came up to me, and bit me on the right leg. He quickly ran off, leaving me to stop the flow of blood with my handkerchief. The thought immediately occurred: rabies! A year earlier in Rangoon, I had encountered a mad dog at a dinner party; he bit a half dozen guests, including me. Twenty-one shots in the stomach of antirabies serum, on successive days, followed—an experience I did not enjoy. The club manager came running up to me full of apologies for what the poor man in any case could not have prevented. Ten minutes later he told me that a policeman had shot the dog, the head of which would be examined, but that he regretted to tell me that every indication pointed to rabies. I knew that a principal carrier in Burma of a particularly virulent form of rabies was the jackal, and the wandering pie dogs were often infected by jackal bite. I feared the worst.

Once it was clearly established that the dog indeed was rabid, the British doctor whom I consulted insisted that, in the absence of any Pasteur Institute in upper Burma or China, there was no alternative but to get to Calcutta as soon as possible for the usual twenty-one shots in the stomach. The China National Aviation Corporation (CNAC), with exclusively American pilots, was still flying daily to Calcutta from Lashio on the Chinese-Burmese border. After meeting with my colleagues, who all agreed I must get to a Pasteur Institute as quickly as I could, I took off for Lashio in a jeep. After a night there, I was fortunate enough to find space on the next DC-3 to Calcutta.

Thus my Burma experience ended. It had been a hectic and sometimes tumultuous eighteen months. I had found a bride, but our first year of marriage had been engulfed in the collapse of British rule in Burma. My feelings, as the plane left the Lashio runway, were admittedly confused. The need for my departure had happened so quickly. I was happy to be seeing Faith again; I knew that she had managed to stay on in Calcutta by getting a job with U.S. Army headquarters in that city. I was definitely not looking forward to twenty-one shots in the stomach on successive days. What could one think about the country I was leaving behind, soon to be completely in Japanese hands? A gifted British official and writer at the turn of the century, H. Fielding Hall, had called it "sad, silly Burma." His adjectives were aptly chosen and prophetic. The post–World War II history of the country has been, for those who believe in conventional progress, both sad and silly—a deliberate opting out by its leadership from the economic development of its neighbors. I had few concerns about the postwar future of Burma as we flew over the northern part of the country, a route soon to be denied to the CNAC, which then had to resort to perilous flights "over the hump" of high mountains even further to the north, in order to keep open air transportation between India and Kunming-Chungking. The horizon of my thoughts was much more limited. I had witnessed the collapse of a colonial regime attacked by a determined foe, and I saw little at that point that would prevent Japanese action against India, the logical next target.

The Chinese army front south of Maymyo was soon to fall apart, and General Stilwell and his headquarters group could only escape to India on foot through the rugged Naga Hills—a march that demonstrated the personal courage and driving leadership of "Vinegar Joe."[5]

India: The Raj before Sunset

Our plane arrived at Calcutta's Dum Dum Airport late in the evening. The unique smells of India at night hit me at once. The airport seemed half deserted, and there were no taxis in evidence. I managed to hitch a ride into the city with an American whose firm furnished the CNAC with supplies. Faith had rented a small apartment in the grandiloquently named Chowringhee Mansions. I was happy to see her and slept well that night.

The next morning I went to the Pasteur Institute and had my first shot. The Indian doctor was an excellent practitioner of gallows humor, telling me that, although the serum worked in 90 percent of all cases, it could also fail. If one morning I was preparing to shave and noticed foam coming out of my mouth before I had applied my shaving brush, I would know that I was in the minority of failed cases. My thanks for this advice were not heartfelt.

The sheer weight of Calcutta's collective humanity dominated my first impression of the city. There were masses of people everywhere, on the sidewalks, on the streets, and anywhere else they could crowd. Cars edged carefully through them; there were no Burmese drivers. In the midst of all this teeming turbulence loomed the physical presence of British rule. India was big-time imperialism compared with Burma. Government House (the home of Bengal's provincial governor), the British clubs, and the office buildings (as visible signs of British business dominance) were all overwhelmingly larger. Despite all the exploitation involved in classical British imperialism, one could not deny the fascination of empire, its appeal to the romantic streak most of us possess. The British had transferred their flair for pomp and spectacle from London to their colonies, and India was clearly the brightest jewel in the crown. The way of life that senior officials had developed, as well as those further down the hierarchical line, was both gracious and outwardly pleasant, staffed by many servants. Yet it was not without its price in diseases acquired, discomfort felt during the hot season and the damp of the following monsoon, and the restless unhappiness of the uprooted expatriate away from home, dreaming of ultimate retirement in England or Scotland. I had already noted in Burma the disproportionate number of Scotsmen both in government and business. It almost seemed as if the Scots had volunteered to be the vanguard of British imperialism.

Rudyard Kipling and many other writers had written of the glory days in India. Generation after generation of young Englishmen and Scotsmen had come to this far-off subcontinent to fight and to rule. Many had brought their wives and raised families. Many had died in the heat and epidemics of a cruel environment, but there were always others to carry on, attracted by mixed motives of duty and the reality of power. At the top stood an elite corps of ICS officials who, under the viceroy, in effect ran the country. The British constructed their own exclusive subculture of clubs, schools, and hill stations drawing on Indian labor, of course, to keep things running. The clubs were strictly for non-Indians, a major factor behind the deep resentment of British rule by educated Indians.

Much has been written about the effect on British psychology of loss of empire in the aftermath of World War II. Not only was an important career path closed to ambitious and bright young men, but a whole complex of stores in London and abroad specializing in supplying the colonies with tropical clothing, tinned foods, liquors, and other gear disappeared. The collapse of the mythology of empire left a void in Britain. Dean Acheson, somewhat cruelly but accurately, commented that "Britain had lost an empire but had not yet found a cause." He was right, of course. The discontents of postwar Britain have reflected that lack, at least in part. The dark shadows of colonialism were largely forgotten. One remembered only the faded glories of the past.

Reflections on the course of empire were not, however, my principal preoccupation during those first days in Calcutta. The consul general thought he needed another officer, and his request for my transfer received a quick reply from Washington in the affirmative. A month or so later, the governor general of Burma and his entourage of senior officials set up shop in Simla, the hill station for New Delhi, and I was told to act as observer to the government of Burma in exile—a not overwhelming responsibility that required only occasional travel to Simla. When it became vacant a month after my arrival, Faith and I moved into the penthouse on top of Tower House, the tallest building (nine stories) in Calcutta. Situated on the corner of Chowringhee and at the southern end of the Maidan (a large central park and exercise ground), our new apartment, with spacious balconies, provided panoramic views over central Calcutta. The seething street life floors below sometimes seemed like an Indian version of a Brueghel painting. When the Japanese bombing of the city began, we had an incomparable observation post.

In those early days after the fall of Burma, no one could be sure what the Japanese would attempt next. Would they try to move through Assam into Bengal, or would they instead launch an invasion by sea farther to the south? After his arrival in India, Stilwell continued in his somewhat anomalous position vis-à-vis the British military command structure. As commander of the new American China-Burma-India theater, he reported directly to the Joint Chiefs of Staff in Washington and was not responsible to any British authorities in the area. In practice, this meant, as Professor Callahan has put it, "Stilwell was to control not only any American forces sent to China or South-East Asia, but a base area in India that would support these operations and the trans-Himalayan Airlift" that replaced the "defunct Burma Road."[6] Needless to say, this was not an arrangement that pleased the British, convinced as they were that the American fixation on China was unrealistic. Churchill, however, did not feel himself to be in a position actively to oppose American plans, which, in Stilwell's view, involved reopening the Burma Road with a reconstructed Chinese army based initially on the Chinese troops that had retreated from Burma into Assam. Reports of stresses and strains between Americans and British, as well as within the American camp, reached us in confusing abundance. British prestige was at a low point, and Stilwell's assessment of the "Limeys'" military potential was derogatory.

I began to keep a detailed journal reflecting some of the current speculation and strategic concerns. But daily life went on. Faith continued to work in the Calcutta office of the Stilwell mission for several months, and we enjoyed the club life together and entertaining in Tower House. A favorite nightspot was the ballroom of the Grand Hotel, where Teddy Weatherford, a talented American black jazz pianist and bandleader, provided the entertainment. After the war he was to die in an outburst of cholera that hit many guests and employees of the Grand Hotel from a polluted water supply.

One feature of life in Calcutta that we noticed fairly early on was that a popular route to the burning ghats near the Hoogly River to the north of the Maidan (where bodies were cremated) went past Tower House. It was the custom in the case of deceased well-to-do Indians to have a band lead the funeral procession. Its repertoire was not extensive, but it came as something of a shock to observe a particularly spectacular procession led by a band blaring out "There'll be a hot time in the old town tonight."

We developed close friendships with Colonel Paul Freeman (later to become a four-star general and U.S. Army Europe commander in the postwar period), for whom Faith worked, and with other military and CNAC pilots who came into and out of Calcutta. Freeman was one of Stilwell's Chinese-speaking bright, young officers charged with training Chinese troops in Assam. His healthy skepticism proved much more realistic than the enthusiasm of some of his colleagues.

I began the onerous task of beginning a new cycle of research for my Ph.D. dissertation to replace the materials lost in Burma. The Royal Library in Calcutta, it turned out, would be my principal source of books and periodicals, and it quickly became clear that I would have to give some Indian content to the new work if I was to use the available research materials fully. This proved no hardship, for I quickly developed an interest in the classical philosophies of Hinduism. Language was no immediate barrier, since I found that not only were most of the great writings available in English translation, but most of the learned commentaries were the work of such British scholars as Keith, Farquhar, McNicol, and Urquhart, some of them Anglican divines, as well as such Germans as Muller and Winternitz. Two Belgian Jesuit scholars, Dandoy and Johanns, were also helpful with their numerous writings. I began collecting a small personal library of works on Indian thought that I found, sometimes in musty condition, in Calcutta's secondhand bookshops. At one point, I thought of studying Sanskrit or Bengali, a sophisticated language with a distinguished literary tradition, exemplified by the poet Rabindranath Tagore. Alas, my intentions exceeded my possibilities. In the two years we were to stay in India, given the pressures of work in the consulate general and my reporting on the exiled Burma government in Simla, I had to be content with learning some Hindustani (coolie Hindi that served a general functional purpose). I got a good deal of research done in such spare time as I found, and became quite accustomed to the unique smell of mildewed books, the product of successive monsoon seasons.

Faith and I did find the time to spend a month on a houseboat in Kashmir—a substitute for the honeymoon we never had in Burma. This is not a travelogue, but if any place in the world is likely to inspire rhapsodic descriptions of mountain scenery, moonlight on glistening lakes, and colorful native people and crafts, it is Kashmir. Behind our houseboat and its operation, including daily calls by food suppliers and, when required, a barber, stood British entrepreneurial organization. Vacations for representatives of the raj were meant to be pleasant and relatively effortless, once the drive to the vale of Kashmir by a winding, climbing road had been accomplished. The fate of Kashmir in the postwar period has provided a sad illustration of the difference between profession and practice not uncharacteristic of successive Indian governments.

Another memorable experience was our two-week trek starting from Darjeeling into Sikkim, Bhutan, and along the border of Nepal (then still "the forbidden kingdom"). A team of Sherpa porters served as guides and bearers of burdens; we enjoyed the incomparable views of the high Himalayas, spread across the northern horizon in white majesty. Darjeeling itself was a splendid relic of former glories when it was the primary hill station for the government of India, then located in Calcutta, rather than New Delhi. Government House, the hotels, and the clubs were all on a grand scale. One could appreciate why tired British officials and businessmen would come to Darjeeling to escape the oppressive heat of the plains during the months before the monsoon broke.

My views about the internal political situation in India inevitably reflected, it seemed to me, the clear exigencies of war for a responsible leadership. I could understand why educated Indians disliked the British, who had ruled their country for so long and who refused to treat them as equals. In 1942–43, however, the indicated choice should have been the lesser of evils. Freedom would certainly not come under Japanese domination, and the Japanese military would scarcely have tolerated civil disobedience to the same extent as the British, who were highly sensitized to the use of force in India ever since the Amritsar massacre of 1918. They would have been ruthless in suppressing dissent, and gentlemanly imprisonment of India's political leadership could hardly have been a realistic expectation.

Gandhi had, of course, launched a limited civil disobedience campaign in 1940 before the war began in Asia, and the discussions of 1941 were inconclusive.[7] In March 1942, Prime Minister Churchill announced that Sir Stafford Cripps, a Labour Party member of the British war cabinet, would go to India "to satisfy himself upon the spot, by personal consultation, that the conclusions upon which we are all agreed, and which we believe represent a just and final solution, will achieve their purpose." The failure of the Cripps mission led to impasse. It did not obtain the desired truce from controversy as long as the war continued given Indian nationalist insistence on immediate political change and the creation of a national government. Historians (and several of these were involved in the negotiations) have provided various explanations for the breakdown; it was a classic case of failure to communicate precisely what the two parties had in mind. At the time, it seemed that Gandhi and some other Congress leaders had concluded that a successful Japanese invasion of India was likely and that to deal with the British at this juncture would be foolish. Subhas Bose, the Congress leader, had, in 1940, already come to the conclusion that the Axis powers would win the war. After an interlude in Nazi Germany, he turned up as a Japanese propagandist, urging the Indians who were prisoners of war to rise and form the so-called Indian National Army to fight against the British. It fought alongside the Japanese with varying degrees of effectiveness.[8]

Ironically enough, it was the generally uncompromising Nehru who opposed the Gandhi line, arguing that any hope that the Japanese would liberate India from the British, and grant the country freedom, was illusory and distressing. He advocated keeping the door open for further negotiations with the British against Gandhi, whom he saw advocating a policy that would plunge India into "anarchy and chaos." What neither he nor Gandhi, nor, for that matter, the British, seemed to understand was that while this tug-of-war between Congress and the raj was proceeding, Mohammed Ali Jinnah, head of the All-India Muslim League, was gathering support and moving toward the accumulation of power that made partition inevitable once the British were actually prepared to grant independence to India. Gandhi, in the meanwhile, had coined his slogan "Quit India" vis-à-vis the British, while advocating nonviolent resistance to the Japanese. The sanction behind his slogan was to be a new mass civil disobedience campaign. The government of India reacted vigorously, declaring the whole Congress an illegal organization and imprisoning its leaders. Violence prevailed over nonviolence. Large-scale rioting and attacks on public facilities took place in several provinces, including Bengal; more than one thousand were killed and many more injured.[9]

Calcutta itself became a center of turbulence. We did not know precisely what to expect, but we knew that, despite Gandhi's verbal commitment to nonviolence, widespread violence was likely. It was not reassuring to see wildly dressed and painted devotees of Kali, the goddess of death and destructive forces, running up and down Chowringhee, shouting for revenge. The Indian police and security forces generally kept the rioting under some control, but on one occasion Faith and I found ourselves suddenly caught up in the midst of an unruly and threatening mob on a main street in Calcutta. It looked like we would be swept away, but a police charge with lathis swinging came to our rescue. The mob leaders undoubtedly thought we were English. The emotional intensity of the mob presaged the eruptive and murderous violence of the rioting and terrible communal slaughter between Hindus and Muslims that so marred the months after independence.

I could not help but ponder the ambivalence of nonviolence as a program for action. Time and again in India it had proved to be the prelude to violence. Gandhi himself seemed an enigma, a peculiar combination of saint and charlatan, not at all committed, despite his legal training, to the syllogistic methods of Western logic. He was prepared to say in July 1942, "If, in spite of precautions, rioting does take place, it cannot be helped." [10] The Methodist bishop Wascom J. Pickett told me that he had once witnessed a mass meeting to which Gandhi spoke ending in a riotous mob looking for blood. The major thrust in the man's life and teaching, however, was certainly against the use of violence to achieve political ends. My study of his thought within its Hindu context appeared in 1949 as a chapter of my book *Power and Morals*. In it I concluded that "the Indian philosophy of non-violence is more than just another variety of pacifism as the term is used in the West. It embodies a distinctive world outlook some of the basic concepts of which may well appear unacceptable to the Western mind." [11] After analyzing those distinctive features, I went on to argue that an approach consistent with sound moral principle must allow for a legitimate and strictly proportionate use of counterviolence in a clearly defined situation of self-defense against the imposition of violence. I did not discuss the possibility, clearly observable in India, that advocacy of nonviolence might camouflage positions that actually lead to violence.

Against this background of political impasse, British officers continued to train new Indian divisions that were to play an important role in the victories to come in Burma. After a few months, the turbulence in the country quieted down. At least temporarily, the raj had won. Apart from Japanese naval activity in the Bay of Bengal, supplemented by sporadic bomber attacks on Calcutta and Madras, the expected land offensive against India did not materialize in 1942. That was to come only early in 1944, by which time British and Indian army units were much better prepared. Moreover, General Sir William Slim—the only real military commander of genius that the theater was to produce—had taken over command of the Fourteenth Army. He provided the leadership that was to repel the Japanese offensive in Assam and eventually to retake Burma in a brilliant campaign. [12]

I could see that, on the American side, both in India and in Washington, the obsession with the overriding importance of China as a factor in the war against Japan continued. General Stilwell could not conceal his disdain for the British but in a strangely perverse fashion was also vocal in his criticism of the Chinese leadership. This colorful curmudgeon of a general with a genius for invective left a trail of bruised feelings wherever his private epithets leaked to the individuals concerned, as they inevitably did. His tongue finally did him in. His emphasis was entirely on reopening a land route into western China. What the British and Indian armies did was only important in relation to that objective. He also found that he was at strategic loggerheads with Chennault (now a general), who apparently believed that, given sufficient planes, supplies, and trained pilots, his China-based air force could knock Japan out of China by blocking the movement of war matériel through the South China Sea. This competition over strategic emphasis and relevant supply priorities was to continue, in one form or another, until Stilwell's departure from the theater late in 1944.

We sat in the Calcutta consulate general observing all this and tried to keep the State Department informed as best we could. Stilwell had, attached to his staff as political officers, two bright Foreign Service officers, who were both China experts and fluent in Chinese: John Paton Davies Jr. and John S. Service. Both were to suffer bureaucratic decapitation, along with other old China hands, in the aftermath of the Communist takeover of China. Their personal tragedies have been the subject of several books, most notably *The China Hands*, by E. J. Kahn Jr.[13]

My first trip to Simla, to visit the Burma government in exile, impressed me with the durable quality of existing bureaucracies. Ensconced in the overblown splendors of the viceroy's hill station, the governor general and his senior officials, with appropriate secretarial and clerical assistance, went dutifully to their offices and carried on as if they still had important functions to perform. Their assumption was that sooner or later they would return to Burma and resume where they had left off. My lengthy report of conversations and observations contained some sarcasm and a few cheap shots. These were, after all, honorable men who found themselves in an impossible situation. They had suddenly been uprooted from positions of real power. Now it was all show and shadow. Eventually, some of them did return to Burma, but their stay was short, as British rule quickly ended in the postwar era. In 1942, it all seemed like make-believe.

The year 1943 proved to be essentially one of waiting and preparation—waiting for the Japanese invasion that did not come, and preparation, on the British side, for the eventual recapture of Burma. It was also the year of the great Bengal famine that brought untold misery to the province and the death from starvation of at least a million and a half people. The causes were manifold and complex. Starting in 1938, there had been a series of crop failures in Bengal, but the cutting off of rice imports from Burma (normally in the range of several million metric tons per year); the railway transport crisis, precipitated by massive troop and supply movements to the Eastern front as well as by mob action against depots and other facilities; and speculator control of the surplus stocks theoretically available vastly worsened the situation. It was also said that the rice-eating Bengalis refused to eat wheat, when provided. The central government in New Delhi, under the viceroy, Lord Linlithgow, proved dilatory in its reaction, claiming that the food supply was essentially a problem for provincial management. Only after Lord Wavell took over as viceroy in October 1943 did New Delhi take vigorous action, imposing food rationing on all large Indian cities and using British forces to provide famine relief in Bengal.

Calcutta was a city of death. Starving peasants and laborers poured into the provincial capital to die in the streets by the thousands. On my morning walk from Tower House to the consulate general, only a few blocks away, I would see the many bodies, on sidewalks and streets, of those who had died during the night. They would be piled into trucks and carted off to the burning ghats. One had an awful feeling of helplessness and anger at the seeming ineffectiveness of public authority. It soon became clear that the provincial government was not only inefficient; it was also corrupt. Colluding Indian grain traders made enormous profits holding back supplies until prices rose to record levels. After the worst was over, the British governor of Bengal, Mr. R. G. Casey, publicly admitted the moral breakdown, stating, "It is common knowledge that there is a great deal of corruption in Bengal, and together with the great mass of decent people I very greatly deplore it." [14] He did not deal with the question of why the British at the top had not been able better to combat this corruption and profiteering. The fact was that British senior officialdom represented only a thin veneer of control over the behavior of Indian officials down the line, including members of the provincial cabinet. In the absence of any major crisis, the governor and his staff could maintain a semblance of order and effectiveness. The combination of war, failed crops, blocked imports, disruption of railway transport in India, and the remnants of civil disobedience, however, proved overwhelming.

Nineteen forty-three was also the year of the first Chindit foray, led by Brigadier Orde Wingate, proving that land operations behind Japanese lines were possible. The effect was, perhaps, more psychological than strategic. Another Wingate expedition, and an American operation led by then Brigadier General Frank Merrill (Merrill's Marauders), took place in 1944. Both proved costly in manpower and controversial as to their real effectiveness. Wingate himself became either a romantic hero to his supporters or an arrogant prima donna to his critics. [15]

Our life in Calcutta in the midst of war, civil disobedience, and famine was not without its domestic drama and absurdities. One day, as we were sitting down to lunch, we suddenly saw our cook, Joseph, come running out of the kitchen with our Muslim bearer right behind him, brandishing a large kitchen knife and shouting imprecations. We got them apart before any damage was done but were never able to determine the cause of this explosion. It revealed, once again, the eruptive nature of the Indian temperament, to be displayed so tragically at the time of independence.

Tower House had a large terrace on both floors. In the pre–air-conditioning era we normally kept the balcony doors open. Early one morning a huge bird flapping at the foot of our bed awakened us. It was a vulture, an unclean bird by any definition, probably fresh from the burning ghats. It refused to be chased out onto the terrace but fluttered around the room, obviously wounded, perhaps by flying into the side of the building. Finally, we forced it out a door, and it took off, hurt but still able to fly. Cleaning up was another matter. Our bed and the room were a mess. (We bathed and slept in our sitting room the rest of the night.) Our staff used a lot of disinfectant that day.

By the end of 1943, reports began to come in of a possible major Japanese offensive in Assam. Engineered by General Renya Mutaguchi, with whom such an action had become an obsession, the attack actually came in March 1944. After some anxious weeks, it was to end with a major Japanese defeat, in which they suffered more than fifty-three thousand casualties.[16]

By this time we were on our way back to the United States en route to a new assignment. Our experience in that land of fascinating contrasts had been intense. We could not be present for the months of victory as, in a brilliant campaign, General Slim recaptured Burma. When it no longer really mattered, U.S.-trained Chinese forces were finally able to reopen the Burma Road. The Chiang Kai-shek government was doomed to ultimate defeat by the Communists, and the collapse of Japan came as a result of neither Chinese engagement in Burma or China nor the use of Chinese airfields for American bombers. The British regained respect and dignity in Burma, but final military victory could not preserve the empire. Lacking was a realistic political goal, and the verdict would have been the same if the British had not been constrained to abandon their preferred strategy of amphibian attacks, rather than a major land campaign, because of the American emphasis on reopening ground access to China. The judgments of historians vary, but there can be little disagreement about the ultimate futility of it all. Many brave men died in what was, in the final analysis, a largely irrelevant strategy. India had not been conquered, at least, and could move toward independence without the burden of defeat and Japanese military occupation.[17]

We sailed from Bombay in February 1944 on the SS *Hermitage*, a naval transport. Our route took us south around Australia through a very rough Tasmanian Sea. After a few days' stop in Melbourne, we proceeded to Los Angeles via the South Seas. The great fear, of course, was that a Japanese submarine would approach and fire a torpedo. There were a number of alerts stimulated by rather primitive radar equipment, and, at one point, a lookout actually saw a submarine on the surface (he could not identify its nationality). In any event, after some forty days en route, we arrived at our destination none the worse for wear. Faith was pregnant, and we looked forward to having our first child in Washington. Perhaps the most memorable part of the trip was the highly pungent cooking smells provided by a crew of Lascar sailors being transported from Bombay to Melbourne. They literally lived on deck, preparing their meals in the open—an accepted fire hazard, no doubt.

I thought India was part of our past, but when I reported to the department, I found myself assigned temporarily to take over the India desk to replace an officer absent on sick leave. I now saw the reports coming in regularly from our mission in New Delhi, as well as those filed by Stilwell's political advisers. They did not really add all that much to what we had been able to learn in Calcutta. British-American differences on strategy in Burma continued. It also became clear that the Stilwell era in China was approaching its end. Chiang Kai-shek kept pressing for his replacement and finally succeeded in persuading President Roosevelt that Vinegar Joe must depart (his recall took place in October 1944). His replacement was General Albert Wedemeyer, a hard-driving, ambitious American officer, described by contemporaries as something of a martinet. In typical blunt fashion, Stilwell exclaimed, when rumors reached him in June that he would be relieved: "Good God—to be ousted in favor of Wedemeyer—that would be a disgrace." [18]

After some months on the India desk, I learned that my next posting would be to the American embassy in Lima, Peru. Once again, as in the case of Baghdad, I was never to arrive at my original assignment. Instead the department, at the last minute, changed my assignment to Lourenço Marques, Mozambique.

Mozambique

I must concede that I did not know very much about Mozambique when I got there. I had read the post report and other materials prepared by our consulate general, but there was not much information about the neutral

Portuguese colony floating about Washington in 1944, other than that Lourenço Marques, the capital, was a little Lisbon in the sense of being a spy center for German and Japanese intelligence operations all over southern and central Africa.

My arrival took place in the summer (actually winter in the Southern Hemisphere), after travel by a circuitous and prolonged route that carried me from Miami, over Belem and Natal in Brazil, to Accra, via Ascension Island (in a B-24 bomber), then on to Lagos, Leopoldville, and finally Lourenço Marques. From Lagos on, I traveled in a Lockheed Lodestar plane, piloted by a Czechoslovak who seemed to know his way around Africa and could spot landing strips for refueling that suddenly appeared out of the jungle. The destruction of Africa's tropical rain forests had not yet begun in that distant era.

Lourenço Marques turned out to be more pleasant than I had anticipated. Located at nearly twenty-six degrees south latitude, the city actually had a reasonably mild climate, with many miles of sand beaches stretching to the north. The Polana Hotel, where I spent my initial months, enjoyed the reputation of having the best kitchen and other facilities in Africa. The Portuguese colonial administrators had provided the city with broad boulevards and fine villas. The wartime espionage activities of the Germans, Japanese, and, of course, the British, Americans, and South Africans added spice to what might, in more normal times, have been a fairly bland existence. I found both the U.S. Office of Strategic Services (OSS) and Naval Intelligence operating in the city; one of our tasks in the consulate general was to make sure they did not go off the rails. While Portuguese neutrality involved considerable leaning in our direction, particularly after the war in Europe seemed to be turning against Germany, the governor general insisted on maintaining an orderly surface appearance. The Nazi network was clearly the most extensive and included the usual party breakdown into gauleiter and other distinctive ranks.

In the meantime, Faith and our baby daughter had begun a long and arduous trip to join me in Lourenço Marques. The State Department had officially advised against it, but a sympathetic Foreign Service officer on the African desk, Perry Jester, to whom I shall be eternally grateful, furnished informal help in getting them on a Portuguese passenger vessel bound for Lisbon. After considerable delay in Portugal, they were able to fly from Morocco to Cairo, where Faith was hospitalized for some weeks. After further delay, she and Ruth obtained space on a British Overseas Airways flying boat. I was happy to greet them upon arrival after their months en route, which had tested my wife's ingenuity, endurance, and resolve. It was a tribute to her possession of all these qualities that they made it.

Work in Mozambique proved varied and frequently interesting. Among other things, I handled the political and economic reporting. The consul general handled the golf playing and the socializing at the numerous so-called sundowners that the large South African and British business communities inflicted on each other. It took no great powers of discernment to observe that the colonial government was a tightly run operation under Governor General José Tristao de Bettencourt, who reported directly to the all-powerful minister of colonies in Lisbon. The ruling Portuguese, I found, did not mingle much socially with the largely non-Portuguese business community; their emotional and family ties were mainly with the mother country, and periodic trips home represented the most cherished reward for service in exile. The government's policy toward the native population sounded better in theory than it proved to be in practice. Only a relatively small proportion of the African population (less than 1 percent) qualified as assimilated (*assimilados*), with full privileges of Portuguese citizens, while the vast bulk of the population remained classified as indigenous (*indigenos*), with limited privileges. One could argue, as some Portuguese officials did, that their approach was essentially paternalistic, without racial prejudice (after all, there were the *assimilados* to prove the point), but the reality of harsh labor codes and generally discriminatory treatment of blacks was all too apparent. Those same officials could point to rather good hospital facilities in the capital city for Africans (in some respects actually better than for the white population) but made no similar claims for up-country and out in the bush.[19]

I found this latter colloquialism in the form of "back to the bush," borrowed, apparently, from South Africa, not inappropriate to describe the behavior of black servants and employees, who, after working for a few years, would suddenly disappear without warning. The legitimate assumption was that they had returned to their native villages. Somewhat to my shock, I discovered that the menials employed by the consulate general did not correspond to the names on the payroll; the real possessors of those names had long since gone back to the bush. Since only an X was required in lieu of signature on the payroll, the chief clerk, a Goanese Indian, had simply tolerated the practice, arguing that it did no one any harm. I was already enough of a bureaucrat to insist that we get the right names on the payroll, an objective we achieved only after considerable correspondence with Washington. We had telegraphic communications with Washington, of course, but basically we lived by the weekly diplomatic pouches brought by courier from Cairo. Sea pouches delivered by

American freighters would periodically deposit a month's supply of welcome magazines and back issues of the *New York Times*.

While gathering material for economic reports, I was able to travel fairly extensively to the north of the colony and into the hinterlands. Mozambique is an elongated country with an area of more than three hundred thousand square miles, stretching for more than a thousand miles along the Indian Ocean and to the north into the deep tropics. In 1944–45, one got around either by plane or by coastal steamer. All the passable roads and railway lines ran from east to west, into either South Africa or Southern Rhodesia. One question I tried to explore was the reality of the claim that Mozambique possessed vast reserves of valuable minerals that had not been exploited, a belief that had existed since the early days of the Portuguese colony. I concluded tentatively that the vast reserves were mythical and so reported. Even today one hears similar rumors, but apart from minor coal and oil deposits, little tangible has turned up.

Faith and I made the obligatory visit to Krueger National Park to see the wild animals and to hear the lions roar at night. We also traveled frequently to Swaziland, where some retired American friends had built a modern house on the brink of the Great Rift Valley, that spectacular geological phenomenon extending some three thousand miles to the north across most of East Africa and into Southwest Asia. One could descend to the bottom of the depression by jeep to observe the huge herds of impala and other game at first hand, and the views from the top were breathtaking. Our visits to Swaziland and the Great Rift Valley are among my most pleasant (and still vivid) memories of a distant past.

Our own house, rented from a Swiss businessman, was built in typical colonial style, with large screened verandas. With it came a well-tended tropical garden that provided fruit and colorful foliage in abundance. We were pleased when a local publication featured it as the best example of an old-style colonial garden in Mozambique, but could claim no personal credit for it. We had running water, but cooking had to be done in a separate kitchen over a coal fire. We were lucky to inherit a reasonably good native cook, although he tended, in Portuguese fashion, to be a bit heavy on the olive oil. Swimming in the ocean provided a welcome diversion, although everyone knew that the Mozambique Channel boasted a large shark population. We had a few scares, and one tended to look over one's shoulder frequently to make sure that a telltale fin did not appear. The Polana Hotel had its own swimming area surrounded by a large shark net, but it lost its attraction when a good-sized shark entered through a hole in the net. Thus our days passed with a mixture of pleasant living and hard work.

Ironically enough, what had already seemed like a work overload at a two-officer post in wartime turned into an even heavier burden with the end of the war. The consul general had had a heart attack while vacationing in South Africa, and when he finally returned, he performed in low gear. With the end of the war, OSS operations in Mozambique vanished overnight. I soon learned why. While the governor general was favorably disposed toward the victors, he could not tolerate the subornation of some of his senior officials, including the chief of police. How he came by the evidence I do not know, but they were unceremoniously relieved of their duties and dispatched back to Lisbon for whatever fate awaited them there. Under instructions from Washington, I went down to what had been the OSS office. It was a mess, with papers scattered all about. The large safe was locked, and, of course, I did not have the combination. There was nothing to do but to bring in someone with an acetylene torch. I made sure that one of the remaining members of the U.S. Naval Mission—itself in a stage of urgent liquidation—would be present to witness whatever might come out of the safe.

The man with the torch finally burned out the locking device and swung the door open. To our amazement, hundred-dollar bills tumbled out onto the floor in profusion. Money used for payoffs to agents and officials no doubt! We counted the bills carefully twice, and I had the naval officer countersign the inventory. The State Department response to my telegraphic report was to request that the money, a considerable amount, be forwarded to Washington by the next diplomatic courier. The remaining contents of the safe, some of them incriminating for local officials, I either destroyed or sent to Washington. It was not an inspiring conclusion to what, on the whole, had been a fairly successful operation, if somewhat jazzy and "old boy."

Just as the demobilization of our victorious forces in Europe took place at pell-mell speed, in far-off Mozambique soon only the consulate general was left to constitute the American presence, or, in some cases, to hold the bag. Word came to us through various channels that further payoffs were expected. Our main burden, however, derived from the American government's request that all German-owned business and official properties in the colony, including, of course, the German consulate general, be turned over to us. The governor general quickly complied, and I found myself, among other things, responsible for some nine up-country German-run sisal plantations. I also found that all nine of them had regularly been delivering sisal to the port of Beira for shipment to the United States, an OSS achievement of some importance. With the fall of the Philippines after Pearl Harbor, we had lost access to Manila hemp, the principal source of naval rigging. In the pre–nylon-rope era, sisal had become a critical material as the next best thing, just as Bengal jute (as the principal source of burlap) had appeared on the critical materials list. The German plantation owners, whether or not they were ideologically anti-Nazi, had apparently had few scruples about aiding the enemy.

Taking over and analyzing the voluminous documentation left in the German consulate general proved to be an arduous and complicated task. The staff had managed to burn what (we could only assume) were some of the most sensitive materials, but they had obviously been interrupted by the Portuguese authorities, since much remained. The building itself dwarfed our modest office. We obviously could not expect any help from the German staff, which had been interned temporarily by the colonial government and would soon be shipped back to Portugal for repatriation to Germany. Years later, during the mid-1960s, when I was in Bonn as deputy chief of mission, I was to run into the former German consul general Heinrich Wirtz. He had remained in the Foreign Office and was on the verge of retirement. We could only exchange a few rueful reminiscences of our time in Mozambique where as wartime enemies we had never met.

I obviously needed help and was fortunate to be able to enlist the services of Werner von Alvensleben, a white hunter and political refugee from Nazi Germany, who had been condemned to death in absentia. He had been working on dangerous missions for the OSS during the war and was now at loose ends. It turned out to be an association that was to lead us, when we arrived in postwar Germany, to some of the best and most enduring friendships of our lives. Werner worked untiringly, going through the archives of the consulate general, categorizing the various documents, and separating the wheat from the chaff. Some identified individuals and organizations with Nazi affiliations, both in Mozambique and in South Africa. I dutifully sent the interesting items back to Washington, but I never found out if they had served any useful purpose. I could not be surprised at the degree of South African involvement; many Boers seemed to have a natural affinity for the German cause.

Our association with Werner and his lovely Portuguese wife, Bibla, caused some problems with the English and South African community in Lourenço Marques. After all, he was a German, and no matter what his wartime record, it was not cricket to use him as we were doing. At first, the consul general joined us in efforts to rehabilitate him and his wife socially, but when the protests started, he quickly retreated, leaving Faith and me to take the flack. In any event, our time in Africa was coming to an end. My next assignment would send me to postwar Germany.

Saying goodbye to the von Alvenslebens in Lourenço Marques was the hardest aspect of our departure. We had become close friends, and good friendships, we had already learned, are to be cherished! We had the names and last addresses of Werner's parents and sisters, but whether they were still alive in the turmoil of German defeat and disintegration he did not know. Getting to Germany did not prove to be easy. After a considerable delay in Cairo, we finally boarded a military transport bound for Genoa. From there we flew to Frankfurt on a U.S. military plane.

3

Postwar Germany

. . . .

We landed in Frankfurt early in June 1946. The American officer at the airport inspecting documentation seemed surprised that Faith was with me. "Dependents are not yet authorized to come to Germany," he said, but added, "Well, she's here with your daughter, so they might as well stay." Once again, as when she remained in Calcutta, Faith's presence constituted a fait accompli. We were to become very accustomed to the term "dependent" in a military-dominated, occupied Germany; it defined the limits of the possible for women and children. Dependents could do some things but not others.

We took an army bus into Frankfurt to spend the night at a military hotel before proceeding to Berlin. First impressions are sometimes misleading, but in this case they were not. Frankfurt overwhelmed us as a city of bleakness and ruin. The streets were unlit, but, in the dim moonlight, huge piles of rubble reared up on all sides. Our hotel was near the partially destroyed, but still used, main railway station. The square in front had already become the center of the city's black market—a dominant feature everywhere of postwar Germany's economy, as we were to learn very quickly.

The hotel proved comfortable enough; it had escaped British and American bombs during the entire war. Inevitably, the story spread that it, along with several others, had been spared so that the American military could use them as officers' quarters after the victory. Such confidence in Allied accuracy was touching but hardly persuasive, given the general promiscuity of strategic bombing by both sides. We slept well that night under old-fashioned German feather comforters that had not yet been replaced by American blankets. The following morning we flew into Berlin on a dark, damp, and dreary day.

The scene below, as we circled over the city before landing at Tempelhof Airport, seemed one of utter desolation. Nothing appeared to stand undestroyed (actually more than 25 percent of the city survived, mainly in the suburbs). Tempelhof itself had obviously received many direct hits, but its main structure stood together with the enormous overhang that had made the airport, built in 1936, such an advanced architectural design. We took an army bus to Harnack House, formerly the guest house of the Max Planck Institute but now an officers' club, where we were to stay. En route, we noted that the suburb of Dahlem, in which Harnack House and the headquarters of the Office of Military Government United States (OMGUS) were located, had come through the war with many fine villas still relatively intact. But even there, the travail through which the city had passed evidenced itself in the heaps of rubble and partially destroyed buildings between those that by luck had survived.

That afternoon we obtained transportation to look for Werner von Alvensleben's parents and sisters in the Kurfuerstendam area of the city. The street where the address he had given us should have been located had completely disappeared under huge piles of rubble with not a building left standing. If they had still been there when the destruction took place, none of them could have lived. Later, walking about alone after dark, I soaked up impressions frequently to be duplicated in the ruined cities of Germany. The lingering aura of death seemed all-pervasive, together with the frequent stench of rotting potatoes, seemingly the only food that the still surviving Germans, in the remnants of their houses, had been able to salvage. It was a smell we were to encounter often enough in the next few years as we entered unheated German houses. As I walked, I noted that streetlights were nonexistent; only a partial moon provided light and lent a hazy gloss to the rubble and empty shells of buildings. Occasionally a light became visible, revealing the location of a black market nightclub or restaurant. My thoughts were disjointed; utter desolation and demoralization prevailed, and I could only absorb fractured impressions in the midst of chaos. I later observed how well the movie made from Graham Greene's novel *The Third Man*, though photographed in Vienna, caught the eerie, dark atmosphere of those early months in Berlin and the other destroyed cities of Germany.

After some days in Berlin consulting with Robert Murphy, political adviser to the military governor and the senior State Department official in occupied Germany, and members of his staff, we departed for Bremen, where as consul I was to assist with the opening phases of the tasks and duties of the American consulate general in that city. Bremen, too, was a city largely in ruins, but with strange pockets of survival; these included the suburbs where the American occupiers lived. The consul general, just arrived from Switzerland, turned out to be Maurice W. Altaffer, who had been the number two man in Zurich during my months there in 1939–40. He was a man of strong convictions and prejudices, thoroughly honest and frequently unbending. He found cooperation with Military Government, and the amateurs and bunglers whom he believed to be running it, difficult.

The American military government establishment in Bremen, and indeed elsewhere, had its share of misfits, but it also had some talented and dedicated officials who tried their best to carry out the instructions they received, no matter how contradictory (or in some cases downright absurd) they turned out to be. Some were returned refugees from Nazi Germany who understandably bore little good will for the conquered German people; they seemed to be mainly in the Information Control or Political Divisions. Invited to attend the weekly staff meetings of the military governor for Bremen, a civilian former shipping executive, I observed at first hand the dissensions within his organization and the incompatible directions in which they were trying to move. It quickly became clear that the assumptions under which a triumphant American army had entered a conquered Germany had little relationship to reality or to basic long-term American interests. Joint Chiefs of Staff (JCS) Directive 1067, the bible of the American military government, issued in April 1945, was essentially punitive in intent. It stipulated, inter alia, that Germany was to be occupied not "for the purpose of liberation, but as a defeated enemy nation," that "fraternization with the German officials and population" was strongly to be discouraged, that Germany was to be industrially disarmed and demilitarized, and that a "program of reparations and restitution" was to be enforced. The only positive note was to list, along with denazification, demilitarization, punishment of war criminals, and industrial disarmament, as essential steps in the achievement of the principal Allied objective of preventing "Germany from ever again becoming a threat to the peace of the world . . . the preparation for an eventual reconstruction of German political life on a democratic basis."[1]

Reality quickly caught up with abstract formulations of policy. Nonfraternization could not stand up long in the face of the human propensity for sympathy and affection. Moreover, the plight of the civil population in the midst of destroyed buildings, food and fuel shortage, and economic collapse so obviously called for help that further punishment seemed irrelevant in what had become a battle for survival. The denazification effort and the Nuremberg Trials continued, of course, along with other programs of Military Government, but the emphasis inevitably shifted to the provision of minimal supplies to avoid mass starvation. The outset of the cold war was soon, in any event, to inject a whole new set of priorities that radically altered American objectives with respect to Germany.

The district of the Bremen consulate general included most of the British zone of occupation. We had no office in Düsseldorf, and our consulate general in Hamburg had jurisdiction only over Schleswig-Holstein, the city of Hamburg itself, and a slice of Niedersachsen. This, in effect, meant that we in Bremen were responsible for political and economic reporting on the area that later became North Rhine–Westphalia, including the Ruhr, as well as on the relevant activities of the British military government. Frequent trips by car to Düsseldorf, Cologne, and the Ruhr became essential to establish contacts with German industrialists and politicians. I did not keep a record of how many times I traveled south, but it seemed to me that I was more on the move than at home. As the occupation zone began to divide organizationally into *Länder*, or states, and North Rhine–Westphalia emerged as clearly the most important of these administrative areas, our reports provided the only comprehensive information about it for the U.S. government. I was repeatedly surprised, while attending conferences in Berlin and later Frankfurt, at how little our military government, or even State Department people, knew about what was going on in the British zone or, for that matter, even seemed to care. The zones of occupation appeared to be largely sealed off from each other, even after the creation of Bizonia in the autumn of 1946.

My circle of contacts expanded rapidly. One of the first was Dr. Konrad Adenauer, recently ousted by the British as mayor of Cologne, who was beginning the process of organizing the Christian Democratic Party in North Rhine–Westphalia. He turned seventy in 1946, and the tendency was to write him off as a member of the older generation. When I would describe him as a politician who might still play a role in postwar Germany, my colleagues in Berlin and Frankfurt would only laugh. In any event, I met with him regularly on my trips south at St. Elizabeth's Hospital in a suburb of Cologne, one of the few buildings in that blighted city that seemed to have survived unscathed. I cannot claim specific prescience about the future first chancellor of the Federal Republic of Germany, but from the outset he impressed me as a man of great ability, determination, and political skill. As I came to know him better, I was more and more persuaded that he would emerge as an important political figure in Germany.

Other Germans in North Rhine–Westphalia whom I came to know well were Karl Arnold, the first minister president of the state, and his political adviser, Dr. Hans Kroll, an experienced former diplomat, as well as a whole bevy of British military government officials and Ruhr industrialists who were trying to save the remnants of their factories and mills from dismantling for reparations as well as to bring them back into at least minimal production. In the Bremen area itself, Mayor Wilhelm Kaisen, truly a grand old man of his party, the Social Democratic Party (SPD), became a regular contact along with members of his staff. As a young American official who made no pretense about possessing decision-making authority in Military Government, I provided a sympathetic shoulder to cry on and an assured channel of communication—directly to the State Department in Washington.

We made many German friends. It was a time when elemental human needs drew people together; the friends we made in those early postwar years were among the best and most lasting of our diplomatic experience. We had found Werner von Alvensleben's sister Lexi, and their parents, living north of Bremen in Vegesack in a country house belonging to William Roloff, Lexi's husband. There must have been at least fifteen other relatives and children who had taken shelter with the Roloffs. Lexi, we soon found, was a woman of great resourcefulness. Along with her father, she had been imprisoned by the Nazis in Berlin; her escape and move to the West was a drama in itself. Roloff himself had been designated as minister of fisheries by the Twentieth of July plotters against Hitler; he also ended up in prison when the takeover failed, but he escaped execution. Other close friends were Helmut Schnackenburg and his wife, Isolde, and Dr. Kurt Jackle. Helmut was director of the Bremen Philharmonic Orchestra and was later to become the general music director for the city, while Kurt was head of obstetrics at Saint Joseph Stift (a principal local hospital). He brought our two sons into the world when Faith chose to have her children in a German hospital rather than in the American military hospital in Bremerhaven.

We had a large house in a Bremen suburb and tried our best to feed as many friends as we could. Providing hot water for at least a weekly bath turned out to be a major contribution that we could make. When Faith discovered that there were a large number of celiac babies in the Bremen area, she instituted a "banana lift" from Amsterdam that undoubtedly saved the lives of many. Funds for this were raised by the American Wives Club.

As part of the occupation establishment, we lived well. There might be occasional shortages of coal or luxury items, but small inconveniences in the midst of the misery and need that surrounded us seemed so trivial that our discontents could arouse only personal shame. The consulate general had its own club staffed by expert German cooks and waiters who were glad to be so near good food. We tolerated expenditures for meat and canned goods at the army commissary far in excess of what we could reasonably consume on the assumption that our staff and their families would benefit. We did not want our supplies to be sold on the black market, however, and our first real crisis at the club came when an observant American discovered that sizable pieces of meat were being secreted in a large hollow statue with detachable head that stood in the hallway. I remember having to deliver a solemn lecture to the staff saying that, while we could be generous, we could not accept being exploited. How ridiculous my somewhat pompous and patronizing remarks seemed to me after I had made them! Most Americans would have attempted precisely the same thing under comparable circumstances.

One lesson we learned quickly was that being close to Bremerhaven, the American port of embarkation and disembarkation (the so-called reppledepple), did not guarantee access to the best American supplies, whether of food or post exchange merchandise. In life, military or otherwise, the best follows the brass. The commissaries and PXs in Berlin and Frankfurt and points south, where the senior Military Government officials and military commanders held forth, were much better stocked, we discovered. That reality could justify an occasional special shopping trip to a point three hundred miles away in search of scarce items. There was no shortage of gasoline for Americans.

The German autobahn system had survived the war reasonably intact with the exception of some key bridges that the Nazis had blown up during their last chaotic months in power. This necessitated some difficult and precipitous detours down into and up from river valleys that put harsh strains on one's brakes and transmission system. A particularly bad example was at Minden on the main north-south route. We generally drove the red Studebaker that we had shipped up from Mozambique; it broke down on a number of occasions, but we were always lucky enough to find a skilled German mechanic who could perform wonders at patchwork repairing, sometimes even with Jeep parts. The official car fleet of the consulate general was not impressive, but it did boast one huge, elongated Maybach limousine—allegedly the former property of a senior Nazi official—that could be used for business trips. I used to feel somewhat ashamed, as I arrived in chauffeur-driven splendor at British military government headquarters at Bad Oeynhausen or at other stops in North Rhine–Westphalia that I would visit regularly, but the quest for comfort would generally prevail when a lengthy trip was in prospect, and the alternative was a considerably less commodious car.

The State Department had some interesting characters scattered around Germany in those early years. One of the most colorful was certainly our consul general in Hamburg, Edward Groth, known to his contemporaries as "Eddy the Ready." He was an indefatigable walker and explorer. His travels to obscure places around the world have become the subject of many tales. He had a great love of opera and, for the first years after the war, literally fed many of the singers of the Hamburg State Opera. He had established such a close relationship with some of them that, as Faith and I observed one night, when a Wagnerian soprano (Ilse Schluetter) was in bad voice during the first act of *Tristan und Isolde*, he personally delivered a package of cough drops between the acts to ensure improved performance.

I did not come to know General Lucius Clay well. Although I met him a number of times, it was always in groups or at conferences. My relations with Robert Murphy became somewhat closer, allowing for the fact he was primarily in Berlin and I in the West. After all, as the principal State Department representative in occupied Germany, he was in effect our chief of mission. He did not always enjoy a comfortable position. U.S. Military Government received its instructions from the Pentagon. Murphy, on the other hand, reported to the Department of State, which played an increasingly important role once the war was over, and attended frequent four-power or three-power meetings at the foreign-minister level. There were inevitable tensions and disagreements, but, on the whole, Clay and Murphy worked well together.

So life went on during 1946. It was a fascinating and sad time. A destroyed Germany had not yet begun to climb out of its paralysis, and even the process of clearing away the rubble seemed endless. In every city I visited during that first year, I found the oppressive reality of ruins. These were not the historically picturesque ruins of Rose Macaulay's later book *The Pleasure of Ruins*, ruins mellowed by time and the passage of many centuries. These were man-made ruins achieved in a few years of warfare, a reflection of the enormous destructive power of modern explosives, of humankind's ability to destroy, within a relatively few days, the accumulations of urban civilization over hundreds of years. A typical street scene would be of a group of slow-moving elderly women piling rubble into wheelbarrows and then wobbling off with them to some central collection point. I bought a painting by Martin Koblo, an artist of the Worpswede school, entitled *Truemmerstadt* (city in ruins). It captured, better than words could express, the eerie mood and atmosphere of a destroyed Hamburg at night. In the painting, haze diffuses the moonlight; only a few barely distinguishable figures slink along a street that was once a thoroughfare. A steeple and a few partly demolished buildings loom up amid the piles of rubble. All is quiet in this picture of desolation—a city seemingly mortally wounded. No one could imagine that within a decade or so life in Germany's destroyed cities would have revived to the extent it did, even though many of the new apartment houses and high-rise office buildings would be ugly, along with artfully reconstructed historic churches and public edifices.

An intriguing question is what might have happened if the Soviets had played their cards differently during those early years in Germany. Policy making in Washington in 1945 suffered from the tug-of-war between Secretary of the Treasury Henry Morgenthau and his followers, who wanted to punish, deindustrialize, and ruralize a rump Germany,[2] and those who saw the task as essentially a rescue operation to avoid mass starvation and total economic collapse. Even many of the latter, however, did not originally think in terms of a lengthy occupation of the country. American demobilization of our victorious armies in Europe had been pell-mell, and there were voices in the United States that suggested we should quietly get out and leave the Germans to the not-so-tender mercies of the Russians, and perhaps to the French, who would know how to treat them properly. One could argue that the Soviets really blew a golden opportunity. If they had been more obliging and less bullying in their behavior in the four-power Allied Control Council in Berlin, if they had not in their own zone of occupation behaved in a way indicating they intended to Sovietize it completely, they might have come much closer to achieving, by default, the objective—which later seemed to emerge—of dominating all of Germany and Western Europe in such a way as to incorporate their economic strength and military potential within the Soviet sphere of influence and thus unbalance completely the relationship between the two superpowers. In June 1945, General Clay still expressed his determination to make quadripartite government function. As late as November of the same year, he stated his view, during consultations in Washington, that the French were the real stumbling block to economic unity of the four occupation zones and that Soviet barriers to interzonal trade and travel had a rationale. He still apparently felt this way in May 1946.[3]

Soviet strategy, of course, also seemed to involve the assumption that growing Communist Party strength in Western Europe would sooner or later lead to governments strongly supportive of Soviet objectives. That fear was common in the West during the early postwar years; it seemed as if Communist Parties in a number of countries, especially France and Italy, with their control of strong labor unions, might well be able to take power. The unfolding reality demonstrated that these fears were unfounded. No Communist Party in any Western democracy ever came close to a political takeover, but this did not seem so clear in the late 1940s; the concern was sincere, just as the concern about the possibility of Soviet military aggression against Western Europe was sincere, whether or not the Soviet leadership ever seriously contemplated such action.

What brought about a gradual change of attitude on the part of General Clay and other senior American military government officials is a complicated story. Soviet intentions in Eastern Europe and their zone of Germany seemed less and less benign, but the harsh realities of life in West Germany developed a momentum of their own, requiring action that was bound to run counter to Soviet interests, as defined in Moscow. On the political front, the United States had already, in November 1945, authorized the creation of a *Länderrat* (Council of the States) to represent the minister presidents of the three states in the American zone, but a continuously deteriorating economic situation during 1946 demanded a basic redefinition of objectives. It had become clear that a major food crisis was inevitable despite American and some British grain deliveries. The whole population faced slow starvation at the daily level of 1,275 calories anticipated for the American zone. Available statistics indicated that 30 percent of every thousand children born in Germany died before reaching the age of one. Moreover, Ruhr coal production, important not only for Germany but for Western European economic recovery in general, continued to lag. Economic union of the four zones called for by the Potsdam Agreement (and considered essential by General Clay) seemed a remote prospect. An atmosphere of crisis prevailed, and even greater U.S. subsidies for its zone, if available, than the some two hundred million dollars per year already in effect could do little in the short term to improve the situation.[4]

The official redefinition of policy came on September 6, with the speech in Stuttgart of Secretary of State James Byrnes. Although Military Government practice had already begun to water down JCS Directive 1067, Byrnes, in effect, delivered its death knell (although formal repeal did not come until early 1947). An invitation had gone out to all State Department officials in Germany to attend the speech to be given in the Stuttgart opera house, which had suffered only slight damage in the war. I can recall driving down from Bremen with some of my colleagues in our red Studebaker, which, obligingly, did not break down en route. We did not know what to expect from the secretary, but our hope was that he could inject greater realism into our policy toward Germany. We were not disappointed. He stressed that, although the United States was "prepared to carry out fully the principles outlined in the Potsdam Agreement on demilitarization and reparations," this had to be consistent with levels of industry agreed on the assumption that reparations would not be made from current production. He went on to say that "the German people were not to be denied the right to use such savings as they might be able to accumulate by hard work and frugal living to build up their industries for peaceful purposes." In the absence of that economic unity for Germany that the United States favored, we were now prepared to unify the economy of the American zone "with any or all of the other zones willing to participate in the unification." He noted that "it never was the intention of the American Government to deny to the German people the right to manage their own internal affairs as soon as they were able to do so in a democratic way with genuine respect for human rights and fundamental freedoms." Hence we favored "the early establishment of a provisional German Government for Germany."[5]

I have quoted at some length from Secretary Byrnes's speech because it had historic significance and certainly created a sensation in Germany. Rereading the text and looking back, I find it easy to understand why. At a dismal time and with little prospect for immediate improvement, it struck a note of forgiveness and hope.

As an American who had been physically present in 1946, I returned in the fall of 1996 to be the opening speaker in Stuttgart at the fiftieth anniversary celebration of Byrnes's speech. Although over the years I have made more trips to Germany that I can even begin to count, this visit proved particularly evocative as it brought back intense recollections of the postwar history of a country that still remains an enigma to many Americans.

The winter of 1946–47, however, proved to be the low point in postwar Germany. It was the most severe in decades, with unbroken months of subfreezing weather, as a seemingly perpetual high-pressure area hung over northern Europe. Whatever reserve stocks of food and fuel had survived the war were exhausted. Even the American military government doled out coal by the sack to its members, although army commissaries were able to keep essential food shipments flowing from the United States. The demand for cigarettes, coffee, fats, and chocolate bars in military commissaries and post exchanges must have been extraordinarily high, for these were the staples of the black market in Germany, the only source of them for those who could afford to pay. By the end of 1946 even the vestiges of nonfraternization had completely disappeared, and German girlfriends of GIs were the beneficiaries of typically American generosity in the distribution of military supplies.

The black market—or the free market, if you will—is a phenomenon that springs up almost automatically in an economy of scarcity. We have seen it in Eastern Europe and other parts of the world where demand exceeds supply. In postwar Germany, except for tightly rationed food, it dominated the distribution system, frequently in a sleazy atmosphere of dimly lit cafés or public squares. Many of the transactions were essentially barter, sometimes of intrinsically valuable family possessions, for items become valuable only because of dire need. Nearly every German bought and sold on the black market, but the professional black marketeer was a distinctive type (a so-called *Schieber*), with seemingly inexhaustible sources of supply, if the price were right. The right price was usually so many packages or cartons of American cigarettes, a much more prized medium of exchange than the virtually worthless reichsmark. Cartons of cigarettes revolved around and around in transaction after transaction. After reform of the currency in 1948, it turned out that many of the cartons had been skillfully opened, their contents removed and sold separately, and the empty space stuffed with filler. The carton (*Stange*, as it was called) would be just as skillfully resealed, so that, to the naked eye, no sign of tampering was visible. Such is the role of illusion in economic life: the empty cartons served precisely the same function as a medium of exchange as those with their original content.

The destroyed German cities provided an atmospherically appropriate setting for all of this technically illegal, but almost universally practiced, trading activity. Streets and squares in the vicinity of railway stations, or the space under viaducts, seemed to be particularly favorite locations, usually after dark and late into the night. The trading also went on in black market restaurants and nightclubs, some shady and some elegant, but all with that peculiar atmosphere of furtiveness that tolerated illegality seems to engender. In more recent times of relative prosperity and plenty in the Western democracies, we experience the contemporary counterpart of the black market in the so-called unrecorded or black economy. The motive here is primarily to escape taxation or to hide criminality, rather than to extract profit from scarcity. Economics as a social science has little useful to say about this not unimportant segment of economic activity, or why, in some cases (as in contemporary Italy), it may well be among the most dynamic and creative parts of the economy. In postwar Germany, it was both inevitable and necessary to the process of distribution.

During that dark and dreary winter, a major sustaining force, particularly for the educated middle class, was the availability of music and theater performed in whatever ramshackle and unheated auditoriums had survived the bombings. I came to appreciate this more and more, as I would sit along with the German audience, all of us in overcoats, at concerts and at plays. Listening to music was like an infusion of plasma to enraptured audiences. Our friend Helmut Schnackenburg, who conducted the Bremen Philharmonic in the conventional white tie and tails (without an overcoat but with a sweater underneath), used to say that only the great classics of German music could carry his compatriots through bad times by reminding them of the better part of their heritage. The contribution to morale of conductors and musicians in their shattered country was important at a time when there seemed to be little basis for hope. The revival of many classical German plays by theater groups that organized themselves out of the ruins also helped to give this seemingly hapless people some living link with their pre-Nazi past.

During 1946 and into 1947 a constant stream of German refugees returning from the United States flowed through Bremerhaven. Some came to recapture the past, others to influence the future. A number ended up in East Germany, a few to play a prominent role during the early years of the German Democratic Republic. They had not forgotten their left-wing antecedents. The majority, however, stayed in the West and identified themselves with the developing institutions of the new democratic Germany. Among the most spectacular was Prince Hubertus zu und von Loewenstein who, in his youthful Berlin days, acquired the sobriquet the "Red Prince" because of his courageous political opposition to the Nazis. A scholar, a fine speaker, and a somewhat quixotic character, Hubertus never quite made the mark in postwar Germany that his talents might have indicated. He did become an FDP (Free Democratic Party) member of the Bundestag for four years, wrote many books, led successful agitation against British use of Heligoland as a target for bombing practice, campaigned for return of the Saar to the Federal Republic by France, and, as he grew older, became an indefatigable traveler around the world as a speaker for the Federal Information Office. His career was not atypical. Unlike Willy Brandt, a returned refugee from Scandinavia, the American contingent of refugees did not contribute anyone who was to play a major role in West German political life.

Meanwhile, to the south, a contrary process to rehabilitation was under way: the Nuremberg Trials. The accused were presumably the worst of the surviving Nazis who had not escaped the country. The millions of others who had given some form of support to Hitler's regime fell within the scope of the general denazification program. Held in the Palace of Justice in Nuremberg, the trials began in July 1945 and did not conclude until four years later. They resulted in the acquittal of 38 (out of a total of 199 defendants in twelve successive cases), with 36 defendants being sentenced to death (18 were actually executed), 23 to life imprisonment, and 102 to prison terms ranging from one and one-half to twenty-five years. We read about all this and generally, I think, felt that rough justice demanded punishment of the clearly guilty. There was some uneasiness about having a Soviet judge sitting on the International Military Tribunal that tried the leading surviving Nazi political and military leaders, and it seemed inevitable that the proceedings would in subsequent discussion be criticized as essentially "victors' justice." The legal framework of international law had simply not kept pace with the behavior of Hitler and his associates in providing clear criteria that would brand their actions as illegal, yet the moral sense of civilized people seemed to require that crimes against humanity, crimes against the peace, and the more definable category of war crimes be brought within enforceable legal categories. Whether the decisions of the various tribunals were just and proportionate was another matter. It was also evident that the Nuremberg research material (some forty-two thousand court exhibits of various sizes, mainly of German origin) would provide an inexhaustible source of data about the Nazi era.[6]

Much closer to home were the denazification proceedings applicable to broad groups of Nazi-affiliated individuals. From the early days of Military Government, this attempt to purge and punish those associated with Hitler's Reich had top priority, and directive after directive tried to close off loopholes that had emerged. As redeployment of American military personnel took place, gradual assignment of denazification to German screening boards became necessary. Moreover, with the growing need to enlist Germans in the management of their economy and incipient political institutions, the tendency to overlook or to conceal minor transgressions became more common. Pressures from the American side and counterpressures from the German side led to frequent impasse. The problem was not essentially with former leadership groups, though many of their members had left the country, gone underground, or assumed different identities, but with the large marginal groups who, though tainted, could argue that the time had come to draw a line under the past and let them make their contribution to the reconstruction of Germany. This line of argument had wide appeal to most Germans, including those with no Nazi record, and by 1947, American congressional visitors to Germany were criticizing the denazification program for its negative effect on economic recovery. By 1948, pressure in Washington and Germany had built up to the point that rapid liquidation of the program seemed the only acceptable option, despite the fact that 28,065 hard-core cases were still awaiting trial and that more than 100,000 cases remained on which the paper work had not been completed. Before the end of the year the still outstanding cases were pretty much left to the Germans to decide as they wished.[7]

Needless to say, the British and the French, while paying lip service to denazification and implementing their programs in egregious cases, were generally much more relaxed on the whole subject. While their zones of occupation did not exactly become safe havens, they seemed willing to accept that guilt deserving punishment did not penetrate as deeply into German society as the Americans, in their initial casting of the denazification net, evidently believed.

The whole question of German guilt for the iniquities of the Nazis troubled me in those early postwar years and continued to be a problem within the broader framework of responsibility for the Holocaust, as we have come to know more and more about that monstrous blot on human behavior. Here we run head-on into the mystery of moral evil, an obvious reality in the world as we know it. The whole concept of moral evil makes no sense, of course, in a determinist world devoid of free choice of good or evil, and those who deny freedom of the will lose all basis for making moral judgments. The very immensity of the Holocaust demands the assumption of free choice; the whole tragedy becomes a complete absurdity if the Nazi leaders did no more than act in accord with preordained causation, lacking all moral content.

In her controversial book published in 1963, *Eichmann in Jerusalem: A Report on the Banality of Evil*, Hannah Arendt made the point, however, that even the most intrinsically atrocious misdeeds do not require a Lucifer-like figure to perform them.[8] The *Spiessbürgertum* of Germany provided much of the mass Nazi following. An immediately relevant question, which the denazification program in its various phases could never satisfactorily answer, was the depth of real guilt that could legitimately be attributed to those who, in one way or another, supported the Nazi regime. If one started with the assumption, as some did, that the German people were collectively guilty for all that the Nazis did, then gradations tended to blur, and harsh treatment of all Germans became logical. In real life, however, that proved to be an impossible position for Military Government to maintain, and since there could be no doubt that most Germans had to endure much hardship in those early postwar years, the normal American tendency to kindness and pity took over. Forgiveness came easily under the circumstances, and the evil involved in immoral behavior under the Nazis, with the exception of the really glaring cases, was left largely to burden the individual conscience.

How much sense of remorse and shame the average German felt for the behavior of his or her country was difficult to discern. Years later in his 1970 book *Germany in Our Time*, the French commentator Alfred Grosser wrote that German gratitude for the aid they received during those early years "was on the whole somewhat tepid, and foreign help was accepted as though it were a very inadequate atonement for undeserved suffering."[9] I found this generalization somewhat absurd in the light of my own experience. A measure of self-pity was inevitable under the circumstances, but the postwar generation of Germans who lived in the American zone were almost embarrassingly profuse in their expressions of gratitude for American help in their hour of greatest need. Even twenty-five years later, when I was in Bonn as ambassador, hardly a public occasion went by without some German reference to American assistance after the war. If they did not seem very grateful to their French occupiers, perhaps it was because they had very little to be grateful for. For that matter, given the experience of World War II, there was not much reason for the French to behave in a manner to elicit gratitude.

During 1947 I made many trips to the Ruhr and the Rhineland to see Dr. Adenauer and other German politicians as well as industrialists and labor leaders. My reports provided what I believed was useful information about their activities and thinking. There seemed to be little love lost between leaders of the new party, the Christian Democratic Union, and the British occupation authorities. Adenauer had himself been ousted at an early point from his position as mayor of Cologne by a British brigadier (something he never mentioned), but he deeply suspected that the British Labour government of Clement Atlee could be up to no good. British emphasis on deconcentration of the Ruhr coal and steel industry, with its typical vertical integration, provided a particularly sore point.

After one of our meetings in Cologne, Dr. Adenauer walked off with my trench coat and I with his. We communicated with each other and agreed to exchange coats during our next meeting the following month. So for four weeks or so, I wore his coat and he mine. I am still not sure who got the better deal; both our coats had been much used, and he was taller than I.

I thought it made sense to keep in touch with leaders of the reorganizing German trade union movement, particularly Hans Boeckler, first chairman of the German Trade Union Federation for the British zone, later, in 1949, to become chairman of the German Trade Union Federation for the entire Federal Republic. We, and for that matter the British, had much concern over the infiltration of Communists into the Works Councils in individual plants, particularly in the Ruhr, and a strong, democratic union movement was obviously the best safeguard against total radicalization of the workforce. The record of most of the reemerging union leadership had been exemplary during the Nazi period. In those early postwar years, as I have already noted, fear of Communist Party takeovers, abetted by the Soviet Union, in a number of European countries was widespread. Those fears proved to be misplaced; European social structures showed themselves to be remarkably stable, but there was no way of knowing in 1946–47 that this would turn out to be the case. The societal and economic destruction left by World War II seemed not only enormous but beyond repair.

A group of eminent American economists from Harvard and other universities came to Germany to study the economic situation and make recommendations to Military Government. Fortunately for their collective reputations, their report must now lie buried under tons of retired Military Government files in some obscure warehouse. In their totally gloomy assessment of Germany prospects, they could not have been more wrong—

but they were in good company. Gloomy prognostications prevailed at all levels of sophistication and learning.

Adding to the pessimism was the seemingly insoluble problem presented by the millions of German refugees who had streamed westward after the war from the lost Eastern territories. Located mainly in refugee camps, they seemed nonabsorbable in a prostrate economy. Once again the predictions of the experts turned out to be far from the mark. One of the factors that contributed to the phenomenal West German economic growth characteristic of the 1950s and 1960s was the skilled labor supply required by developing industries and provided by the refugees.

There were a few gleams of light amid the encircling gloom. The saturation bombing of Cologne had severely damaged the city's cathedral, although the two steeples and the walls of the nave remained standing. The entire structure was severely pockmarked and the roof largely destroyed. Repair work began almost with the end of the war, and by 1947 the cathedral—so symbolically important to the city and the Rhineland—was ready to be opened to the public. Cardinal Frings and the city authorities arranged a solemn rededication, to which I was invited. The entire population joined in the celebration. Before high mass, we were able to observe the reconstructed church, now saturated with light, through the plain glass side windows that had replaced the destroyed stained glass. The interiors of cathedrals are usually dark and mysterious, as little light penetrates the stained glass windows that have become less and less translucent through the centuries. One could imagine that, in medieval times when these magnificent Gothic structures came into being, their interiors were much brighter than we have come to know them.

Once again, I felt at first hand the enormous psychological role that music plays in Germany. The Cologne Gurzenich Orchestra (the city's main symphonic group) played Bruckner's Fourth Symphony (the "Romantic Symphony") in the open air to assembled dignitaries and, seemingly, a large portion of the city's population. The orchestra outdid itself, and the vast sonorities of Bruckner evoked an almost tangible response; as part of the audience, I could feel the same emotional empathy. In some inexpressible way, a whole culture and way of life experienced a high point in a time of despondence. The renewed Kölner Dom symbolically expressed the need for renewal of a depressed and stigmatized people.

As 1947 went on, the need for some more fundamental approach to the economic morass of the three Western zones became more and more apparent. The British and the Americans had, in 1946, already created the Bizonal Economic Administration located in Minden (a city in North Rhine–Westphalia), but stubborn French resistance held up a comparable trizonal arrangement until 1948, after the United States had accepted de facto assimilation of the Saar into France. The problem of providing some more acceptable medium of exchange than the cigarette carton remained, however, to plague the German economy.

Meanwhile, at the four-power level, successive meetings of the Council of Foreign Ministers—in Moscow from March 10 to April 24, 1947, and in London from November 25 to December 16, 1947—brought Secretary of State George C. Marshall reluctantly to the conclusion that any movement toward German political and economic unity had become impossible in the light of the position taken by Soviet foreign minister Vyacheslav Molotov. Given this realistic assumption, the logical next step, as Marshall put it, was to "do the best we can in the area where our influence can be felt." [10] The chain of causation leading to the decisive events of 1948 began ineluctably to unfold.

A climactic event at the family level was the birth of our son David in Bremen on June 10, 1947. During the late autumn, we took our first home leave since going to Africa in 1944. Luckily, we were able to book a cabin on the SS *America*, returned to service by the United States Lines as a regular passenger ship. Although an infant and a three-year-old daughter kept us on the run, the crossing proved pleasant enough. Once again, we enjoyed an experience denied first to diplomats by administrative fiat and to everybody else by the paucity of passenger ships as well as the psychological burden of seeming to waste time en route in the jet age.

We returned to Germany early in 1948, after spending the holidays with collected family and relatives in Louisville, Kentucky. Nothing much seemed to have changed during the two months we were gone, but there was a feeling that important developments would soon occur. The winter had proved considerably milder than the previous one, and American aid had at least maintained minimum standards of subsistence. The black market continued to prevail, however, and Allied and German economics officials were giving urgent attention to the possibility of instituting a new currency that would have stable value. I picked up where I had left off in terms of travel and contacts in the British zone. The word from Berlin was that the Soviets had become less and less cooperative and clearly had in mind the isolation of their own zone from the Western part of Germany.

All this provided a prelude to the London Six-Power Conference that began on February 23, 1948, between representatives of the United States, the United Kingdom, and France and, from February 26, with representatives of the Benelux countries. Both Belgium and the Netherlands had troops stationed in West Germany, mainly in the British zone; the cognoscenti quickly learned that the Belgian Officers Club, which was in a Cologne suburb, and the Belgian Rest Center on the Petersburg possessed the best restaurants and wine cellars in the country. The London meetings, chaired by the United Kingdom representative, Sir William Strang, were held at the ambassadorial level. The first session adjourned on March 8, and the discussions resumed in April. On June 2, the representatives of the six countries submitted agreed recommendations to their governments calling, inter alia, for the three military governors to hold a joint meeting with the minister presidents of the Western zones in Germany. At that meeting the minister presidents were to be authorized to convene a constituent assembly to prepare a constitution for the approval of the participating states.[11]

Thus the process began that led to the creation of the Federal Republic of Germany. The various ambassadors meeting in London were, of course, acting under instructions of their governments, so that their agreed recommendations were expected to receive more or less automatic approval in their capitals. Detailed instructions went out relatively quickly to the American and British military governors, who were told to have their meeting with the minister presidents by June 15. Last-minute French hesitation, however, delayed the meeting until July 1. Although the London conference had been essentially a State Department operation, with some collateral inputs from the military governors, a strong-minded General Clay would still receive his instructions directly from the War Department. This, in effect, gave him more autonomy in the constitution-making process than the State Department would have liked.

Meanwhile, considerable momentum began to gather in the West for a move toward currency reform. Somewhat reluctantly, the French agreed to join the British and the Americans in the necessary planning. The thinking that went into the currency reform announced on Saturday, June 19, 1948, had various sources, but the primary impetus came from the United States. Reading the various historical accounts of who did and advocated what, a skeptic might conclude that we had here a Rashomon effect: different versions of what actually happened depending on the observer and his point of view. General Clay in his book *Decision in Germany* mentions Dr. Ludwig Erhard, head of the Bizonal Economic Administration, only once, and then only to say that his influence was to be of special significance after currency reform. On the other hand, German historians typically credit the future economics minister and chancellor, as well as Professor Wilhelm Roepke, with being the ideological fathers of the reform.[12]

A spectacular success, as currency reform turned out to be, breeds many claims of authorship. Rumors floated around Germany that such and such a brilliant young member of the Economics Division of OMGUS had really come up with the basic ideas that determined the precise configuration of currency reform. I prefer to think of it as an Allied and German collective enterprise. For two years or so before June 1948, General Clay and his advisers had pushed for measures to create the banking infrastructure without which implementation of the reform would have proved impossible.

On the surface, the specifics of reform embodied in four separate military government laws seemed harsh. The old reichsmark became invalid on June 21, 1948, but each person could exchange on a one-to-one basis 60 reichsmarks for the new deutschemarks. For every 100 tax-clear reichsmarks on deposit, 6.5 new marks were to be made available, in part only for investment purposes. There were many other details, of course, but the net effect was to extinguish some 93 percent of the paper wealth of West Germans expressed in reichsmarks in either cash, bank savings, or securities.

It is hard to forget the almost instantaneous results of currency reform. One heard outcries on all sides against its confiscatory nature, but the reichsmark had become almost totally worthless, even when still nominally quoted. On the black market, barter and the American cigarette had reigned supreme. Suddenly, goods of all sorts appeared on store shelves, and one had the feeling that the West Germans had crossed a real economic watershed. Military Government did recognize that justice required some burden-equalizing measures (*Lastenausgleich*), but these were left to the German Trizonal Administration to develop. Much more had to be done, of course, to ensure that the reform would have its intended broader effects. Here Dr. Erhard entered the picture with a courageous program of deregulation and liberalization. In an encrusted economy, with many controls still in effect from the wartime period, his initiatives released dynamic economic forces.[13]

I do not think, however, that conventional economic theory can adequately explain the spectacular aftermath of currency reform. Psychological factors undoubtedly played an important part. The suppressed wants of the average German provided extraordinary consumer stimulation, once goods became available again outside the black market, but there was, obviously, a powerful popular desire to return to the relatively normal and to have a currency of value. Once consumer goods came onto the market, sellers could be assured of customers. Explosion of demand manifested itself in some peculiar ways. A public deprived during years of wartime and postwar scarcity suddenly rediscovered its collective sweet tooth. The *Schlagsahneepoche* (the whipped cream era) of the early fifties, when German men and women stuffed themselves daily in restaurants and cafés on rich cakes heaped with whipped cream, had both its ludicrous and pathetic aspects, but the need for this kind of sustenance was more than purely physical. Whipped cream became the symbol of both a new prosperity and a need for personal security.

The black market vanished almost overnight. As the *London News Chronicle* put it, "In this week the most stable currency in Europe was destroyed. It is the currency of the cigarette."[14] Ironically enough, even today a black market or unregistered economy exists in many countries, this time driven not by the valuelessness of the currency but by the desire to keep more of it through avoidance of tax payments.

Berlin Blockade and Airlift

The Soviets' reaction to all this came quickly and more dramatically than anyone had anticipated. They moved in an area where they thought they had both a geographical and tactical advantage: the Allied enclave in West Berlin surrounded by the Soviet zone of occupation. On June 22, the Soviets told the Western powers that they intended to carry out a currency reform in East Germany and in all of Berlin. The German authorities in Berlin, led by the charismatic Ernst Reuter, soon to become governing mayor in West Berlin, categorically rejected having the Eastern currency applicable in the Western sectors, arguing that this would inevitably lead to absorption of the whole city into the Soviet zone. The deutschemark thus became the currency of West Berlin as well. Although harassment by the Soviets of both personnel and goods traffic to and from Berlin had begun in March, they now moved quickly to tighten the noose. By August 4 the blockade of Western sectors had become total; West Berlin officials were forced out of the city magistrate, then meeting in East Berlin; they then proceeded to set up a separate West sector administration in the Schöneberg district *Rathaus* (city hall).[15]

I happened to be in Berlin during early August, attending a conference called by Mr. Murphy, which was held in an atmosphere of tension and foreboding about impending events. Word reached us that the Soviets were constructing new barriers at the Marienborn checkpoint, where the principal autobahn from the West entered East Germany. The conference adjourned in some haste, and on the morning of August 4, Consul General Edward Groth, with whom I had hitched a ride back, started to drive westward. We noted a great deal of agitated activity at the outgoing Soviet checkpoint but were waved through. When we arrived at Marienborn two hours later, we saw a number of Soviet officers milling around newly constructed barricades. One of them finally approached us grinning. He took out a pack of Russian cigarettes and offered them to us. Groth, a man of rectitude and rigidity, declined with demonstrable indignation. The Soviet officer bridled and exclaimed, "You not like Russky cigarettes." Although I had not smoked in some years, I succumbed to a wave of diplomatic flexibility and loudly said, "I like Russky cigarettes." I took one, which he lighted for me with a smile. After a pause for reflection, he lifted the barrier and let us through. We later found out that our vehicle was the last to pass through the checkpoint; a number of other westbound Allied cars could not make it and had to return to Berlin. The blockade was in full effect. I was never quite sure what our experience proved other than that a friendly gesture deserves a friendly response.

Those were dramatic days. It seemed as if the Soviets had the Western Allies by their jugular, threatening some two and a quarter million West Berliners with slow starvation, as food stocks in the city ran down. No one doubted that the Soviets had the will to carry their action to the point of Western surrender to the inevitable. Fears of broader Soviet military action against the West grew. A country capable of blockading a whole city in peacetime seemed capable of anything. Yet, as it turned out, the Soviet Union had made a miscalculation of major historical significance. It did not anticipate that the Western powers, led by the United States, would mount an airlift that successfully supplied the city's population with at least minimum requirements of food and fuel. Nor could it have foreseen the worldwide revulsion against the blockade and the growing sympathy for the Berliners, who now, in the media, took on a heroic posture. As I noted in the book *The Future of Berlin*, "Thus fairly early on, the city began to acquire the symbolic significance which has given the struggle over its past and future an importance transcending the urban geography involved." [16] Another consequence was that the blockade removed any lingering French doubts about the need to proceed with setting up a German government for the three Western zones. Finally, the success of the airlift gave a great boost to Allied morale at a time when the situation in Germany still seemed gloomy.

One is tempted to speculate about the precise Soviet motivation that led to the colossal mistake of the blockade. The Soviets obviously wanted to get the Western powers out of Berlin and to incorporate the entire city in their area of control, but what impelled them to move precisely when they did? The Western determination to proceed with currency reform in the three zones, and finally in West Berlin, undoubtedly played a causal role, and the Soviets later claimed that they had imposed the blockade in order to prevent the currency reform in West Germany from disturbing the economy of the Soviet zone. Some writers, such as Daniel Yergin, have argued that Stalin's concern about the possibility of a separate government being established for the three Western zones of occupation provided the driving force.[17] We shall probably never know for sure. Stalin left no memoirs, but what we have come to know about his character requires an interpretation within a broader context.

If Stalin was clearly paranoid with respect to imagined or real domestic enemies, whom he purged mercilessly, is there any reason to think that he was not equally paranoid with respect to imagined external threats? I am normally wary about dogmatic assertions by so-called psychohistorians, but any analysis of the causes of the cold war can scarcely leave the pathology of Josef Stalin's mind out of reckoning.

In allocating responsibility for the cold war, revisionist and postrevisionist historians usually fail to take sufficiently into account the enormous political and psychological consequences of the Berlin blockade and airlift. Any country that would, in peacetime, attempt to starve into submission the population of an entire city was obviously beyond the pale. In general, I have been impressed by the systematic underestimation by historians of the centrality of the Berlin-German issue in the chain of causation leading to the cold war.[18]

What I also find lacking in virtually all of the books and articles about the origins of the cold war, as impeccable as their documentation may sometimes be, is the sense of drama and emotional intensity shared by Western participants in the events of those days. In the light of hindsight, it is easy to say that their fears, anxieties, and animosities were exaggerated, based on too simplistic an interpretation of real Soviet intentions. Those fears, anxieties, and animosities were, nevertheless, genuine and deep seated, created by what seemed logical deductions from Soviet behavior in Germany. Emotional intensity, on the other hand, is not self-sustaining over time; it requires periodic reinforcement, and this the Soviets provided. The cold war was, after all, a continuum, not merely a mechanical chain of causation that, once set in motion, moved inexorably step by step to its conclusion. There is, therefore, something constricted and even unhistorical about discussions of the cold war limited exclusively to the very early postwar years. Soviet behavior in Germany, most notably in the great Berlin crisis of 1958–63 but also in persistent harassment of Allied military traffic into and out of Berlin during the early and middle fifties, strengthened the views of those in the West who felt that Soviet intentions were essentially aggressive. The death of Stalin and the advent to power of Nikita Khrushchev, despite the early promise of de-Stalinization, brought no essential change of Soviet behavior in Germany but, over time, actually reinforced negative American impressions of Soviet policy.

The airlift was a triumph of both daring and technical competence. The C-47 planes already in the theater (the military version of the DC-3), which had performed so well as workhorses in World War II, provided the basic initial transport for the airlift that as early as June 26 became an organized operation. They were soon to be supplemented by a contingent of C-54s (the DC-4 in civilian usage) that could carry greater tonnage per flight, as well as U.S. naval planes and British Flying Boats that could land on the Wannsee. General William Tunner provided the organizational and command leadership that such an undertaking required. In later years he was to express some resentment that his vital role had never been sufficiently recognized in accounts of the airlift. He had a point. One sees little or no mention of his name in many of these accounts.[19]

A question that arose at the time, and has not been answered since, is why the Soviets did not attempt to interfere with the constant procession of Allied planes in the three air corridors to Berlin. Having blockaded the city on land and canal, they might have been expected to harass air traffic in various ways (as they did during a different Berlin crisis in 1962). Undoubtedly somewhat bewildered by the Western logistical feat, they were not prepared in 1948–49 to take the final confrontational step to make their blockade complete.

Constitution Making in Germany

As the airlift moved into full gear, the constitution-making process in the three Western zones gathered momentum. The road to a final document proved to be bumpier than anticipated. As envisaged by the London Agreement, the military governors met with the minister presidents of the various states on July 1, 1948, and handed them documents directing the convocation of a constituent assembly. Somewhat to the surprise of the military governors, the minister presidents did not rise to their feet with enthusiastic shouts of endorsement. In their written reply they accepted the concept of trizonal fusion but expressed some apprehension about moving toward the creation of a full state that might widen the rift between East and West. After further exchanges, the military governors agreed that the body drafting the document would be called a *Parlamentarischer Rat* (Parliamentary Council) rather than constituent assembly and that the final product would be called a *Grundgesetz* (Basic Law) followed in parentheses by "Provisional Constitution." All of the participants in this early debate over nomenclature would probably have laughed in derisive rejection of the very idea if a prophet had come along and predicted that forty years later the Basic Law would have become the institutionalized constitution of a prosperous West Germany still divided from East Germany. Once again, *C'est le provisoire qui dure.* In any event, the sixty-five members of the Parliamentary Council met in Bonn on September 1 and promptly elected Dr. Konrad Adenauer president.

My established contacts with German officials in the British zone, particularly with Dr. Adenauer, proved useful in providing the State Department with points of view not otherwise available, since the U.S. liaison group with the Parliamentary Council was dominated by academicians or employees of Military Government reporting through Defense Department channels. Murphy, of course, kept himself generally informed, and during the crisis of 1949 he and his successor as political adviser, James Riddleberger, became directly involved.

This is not the place for a detailed account of the tug-of-war that developed between the Parliamentary Council and the military governors over such issues as the degree of federalism, the fiscal powers of the central government and its relationship to the states, and the contents of the Occupation Statute to come into effect at the same time as the Basic Law. The existing literature is fairly extensive, and the essential German and American documentation is now available for researchers.[20]

Suffice it to say here that, by early 1949, the Parliamentary Council seemed to be moving rapidly toward a final draft when the military governors reacted strongly and adversely to the text that had informally been passed to them. The thrust remained too clearly in the direction of central control of taxes and fiscal administration to meet the requirements of either General Clay or the French military governor, General Koenig. The British military governor, General Robertson, was much more relaxed and urged approval. It became clear during the verbal battle of late winter that only intervention at a higher level could break the deadlock. The French, British, and American foreign ministers met in Washington in early April and provided what they hoped would be definitive guidance to the three military governors. Further complications developed, however, and it was only when Secretary of State Acheson, prodded by British foreign secretary Ernest Bevin, had the secretary of the army instruct General Clay to convey to the Parliamentary Council a portion of the foreign ministers' instructions, which he had withheld up to that point, that a draft acceptable to all parties quickly emerged. General Clay himself was able to play a conciliatory role in reaching agreement during the final days.

Thus it was that the military governors approved the final German text on May 12, 1948, and within ten days all the state legislatures had ratified the Basic Law with the exception of Bavaria, which, however, agreed to abide by the action of the majority and to adhere to the new state.

Whatever one may think about the hesitation along the way and the procedures by which the military governors and the Parliamentary Council interacted, the Basic Law proved to be an ideal constitution for the new West German state. It provided a framework for reasonably efficient government without the fundamental weaknesses of the Weimar constitution that led to systemic regime instability. Despite all the pressures on the council from the military governors, the document that emerged fell largely within the German constitutional tradition. There were some exceptions, of course. One of them was the exclusion of Berlin from full membership in the new state, although the necessity for close political and economic ties was clearly recognized. The military governors simply suspended those articles of the Basic Law that would have given Berlin such full membership, particularly popular election in Berlin of the city's representatives to the Bundestag and denial to them of full voting rights in the legislative procedures of the Bundestag. This exclusion survived up to reunification in 1990 despite periodic German restiveness over the issue, along with the retention of ultimate authority for West Berlin by the three occupying powers. The inevitable ambiguities involved in the relationship between the Federal Republic and a West Berlin economically integrated with it, and dependent on its subsidies, were to be a continuing source of difficulty in the decades to follow.

An intriguing question that interested me during the life of the Parliamentary Council was the precise relationship between the SPD in Germany and the British Labour government headed by Prime Minister Clement Atlee. The ailing SPD leader, Kurt Schumacher, was not a member of the Parliamentary Council, but, from his sickbed in Hannover, he pretty much dictated his party's policy. He favored a strong central government, presumably in the expectation that the SPD would win the first election and then be in a position to carry through a wide-ranging program of social and economic reform. British support for such a strong central authority and seeming indifference to the American and French emphasis on a federal system, it was suspected, reflected Atlee's ideological sympathy for the Schumacher position. Dr. Adenauer clearly felt this to be the case. The SPD electoral victory did not occur, of course, and it was Dr. Adenauer who became the first postwar German chancellor.

I should add that, whatever the degree of collusion between British Labour and the German Social Democrats, this did not mean that the British government in any way was soft on Communism. As a matter of fact, British Foreign Office documents released under the thirty-year rule indicate quite the opposite. The British authorities were actually worried during the early postwar years that American leaders would be soft-headed about the Communist threat.[21] Moreover, many SPD officials had been in the forefront of opposition to the Communist Party, both before Hitler came to power in 1933 and after 1945, both in the Soviet zone and in the West. Needless to say, all of this runs directly counter to a basic tenet of some historians: that the United States forced its unwilling European allies, against their better judgment, into taking a hard-line position with respect to the Soviet Union.

In left-wing circles, including the Catholics associated with the *Frankfurter Hefte*, a monthly that quickly became an important influence among German intellectuals, an early criticism of the new German order was that it represented essentially an attempt at restoration of the old system. An article entitled "Die Restaurative Charakter der Epoche" (The Restorative Character of the Epoch) aroused much discussion. Walter Dirks, its author and a coeditor of the *Hefte*, had a good point. The fathers of the new West German republic, which most of them hoped would be only provisional prior to the reunification of Germany with Berlin as its capital, wanted viable democratic institutions and economic recovery but obviously did not think in terms of radical innovation. Some of them undoubtedly wanted a return to the good old Germany of pre-Nazi and pre-1920 inflation days, as dubious as their recollection of earlier times may have been, but the essential desire of the majority was to make possible again honorable work for good pay sufficient to satisfy middle-class consumer wants. The idealism of the *Frankfurter Hefte* group and such writers as Heinrich Böll, which looked to a more fundamental transformation of German society, did not have much impact on actual developments. It did provide a continuing critique of the materialism and consumerism that it saw as characteristic of that society—a critique that markedly affected the attitude toward the Federal Republic of successive generations of German intellectuals, writers, and artists.

An interesting question, not unrelated to the periodic outbursts of controversy in the Federal Republic over alleged lost golden opportunities to achieve German reunification, is why Stalin made such a point of opposing Western determination to go ahead with building a central government in three zones of occupation. Was it because he still cherished the hope of a united Germany under Soviet dominance? Or because he foresaw an independent West Germany bound to become more powerful and influential than East Germany? Or because he still believed in the utility of the Potsdam Agreement, on claimed violations of which the Soviets hinged their protests? We shall probably never know for sure. The climactic developments of 1948–49 obviously had a direct bearing on the fundamental question of German national unity. In the face of observable Soviet behavior, it would be hard to argue that the decision to move ahead with the creation of the Federal Republic lost any real opportunity at the time to achieve a unified country. Whether the development of the German Democratic Republic would have come as rapidly as it did is not so important as the fact that the Soviets had already embarked on a course of action that would inevitably have led to the creation of a separate state in their zone of occupation, unless the Western powers had been prepared to concede Soviet control over all of Germany. I shall come back to the problem of a divided Germany at a later point in discussing the situation prior to, and in the aftermath of, Stalin's death in 1953, when the opportunity to gain national unity, one school of publicists claims, was the greatest.

While the Parliamentary Council and the Allied military governments were taking the final steps toward the Basic Law, the Soviets had decided to cut their losses on an obviously futile blockade. Informal conversation between Ambassador Philip Jessup and Soviet ambassador Jacob Malik on the margin of the United Nations in New York led to the announcement on May 4 that the Berlin blockade had ended and that the foreign ministers of the four occupying powers would meet in Paris on May 23. The Paris conference did not accomplish very much other than to confirm the Jessup-Malik Agreement of May 4, 1949, and to provide for continuing four-power consultations aimed at achieving the restoration of the economic and political unity of Germany. The Western foreign ministers had proposed extending the Basic Law to the entire country, making it one political and economic unity. Free elections would follow to establish a national government under four-power supervision. Soviet foreign minister Andrei Vishinsky rejected this but continued to call for a return to the old system of four-power control. This to the Western side simply meant perpetuation of a split Germany.

The End of Military Government

With the coming into effect of the Basic Law, the bureaucratic guillotine descended swiftly on Military Government. President Truman accepted General Clay's resignation as early as May 15, and on May 18 he announced that he was sending to the Senate the nomination of John J. McCloy to be United States high commissioner for Germany and chief of mission. He was to be under the immediate supervision and direction of the secretary of state, rather than the secretary of defense, and was to represent the United States on the newly created Allied High Commission for Germany (HICOG). General Clay departed for the United States shortly after May 22.

Thus without much fuss and bluster the era of Military Government came to an end. After a rocky start, American policies in Germany had been on the whole constructive and probably essential in bringing the population of our zone, and ultimately of the three Western zones and West Berlin, through those difficult early years. Humanitarian considerations generally outweighed the desire to punish or to reprimand. Without American aid difficult conditions might well have become impossible conditions.

There was, of course, a darker side to the Military Government era. In an economy where the reichsmark drew only scorn and the cigarette carton, the coffee can, the whiskey bottle, and the chocolate bar reigned supreme, the temptation was great to barter supplies readily available in post exchanges for valuables that hard-pressed Germans had channeled into the omnipresent black market. Shady operatives as well as just plain needy Germans appeared from everywhere to offer goods; their very ubiquity and the range of products available attested to a greater underground abundance than the empty shelves of shops and the meager level of rationed items indicated. The professional black marketer—the *Schieber*—quickly emerged to take advantage of the peculiar kind of economic opportunity that the market provided, but often enough middle-class Germans swallowed their pride and went door to door in American settlements to peddle their prized family possessions for cigarettes, coffee, or fat.

Thus massive corruption of the occupiers (whether American or, for that matter, British or French) became inevitable. The wives of generals as well as of sergeants gathered in the loot. In Berlin, the American military government even went so far as to organize a legal black market where the wives of senior officials could barter without fear of getting caught. As consul in Bremen I could observe the peculiar predilection of a few select generals for grand pianos, as shipments of their effects passed through the port. Their desire for Bechsteins, Steinways, and Boesendorfers did not derive, I feared, from a sudden development of musical culture but rather from their potential resale value in the United States. Whatever moral scruples individuals might have entertained were easy to put aside. After all, everyone from the top down was doing it, and if the exploitative aspect sometimes sharply intruded in individual cases of obvious dire need, one could always fall back on the argument that, after all, we had won the war and to the victor belongs the spoils. I should not have been surprised by this American proclivity for the fast buck. In India I had observed some of my compatriots making small fortunes while flying "over the Hump," by smuggling gold, wristwatches, fountain pens, and other items prized on the Chinese black market.

In contrast to this wholesale plundering of Germany via the black market, many individual Americans displayed warmth, sympathy, and generosity in helping Germans and their families living in semistarvation and without fuel. Some found lasting friendships in the process, and thus in adversity was born that network of personal relationships between Germans and Americans that played such an important part in the bridging of differences and the growth of understanding in the subsequent thirty years.

After our more than three active years in Germany, the time had come to think of moving on. I had put in a request for a year of advanced economic studies under a regular State Department program, and affirmative word soon came that I would be spending the next academic year at Harvard, beginning with the fall semester. I was pleased at the prospect of returning to an academic setting after a break of ten years. Meanwhile, I would still be in Germany long enough to witness the transition from Military Government to High Commission. Our third child, John, had been born in March 1949, with Dr. Jackle again performing the honors. While on home leave in 1948, I had successfully defended my Ph.D. dissertation at Columbia and would thus technically be enrolled as a postdoctoral student at Harvard. The Columbia University Press in 1949 published a slightly abbreviated version under the title *Power and Morals*.

The American HICOG advance group took over like the Republican Party from the Democrats after a victorious presidential campaign. The new broom complex dominated, although a few familiar faces turned up again. The State Department was now running the show, and little room remained for the stalwarts of Military Government. The three Allied high commissioners and staffs would have to move to Bonn—the capital of the Federal Republic—as soon as adequate housing and office space became available. In the meantime they would be represented by a smaller contingent while the bulk of personnel remained elsewhere—in the American case in Frankfurt. There was considerable grumbling about the choice as capital of Bonn, a rather sleepy university town on the Rhine with little public infrastructure. Stories spread that Dr. Adenauer had bullied through the selection of Bonn largely because of its convenient proximity to his home in Bad Honnef on the other side of the Rhine. Adenauer had advanced another argument that, in the light of experience, proved to be a farsighted one. He had fought against the choice of Frankfurt, favored by most Americans, on the ground that a fledgling West German government would be swamped by the continuing large-scale American military presence, including an army corps headquarters, in the Frankfurt area. Despite all the snide remarks about Bonn as the federal village (*Bundesdorf*), it actually turned out in many ways to be an ideal capital for the Federal Republic. Without any imposing public buildings, it provided an appropriate setting for a government that could not afford to have any pretensions or illusions of grandeur.

This was unfortunately not the case with U.S. HICOG. Its bureaucracy remained formidable in size, although somewhat smaller than the OMGUS establishment it replaced. The existence of a functioning German central government, however, meant that it really had less to do. Hence officials had more time to write reports that came out in a veritable flood. Not that Military Government had been remiss in the production of paper. As a result, the American documentation for the years 1945 to 1955, when HICOG came to an end, is enormous.

HICOG also produced some grandiose construction schemes for Plittersdorf and Mehlem (two areas of Bad Godesberg long since absorbed into the growing capital of Bonn). Along with some others, I opposed the housing project on the ground that it would commit the staff of a future embassy to a segregated pattern of living, but we quickly lost out. Given the need for adequate quarters for a huge staff and the scarcity of available housing in the Bonn area, we were probably wrong. The Plittersdorf complex of apartment buildings with a few so-called position houses added as icing quickly became known as the American settlement (*die amerikanische Siedlung*) and remained over the years as the primary source of housing for American embassy staff. As that staff declined in size, we returned blocks of apartment houses to the German economy, and the embassy made efforts to provide housing scattered around town for its political officers.

The embassy office building itself (or chancery, to use the classic diplomatic term) is an aesthetic monstrosity. The central part, allegedly constructed to last fifty years, was at some point to be turned over to the Germans for service as a hospital. The four wings, on the other hand, were jerry-built and not intended to last. Sagging floors quickly developed, but as the embassy staff diminished, the German government gladly took them over and periodically propped them up to provide office space for one of its ministries. So even today that ugly chancery rears up over the Rhine, still functional but not particularly comfortable. The HICOG major domo, who presided over all this construction—paid for by the Germans, of course—was the director of administration, Glenn Wolfe, later to become an administrative officer in the U.S. Foreign Service. The tripartite High Commission itself found itself magnificently, if somewhat remotely, ensconced in the luxurious Petersburg Hotel, some one thousand feet above Bonn on the other side of the river, with a splendid view up and down the Rhine.

Almost while we were packing to leave Germany, I found myself temporarily in charge of the consulate general and having to entertain a number of dignitaries of the new Germany as they traveled about. I remember well one lunch at which the guest of honor was Theodor Heuss, the leader of the Liberal Party (the FDP), who had played a constructive role as member of the Parliamentary Council. He brought a number of his party colleagues with him and put on an impressive display of wit and verbal pyrotechnics, a talent he was subsequently to display as the first president of the Federal Republic of Germany.

We could not help but be sad as we said goodbye to our friends in Bremen before embarking on the SS *United States*, now reconverted to civilian status after serving in the war as a troop transport. As we sailed from Bremerhaven, I had a strong intuitive feeling that we would one day return in an official capacity to this fascinating country of many contradictions and troubled history.

4

Cambridge, Washington, Paris

. . . .

Our family disembarked in New York along with our still trusty red Studebaker, now equipped with a Jeep motor installed by an ingenious German mechanic. Faith drove immediately up to Boston while I went to Washington for a few days of what, in the language of the trade, is called consultation. When I arrived, Faith had already found a fine old frame house for rent in Newtonville, and we quickly settled in for an anticipated vigorous New England winter. It also proved to be a winter of considerable sickness in the family and consequent disarray and strain.

The academic year at Harvard began smoothly enough; as a post-doctoral student I could pretty well call my own shots when choosing specific courses. Apart from advanced studies in economics, the department had asked me to scout the possibilities of organizing a German area studies program for the Foreign Service. This required considerable shopping around the curriculum as I audited courses in several departments. I found Professor Carl Friedrich of the Government Department, who had been among the more useful academic advisers to Military Government, a source of good counsel as well as the single most interesting professor that I met on the campus. He was a burly German, eloquent in a slightly accented English and a real polymath. He could sometimes be arrogant in a teutonic, professorial way but was helpful and kindly to serious students. A first-class political theorist and student of totalitarianism, he demonstrated his versatility and breadth of culture by writing *The Age of the Baroque, 1610–1680* in the Rise of Modern Europe series, a classic in its combination of conventional political history with a deep knowledge of baroque art and literature.[1]

The Economics Department proved generally less satisfactory. With some exceptions, the great names had apparently long since passed the point when they felt any obligation to provide their students with an organized presentation that had pedagogical coherence. They frequently just rambled on, mixing worn-out jokes with platitudes. Absenteeism was chronic because of consulting or other business away from the campus, and the burden of substituting fell on young teaching assistants who were sometimes better prepared than their supervisors. As I recalled my days at Columbia, the professors there had a much better attendance record and were generally more available. One thing at least I could say for the economists: they had not yet succumbed to the current academic predilection to substitute econometric models for the obstreperous real world.

I found the historians, sociologists, and social psychologists whose courses I audited more satisfactory as teachers. They usually came prepared and kept their talking notes reasonably up to date. It was the heyday of structural functionalism in the Sociology Department, over which Professor Talcott Parsons reigned. He had developed a unique jargon that made the obvious sound esoterically profound, if one could figure out what he was saying, but he seemed to fulfill that need social scientists apparently have to believe themselves to be in the same league as the so-called hard scientists. A short, roly-poly man, Parsons did provide some valuable insight into societal structures that subsequently proved helpful in my understanding of national societies. Particularly impressive to me as teacher was Professor Gordon W. Allport, a psychologist and social psychologist, who did not believe that the study of human behavior began and ended with watching rats find their way through mazes.

My year at Harvard passed quickly enough, as I have generally found the rhythms of academic life to do. Despite disappointments, I had undoubtedly benefited from those months of study, reflection, and exposure to some stimulating minds. I also knew considerably more about economics, bad teachers notwithstanding, than when I arrived in Cambridge. The numerous bookshops ringing Harvard Square had provided a frequent source of pleasure to this dedicated browser. Their presence also reminded me that Harvard, with all its faults, was still a serious university that attracted fine talents from around the world, just as that marvelous bookshop Blackwell's brings home to the visitor to Oxford the depth of tradition and learning that must be necessary to support such an establishment. In the spring, I received word that my next assignment was to be to the Department of State, where I would become chief of the Division of German Government and Administration in the Bureau of German Affairs. I looked forward to a genuine Washington assignment. Faith was somewhat less excited. With three children and a German shepherd, she knew her hands would be full.

Washington

The Bureau of German Affairs in the department (to members of the Foreign Service there was only one department and that was State) represented the Washington counterpart of the U.S. High Commission in Germany. It was the only bureau in the department dedicated to a single country, but given the size of the American bureaucracy in Germany, it kept busy enough and was, of course, in the middle of important policy formation. As the cold war progressed and the Korean War began, President Truman and Secretary of State Acheson became more and more persuaded that a German military contribution to the newly created North Atlantic Treaty Organization could be crucial to Western security. The Defense Department had for some time advocated bringing the Germans into any defensive arrangements for their country, but the political obstacles to doing this—primarily understandable French hesitancies—seemed formidable. When I arrived in Washington, attention focused on military developments in Korea, but by August the debate centered on the modalities of a German contribution to the defense of Europe. High Commissioner McCloy bombarded Washington with cables advocating action, and Henry Byroade, director of the Bureau of German Affairs, strongly pushed his point of view.

I quickly learned about the lines of influence in the department. To the outside observer of bureaucratic decision making, the official who produces the most documents that, at some later point, become available to scholars may well be regarded as most influential, and this can sometimes be the case. On the other hand, his or her papers may have been only marginal to the decision-making process. For example, the index of John Lewis Gaddis's *Strategies of Containment* makes no reference to Byroade, who in reality played a key role under Secretary Acheson in the decisions affecting Germany during the period 1950–52.[2] He seldom drafted memorandums or position papers, yet as an advocate and message bearer between the Pentagon, Germany, and the State Department, his influence was great. A West Point graduate and a brigadier general who did not retire from the army until 1951, Byroade did not know too much about Germany, but he certainly knew his way around Washington. Acheson prized him highly as someone who could get things done. He was later to join the Foreign Service and become ambassador to a number of countries, generally far removed from Washington. One's moment of greatest glory passes, and what follows may never quite live up to the promise.

The understandable fascination of historians for the written record can lead to some serious distortions of the way things really were. The name of George Kennan appears profusely in accounts of the early postwar years as if everything he wrote had enormous impact on policy. His elegant prose style and obvious depth of intellect cannot help but impress, and his famous article in *Foreign Affairs* signed X undoubtedly helped to form the conceptual basis for the American position in the cold war.[3] His influence on policy toward Germany, however, was clearly marginal. He himself notes in his *Memoirs* that his Plan A (to be proposed to the Soviets at the Paris Council of Foreign Ministers in 1949) never had any serious chance of adoption.[4] If it had been put forward, the Soviets would never have agreed to it, since it involved the holding of free, internationally supervised elections in all four zones—something the Soviets were not prepared to accept. I can recall having lunch with Kennan at Consul General Altaffer's residence during his visit to Germany in the spring of 1949. He talked eloquently, but neither Altaffer nor I was impressed by the practicality of the program for Germany he was advocating. He left the State Department to go to the Princeton Institute of Advanced Study at the end of August 1950, persuaded that American foreign policy was in a state of utter confusion.

At my level in the department, I knew generally what was happening and contributed to the inevitable bureaucratic paper flow to match that generated by the U.S. High Commission. The early fifties were to be a period of major travel by German politicians, paid for by an HICOG anxious to bring them into presumed beneficial contact with American ways. Most of the visits proved to be helpful in molding the attitudes of a whole generation of German parliamentarians—but not all. I can recall the arrival of a high-powered Social Democratic group led by the chairman of the party, Erich Ollenhauer. A difficult delegation member, Herbert Wehner, came with a chip on his shoulder. Everything we did or arranged for him seemed doomed to go badly. During one crucial session with senior departmental officials at which Wehner was to present his views, four or five stalked out at the halfway point because they had another meeting scheduled. Wehner thought they were deliberately walking out on him, and after his return to Germany he commented with disdain about such discourtesy. He did not believe his fellow travelers who tried to assure him that coming and going at meetings was standard American practice. At a later time, I came to know Wehner well; for many years he performed capably as leader of the SPD *Fraktion* in the Bundestag. He never ceased to be crusty and unpredictable in his reactions, but he was a man of honor and integrity. I do not think, however, that he ever completely shed his initial bad impression of life and bureaucratic practice in America.

The German government had opened a diplomatic mission in Washington but did not call it a full-fledged embassy. That was to come only later with the ending of the High Commission. Hans Krekeler was the special representative, and he cut a reserved figure on the local diplomatic scene. The house out on Reservoir Road that he acquired remained for many years as the residence of the German ambassador, an appropriately modest counterpart in Washington to the modest West German capital in Bonn. Any observer of the Washington diplomatic establishment could, over the years, contrast ironically the far more splendid residences of many ambassadors from the poorer countries of the world that an ever more prosperous Federal Republic could swallow economically without a gulp. I was to know that residence well under successive German chiefs of mission.

Washington in 1950, a time when air-conditioning did not yet prevail over the humid heat of summer, was still a city with few cosmopolitan pretensions. The cuisine of France also had not yet left its mark on restaurant life, and dinner at Harvey's or the Occidental was about as well as one could do. The Mellon Gallery had an impressive collection of classical art, but the city's cultural life did not overwhelm one with its variety or depth. We lived off McArthur Boulevard near the old Cabin John streetcar line. It provided my daily transportation to and from the State Department, now moved into what had once been the so-called New War Department Building. Our Bureau of German Affairs had its office in one of three red brick former apartment houses immediately adjacent to the department. Part of the one we occupied allegedly had been a brothel at some point in the past, but this was probably apocryphal. Coming into town on the tram provided plenty of time for reflection about the forthcoming events of the day, but the cars swayed too much to permit any writing or even comfortable reading.

Arranging for a German defense contribution proved to be a prolonged and arduous task. The process became entangled with the making of postwar Europe in a way that was to test the patience of governments and to involve me personally in Washington, and to an even greater degree when I went to Paris in the summer of 1952. The generations of Western Europeans that had survived the war shared a more or less common resolve to create a new European order that would prevent any recurrence of conflict and at the same time build new institutions of cooperation. The Marshall Plan had already led to the founding of the Office of European Economic Cooperation (OEEC) in Paris, but there was also a feeling that the new order had to go beyond the mere creation of more conventional international organizations and to involve some derogation of national sovereignties to an institution possessing real supranational powers. The French foreign minister, Robert Schuman, influenced by the dynamic and memorable Frenchman Jean Monnet, proposed on May 9, 1950, the creation of the European Coal and Steel Community, to which the member countries would entrust sovereign powers in the relevant economic area. In Monnet's mind this could form the nucleus of a future European government.[5] The negotiations on the Schuman Plan between France, the Federal Republic, Italy, and Benelux, complicated by the issue of German coal and steel production, took nearly a year, but on April 18, 1951, the treaty establishing the European Coal and Steel Community was finally signed. London would have nothing to do with the whole business, an attitude that many observers believed to be mistaken and ultimately contrary to British interests. British negativism with respect to supranational institutions was to play a continuing role in the years to follow.

Meanwhile, the United States had pushed ahead with its effort to clear the way for a German defense contribution. The French responded to American pressure by proposing what became known as the Pleven Plan, after the French prime minister of the moment, René Pleven. The guiding hand of Jean Monnet was plainly to be seen behind the key idea of creating a special European force, with its own command structure, under an American Supreme Allied Commander. All the German contingents, along with force contributions from the other Allies, would go into this European army. The attractiveness of such a concept to the French should theoretically have been obvious: it would eliminate the necessity for a German general staff or even Ministry of Defense. In Washington, as Dean Acheson put it in his *Present at the Creation*, the Pleven Plan caused "consternation and dismay,"[6] but in this way a process began that was not only to become inextricably linked to the progress of European integration but one that, from such an adverse beginning, became a major American cause. It took some eighteen months before the six countries concerned (France, Italy, Benelux, and the German Federal Republic) could agree on the final version of the treaty establishing the European Defense Community (signed on May 27, 1952).[7] Assuring ratification by the signatory states of the EDC Treaty (as it quickly was called), particularly by the French National Assembly, immediately became a high American priority. The distractions of the 1952 electoral campaign in the United States, and the defeat of the Democratic candidate, Adlai Stevenson, by General Eisenhower, meant in practice that not much could be done, until the new administration took over, to apply pressure on the French government to move ahead with the ratification process.

My principal task in the department was to follow internal German political developments closely and to see to the preparation of relevant guidance and instructions for the U.S. High Commission. After a shaky start (he had only become chancellor by the margin of a single vote, presumably his own), Konrad Adenauer quickly established his dominance over the German political scene. He seemed like a rock of firmness and stability to most of his compatriots and, with as much passion as he could muster, sought rapprochement with France and the acceptance of his country in European counsels. Along with Schuman, Spaak of Belgium, and de Gasperi of Italy, he was one of an extraordinary group of gifted and idealistic statesmen who emerged from the ashes of war to espouse the cause of West European integration.

Somewhat inconsistently, I suppose, given the strong American commitment to support efforts toward unity in the West, we also continued to discuss and to formulate proposals that might, in theory, lead to the reunification of Germany should there be any detectable change in Soviet policy. All of these, of course, involved holding truly free elections in both East and West Germany as the basis for establishing an all-German government. We did not expect the Soviets to accept anything of the kind, but we wanted to be ready for any resumption of four-power talks. This conceptual dualism in the American approach, at least at the working level, where the actual drafting of position papers was being done, opened American officials dealing with Germany to the possible charge that their recommendations smacked of schizophrenia. There was always the assurance, however, that Soviet obduracy would prevent any real testing of our will.

During the first part of 1951, the Soviet Union pressed for a four-power conference to discuss the German question. The Western Allies proposed a preliminary meeting of deputy foreign ministers to fix an agenda for an eventual conference of foreign ministers. The deputies met in Paris on March 5, 1951, in the Palais Rose but, after seventy-four frustrating sessions, adjourned on June 21 without ever reaching agreement on an agenda. It was a classic exercise in diplomatic futility; the Soviets obviously hoped to block the NATO decision to move toward a German defense contribution by manipulation of the agenda wording. My immediate superior in the Bureau of German Affairs, Perry Laukhuff, was a senior member of the American delegation. His description of the Palais Rose conference, after his return to Washington, provided both comic relief and constructive insights into Soviet negotiating tactics. The Soviet deputy foreign minister at the time was Andrei Gromyko, whom we were to see around as a formidable, hardheaded foreign minister for some twenty-nine years (1957 to 1986). Diplomats used to call Molotov, his predecessor as foreign minister, "Old Iron Pants." Gromyko deserved the same appellation as an indefatigable negotiator, prepared to outsit American, French, and British diplomats until they conceded his point in sheer boredom or exhaustion.

The year 1952 turned out to be one of major diplomatic exchanges on Germany between the Soviet Union and the Western powers. I became heavily engaged in the analysis of Soviet notes and the preparation of our responses. The process began with a note from the Soviet Union dated March 10, 1952, transmitting a Soviet draft of a peace treaty with a united Germany. The draft said nothing about free elections, and the identical notes in reply sent by Britain, France, and the United States on March 25 proposed the creation of a freely elected all-German government, after completion of its work by a UN commission of investigation and prior to negotiation of a peace treaty. The Soviet riposte of April 9 in turn proposed four-power rather than UN investigation of conditions for free all-German elections; the tripartite note of May 13 reasserted the authority of the United Nations to investigate conditions for free all-German elections. A lengthy Soviet reply arrived on May 24; it proposed simultaneous four-power discussion of a German peace treaty, German reunification, and formation of an all-German government. A further exchange of notes in July, August, and September left the position of both sides unchanged. In their note of September 23 the Western powers urged "a single minded effort . . . to come to grips with the problem of free elections in Germany."[8] The United States was now on the eve of presidential elections, and no further exchanges took place until after the Eisenhower administration had come into office.

While this diplomatic volleying went on, we were also heavily engaged in providing guidance from Washington to our High Commission for its negotiations with the Federal Republic, first on termination of the state of war between France, Britain, the United States, and the Federal Republic (declaration issued October 24, 1951) and then on a new contractual relationship between the three powers and the Federal Republic to replace the Occupation Statute and to bring the High Commission to an end. This Convention on Relations and attendant conventions (signed May 26, 1952) would not enter into force until ratification of the EDC Treaty.[9]

One did not require clairvoyant powers to see that the flurry of Soviet notes in 1952 aimed at aborting movement toward a West German defense contribution. A broader question that has arisen periodically in Germany is whether, behind the veil of Soviet propaganda and rhetoric, a real opportunity existed in 1952–53, and was lost, to achieve the reunification of Germany under conditions acceptable to the West. In the absence of any authoritative Soviet documentation about the thinking in the Kremlin, we can only conjecture at best. A German publicist, Sebastian Haffner, made the claim in a 1961 *Encounter* article, and later in his book *Der Selbstmord des Deutschen Reiches* (The Suicide of the German Reich), that Stalin's proposal of March 10, 1952, for a peace treaty with Germany (the Deutschland Plan, as it became known in Germany), and the subsequent clarifications of that proposal, constituted a genuine Soviet offer to dump the GDR, to permit free elections, and to accept a unified, neutralized Germany.[10]

A more recent book, written by an Austrian scholar, Rolf Steiniger, revived the discussion of an alleged lost opportunity. The very title of his book, *Eine vertane Chance: Die Stalin-Note vom 10. März 1952 und die Wiedervereinigung* (A Frittered Away Opportunity: The Stalin Note of March 10, 1952, and Reunification) shows the thrust of his thesis.[11]

I have over the years given some thought to this important question, which rose again during the last years of the Khrushchev era (a point neither Haffner nor Steiniger makes). Needless to say, if Western determination to push ahead with its German policy resulted in a preventable, indefinite division of the country, that policy would have suffered from a fundamental flaw—a flaw that could provide ammunition for those members of the oncoming German generation who questioned the desirability of the postwar order of things in Germany and in Europe.

It is difficult to describe past human intentions with cocksure precision. Our motivation is often ambiguous, and even the seemingly most certain can have secret doubts. An underlying reality during the cold war years that conditioned the behavior of the Western powers was deep distrust of Soviet intentions. Whether that distrust was warranted or erroneous, it was genuine enough and derived from a reasonable assessment of Soviet conduct in Eastern Europe, including the Soviet zone of occupation in Germany. Writers like Haffner and Steiniger attribute to the Soviets a basic beneficence of purpose that their practice failed to evidence. A few of us in the department favored calling the Soviet bluff by agreeing to a conference of foreign ministers in 1952, but the prevailing mood clearly ran counter to anything that portended further delay in obtaining a German defense contribution. People get committed to a course of action, the momentum builds up, and it becomes almost impossible, not only to reverse directions, but to brook any possible diversion. Chancellor Adenauer feared a Soviet trap; he had genuine concern that the West, and particularly his susceptible compatriots, would be bamboozled into accepting protracted negotiations in pursuit of the will-o'-the-wisp of unobtainable reunification, except under conditions that would lead to Communist hegemony over all of Germany.

We cannot know for sure what Stalin, and after his death early in 1953, his contending successors in the Politburo, had in mind with their flood of notes and proposals, but, given the prevailing atmosphere, there was little reason to expect that they were prepared seriously to discuss the modalities of reunification in terms acceptable to the West. That essentially meant a willingness to hold free, supervised elections in all four zones of Germany, elections that, in the light of their own experience in Berlin in 1948, they had little reason to believe would result in a Communist victory. The Western powers had the advantage, of course, of knowing that free elections in all of Germany would, in all probability, result in the election of a democratic, anti-Communist legislature (and hence government) that would move a united Germany in an anti-Soviet direction. Moreover, Soviet delaying tactics at the Palais Rose negotiations in 1951 had confirmed the impression that the Soviets' essential purpose was to halt progress on building new institutions in the West, rather than to move forward on German reunification.

Although the SPD, led by Kurt Schumacher, strongly opposed a West German defense contribution and Adenauer himself distrusted the steadfastness of his compatriots in the face of blandishments from the East, the majority of Germans in the Federal Republic clearly favored the policies of his government. The chancellor was to gain major electoral victories in 1953 and 1957 in support of his basic position. I could well remember the intensity of anti-Soviet feeling in Germany during the early postwar years. A population in the East overrun, mistreated, and often fleeing to the West from a brutal Soviet soldiery could not, in mitigation, put itself in the place of a Russian people who, only a few years earlier, had been overrun by a brutal German military machine.

In assessing where to come out on all this, I am persuaded that Soviet actions in 1952 were basically tactical. After all, the draft treaty of March 10, 1952, did not differ essentially from Soviet positions taken on various previous occasions such as the Prague Declaration of October 1950. The content of the notes, as well as general Communist activity with respect to Germany, make it appear highly probable that the Soviet objective was to play up to the nationalism of West Germans, to retard their contribution to Western defense, to stimulate Western European fear of Germany, and to divide the Allied powers. The Soviets obviously achieved none of these objectives; the delay in ratification of the EDC Treaty had very little to do with Soviet initiatives but much to do with the internal political situation in France.

We later became aware of some evidence that, for a brief period following the death of Stalin in March 1953, a few Soviet leaders, particularly Lavrentii Beria (head of the Soviet secret police), might have been willing to go further than in the past in considering the reunification of Germany in exchange for German neutrality. The principal source of this was Nikita Khrushchev, who charged that, shortly after Stalin's death, Beria began his effort to destroy Soviet relations with such fraternal countries as the GDR. After his arrest in June 1953, Beria served as a convenient whipping boy for alleged efforts to sell out the Ulbricht regime in East Germany.

Ulbricht himself, in a speech he made years later, implied that Beria was involved in such a plot, and we do know that considerable turbulence existed among the East German leadership in 1953, with one group allegedly having ties with the Beria faction. We shall probably never know for sure what might have emerged if the power struggle between Beria, Georgi Malenkov, and Khrushchev had come out differently. Beria's arrest in June 1953, the East German uprising on June 17, and Beria's execution late in 1953 presumably put an end to whatever possibility of movement toward German reunification Moscow may have entertained.[12] Ironically enough, in the declining years of his power, Khrushchev himself came under attack for alleged softness on the German issue.

As I recall the prevailing judgment at the time, few of us thought that, in the final analysis, the Soviets would agree to any solution of the German problem that entailed surrender of Soviet control over East Germany, or for that matter, would create a unified, supposedly neutralized Germany that inevitably would have continuing strong ties with the West. When it actually came in 1990, German reunification made this whole question of lost opportunity in the past largely academic.

A question related to all this, posed by some critics, was whether Chancellor Adenauer really wanted a unified Germany, knowing that the addition of the dominantly SPD population of the GDR might destroy the CDU/CSU–FDP (Christian Democratic Union/Christian Social Union–Free Democratic Party) majority that kept him in power. Did he really believe that building a position of strength in the West provided a workable path to reunification? His primary concerns, I believe, were Franco-German rapprochement and integration of the Federal Republic into the West. Even Haffner, however, has conceded that Adenauer was never known to have expressed any reservations he might have had about the desirability of German national unity.[13]

To move backward in time, by the summer of 1952 I had received word of my transfer to Paris. Our delegation to NATO, the headquarters of which had just moved from London to Paris, was building up its strength, and Ambassador Livingston Merchant had asked that I be assigned to his political staff. Before leaving Washington, I discovered what a complicated organizational structure would face me in Paris. The special representative Europe (SRE) stood at the top of the pyramid. He dispensed American aid and would also become our permanent representative to the NATO Council. Merchant would serve as his deputy and effectively run the U.S. delegation. It seemed like an exciting assignment, and the prospect of some years in Paris—a city Faith and I had only occasionally visited—could hardly displease.

Paris

Our arrival in the City of Light was inauspicious. We drove down from Le Havre and arrived at the Place de la Concorde in the early afternoon with three children and a German shepherd. After finding a parking place, I entered the Hotel Talleyrand (on the extreme left of the Place facing toward the Seine) where SRE had its offices, only to discover that word of our arrival had fallen by the wayside and that no one had made any hotel reservations for us. We sat through a long afternoon but finally ended up with two rooms in the Hotel St. James et d'Albany. A former nobleman's palace on the Rue de Rivoli, it was to be our home for more than two months, until we located a rental property nearly twenty miles to the south from my office—La Maison sous l'Eglise in Epinay sur Orge. Living in a hotel for a protracted period with three children and a dog inevitably strains both patience and vitality, but we managed. Our biggest upset came when our youngest son, John, wandered off into the hotel's subbasement, precipitating a frantic search in fear that he might have found his way into the main Paris sewer system, to which, apparently, the subbasement had access. To everyone's great relief, an employee found him short of the entrance.

At the Hotel Talleyrand, I quickly became fully engaged in the routine of many regularly scheduled NATO meetings. Although I was technically assigned to Paris as first secretary of embassy, it quickly became evident that, unless some other duties came along, my official life would involve mainly my office and the Palais de Chaillot, where the NATO organization had its headquarters. The Hotel Talleyrand was a splendid old palace (which Talleyrand himself had occupied for some years), with magnificent main salons on the Rue de Rivoli side under the protection of Beaux Arts (the Administration for Fine Arts). Nothing could be changed or even moved in those frozen rooms, splendid to look at but impractical as working offices. This was not my problem. Most of the SRE staff worked elsewhere in the building in offices that had been put together out of wallboard in various, peculiarly ungeometric shapes.

Relief from what promised to be a rather routine set of duties came quickly enough. The Bruce Mission, named after its head, Ambassador David Bruce, was being set up in Paris, attached to the embassy for administrative purposes but with independent status, its own telegraphic reporting series, and a separate location in a former Rothschild mansion on the Rue de Faubourg St. Honoré, destined at a later time to become the residence of the American ambassador. The Bruce Mission was nominally designated as the U.S. mission to the newly created Coal Steel Community (CSC) (which required maintaining a separate office in Luxembourg City).

The primary function of the mission, as everyone knew, was to do all in its power to assure ratification by the French National Assembly of the treaty establishing the European Defense Community. An even broader writ was to follow and to encourage all efforts toward European supranational integration. Once the Interim Commission to the European Defense Community set up its headquarters in Paris, staffed by personnel from the six signatory states, the Bruce Mission automatically took over representation to that body—a body intended to turn into the Permanent Commission of the EDC when the treaty came into effect. Ambassador Bruce was looking for a German expert to add to his staff, and I seemed to fit that requirement. Thus I ended up with two offices, one in the Hotel Talleyrand and one at 41 Rue du Faubourg St. Honoré, but in practice spent most of my time in the latter. The arrangement proved to be ideal for me, as I became progressively more wrapped up in the goals and operations of the Bruce Mission, while at the same time maintaining my interest in NATO affairs.

My colleagues in the mission were an able group of officers, some of them destined later to become ambassadors. Tommy Tomlinson, Bruce's deputy, had been treasury attaché in the embassy; he brought to his position an unusual degree of dedication to the ideal of European integration and a willingness to cut bureaucratic corners in order to achieve results. He suffered from a chronic heart and circulatory problem that, in the aftermath of the EDC's collapse, was to bring on a stroke and shortly thereafter his death. I need not add much here to the many encomiums that others have written about David Bruce, whom I came to admire as a paragon of diplomatic skill and personal kindness. I was to work closely with him in a later capacity and to count him as a friend. A person of considerable means and impeccable taste, he enjoyed life to the full aesthetically and culinarily. His leadership in the Bruce Mission provided both clear general direction and a willingness to let individual officers exercise considerable personal initiative. After many embassies, and the rare distinction of being a noncareer ambassador who had the full approval of the career service, his last few years were marked by personal tragedy.

Meanwhile, the Hillenbrand family had moved to La Maison sous l'Eglise to confront the rigors of an exceptionally cold and stormy winter. Our estate, behind a high wall, was picturesque enough, with the village church extending directly into a part of the wall. The house, however, had preceded the era of central heating, and we found, to our dismay, that the heating system a previous occupant had tacked on displayed an egregious disregard of the laws of thermodynamics. A relatively small, coal-burning stove stood in the kitchen to heat a hot-water tank, and from the tank ran a pipe that snaked around the outer wall of the building, to enter it again some fifty feet away. The colder the weather, the cooler the water was that supposedly heated the main salon. This alleged system forced us to rely entirely on electric heaters, with a resultant enormous electric bill each month. Another disadvantage of our country house, we discovered, was the long daily round trip into Paris, either by suburban train or car, and sometimes back again in the evening for a social engagement. Our son David, who had entered the local elementary school, found that, as the sole American, he quickly became the object of abuse from the well-indoctrinated children of what turned out to be a largely Communist village. All in all, we concluded, we would want to move into Paris when our lease expired, despite the undoubted pleasure of semirural life in a semichateau.

As we moved into 1953, ratification of the EDC Treaty by the French seemed to recede farther into the future. Our small group in the Bruce Mission became dedicated advocates of a supranational European Defense Community. It seemed to us that, once in being, the community would provide both a significant step forward and a symbol in which the idealism of a whole generation of young Europeans could find a central purpose. Like most people committed to a cause, we had little tolerance for opposing arguments, nor did we assess the political forces opposed to ratification with complete realism. When I look back, the mistakes of judgment that we made are now apparent, but caught up as we were in what seemed like a righteous cause, the wisdom that hindsight provides escaped us at the time.

At the beginning of 1953, the Eisenhower administration took over in Washington. John Foster Dulles became secretary of state and issued his demand for "positive loyalty" from all State Department employees. He did not define what he meant with precision, and the secretary's new requirement did not affect us very much in Paris, although it ended the careers of a number of Foreign Service officers who had been involved in Chinese affairs during and after the war.[14] The whole idea could not help being insulting to a professional diplomat trained to serve successive presidents and secretaries of state with loyalty and impartiality. Did it mean that allegiance to the Republican Party was now required?

Dulles also brought Ambassador Merchant back to Washington to become assistant secretary of state for European affairs. Livy Merchant had been a good boss, articulate, realistic, and understanding. A few regarded him as somewhat mercurial, but I found him a steadfast and disciplined public official. Both he and his deputy, C. Burke Elbrick, had personal doubts about the EDC Treaty that, they feared, would weaken the U.S. role in NATO. When he took over as assistant secretary, however, he loyally supported American efforts to have the treaty come into effect—an objective that Dulles accepted from his predecessor as an important national interest.

The French political scene had also undergone some significant changes since the proposing and the signing of the EDC Treaty that were to affect both governmental and legislative attitudes toward the EDC in a negative way. When René Pleven made his proposal for the Europe Defense Community in 1950, the parties that supported him in the National Assembly represented a coalition favoring supranational institutions (the MRP [Mouvement Républicain Populaire] alone had some 160 deputies). By May 27, 1952, when M. Antoine Pinay, as prime minister, initialed the treaty establishing a defense community, the Socialist Party had already begun to think in terms of *conditions préalables* (preliminary conditions) for its support. Then, for reasons not entirely clear, Foreign Minister Robert Schuman delayed sending the treaty to the parliament for ratification until January 29, 1953. Perhaps he was waiting for the separate discussion of a European Political Community to make headway, or perhaps he already felt the climate in the National Assembly had turned unfavorable.[15]

In any event, Georges Bidault replaced Schuman early in 1953 as foreign minister in the René Mayer government. Bidault was a strange and brilliant man of small physical stature but great eloquence. A leader of the Resistance, he later became an exile from his own country because of his opposition to Charles de Gaulle's Algerian policy. He displayed some ambivalence on issues we thought important, seeming to do what he could to make progress on EDC ratification while, at the same time, showing hostility to the idea of broader European political union.

Perhaps the most important negative development was the splintering of the government coalition precisely on the ratification issue. The Socialists (the majority of whom still favored the EDC, although some prominent members of the party were strong opponents) had moved into the opposition against Pinay, while some Gaullists, all of whom opposed the EDC, had joined the government majority.

We in the Bruce Mission were to become thoroughly sick of the term *conditions préalables*, although we generally ended up by urging their successive acceptance as necessary to that ever more elusive ratification of the EDC Treaty. Whether it was demands regarding the Saar, guarantees of a continuing U.S. commitment to the defense of Europe, some form of British association with the EDC, or more American aid, we argued that, as distasteful as this French extraction of ever more concessions might be, achievement of our overriding objective justified their acceptance. Psychologically, we were in that situation one encounters frequently in life in which, with each passing day, the goal of one's striving becomes less likely of attainment, but one does not give up the struggle and grasps at straws to maintain at least a modicum of optimism. Looking back, I recall how our small, heavily engaged group managed to be of good cheer. Perhaps we did not fully appreciate how dark the prospects actually had become.

We should have seen a clear warning in the fate of the European Political Community. Article 38 of the treaty establishing the European Defense Community had stipulated that action should be taken to move toward a "federal or confederal structure" for the six member countries, and on September 10, 1952, the six foreign ministers asked the members of the Common Assembly of the European Coal and Steel Community (a body constituted by parliamentarians from the member states) to draw up a draft treaty setting up the European Political Community. An ad hoc assembly was then formed with representation in the same proportion as proposed for the Assembly of the European Defense Community. The ad hoc assembly held its initial meeting in Strasbourg on September 15, 1952, and chose M. Paul Henri Spaak of Belgium as its president. After setting up committees and subcommittees to handle the basic drafting, the assembly met periodically during the next six months until adoption of a final draft treaty embodying the Statute of the European Community on March 10, 1953.

I made a number of visits to Strasbourg for the Bruce Mission to observe the proceedings of the ad hoc assembly. In a way, these sessions were really a high point of the European movement. Idealism and good will flowed through the halls of the l'Orangerie, the home of the Consultative Assembly of the Council of Europe, where the ad hoc assembly met for its plenary sessions. With only a few exceptions, the engaged parliamentarians really believed their work would lead to a new and unified Western Europe; their debates reflected a high degree of commitment and intelligence, and gradually they hammered out a draft treaty. As presiding officer, Spaak skillfully directed the discussion, and the adoption of specific language, toward the objective of a true federal system. The whole process proved infectious for the Bruce Mission. We were enthusiastic about the achievement and, to a slightly lesser degree, about the prospects. I came to know Heinrich von Brentano, chairman of the Important Constitutional Committee of the ad hoc assembly (later to become West German foreign minister), as an important source of information about problems and prospects.

The cold shower came on March 9, 1953, with the speech to the ad hoc assembly by French foreign minister Bidault, president of the Special Council of Ministers of the European Coal and Steel Community. Commenting on the treaty draft just completed, in elegant but evasive language, he noted the "inevitable division of labour between men with bold and independent minds and Governments whose honour and impediment it [was] to carry the responsibility" and "that it should be left to governmental circles . . . to determine how the Treaty should be drawn up." He added the warning, "Let us beware of thinking, if I may say so, that all things are possible to hearts that are sincere," before concluding with a rhetorical salute to the destiny of Europe. The applause was vigorous; only afterward, when one had time to read his precise words beneath the rhetoric, did the impression emerge that this was really a brush-off, an injunction to cool it. The "governmental circles" to which Bidault referred never got around to the final drawing up of the treaty, and the whole project (which was supposed to provide a political roof for the EDC Treaty) collapsed along with the idea of an integrated defense community.[16]

We should have taken heed from this experience. Despite all their fears of a resurrected German army, the French aversion to any derogation of their own national sovereignty in the political-military area would, in the final analysis, prevail—but this lesson we learned all too slowly. Who remembers today the efforts of the ad hoc assembly, now more than forty years buried in the past? The principal actors are nearly all dead and what they tried to do in Strasbourg forgotten, hardly deemed worthy of a footnote by historians. If they had succeeded, and perhaps there was never any realistic chance of this, the shape of Europe in our time would be quite different from that which it is.

One impression I carried away with me from Strasbourg: Frenchmen infected by Gaullism were prepared to vote their views even if part of a ridiculously small minority. Michel Debré, representing the Gaullist Rally of the French People, steadfastly voted against any draft language that smacked of supranationality. In the final ad hoc assembly vote on the treaty text (90 to 1 in favor), his was the single negative vote. We were to hear much of Debré later in his various capacities as a senior member of French governments, including a period as prime minister; his stubborn individualism and obstructionism at times irritated, but at least he could plead consistency.

Another memory of those days in Strasbourg that I carried with me had to do with its fine restaurant life. Alsatian cooking tended to be a little heavier than that we had found in Paris, but it went down easily. Dinners at Zimmer, sometimes with von Brentano, proved both gustatorily and intellectually stimulating. I also learned the practical lesson that the relationship of transportation to position is not always what one would think. One day I was having lunch at Zimmer with Victor Preusker, a German FDP member of the Bundestag and a Ruhr industrialist, later to become a minister in an Adenauer cabinet. We arrived and later returned to the l'Orangerie by streetcar. We came out of the restaurant at the same time as several German Social Democratic members of the assembly and noted that they were picked up by a chauffeur-driven black Mercedes. We could not help but laugh as we boarded our streetcar. In my experience, love for austerity is not a noteworthy characteristic of many left-of-center European politicians.

Anyone who reads through the voluminous cable traffic between Paris and Washington during 1953–54 (contained in *Foreign Relations of the United States*) cannot help but be impressed by the intensity of American concern over ratification of the EDC Treaty.[17] Bruce Mission telegrams that went out under the acronym COLED, and those from the department to the mission under the acronym EDCOL, as well as those from and to the American embassy in Paris, provided a detailed running commentary on the seemingly endless ebb and flow of argument and manipulation with respect to the EDC. There comes inevitably, and periodically, a weariness of the flesh and spirit in pursuit of a goal that seems to be ever receding, but between the Bruce Mission and the State Department the stream of recommendations and endorsements continued without diminution. Toward the end of 1953, however, when the prospects seemed bleak in the face of every new French delay in presenting the treaty to the National Assembly, Secretary of State Dulles, in an obvious effort to shock the French government into action, stated to the North Atlantic Council, meeting in Brussels at ministerial level on December 14: "If, however, the E.D.C. should not become effective; if France and Germany remain apart, so that they would again be potential enemies, then indeed there would be grave doubt whether continental Europe could be made a place of safety. That would compel an agonizing reappraisal of basic United States policy."[18]

The expression "agonizing reappraisal," which Dulles used again at a press conference in Brussels after the council meeting, obviously created a sensation. There was a great deal of diplomatic scurrying around, but the emphasis shifted in January 1954 to Berlin, where the foreign ministers of France, Britain, the United States, and the Soviet Union met once again to discuss the question of Germany. Bidault attended for France, Anthony Eden for Britain, Dulles for the United States, and Molotov for the Soviet Union. We could only watch from Paris, but I knew enough about the frozen positions of both sides to have low expectations of any significant agreement being reached. The Western ministers put forward the Eden Plan for German Reunification through Free Elections, and the Soviets responded with another version of their draft peace treaty.[19] Although the Eden Plan contained some new elements on which we were to draw at a later point, the conference proved to be just another turn of the old four-power merry-go-round. In its way, however, the fact of the conference contributed to a more general feeling in France that East-West tensions had somewhat relaxed and that therefore the need for a German defense contribution, and hence the EDC, had lessened. Another French distraction from the business of EDC ratification was the deteriorating military situation in Indochina. The Battle of Dienbienphu began on March 13, 1954, to end on May 7 with the collapse of French resistance in the beleaguered camp.

Apart from the pressures of work and premonitions that we were pursuing a losing cause, life in Paris had both its highlights and shadows. The sheer beauty of the city, the vistas that suddenly opened up, the intensity of its restaurant and street life—all captivated us. When we moved into the city from the countryside in the fall of 1953, we looked forward to an even greater measure of participation in all this. We had found a house in the Sixteenth Arrondissement that seemed to meet our family needs. I had been alerted to the guile that otherwise perfectly respectable French citizens displayed in cheating on their income tax. Landlords, I had been warned, would almost automatically insist that the prospective tenant sign two leases, one containing the correct amount of rent, and the other with a lesser amount intended for display to an inquisitive tax agent. My exposure to this common practice, developed to an even higher degree of psychological subtlety, came when I called on the eminently well-known doctor who owned the house on the Rue Henri Heine into which we hoped to move. After some preliminary harrumphing, he pulled three pieces of paper out of a desk drawer. The first lease form, which he handed to me for signature, contained the rental amount on which we had previously agreed. The second, as I expected, contained a considerably smaller amount. I signed it as well. Then he handed me the third paper, also a lease form with an even smaller rental amount on it. When I looked somewhat quizzically at it, he explained, with a smile, that it was somewhat unusual, but he had found it to be a good system. When the tax inspector asked to see his lease, he handed him the one with the lowest amount on it. Then when the inspector said, "And now show me the real lease," the good doctor would give him the one with the intermediate amount. With a laugh, our future landlord commented, "They never suspect that I really have three leases." I surrendered to harsh reality and signed the third lease as well.

As do most Americans in Paris, we developed our favorite restaurants and cafés. The rituals of good eating have traditionally played a major role in French culture; they have produced a cuisine that we found it easy to enjoy. One was always searching for that unique little, still undiscovered bistro with a talented young chef, but the really good ones sooner or later, and usually quickly, became discovered. The inexorable cycle seemed to be obscurity, fame, decline, and often eventual closure. Our favorite night-spot was the Mars Club, now long defunct, just off the Champs Élysée. American jazz pianists frequented the place. A regular performer was Bobby Short, with his impressive repertoire of songs and breezy manner. Many New Yorkers have enjoyed him over the years as a popular enter-tainer at the Hotel Carlyle.

Whenever enough Americans have been around to form at least two teams, I have tried to organize some baseball competition. This proved easy enough in Paris, and our league played its games regularly on a large cleared area in the Bois de Boulogne. One Sunday afternoon, with my team at bat, we were startled to see about fifty American Indians, in full war paint and regalia, burst out of the woods and race across our ball field with loud war whoops. They effectively disrupted our game until they dis-appeared again into the woods. We could only laugh at this exposure to an organization of Frenchmen, so infatuated with Indian lore that each Sunday they roamed the Bois de Boulogne in full costume. America's Wild West and Indian lore has exercised a peculiar fascination for some in France, as it has for generations in Germany, where the imaginative, and not entirely accurate, writings of Carl May about our Indians have con-tinued to enjoy popularity.

Any observant American living in Paris during the mid-fifties could not help but note a strong undercurrent of anti-Americanism among a sizable segment of the French population. Some 25 percent of the population voted for a Communist Party that endorsed Soviet policy without qualifi-cation. Painted slogans proclaiming "Ridgway Go Home" appeared on every available wall, aimed at the American general who had become Supreme Allied Commander Europe, with his headquarters some fifteen miles from Paris. Massive demonstrations against various aspects of U.S. policy, including the sentencing of the Goldbergs for espionage, would stream past our embassy and the Hotel Talleyrand, tying up traffic for hours on the Place de la Concorde. After our experience in India, we did not feel very threatened personally by all this, but some of our colleagues and their families became jittery. The French riot police always turned out in force around the embassy on the days of demonstrations. An effective way to break up a hostile crowd, they discovered, was to put the vanguard into a fleet of assembled paddy wagons and deposit them in a remote part of the Bois de Boulogne, far from the subway or other means of transport. By the time the weary demonstrators reached the center of Paris again, they had little heart or feet left for further marching.

Collapse of the EDC

As we moved into the spring of 1954, it became evident that the government of Prime Minister Laniel (which had been in office since June 26, 1953) could not be certain of its ability to deliver a majority of the National Assembly in favor of the EDC. Laniel had proved to be a man of many hesitations. The growing importance of EDC opponents in the governmental majority and the apparent easing of East-West tensions in the immediate post-Stalin years were realities that we could not ignore. Moreover, French official attention more and more focused on the military crisis in Vietnam. The Laniel government fell on June 12, and on June 18 Pierre Mendes-France formed a new cabinet. On July 20 an armistice was signed in Geneva ending hostilities in Indochina.

It was not clear to us what Mendes-France would do with respect to the EDC. In his inauguration speech, he stressed the necessity for a compromise that would win a large majority in the National Assembly.[20] He also provoked considerable ridicule in the French press by advocating in an interview the consumption of milk by his wine-drinking compatriots. We do not know with certainty even today whether the prime minister really wanted a defeat of the EDC or simply found himself overwhelmed by the forces opposed to it. The three modifications to the treaty that he proposed raised both constitutional and practical problems for the three signatory countries that had already ratified the treaty. We members of the Bruce Mission should have been able to read the handwriting on the wall, but we were reluctant to give up or fully to recognize that a radical transformation of the issues had taken place. What had started out to be a scheme for harnessing a West German defense contribution within a supranational framework had now become an unacceptable infringement of French sovereignty.

The prelude to the end came at a meeting in Brussels of the heads of governments of signatory states. Mendes-France was unable to obtain the watering down of supranationality that he claimed to be essential to win approval in the French assembly. After returning to Paris, he submitted the treaty to the assembly without a decision by his divided cabinet, and on August 30 the EDC fell with the rejection of a preliminary procedural motion made by proponents to defer the debate that they feared would inevitably end with a negative vote. Thus ended with a whimper what many had believed to be a noble design destined to bring Europe together in a binding union.[21]

Those frenetic last days left the Bruce Mission in a state of shock. We had had observers in Brussels who came back with tales of British perfidy behind the scenes. We knew that Mendes-France had made a quick trip to London to see Prime Minister Churchill, and friends of the treaty reported that British maneuvering in Brussels went in a hostile direction. It was no secret, of course, that the British looked askance at the idea of a truly supranational Europe—the forerunner of subsequent reluctance to join the European Economic Community until the perceived advantages of membership became overwhelming. We were obviously looking for a scapegoat, but the overriding reality was that the French had ultimately rejected their own handiwork.

Postmortems in the aftermath of failure are bound to be painful. Given the intensity of commitment and of opposition, strident recrimination was inevitable. Supporters of the EDC could not help but feel that a tragic event had occurred, that an opportunity had been lost that perhaps would never come again. We in the Bruce Mission were emotionally exhausted, depressed by a deep sense of failure. We obviously tried to analyze what had gone wrong. Like most people dedicated to a cause, we had had little tolerance for contrary arguments, nor did we perhaps assess the forces opposed to French ratification with complete realism. When I look back, our mistakes of judgment seem apparent, but caught up as we were in a dynamic and fast-moving process, those mistakes escaped us at the time. We were, of course, far from alone in our disappointment. The EDC had become a righteous cause to dedicated officials and leaders in all six proposed member countries. Among them was Hervé Alphand, the French representative to the Interim Commission of the EDC and later during the 1960s French ambassador in Washington. During the 1952–54 period, he had been an important contact with the French government. It was usually he who came to us with the first word of a new *condition préalable*. A man small in stature and cynical in manner, Alphand had both friends and enemies within the French establishment. We generally judged him to be sincerely committed to the EDC. A few thought he was just stringing us along, but as I look back, I am inclined to believe that his cynicism did not extend to the defense community. He and Tomlinson had developed a particularly close relationship, and he sometimes seemed exceedingly frank, if not indiscreet, in his comments about French politicians.

Perhaps the best immediate analysis of the EDC debacle came from Second Secretary of Embassy Martin Herz, whose lengthy memorandum was transmitted to the State Department in a dispatch dated September 16, 1954.[22] Martin, a valued Foreign Service colleague over the years, concluded that there had at one time been a majority in favor of the EDC in the National Assembly but that it had gradually been lost; that Mendes-France did not go to Brussels with the deliberate intention of torpedoing the treaty but went there with no keen desire to succeed; that after the failed Brussels meeting, his actions were effectively directed to defeat of the treaty; and that Mayer, Bidault, and Laniel all must share some responsibility for delay and dilution of the European idea. In other words, nothing had been inevitable, but given the personalities and forces involved, one could detect an almost fatalistic thread of inactivity and misdirected activity that in combination led to the deadly procedural vote of August 30, 1954.

The collapse of the EDC inevitably produced many books and articles, mostly in French but some in English, purporting to explain how it all happened. Before writing this section, I have gone through a number of these and have tried to think back, more than forty years later, into the atmosphere and pressures of the early fifties. One might today wonder at the seeming arrogance of the role we tried to play, but it was the era of clear American hegemonial power, political, military, and economic, with respect to Western Europe. Rereading the voluminous exchanges of messages between Washington and Paris, one can note the differences of emphasis and occasionally of tactics to be followed, but there was no challenging the idea that we ought to intervene to the extent that we did. The National Assembly, whatever its confusions and perversities, punctured any illusion of American omnipotence in forcing our views on French behavior.

Our purpose lost, the Bruce Mission quickly dissolved, and I went back full-time to our NATO delegation. Our last collective activity was a splendid dinner for all staff members given by Ambassador Bruce at his residence. He produced the very best food and wines. The atmosphere, however, was funereal, even to the eulogies exchanged between those who had been most active. We had a last opportunity to talk of what might have been and, as is the wont of the defeated, who the villains were. If there had been a pianist present, he could have fit the mood by playing nothing but dirges. We had, nevertheless, done our best, we thought, and none of us could come up with a different course of action on our part that, given the forces at play, would have led to a significantly different outcome—but that was small consolation. We knew that life must go on and that our tightly knit group must now disperse. Life did not go on very long for Tommy Tomlinson, who, shortly thereafter, suffered a disabling stroke and some months later died.

Picking Up the Pieces

Whatever the degree of Britain's complicity in the demise of the EDC Treaty, it was British diplomacy that came to the rescue of a floundering alliance. The State Department, alone and in consultation with the Foreign Office, had considered some possible contingency plans in the event of French rejection of the EDC, but the National Assembly's action of August 2 resulted in no immediate reaction in Washington other than verbal. Both the British and American governments, and even the French government when it could focus on the problem, had an obvious interest in salvaging as much as possible of the complicated and interlocking sets of agreements, so laboriously negotiated by the three Allied High Commissions with the German government in Bonn, that were intended to restore full German sovereignty when the EDC Treaty came into effect. To find another way to achieve a German defense contribution obviously also remained a high priority.

In his *Memoirs*, Anthony Eden describes in some detail his peripatetic diplomacy of September as he traveled from capital to capital to meet with European leaders.[23] He and Chancellor Adenauer, whom he visited in Bonn, expressed concern that, in disappointment, the United States might be tempted to engage in that "agonizing reappraisal" Secretary of State Dulles had threatened the previous December. There were essentially two options: to water down the EDC Treaty to the point that might make it acceptable to the French, or to move toward direct German membership in NATO with safeguards provided within some other framework. As bitter as the Italian, German, and Benelux leaders were over the collapse of the defense community, they agreed with Eden that the EDC Treaty was dead and that even a watered-down version would probably now be rejected by the French as providing too much scope for an independent German military. The British came up with the idea of reviving the Western European Union organization created by the Brussels Treaty of 1948 (Eden noted that the thought came to him while taking his morning bath),[24] and using it as the framework for certain German commitments and renunciations deemed necessary to obtain French agreement. The first step in this process was to be a Nine-Power Conference in London (Belgium, Canada, the Federal Republic of Germany, France, Italy, Luxembourg, the Netherlands, the United Kingdom, and the United States), which would set forth the main lines of a complex of agreements (some still to be negotiated in detail) that would permit a West German defense contribution.

We could tell from the numerous cable exchanges between the Department of State and Paris that Washington was, at least initially, not impressed by the Eden enterprise. Dulles was not accustomed to being upstaged, and he saw himself doing the rounds of pertinent capitals in Europe in an effort to patch up matters. Eden, however, was on the spot and running; he had clearly seized the initiative and with the help of some personal messages from Churchill gradually obtained a reluctant U.S. government acceptance of the essential course of action that he proposed.[25]

The Nine-Power Conference convened in London at the foreign minister level on September 28 and proceeded rapidly toward agreement by October 3 on a Final Act that, inter alia, invited Italy and the Federal Republic of Germany to accede to the Brussels Treaty and to instruct their representatives in Paris to draw up detailed proposals, for approval by the North Atlantic Council, for a German defense contribution.[26] A principal component of the overall arrangement would obviously be the seven-power agreements, to be worked out within the Western European Union framework, placing certain limitations on the modalities of a West German defense contribution.

Diplomatic agreements of the complexity contemplated can usually only be attained if one party takes overriding control of both procedure and substance. The British are past masters of this, and it was clear to us in Paris that it was they who were the principal architects of the Nine-Power Final Act. Moreover, they would clearly play the dominant role in the negotiating process now moved to Paris. I was designated to be the deputy to Edward Page, the American observer to the WEU (Western European Union) negotiations, but since Page was unavailable, I found myself the only American present at these negotiations, charged with keeping my government informed of what was happening in them.

The chairmanship quickly went to Sir Christopher (Kit) Steel, a senior British diplomat and at the time the United Kingdom permanent representative to the North Atlantic Council. A classic product of the class-structured British system and a graduate of Oxford, Steel was a highly effective chairman. Not an orator but a quiet persuader, sometimes almost diffident in manner, he could usually be relied on to come up with a procedural maneuver or apt phrasing to break a deadlock. In my experience, I have found many British diplomats with the same talents, almost as if a peculiar combination of breeding and elite education tended automatically to funnel young graduates of a certain caliber into the Foreign Office. There have been some notable exceptions to such a background in the more democratic postwar years, but the skills required of them for entry into the diplomatic service seemed essentially the same. Diplomats of other countries have their distinctive strengths and weaknesses, but give me someone English every time when there is need of clever chairmanship.

Kit Steel guided the proceedings with great skill, and after a hectic two weeks the negotiators emerged with four protocols to the Brussels Treaty. The first of these provided for German and Italian accession to the treaty, as well as strengthening the organization and procedures of the Western European Union. The second defined the maximum force levels of the various members to be placed directly under NATO command (actually those already agreed on in an annex to the EDC Treaty). The third, on the control of armaments, specified armaments that were not to be manufactured and those that were to be controlled (a major point here was the German undertaking not to manufacture in its territory any atomic weapons, chemical weapons, or biological weapons). The fourth created the Agency for the Control of Armaments of Western European Union and described its duties. The obvious intent of all this was to provide a limiting framework within which the Federal Republic could make a direct military contribution to the alliance.

I had witnessed a diplomatic tour de force. But who today remembers the conference skills of Kit Steel (who died in 1973), so ably displayed during that concentrated period in October, apart from a few surviving participants or observers? Diplomats know from experience how transient is the glory of their world. The high drama, the anxious moments, the frenetic negotiations, the brilliant improvisations are all swept away by the current of time. The traces they leave in the scribblings of journalists, historians, and memoirists fade as well until only obscure specialists are interested. Ph.D. candidates searching desperately for an unexploited subject on which to write a dissertation might stumble across a forgotten name or skillful negotiation. Given the comparative flood of such candidates in the United States compared with the United Kingdom, American diplomats might have a certain comparative advantage over their British colleagues in their hope for even such slight rescue from obscurity.

So it is, of course, with most achievements in life, whether in government, business, education, or the arts. For everyone who leaves a mark on history, there are millions whose accomplishments vanish into time's maw there to be consumed. This erasure from living memory of so many achievements and talents is an enormously sad reality that contributes to a tragic sense of life. No matter what one's view of the afterlife, most of us yearn for some continuing recognition of what we have done.

Combined with a series of four-power agreements that restored essential sovereignty to the Federal Republic, agreement on the four protocols to the Brussels Treaty opened the way to the signing, on October 23, by the fourteen foreign ministers of the NATO countries, of the Protocol to the North Atlantic Treaty on the Accession of the Federal Republic of Germany. The whole complex quickly became known as the Paris Agreements.[27] It was Anthony Eden's finest hour. He had taken charge and pulled it off. What less than two months before had seemed like an irretrievable catastrophe had been turned into a solution that achieved the essential purpose of obtaining a German defense contribution while giving the Federal Republic its political independence. Who could have imagined then that within little more than two years Eden, become prime minister, would be a ruined man—psychologically crushed and physically sick in the aftermath of the Suez disaster?

The Paris Agreements still had to be ratified, of course, but while this was not a foregone conclusion, the prospects seemed relatively good. Having exhausted itself in rejecting the EDC, the French National Assembly appeared to be in a relatively subdued mood. As a matter of fact, the agreements came into effect on May 5, 1955, all signatory states, including France, having deposited their final instruments of ratification in Bonn. The vote in the National Assembly on December 30, 1954, was 287 to 268 in favor—not an overwhelming margin but sufficient. This did not occur without some anxious moments in both Paris and Bonn. During the debates in the National Assembly before the December 30 vote, apart from the automatic Communist Party opposition, many French parliamentarians demonstrated that they could not accept a German defense contribution in any form. Some observers criticized Mendes-France's tactics, but the final result removed any doubts about French ratification. Contingency planning in Washington for the event of another failure, the subject of many cable exchanges between Paris and the State Department, could finally be discarded.

In the Federal Republic, adamant SPD opposition to the Paris Agreements, plus what some thought was a rising trend toward neutralism, also caused concern in Washington. With his clear majority in the Bundestag, Chancellor Adenauer, however, skillfully guided the necessary legislation through its various readings. In a sense, the Paris Agreements were not as troublesome in themselves as a French interpretation of the Saar Treaty, linked by Mendes-France to acceptance of a German military contribution, which was politically unacceptable to Adenauer. The French wanted a formulation that would, in effect, eventually make the Saar a permanent part of France (through guaranteed U.S. and British support at any eventual peace conference). A compromise formula was finally worked out, but as we know, the march of events settled the Saar issue in favor of absorption by the Federal Republic, after a plebiscite in October 1955, without any relationship to a peace treaty that has never been negotiated.[28] So often in the history of diplomacy, what seems in one context to be an indispensable condition becomes an irrelevancy as time moves on and circumstances as well as the cast of official characters change.

What Did We Gain? What Did We Lose?

Through a diplomatic tour de force, British inspired and American blessed, the Western alliance was able to provide the basis for a West

German defense contribution within NATO while, at the same time, the Federal Republic achieved full sovereignty (with the exception of residual four-power responsibility for all-German affairs, an ultimate peace treaty, and Berlin). For those who regarded the proposal for the European Defense Community as a dubious, if not completely unworkable, construct (Winston Churchill called it a "sludgy amalgam" in a letter to Eisenhower),[29] the outcome represented a considerable improvement. One could not help noting the irony in final French acceptance of direct German membership in NATO, after originally finding it necessary to elaborate the EDC proposal as the only possible context in which a German military buildup would be permissible.

As it turned out, the Paris Agreements worked out very well indeed. The Federal Republic became the major European member of the alliance at the nonnuclear level, a responsible and economically strong democracy that has been an important force for stability in Western Europe. Whatever one's perception of the Soviet threat, NATO provided the sense of security, the psychological shield, behind which its European members have prospered.

But it has not been all gain. In moments of undoubted rhetorical excess, I have argued that the collapse of the EDC destroyed the political idealism, focused on the dream of a united Europe, of a whole generation of young Europeans. It is true, in any event, that the failure of the European Defense Community, and before that of the European Political Community, left a significant void. When an important symbol dies, much of the fervor and hope it produced inevitably die with it. The Rome Treaty of 1957, which created the European Economic Community—the next major attempt to build a supranational Europe—never aroused the kind of enthusiasm identified with the high point of the EDC.

The history of our time is full of lost opportunities. We can never be sure what would actually have happened if the EDC Treaty had come into effect. It was a bold and imaginative venture, and five of the six proposed member countries were ready for it. It might have proved to be unworkable in its blending of forces and military command structure, but the dedicated leaders who committed themselves to it were men of vision and not fools. Responsible statesmen and diplomats do not mourn publicly for long, no matter how deep their regrets. They turn to what is possible, even if they know it to be second best, but, as their memoirs attest, the political supporters of the EDC believed that something important had been irretrievably lost.[30]

After nearly two years of dedicated effort and final disappointment, followed by the frenetic effort to recapture lost ground, my last period in Paris was bound to be somewhat anticlimactic. I quickly fell back into the

NATO routine of regularly scheduled meetings and came to appreciate that the alliance served as much as a psychological as a military necessity for many Europeans. It was also a heady period in the Soviet Union, and we watched the behavior of Nikita Khrushchev with some fascination as he consolidated his control. Word of his de-Stalinization campaign had reached the West, including the text of his denunciatory speech to the Twentieth Party Congress in 1956. As I look back, I am reminded that, in some respects at least, the initial years of Nikita Khrushchev as secretary general of the Communist Party in the USSR resembled the early years in power of Mikhail Gorbachev. Announcements of ambitious reforms poured out of the Kremlin. Few of them succeeded in practice, and, as we know, Khrushchev became enmeshed in foreign policy adventures that basically failed and certainly contributed to his eventual downfall.

One of the experiences to which American diplomats are periodically exposed is the arrival of a team of Foreign Service inspectors making a circuit of posts in an area (most countries, of course, follow the same practice). We received notice that an inspection team would arrive early in 1956. It would be unnatural to assume that field posts greet the prospect with great enthusiasm, but on the whole the process is a salutary one. In this case it turned out to be fortunate for me. The senior inspector, Bernard Gufler, an old Foreign Service hand, noted that I was becoming restive and wanted a change. He knew he would soon be going to Berlin as head of the State Department mission in that city, and he made a mental note to ask for me to come as his deputy. It was to be an assignment that would strongly influence my future as a diplomat.

While somewhat frustrating, our last year in Paris was not wasted. We had more time to enjoy the cultural and other amenities of the city. Our children were getting older, and I was glad to be able to provide increased companionship. Long and leisurely Sunday walks along the Seine became a standard feature, although I usually ended up carrying one of the younger ones part of the way home. The children of diplomats sometimes suffer because their fathers are occupationally and socially preoccupied, so I was glad to have a time of less pressure to share with our three.

There was also time for me to enter a bit into the intellectual life of Paris, particularly that of the organization of Catholic intellectuals. I attended a number of large and animated meetings in the barnlike Mutualité hall and frequented the bookshops in the vicinity of St. Sulpice. The role that intellectuals traditionally play in Europe frequently astonishes Americans, who tend to associate intellectual life exclusively with university campuses. Only New York, among our cities, has produced a distinctive community of at least partly nonacademic intellectuals, and even that group has splintered, and to some extent disappeared, in the past decade.

We all cherish our moments of prescience, and a diplomat ought to be prescient at least once in a while. I came to know David Bane as a colleague. He was the officer in our Paris embassy assigned to follow Indochinese developments. We frequently had lunch together in 1955 and early 1956, and both of us expressed our foreboding that ineluctably, and basically contrary to our interests, the United States would, step by step, be sucked into major involvement in Indochina. The French had tried to bring us in at the time of Dienbienphu, and Secretary of State Dulles had been sorely tempted to provide more assistance than we actually did. Both Dave and I feared that American hubris, added to ignorance, would prevail. How unfortunately right we were sitting at café tables in Paris and expressing our concerns to each other!

5

Berlin, Washington, and the Eisenhower Years of the Berlin Crisis

· ·

It can occur in the life of a diplomat that one becomes engulfed in the handling of a crisis that goes on for years to the detriment of time with family and the general breadth of one's interests. This was to happen to me two years later, but I did not know it when we arrived in Berlin in June 1956. As the number two man in the State Department mission (political adviser and deputy to the minister), I was entitled to a fine house (the housing in Berlin for senior American officials was probably better than anywhere else in the world), and we chose one on the Limastrasse in Zehlendorf district—about three miles from the headquarters of U.S. Military Government, of which the State Department mission (USBER in cablese contraction) was an integral part. Living in a city still under formal military government, with all expenses except salaries paid out of occupation costs, had many advantages. Official cars were plentiful, and once one got used to the ways of the military government bureaucracy, everything needed in the way of supplies, repairs, and other amenities became available. We observed that our British and French colleagues enjoyed similar privileges, sometimes on an even more ostentatious scale, and that fact, I suppose, served as a certain balm to conscience. Until the reunification of Germany in 1990, the continuing necessity for tripartite military government in the three Western sectors of the city, with all the mythology and legal implications attached to that reality, meant that the Allied occupation of the city was still essentially financed by the West German government. But that is all over now.

The legal structure of the three occupation forces in the Western sectors was complicated but, on the whole, worked well over the years.[1] The American, French, and British ambassadors in Bonn, in succession to the former three Allied high commissioners, were the chiefs of mission in Berlin and, when they were in the city, took protocol, as well as command precedence, over everyone else. They had separate and quite splendid residences in their respective sectors and, in practically all cases, came to Berlin on a fairly regular basis. The amenities were great, and the cultural attractions of the city considerably superior to those of Bonn.

Under the ambassadors came the three military commandants with the title of deputy chief of mission. They were the top military officers in the city, exercising this function through their respective brigade commanders. The top State Department official permanently in Berlin was the American minister. He was, in effect, the ambassador's representative in the city but had an independent communications channel directly to Washington or to anywhere else in the world. He had no need to clear his outgoing messages with the embassy in Bonn, although the wise minister would not persistently make recommendations in conflict with the views of the ambassador. Tensions inevitably arose from time to time in this context, just as they did between the commandant and the minister, each possessing his own cable channel to his respective department in Washington, but in my experience over the years, with some few exceptions, differences between Berlin and Bonn, or within Berlin itself, never rose to the point where personnel changes were clearly required.

All this detail may seem somewhat superfluous, but I have found amazing confusion in the press, in the Congress, among other governments, and sometimes even within the U.S. government about where the lines of authority ran in West Berlin. The Soviets had a clear idea of the situation, and despite their abolition of military government in East Berlin in the late fifties, their ambassador in East Berlin, who presided from a huge mausoleum of an embassy on Unter den Linden, still exercised the effective and overriding authority of the Soviet Union. I was to have many contacts with Soviet ambassadors to the German Democratic Republic at a later point, but in 1956, as the American political adviser, my opposite number in Soviet military government was a Colonel Kotsiuba. His headquarters were in Karlshorst, a suburban district of East Berlin within the city limits.

My British and French colleagues as political advisers were Bernard Ledwidge and Raymond Bressier. We worked closely together and quickly became good friends. Bernard was a highly intelligent career diplomat, with a predilection for participation in the amateur theatrics to which the British colony in the city seemed addicted. Recruited after the war, he did not fall into the pattern of the typical Oxbridge-trained British diplomat. Raymond, too, was a career diplomat, fluent in English and German, with a flair for unusual phrasing. Physically sparrowlike in appearance but wiry and tough, he provided a good third to our trio. We met regularly each week and were soon to be caught up in protracted negotiations with Kotsiuba.

Each of the three Western elements maintained a liaison officer in the Schöneberg *Rathaus*—the seat of the West Berlin city administration under the governing mayor, as well as the city legislature (the *Abgeordnetenhaus*). Our liaison officer, Karl Mautner, enjoyed a unique relationship with practically every leading Berlin official and kept us informed on a daily basis about the inner workings of city hall. Otto Suhr, the Social Democratic mayor at the time (Willy Brandt replaced him in 1957 when he became mortally ill with leukemia), was an eloquent and sensitive politician living somewhat in the shadow of the earlier great and deceased Social Democratic governing mayor, Ernst Reuter.

The American minister, Bernard Gufler, was an experienced Foreign Service officer, politically conservative but able to deal effectively with the Social Democratic power structure that ran the city for so many years (actually until the early 1980s, when a CDU governing mayor took over—later also West German president, Richard von Weizsaecker). Gufler was a kindly man, and I could not help but like him even when we disagreed. He gave me a great deal of latitude, but I kept him currently informed of what his political adviser was doing. "Plausible deniability" for a superior has never been an operating maxim in the Foreign Service.

Once again, as we had observed during those early postwar years in Bremen, we were impressed by the important restorative and integrative role that music and theater played in German cultural life. Once sufficiently denazified, and prior to his death in 1954, Wilhelm Furtwaengler had rebuilt the Berlin Philharmonic into a world-class orchestra. Until the construction of a new Philharmonic Hall in the mid-fifties (itself to be replaced in due course by another and larger Philharmonic Hall), the orchestra had to play for nearly a decade in the Titania Palace, a converted movie theater never intended acoustically as a hall for music. In 1955 Herbert von Karajan took over as musical director of the Philharmonic and was to mold the orchestra further into the marvelous instrument that it has since become. Attending concerts, operas, and plays became an important part of our life in the city; the quality was uniformly high and sometimes superb. Generous governmental subsidies, of course, made all of this possible.

In those pre-Wall days, movement into East Berlin and back again was relatively unhampered. The East German government, unable to provide the economic incentives for the rapid construction of new buildings (even if sometimes aesthetically repulsive) that characterized West Berlin, poured state resources into the restoration of the old opera house on Unter den Linden and maintained generally high standards of performance. It was also the heyday of the Brecht Theater am Schiffbauerdam.

The growing contrast, both in appearance and activity, between the three Western sectors of the city and the Soviet sector became ever more glaring. It provided a running commentary on the contrast between the two systems. *"Treffpunkt* Berlin" (Berlin as meeting place) became a much-used slogan, and there could be little doubt that visitors, whether from the West or East, would not note the difference in dynamism. Intelligence activities of all sorts found a natural home in a city some one hundred miles behind the Iron Curtain, and the number of competing American agencies in the business (not to speak of the British or French) sometimes bordered on the ridiculous. It was never clear, for example, why U.S. Naval Intelligence needed such a large and space-occupying establishment in the headquarters complex. The Wannsee had no naval vessels deployed on it. When Kennedy became president, he was astonished to learn that there were sixteen separate American intelligence operations in the city, competing at least to some extent for the same finite amount of information. One rather spectacular coup was the construction of a tunnel from the American sector into the GDR through which our CIA could tap into Soviet military telephone lines. After some interesting listening months, the Soviets unfortunately detected the operation, which quickly terminated.

The whole atmosphere of the city was somewhat wild and woolly, exciting to visitors and residents but obviously less pleasant to the Soviets and the GDR regime, neither of which, of course, were derelict with their intelligence activities in the Western sectors. The blockade was now seven years in the past, and there had been no major threats to Allied or German access to the city in the interim. Of course 1956 was also the year of the failed Hungarian Revolution and the Suez debacle, followed in 1957 by Sputnik. The last came as a great shock to the West, a seeming demonstration of Soviet technological superiority in space and of a Western complacence that boded ill in the continuing competition between systems.

Negotiating with the Soviets

It all began innocuously enough: a slightly more than routine examination of Allied documents by Soviet control officers at the autobahn check points. Then came a claim to an inspection right over Allied military trains moving between Berlin and the Federal Republic, on the ground that they might be carrying escapees from the German Democratic Republic. The three Western political advisers dutifully went over to Karlshorst to meet with Kotsiuba and make a verbal protest at what we could only regard as a violation of existing procedures. He was stony faced and responded that the Soviets had decided to put an end to Western abuses of the transit routes. Moreover, he added, the Soviets had a perfect right to impose such controls as they felt necessary on Allied traffic. The threat was clear. We were only at the beginning of tightening Soviet restrictions on Allied land traffic.

As we consulted after our return to West Berlin, we agreed that, taking advantage of their physical situation, the Soviets seemed determined to assert their right to inspect Allied military trains, to tighten up on our autobahn traffic while leaving German civilian traffic, already completely controlled by GDR officials, relatively untouched. We conjectured that this might be the beginning of a Soviet effort to shift control of Allied traffic into East German hands. We separated then to write long reporting cables to our respective capitals. We did not predict, however, that the situation would develop into a tug of war lasting more than a year that would involve countless meetings with Kotsiuba.

Washington, Paris, and London reacted with predictable alarm. The Soviets were obviously up to something that could lead to a serious crisis, but we could not be certain what their ultimate objective actually was. Were they just trying to harass us, to make our position in Berlin less comfortable and to demonstrate the authority that geography gave them, or were they really moving toward a fundamental challenge to Western rights in Berlin?[2]

Some experiences in life stick in memory. Among mine are those numerous trips to Soviet military government headquarters in Karlshorst, where we would customarily meet across a green-felt-covered conference table after having been ushered through large, gloomy anterooms. Since we were the protesters, we normally called on Kotsiuba. To vary the procedure, my British or French colleagues or I would, by agreement, go to Karlshorst alone. After months of this and continuing Soviet harassment of our trains and motor vehicles, with sometimes lengthy delays, we seemed to be getting nowhere. The one thing we could count on was that, after every business meeting, and no matter how cold, obdurate, and even insulting Kotsiuba had been, we would move to an adjoining room where a table would be full of vodka bottles and glasses. As any Westerner who has had to deal with Russian topers can attest, semicompulsory drinking bouts can be a major trial. Fortunately, the party room was full of large potted plants, and I became quite skillful in emptying my glass repeatedly into the pots. After a few drinks, the Soviets did not seem to notice. Fortunately, the plants did not seem to suffer from such repeated dosages. Although we might have been tempted at times to think that Kotsiuba had engineered the crisis and was prolonging it merely to provide a legitimate setting for his vodka consumption, we knew, of course, that the Soviet military government was getting its instructions from Moscow.

Negotiating with the Soviets can be a unique process. One goes over and over the same ground, repeating the same arguments and listening to the same rejoinders. However, we learned—and future experience was to prove this to me time and again—that the Soviets would normally not close the trap, or take irremediable action, as long as negotiations were in process. So we continued those unendingly repetitious talks to avoid a complete break and what might follow in the way of unilateral Soviet action.

We noted that, despite his unsmiling bluntness and occasional direct threats, during our business sessions Kotsiuba seemed basically unsure of his standing with us. He wanted recognition, not only of the clear Soviet geographical advantage in Berlin but of his own position as an equal. A dumpy man, hypersensitive to seeming slights, even when completely un-intended as such, he could bridle at a stray phrase that struck him as im-plying personal inferiority or that of the Soviet Union. Such sensitivity, undoubtedly related to concealed feelings of inferiority, often evidenced itself in Soviet officials at all levels. It could lead to bluster and threat in negotiations that came across as egregious bullying. It was often said that Soviet negotiating technique involved pocketing your concessions and at-tempting to start out from these without countervailing concessions. An alert Western official would seldom fall for that sort of thing, if attempted, and I generally did not find it impossible in my experience to extract con-cessions from the Soviets for concessions made.

Kotsiuba, however, did not seem to fit into the mold of a flexible nego-tiator trying to arrive at a settlement ultimately satisfactory to both sides. We continued to puzzle over this and the ultimate Soviet objective. Finally, one day as harassments on the access routes continued and our capitals became more and more concerned, we discussed trying to find some de-vice or formula that would cater to the Soviet need for recognition with-out giving up anything important. That was easier said than done. Allied travel to and from Berlin, whether civilian or military, was on the basis of so-called military travel orders issued by the three Western military gov-ernments on mimeographed forms containing the stamped signatures of the respective commanders. We came to the idea that the inclusion of the stamped signature of the Soviet commander (after all, it was an original four-power agreement that dealt with access to Berlin), together with the flags of all four powers at the top of the form, might provide what we were looking for. We prepared a fancy-looking model with four colored flags at the top and with the standard formula for the orders in three languages: English, French, and Russian.

After finally getting somewhat reluctant consent from our capitals, we took the sample form to another meeting with Kotsiuba. His eyes did not exactly light up, but we could see that he was interested. He would obviously need instructions from Moscow. Within a few days, he asked us to meet with him again. It would have been too much to expect that we could have an affirmative response so soon. This was not the way the Soviets traditionally negotiate. He asked a few questions, and that was all. We had the impression, however, that the way had been opened to an eventual agreement. It took a while longer, but eventually Kotsiuba was able to tell us that what became known as "flag orders" would be acceptable. We had already printed up a supply and rushed to have them issued to all Allied travelers by land. We also provided stamped signatures of the Soviet commander. All harassments quickly ceased. We had devised a simple solution to a seemingly insoluble problem—the dream of all diplomats. The system survived for thirty years, up to German reunification, a tribute to the role of psychology in the negotiating process.

I am nevertheless still puzzled by what the Soviets thought they were up to in 1956–57, particularly in the light of Khrushchev's massive attack on the Western position in Berlin less than two years later. During the entire period of Berlin crisis (1958–63), the Soviets never challenged the flag order procedure as such; although had they achieved their objectives, it would have become irrelevant. Were they trying to probe us in 1956–57 to see if the Western Allies would wilt under pressure? Or did they have broader purposes in mind? In any event, we did not wilt. We sat out the Soviets, did not let their border officials inspect our trains, and gave away nothing to achieve what proved to be an enduring solution to the Allied documentation problem.

Last Year in Berlin

James Bryant Conant, an eminent educator become diplomat, was the American ambassador in Bonn and chief of mission in Berlin when I arrived in 1956. David Bruce soon replaced him to my delight. We had no particular problem with Conant, who was both intelligent and understanding, but the prospect of having Bruce again as my superior could not help but please. He did not find everything in the Federal Republic to his liking and felt his lack of German to be a personal handicap contrasted with his fluent command of French. His period in Germany (from early in 1957 to late in 1959) was an interesting one, heightened by the first year of the Berlin crisis precipitated by Khrushchev in November 1958. He enjoyed coming to Berlin, and we enjoyed having him there.

After our extended bout with Kotsiuba, I settled into a more routine pace, following Berlin political developments and expanding my contacts with Berlin politicians, including the new governing mayor, Willy Brandt.

I found him a complicated individual, mentally agile but highly sensitive to what he conceived to be slights. He was obviously a gifted orator who could elicit and maintain the enthusiastic support of his political constituency. In long talks with him, I could never be entirely sure whether he had any master plan for himself and Berlin or whether he thought primarily in terms of immediate tactics. He was, of course, to prove years later, as the proponent of *Ostpolitik* (Eastern policy), that he did have, or at least developed, a comprehensive vision opening the way to a new approach. As governing mayor, he clearly resented some of the restraints imposed on him by the Allied military government, particularly when in 1958 he wanted to visit East Berlin to call on the Soviet ambassador. I favored letting him go, but the weight of sentiment in the three governments was against it. Perhaps I am reconstructing the past in the light of subsequent developments, but my recollection is that there was always a certain ambivalence in Brandt's attitude toward the United States. He knew that the security of Berlin lay largely in our hands, but at the same time our economic system represented something that he, as a Social Democrat, could not totally accept.

The Schöneberg *Rathaus*, where Brandt had his office, was a gloomy, cavernous building with an atmosphere I found depressing. Perhaps the politicians who worked there every day did so as well, for rumor had it that the late night sessions in the governing mayor's office, to which they seemed addicted, featured a certain amount of alcoholic consumption. The advice from our observers at city hall was to avoid early morning appointments with some of the participants, including the governing mayor.

Living in Berlin made it easy to develop a "cold warrior" syndrome. The atmosphere of this exclave city was charged; the very propinquity of an ideologically hostile regime dominated by another ideologically hostile regime made both the threat and the capacity to execute that threat seem larger. The mythology that, even by the mid-fifties, had accumulated around West Berlin and its courageous population could not help but affect officials of the Allied military governments. Even the French, with their historical dislike of all things German, shared some of the same sentiments. As I have already said, it is difficult to reconstruct the atmosphere of the cold war in all its vividness and intensity. Just as most of us thought the Soviets were all true believers in a cause dedicated to achievement of ultimate world hegemony, so our cold warriors were true believers in the righteousness of our cause. Detachment came only with great difficulty amid the constant reminders in Berlin of systemic differences. As it had during the immediate postwar era, boorish and frequently threatening Soviet behavior reinforced the conditioning. Despite all this, I could not help but feel that, in the nuclear age, we must find a better way than continuing confrontation between the superpowers, whether in Berlin or in a broader setting. This was a fine principle, but how to apply it perplexed successive presidents. The Soviets did not make it easy, of course, and Nikita Khrushchev was to heighten the cold war atmosphere considerably in 1958 with his challenge to the Western presence in Berlin.

One aspect of life in Berlin that added to the sense of intrigue and mystery was the seeming presence on all sides, and of all sorts, of both Western and Eastern intelligence operations. Spies seemed to come out of every dark corner. The rooftop restaurant and nightclub of the Berlin Hilton Hotel (now the Intercontinental) quickly developed the reputation (to some extent apocryphal) of being a favorite meeting place of agents from the East and their Western control officers. A related anomaly that continued until German reunification was the existence in Potsdam of British, American, and French military missions that operated primarily as gatherers of military intelligence in the Soviet zone. The Soviets tolerated this because of the compensatory advantages they derived from having similar military missions in the three former Allied zones of occupation. A document (known as the Huebner-Malinin Agreement) signed early in the occupation period formalized the American-Soviet arrangement. There were harassments, of course, resulting in counterharassments of these missions, but year after year they survived crisis and threat—lasting evidence of the reality that mutual advantage can perpetuate institutional arrangements that seem to run counter to the main trend of events. Their continuing existence lent reality to proposals (made originally by General Lauris Norstad when he was the Supreme Allied Commander Europe) for exchanges of military observers between East and West to observe maneuvers and other relevant activities as a confidence-building measure. These became a standard part of so-called confidence-increasing measures in subsequent arms negotiations.

Another four-power anomaly in West Berlin that continued until the death of Rudolf Hess was the Spandau prison regime. An old jail with more than six hundred cells in the British sector of the city, Spandau became the place where those prominent Nazis convicted in the first Nuremberg Trial who were not sentenced to death ended up as prisoners for various terms up to life. Each of the four powers provided a prison commandant and guard unit for a month on a rotating basis. Inevitably, I suppose, a club facility developed, with a well-stocked bar to provide relaxation for the hard-pressed commandants and guards, whose numbers did not decline proportionately as the roster of prisoners either died or served out their sentences. There were no soft-hearted parole authorities to accelerate their release, but finally only an aged and ailing Rudolf Hess remained. Persistent Western efforts to obtain his release and the consequent closure of Spandau ran into a Soviet stone wall. The Soviets' alleged reason was that he might become a symbol of a reviving Nazism if given his freedom, but some of us suspected that attachment to that periodic month in what to the Soviets must have seemed like their town club in West Berlin outweighed any fears they might have had of the symbolism that a man so decrepit and broken in spirit as Hess might provide. Both during my period in Berlin and on subsequent assignments to Germany, I made a number of inspection visits to Spandau during American months. It always seemed reasonably well run, a strange four-power relic in a part of Berlin that had long since shed nearly all vestiges of the four-power era. I might add that one feature of the prison that made its perpetuation easy was that German occupation costs covered all operating expenses. The death of Rudolf Hess at the age of ninety-three on August 17, 1987, brought the whole silly business to an end. Instead of his remains being cremated and scattered to the four winds, as the Soviets had insisted (ostensibly to prevent a neo-Nazi cult from developing around his grave site), the British, who were in charge that August, returned the body to his widow and son for burial.

The four-power Berlin Air Safety Center (BASC) also provided an important air safety function. Housed in the cavernous former Allied Control Commission building in the American sector, BASC provided the instrument by which all French, British, and American flights into and out of Berlin were notified to the Soviet representatives in the center, who transmitted the relevant information to Soviet officials in East Berlin so that Soviet and East European traffic would not try to occupy the same space in the three Western air corridors into and out of the city. The system worked admirably over the years, and even when in 1962 the Soviets tried to harass Allied air traffic in the corridors, they never walked out of BASC. Over the years, we in the West sometimes wondered how long this would go on, but the Soviets obviously attached some value to such a vestige of the four-power regime. It would have been the height of folly to deny that, if it worked to their advantage in ways we may not fully have understood, it clearly worked to our advantage in a very comprehensible way. One could not draw sweeping conclusions about dealing with the Soviets from this example, but it did at least prove that, in an institutionalized setting, cooperation between East and West could continue over the decades.

The city fathers staged a major event during our time in Berlin with the reconstruction of the Hansa Viertel (a quarter that had been destroyed during the war) as an exposition of modern architecture. World-renowned architects such as Niemeyer, Corbusier, and many others contributed designs that became apartment houses, churches, and shopping areas. I have never particularly admired the Bauhaus style, which did so much to make the high-rise architecture, and hence the skylines, of America's cities so bleak and imitative in the postwar era. There have been a few exceptions such as the Mies van der Rohe apartment houses on Chicago's lake front, but our concentrations of office buildings would no doubt look better than the blocks of monotony they are if Gropius and his disciples had not exercised so much influence on American architecture, at least until fairly recently. In any event, the Hansa Viertel exposition, the products of which still stand, some considerably the worse for wear, provided tension-laden Berliners with some distraction. Corbusier's contribution, a huge example of his theoretically integrated apartment houses, was actually located in a different part of West Berlin. Despite all the architect's theorizing about his radiant cities, reports quickly circulated that the new tenants found the place relatively unlivable.

Another product of the era, the Berlin Congress Hall, designed by an American architect, raised some eyebrows with its unusual suspended design. The Berliners, ever ready with a partly derisory and partly playful epithet, quickly labeled it the "pregnant oyster." Years later, fortunately when no one was in it, the building collapsed with a great roar, and for a long time it remained as a monument to the designer's folly. Some years ago, the city fathers had the thing reconstructed, and the hope was that this time the structure would stand.

Life in Berlin, we found, was bound to have something synthetic about it. Things did not come naturally from the West to this exclave. They had to be attracted there—hence the constant need to dream up new ideas, to sponsor expositions, fairs, and conferences in the city. Once a fair or festival had become an annual event, there was no way it could be abolished. The very idea would be described as a potential blow to Berlin morale. Two good examples were the Gruene Woche (Green Week) agricultural fair and the film festival. There was something intrinsically absurd about having an agricultural fair in a city cut off from its hinterland, but it had been an old Berlin custom, and suggestions that it might be terminated aroused indignant editorials and political speeches. So each year the U.S. mission had to persuade the State Department to persuade a reluctant U.S. Department of Agriculture to mount a major exhibit.

American generosity had done much to get the city going again in the difficult early years. The Free University in its origins had been a major beneficiary of American money. The Congress Hall and a major hospital complex came later as symbols of continuing American interest. Little did those who supported the foundation of the Free University know that, during the turbulent sixties, it was to become a center of anti-American student and faculty activity, resisted, of course, by some older professors who were generally shouted down at meetings. Life is full of such ironies: the founders of institutions might hesitate if they had any idea of what their creation might turn out to be.

By the summer of 1958, Ambassador Bruce had decided that he wanted a new man to take charge of German affairs back in the State Department and arranged for my transfer from Berlin. We were sad in a way to leave, but at least I knew that Berlin would continue to be among my responsibilities as director of the Office of German Affairs. We had suffered a great sorrow earlier in 1958 with the death of our infant daughter, Catherine, and perhaps the impending change would be best for both Faith and me.

Washington and Berlin Crisis

Our October arrival in the United States, via the SS *United States* (the last trip by ocean liner we were to take), enabled us to miss the heat of a Washington summer. Many have waxed rhapsodic over the pleasures of transoceanic travel by boat. As one who made quite a few such crossings, I can only confirm that the airplane, while faster, has deprived modern diplomacy of one of its more beneficial perquisites.

We quickly found a house to rent in Chevy Chase, Maryland, thus condemning me to years of commuting by car past Chevy Chase Circle and down Connecticut Avenue—a good forty-five minutes or more each way during the rush hours. The Office of German Affairs in the State Department, facing no major problems, seemed tranquil enough. I was quickly to find out otherwise.

When one is enmeshed for four and one-half years in the handling of a crisis that became a major preoccupation for two presidents and their senior officials, one can only wonder afterward at the rapidity with which such an intense subject of concern drops from view. The flow of events quickly erases the recollections of Washington and its press. Lessons seemingly learned quickly fade away. As someone who lived with crisis for what was one of the most intense and active periods of my life, working weekends and late into the night and making frequent trips to Europe, my memories of more than thirty-five years ago are still vivid. To use a popular contemporary term, I came as close to burnout, or at least physical and psychological exhaustion, as I ever have.

Although some partial accounts of the great Berlin crisis have appeared, I have yet to see a truly comprehensive treatment covering the entire period from November 1958 to September 1963. Some writers tend to distinguish the Eisenhower period from the Kennedy period as two distinct crises, partly, it would seem, because we had a break of administrations on our side between the two presidents.[3] I prefer to think of the crisis as a continuum, with the Soviet ultimate threat merely postponed, not lifted. Crisis management recently became a buzzword on campuses and in Washington. While a cynic might suggest that it is too much to expect that an American administration would ever learn anything from the behavior of past administrations, I would recommend attention to the way two quite distinctive administrations organized themselves to deal with the continuing Berlin crisis. Considerably more has been written about the Berlin crisis during the Kennedy presidency than during the Eisenhower presidency; as a result there are considerably more misconceptions about the former than about the latter.

It all began with a speech given without any real warning by Chairman Nikita Khrushchev on November 10, 1958. While his emotional statement had been preceded by an exchange of memorandums and notes between the Soviet Union and the three Western powers about the possibility of a summit conference to discuss the German question or the process that might lead to an eventual peace treaty, there had been no indication that the Soviet Union would attempt unilateral action aimed at driving the Western powers from West Berlin. In his November 10 speech, Khrushchev stated that the Potsdam Agreement, having been violated by Britain, France, and the United States, by implication no longer bound the Soviet Union with respect to the occupation regime in Berlin. The time had come, he continued, for the four powers to renounce the remnants of the occupation regime, while the Soviet Union "would hand over to the Sovereign German Democratic Republic the functions in Berlin that [were] still exercised by Soviet agencies." This latter, of course, meant that the Soviets would no longer process Allied rail and autobahn traffic. The speech had come like a bolt out of the blue, and the State Department bureaucracy swept into interpretive action. The language was imprecise but the threat to our position clear. We quickly came to the conclusion that a more formal communication addressed to the three Allied governments would be forthcoming shortly. And so it was. Nikita Khrushchev did not disappoint us. The Soviet Union on November 27 transmitted to the embassies of the three Western occupying powers in Moscow a lengthy and highly polemical note arguing that, by their violations of those provisions of the Potsdam Agreement "designed to ensure the unity of Germany as a peace-loving and democratic state," France, Great Britain, and the United States had, in effect, lost their right to remain in Berlin under the 1944 and 1945 agreements. These agreements, the note went on to say, were now null and void, and the Soviet Union would, as Khrushchev had stated in his speech, transfer to the German Democratic Republic the functions performed by the Soviet authorities under those agreements. Having thus lost their right to be in Berlin, the Western powers would have to acquiesce in the creation of a demilitarized free city of West Berlin in the territory of the GDR. If they did not accept this and make the necessary arrangements within a period of six months, then the Soviet Union would "carry out the planned measures through an agreement with the GDR."[4]

The seventeen days between speech and note had not passed without what correspondents call intensive diplomatic activity on the Western side. The immediate question was what to do if the Soviets carried out their threat to transfer control over Allied access to Berlin to the East Germans. With his ever fertile legal mind, Secretary of State John Foster Dulles began to play around with what became known as the "agency theory"; that is, if the transfer took place, the Western powers would simply regard the East German officials at the checkpoints as acting in the capacity of agents for the Soviet authorities. In a conversation with German ambassador Wilhelm Grewe on November 17, at which I was the note taker, he guardedly put out the concept but noted that it did not represent official policy. Grewe noted that any such dealings with East German officials would cause great psychological difficulties in Bonn and later said that he had reported the secretary's remarks as "thinking aloud."

Dulles's statements at his news conference on November 26 sent us diplomatic word jugglers into an exercise in obfuscation. An obviously well-briefed correspondent asked whether the Western powers would deal with East German officials at the checkpoints "as agents of the Soviet Union." He responded, "We might, yes." The secretary further explained that a distinction could be made between dealing with East Germans as agents and dealing with them in a way involving de facto recognition. We knew that his words would cause a storm in Bonn and produced what I thought was a classically obscure explanation. Our guidelines to our embassy in Bonn, also for use in Washington, claimed that the secretary had made it clear that "we would not deal with East German officials in any way which involved our acceptance of the East German regime as substitute for the Soviet Union in discharging obligations and responsibilities of the Soviet Union." The guidelines also pointed out that Dulles's only reference to dealings with the GDR occurred in connection with efforts by correspondents "to elicit detailed analysis of hypothetical situations" and that he was not talking about an agreement to deal with the GDR but the "refusal to exclude insignificant dealings in any and all circumstances."[5]

I mention this in some detail, not only to illustrate the extent to which we had to tie ourselves in verbal knots in order to avoid an explosion in Bonn but because some form of the "agency theory," though never put forward in a Western proposal, continued over the years to exercise a certain desperate attraction for Western planners as an ultimate fallback position. Our dilemma was that any such display of seemingly dangerous thinking immediately aroused the wrath of Chancellor Adenauer, with his strict adherence to absolute nonrecognition of the German Democratic Republic, while on the other hand we were reluctant to take positions that might seem incomprehensible to Western publics not familiar with the verbal subtleties of Berlin doctrine and mythology. In any event, the Soviets wanted us completely out of Berlin, and as long as their threat to turn over their access responsibilities to the GDR remained only a threat, there seemed little point in making a needless concession that could undermine our basic position if the Soviets simply denied that anyone was acting as their agent. As a practical matter, the Soviets continued down to German reunification to carry out the checkpoint procedures that we had worked out with Kotsiuba in 1956–57. They had, in effect, been assimilated into the status quo following the 1971 Quadripartite Agreement on Berlin.

A British Foreign Office memorandum circulated on November 17 to the French and Americans raised another troublesome issue: Was the erosion of the Western position in Berlin inevitable? It became known as the "slippery slope" paper because it postulated inevitable Western capitulation to successive Soviet and East German encroachments. It suggested that it might be better to anticipate this and to strike some sort of deal while we still presumably had some bargaining power left.

Needless to say, these views, which were drafted, we were told, by Deputy Undersecretary Sir Anthony Rumboid, were not well received in Washington. It was not clear whether they represented the policy of Prime Minister Harold Macmillan and Foreign Secretary Selwyn Lloyd, and the assurances that our ambassador in London, John Hay Whitney, received were only partially satisfactory. It seemed to us that conceding complete victory to the Soviets in advance was a formula for disaster. The memorandum aroused suspicions about British firmness, both in Washington and in Paris, which subsequently made suspect the efforts by Macmillan, most notably his visit to Moscow in late February 1959. I think it is fair to say that, during the years of the Berlin crisis, British advocacy in conferences and in the formulation of Western positions generally moved in the direction of compromise and a noncombative statement of issues. How much of this stemmed from a certain failure of nerve in the aftermath of the 1956 Suez disaster, and how much it reflected a mature appreciation of the awesome stakes involved in the nuclear age, I was never quite sure. In any event, we were sometimes to find British support useful against German and French obduracy in our efforts to introduce some flexibility and public appeal into the Western negotiating position. The "slippery slope" memorandum was, in effect, withdrawn, and I do not recall that the British ever made reference to it again. In diplomacy, however, the seeds of suspicion, once sown, tend to have a long life.

Professors Alexander George and Richard Smoke have argued that, if the West had responded quickly to the Khrushchev speech, the Soviets might never have sent their note of November 27—all this on the possibility that Khrushchev had been carried away by emotion on November 10 and had added an unintended demand. I find this rather naive. Although we and our allies were admittedly caught by surprise at the intensity and gravity of the Soviet challenge to our position in Berlin, that very intensity and gravity made it highly unlikely that this was initially merely a reflection of one man's exuberance. Critics of what they regard as too slow diplomatic responses during an incipient crisis fail to appreciate that, in matters concerning Berlin, the United States was not a solo actor. Coordination with the British and French on responses to notes and contingency planning was an essential part of the tripartite process.[6]

Months of Frenetic Diplomacy after the Soviet Note of November 27, 1958

The formal presentation of the Soviet position, foreshadowed by Khrushchev's speech, came in similar notes handed to the governments of the three Western occupying powers on November 27. It was in tone and specific language a tough, unyielding communication that we and the world press interpreted as a six-month ultimatum. Given the warning in the Khrushchev speech of November 10, no one could describe the note as another bolt out of the blue, but its vehemence and ominously threatening tone frankly caught us by surprise, particularly the warning that any aggression (presumably in defense of Allied rights) against any member of the Warsaw Pact would "be regarded by all its participants as an act of aggression against them all and [would] immediately cause appropriate retaliation." It was not clear why Khrushchev had chosen this particular time to issue his challenge, but no one could doubt his seriousness nor the implications of his threats. The occasional niceties of diplomatic language could not conceal the raw menace to our geographically exposed position in Berlin.

After all these years, I still have not come across a completely satisfactory explanation of Khrushchev's behavior. None of us could doubt that the three Western sectors of Berlin were, as he himself put it, "a bone in his throat," a perpetual reminder of the visible political and economic differences between East and West, a meeting place (*Treffpunkt*) between intellectuals, artists, and writers from the East and the West, and the main exiting point for the constant flow of refugees from the East—a drain of talent and skilled workers that, nearly three years before the Wall, had already reached alarming proportions. Moreover, the Communist leadership in the GDR was undoubtedly importunate in urging that the Soviets do something about that den of iniquitous capitalism in West Berlin. But put it all together, and it still doesn't add up to adequate justification for the risky and provocative course of action that he launched in November 1958. Did he think that, by bluster and threat, he could bully the Allies out of Berlin, despite their solemn and repeated commitments to defend the security of the city and our presence there? In his memoirs, Khrushchev throws little additional light on his motives but does seem to stress the economic problems of the GDR as a major factor. He avoids any real discussion of why he did precisely what he did and what forced him to lift his deadlines and finally in 1963 to terminate his threats to the Western position in Berlin. He concedes that through the Wall (what he calls "the establishment of border control between East and West Berlin") "the GDR's economic problems were considerably relieved."[7]

One attempt at an explanation, which has attracted some support among scholars, is that "the main Soviet objective was to secure an agreement that would make it impossible for West Germany to obtain nuclear weapons." Professor Adam B. Ulam, from whom the quotation is taken, then goes so far as to say, "One suspects that for the moment they would have settled for a firm pledge that West Germany would be barred from being a nuclear force."[8] Others link the chain of causation more specifically to the December 1957 decision of the NATO Ministerial Council to station "intermediate range strategic missiles in Europe, with nuclear warheads under American control."[9]

I find this line of argument, especially in its most unqualified form, less than persuasive. Fear of the deployment in Europe of American Thor and Jupiter missiles may have been one of a number of factors that incited Khrushchev to take the action that he did, but he had many other more Berlin- and GDR-centered reasons to act. As a matter of fact, the December 19 NATO Ministerial communiqué, while approving the stockpiling of nuclear warheads in Europe and placing intermediate range ballistic missiles at the disposal of the Supreme Allied Commander Europe, says nothing about the specific countries of deployment other than that they would "be decided in conformity with NATO defense plans and in agreement with the states directly concerned."[10] The emphasis, as far as the Federal Republic was concerned, was entirely on tactical nuclear weapons that could not reach the Soviet Union; the IRBMs were to be deployed elsewhere. In all continental deployments, the United States was to retain custody of the warheads. Certainly the intent of the United States, strongly supported by its European allies, was to create a system that would clearly prevent any unrestricted access to nuclear weapons of any kind by the West Germans, while at the same time satisfying demands for nominal equality of treatment.

Apart from the specific German issue, there was a certain parallel between the American deployment in Europe of IRBMs (admittedly the first generation of highly unreliable Thors and Jupiters) in the late 1950s and early 1960s and the deployment of Pershing II and cruise missiles in the early 1980s. Both were in a sense a response, partly to meet a felt European psychological requirement, to the Soviet deployment of SS-4 and SS-5 missiles in the earlier period and SS-20 missiles in the later period. Although inaccurate, the SS-4s and SS-5s embodied enough destructive power to wipe Western Europe off the map.[11]

Whatever the complex of motives that induced Khrushchev to precipitate and to prolong the Berlin crisis, he clearly had picked the wrong target, just as had Stalin a decade earlier. The city's very physical vulnerability, in a paradoxical sense, constituted a source of its strength. There was no other Western symbol, when threatened, that could so rapidly mobilize the support of governments and public opinion in the free world as this exclave. Even the Social Democratic Party in the Federal Republic, after bitterly opposing the deployment of tactical nuclear weapons in its country, radically changed its position with respect to NATO as a result of the threat to Berlin. Khrushchev obviously knew he was bluffing when he boasted of Soviet nuclear superiority, and there is some evidence that, a few years later, he actually feared a preemptive U.S. strike against the Soviet Union;[12] yet he should have known that, because of its indefensibility, any move against Berlin might more quickly escalate to a nuclear confrontation than anything beyond an overwhelming Soviet ground attack against Western Europe. He should also have been intimately aware of NATO strategic thinking, with its clear limits on nuclear deployments, as he was about Western contingency planning for Berlin, given the presence in NATO headquarters of a high-level Soviet agent, a Frenchman who was head of the organization's document service.

In his writings on the Berlin crisis, Professor Robert M. Slusser sees pressure from hard-liners in the Politburo, led by Frol Kozlov and Mikhail Suslov, to "adopt a hostile stance towards the United States and its allies" as the most important causal factor in the crisis. Slusser also believes that "much of the Soviet hardline on Berlin in the period 1958–59 can be attributed directly to Gromyko, who was far from a negligible factor in the formulation of Soviet foreign policy."[13] Such speculation is interesting but far from convincing. We have had no access to minutes of Politburo meetings, if they exist, and my own impression of Gromyko, from having attended numerous meetings with the Soviet foreign minister as well as from observing him for three months at the 1959 Geneva Conference of Foreign Ministers, does not confirm that he was a potent policy maker in his own right. He was rather the able and articulate executor of policy who needed instructions from Moscow before he took firm stands on Western proposals. As the most experienced Soviet official in the field of foreign affairs, his advice and recommendations obviously carried weight, but I find it difficult to believe that he was the decisive element in formulating the Soviet hard line on Berlin. An explanatory gap remains as far as Khrushchev's behavior in the Berlin crisis is concerned.

The hierarchical organization of the State Department was still fairly simple in those days, and office directors had both authority within their areas of competence and access to the highest levels of the department. Robert Murphy, the undersecretary of state for political affairs, and Livingston Merchant, the assistant secretary of state for European affairs (both career Foreign Service officers), enjoyed great personal prestige and the full confidence of the secretary of state, who, we all knew, had direct and frequent access to President Eisenhower. Murphy and Merchant, in turn, relied completely on the Office of German Affairs to do the paperwork, to come up with recommendations, and, once it became clear that we were moving toward a quadripartite conference of foreign ministers, to represent the U.S. government at international preparatory meetings in Paris, London, and Washington. I quickly found myself participating in small strategy sessions in Secretary Dulles's office.

He was an imposing personality. In the field of foreign affairs he seemed to have great authority within the government enjoying the full support of the president. Having moved from the old State, War, Navy building next to the White House (now the Executive Office Building) to the former War Department building, itself left available when the Pentagon opened, the State Department at its then size luxuriated in reasonably ample quarters. The executive suite of the secretary, two stories high, had impressive proportions. I can recall a number of occasions when a small group of us sat huddled around Dulles's conference table trying to offer analyses and suggestions for dealing with the latest development in the Berlin crisis. After hearing us out, the secretary would rise from the table and begin to pace up and down, his hands behind his back. Livy Merchant whispered to me at the first of such sessions not to be alarmed. This was usual practice. The secretary seemed to think better on his feet. Each time, surely enough, after ten minutes or so of pacing, Dulles would return to the table and, in precise language, state his conclusions and what he wanted done. There was usually no need to remonstrate, but neither Murphy nor Merchant would hesitate to do so if the proposed course of action seemed off course.

So our position would get hammered out. Once we left the meeting, Dulles counted on us to carry out his final mandate without further reference to him. No one knew at the time, of course, that he was already a dying man suffering from terminal cancer. The doctors had diagnosed ileitis.

My own Office of German Affairs was well staffed. Al Vigderman, a highly intelligent lawyer turned diplomat, was an ideal deputy—one on whom I could rely to carry on capably during the many absences from Washington that became necessary for me in 1959. Other officers assigned to German Affairs were both able and knowledgeable about Germany, a collection of experts on that country that probably has never been duplicated since. We could also count on the Office of Soviet Affairs under Ed Freers to provide sound judgments about Soviet behavior.

The obvious first order of business was to prepare a response to the Soviet note of November 27. We decided that it should, in fairly concise fashion, provide a clear statement of the basic Western position on Berlin, but one that the British and French could largely accept for their responses without prolonged haggling. Since the four foreign ministers (including the German, of course) were scheduled to be in Paris in mid-December for the regular semiannual NATO session, this would provide a convenient occasion for discussion of the text. We also proposed that work should be intensified on revising contingency plans to deal with unilateral Soviet actions in and about Berlin.

I found myself representing the United States at a Quadripartite Working Group meeting in Paris on December 13 called to coordinate drafting of the reply to the Soviet note and of the communiqué to be issued by the four foreign ministers. It was pretty heady stuff for an office director. The British, French, and German representatives (Sir Anthony Rumbold, deputy undersecretary of state in the Foreign Office; Jean Laloy, minister counselor in the Ministry of Foreign Affairs; and Ambassador Wilhelm Grewe, the German ambassador in Washington) were all considerably senior to me. This was to be the pattern for the next five months as the Quadripartite Working Group met on a number of occasions in Paris, London, and Washington to prepare for the four-power conference of foreign ministers with the Soviet Union that began on May 11, 1959, in Geneva. Once again I can only note that the absence of hierarchical encrustation on the American side in 1958–59 permitted this, and I would like to think that our side, without inflation of rank, held its own in what turned out to be a fairly star-studded series of Working Group meetings.

The pressures of a Berlin crisis also led to what became an institutionalized prelude to every NATO ministerial meeting: the quadripartite working dinner of foreign ministers on the evening before the NATO sessions. At first the British, French, and American foreign ministers met tripartitely, to be joined later for dinner by the German foreign minister. Although the French held out for a while, the demeaning aspect of this late entry, evident to the Americans and the British, eventually led to inclusion of the Germans from the outset, just as they were, after some further delay, to be included in Berlin contingency planning. In their meeting the four foreign ministers agreed on a quadripartite communiqué that, in effect, stated the determination of the three occupying powers to maintain their rights with respect to Berlin "including the right of free access." A formal reply to the Soviet note of November 27 would be forthcoming after consultation with their NATO allies, it went on to say.

It was not surprising that these quadripartite working dinners did not sit well with the other members of NATO. They claimed that, apart from the food consumed, positions were also being precooked that the four would on the next day try to force on the whole group. There was obviously some truth to this charge, but the dinners also provided a broader opportunity to discuss the Berlin problem than would otherwise have been available. Some might argue that the very term "working dinner" was an oxymoron, given the fine wines and foods customarily provided to foreign ministers by the rotating four ambassadors in Brussels or in other capitals for the NATO spring meetings. The poor designated scriveners of the four powers had a hard time taking notes while trying to get some food down. The practice quickly developed of having organized discussion over drinks prior to dinner and, if need be, with coffee after dinner. Some sessions lasted late into the night. Foreign ministers are generally not an ungarrulous lot and sometimes wandered afield to other favorite subjects, much to the chagrin of their experts. On the whole, however, these affairs served a highly useful purpose, and participants like myself (when not serving as note takers) could also enjoy the accompanying gustatory delights.

When his turn came to speak at the first plenary meeting of NATO foreign ministers, Dulles put on a virtuoso performance. He built the initial part of his presentation around an argument that obviously had captivated his legal mind: that under the agreements of 1944 and 1945 regarding the zones of occupation in Germany, the British and American forces had turned over to the Soviet Union thousands of square miles of territory in return for a "few square miles of what was then rubble in the destroyed city of Berlin." He used a large map to illustrate his point and then noted that the USSR, in denouncing these agreements as null and void, did not propose to "disgorge the advantages which it had obtained under these agreements." Yet the Soviet Union now insisted that the Western Allies should surrender what little they had obtained in this territorial exchange.

Dulles then stressed that the West was faced with what could be interpreted as an ultimatum and that, as a preliminary to any new agreements, the Soviet Union would have to qualify the apparent ultimatum feature of its note. After warning that the West would be subjected to a severe war of nerves and referring to an earlier Soviet threat that it had the capacity to wipe out all of Europe, he stated that it was equally true that the United States could destroy the Soviet Union. The West could proceed in confidence and, drawing on the experience with Hitler, must not allow the aggressor initial success but must discourage him from the outset.

The impact of the secretary's words on the other ministers was dramatic. We members of the American delegation could sense the collective feeling of relief and resurgence of confidence. Dulles had formulated the Western position in the right terms for the occasion. He had obviously not ended the Berlin crisis, but he had given some sense of direction and shown resolve. Surface atmospherics at conferences can sometimes mislead; they can indicate greater support than is actually present in the minds of participants, but in this case he seemed to have swept away, at least for the moment, reservations and hesitations about the need for a strong NATO communiqué, as well as a special declaration on Berlin, endorsing the position of the three Western Allies. There were some aspects of Dulles's record as secretary of state that I did not admire, but this was at least a moment of greatness. Yet who remembers it now except those few of us present who are still living? In the following two months I also came to admire the secretary for his fortitude in the face of acute physical suffering.

In the aftermath of the NATO meeting we pressed ahead to coordinate our replies to the Soviet note of November 27. They went forward to the Soviet Union on December 31. The texts (nearly identical with respect to their central arguments) are public and available in standard collections of documents. Suffice it to say here that the American reply was preceded on December 20, 1958, by a detailed statement issued by the Department of State on legal aspects of the Berlin situation.[14] Carefully drafted, this remains a classic defense of the Western position. Diplomats, journalists, and even scholars are sometimes irked by what they regard as an excessively legalistic approach to political problems. I confess that I have shared this feeling on occasions. However, in the case of West Berlin, having a strong legal case greatly enhanced the effectiveness of Allied arguments. The original Soviet note of November 27 had taken the untenable position that alleged violation of the Potsdam Agreement had resulted in the loss of Allied rights in Berlin. After the Western side had effectively demolished this argument, the Soviet line shifted so that Gromyko at the Geneva Conference of Foreign Ministers then claimed that a new agreement was necessary—one that would substitute for the wartime quadripartite agreements. The object of such an agreement would be the conversion of West Berlin into a free city.[15]

The somewhat shorter note reiterated some of the same arguments and went on to stress that the United States could not consider any proposal (such as the call for a so-called free city of West Berlin put forward by the Soviet Union) "which would have the effect of jeopardizing the freedom and security" of the people of West Berlin and that "the rights of the three powers to remain in Berlin with unhindered communications by surface and air between that city and the Federal Republic of Germany [were] under existing conditions essential to the discharge of that right and responsibility." (This language was to turn up later, in further refined form, in statements of what the United States considered its vital interests in Berlin.) The note offered to enter at any time into discussions with the Soviet government of proposals "genuinely designed to insure the reunification of Germany in freedom" and to treat "the question of Berlin in the wider framework of negotiations for a solution of the German problem as well as that of European security." We were not prepared, however, to do this "under menace or ultimatum."[16] The British note was somewhat more nuanced on this last point and did not use the word "ultimatum."

The Last Journey of John Foster Dulles

So we moved into 1959 in a continuing atmosphere of crisis. It was to be a year of intense activity and much travel for me. An uninvited visitor from the Soviet Union, Deputy Premier Anastas Mikoyan, arrived in the United States early in January, ostensibly to discuss Soviet-American trade problems. The subject of Germany and Berlin inevitably played a central role in two meetings with Secretary Dulles and then a later meeting with President Eisenhower. He repeated the standard Soviet line on speedy conclusion of a peace treaty and action on Berlin but gave assurances that the November 27 note was not intended as a threat or ultimatum. Then on January 10 the three Western powers received a Soviet note, which said little new about Berlin while reiterating the position taken in the note of November 27 but implying a willingness to negotiate. The note also transmitted a draft peace treaty and proposed that within two months a peace conference convene in Warsaw or Prague to consider this draft treaty.[17]

We had, of course, received previous Soviet draft peace treaties, but never one linked so directly to a fundamental change of Berlin's status. As a result of the Mikoyan assurances and the apparent Soviet willingness to negotiate, we moved quickly toward accepting the possibility of four-power discussions. Chancellor Adenauer was not very happy about this prospect, claiming that the Soviet position "was not in the least accommodating and indeed plainly provocative." The British, on the other hand, were all for negotiations. Exchanges between the four Western capitals flew back and forth. In an attempt to bring the German chancellor around, Dulles dispatched a long letter on January 29 to Bonn, containing reassurances about our firmness in the face of Soviet threats but also pointing out the tactical difficulties facing us. The USSR had "by pressing on the West's militarily exposed nerve in Berlin" raised in urgent form "the closely related more general problems of a European settlement." [18] We were of necessity moving toward a conference with the Soviets.

We knew that the secretary, before sending his letter, had already decided that he would make a quick trip to London, Paris, and Bonn to coordinate the Western position and, particularly, to reassure Adenauer. After a few days of frantic preparations in Washington, a small group of us from the department took off for Europe on February 3 in President Eisenhower's plane, the *Columbine*, an old Lockheed Constellation with sleeping accommodations for sixteen. The party numbered fewer than sixteen, so we could all catch some sleep. The jet age was about to dawn, but not quite yet for the president or secretary of state. It took us some sixteen hours to reach Europe, with stops in Newfoundland and Iceland.

We quickly observed that the secretary was in considerable discomfort. He retired early after a brief staff meeting. We wondered how he would stand up under the pressure of lengthy meetings and the inevitable official lunches and dinners. Some of us had been surprised at the flexibility he had demonstrated in the aftermath of November 27, always grasping for new formulations and approaches. Here after all was the father of brinkmanship and massive retaliation; yet he obviously wanted to find a basis for negotiations and to avoid confrontation. Diplomats, and his advisers on this trip were all diplomats, naturally think in terms of finding solutions to difficulties rather than letting them escalate to direct confrontation. We recognized the Soviet threat as serious and one we could not accept, but at the same time we saw little merit in the arguments of some firebrands in the Pentagon that we should simply threaten the Soviets with a military response. Temperamental differences obviously played a role here, but it is the warriors with bold words and seemingly persuasive arguments for action who involve nations in war. We had been glad to note that Dulles had opted to be on the side of the diplomats, even though we would have preferred that he not do his thinking out loud at press conferences or in public remarks. Some have claimed that he was trying to signal the Soviets in ways that could not be embodied in formal notes and exchanges. We will never know this with certainty, since he died without leaving any memoirs or even rough indications in writing of his inner thoughts. Nor would I want to suggest that the professional diplomat, in his quest for solutions, tends to be soft minded, lacking the toughness to stick to a position in the face of determined opposition. I think the record of State Department handling of the Berlin crisis proves otherwise. Our statements were firm, stressing principle, but we did not scorn opportunities for peaceful resolutions.

The meetings in London with Foreign Minister Selwyn Lloyd and Prime Minister Harold Macmillan showed a large measure of agreement, although there were lingering suspicions of British firmness in the pinch. Despite Macmillan's obvious preference for moving directly to the summit level, in the face of Eisenhower's unwillingness to attend such a meeting, the British prime minister finally agreed to a conference of foreign ministers, which, he hoped, would be the prelude to a meeting of heads of governments. The foreign ministers were to meet late in April or early in May in order to give the Soviets a graceful way out of their six-month deadline. Dulles suggested that the Western position, with some embellishments, might start with the "Western Proposal on German Reunification and European Security" presented on October 27, 1955, to the Geneva Conference of Foreign Ministers. All agreed that much work needed to be done by the Four-Power Working Group on the substance of the Western position.

In his conversations in Paris with Foreign Minister Couve de Murville and President de Gaulle, Dulles found general French support for the proposed Western course of action leading, it was hoped, to a four-power conference of foreign ministers. The French stressed the seriousness of the situation, as they saw it, and the need to be prepared with adequate contingency planning should the Soviets proceed to take unilateral action to change the control of Western military access to Berlin.

During all these meetings, one could only admire the fortitude of the secretary of state. He seemed in great pain yet conducted lengthy conversations with complete lucidity and eloquence. Livy Merchant, who of all of us was closest to Dulles, told us that he had difficulty in keeping any food down and that it was a wonder he could keep going. The secretary knew that the stop in Bonn would be the most difficult of the three capitals and steeled himself for some difficult sessions with Chancellor Adenauer, his great friend, whom he had had to reassure by trips to Bonn, or in Washington, during difficult times in the past. The close relationship between the two had not been an automatic one, but over the years, Dulles had won the complete confidence of the chancellor. The latter, however, had been stirred by what he regarded as a dangerous tendency to compromise by the West in the face of threatened action by the Soviet Union, a country whose leadership he distrusted with intensity while fearing the unreliability of his own compatriots.

I had noted this lack of confidence in his fellow Germans during my contacts with Adenauer during the occupation period, a hangover no doubt from personal experience of German aberrational behavior during the Nazi period. Although many politicians are likely to believe that any electorate that chooses them for public office must be ipso facto trustworthy, Adenauer continued to fear that an insecure and disoriented people might be lured by Eastern blandishments into foolish abandonment of their Western ties. These concerns were to be an abiding source of difficulty during the next months as we tried to develop a negotiating position for the Geneva Conference of Foreign Ministers. He always stressed the need for caution in making proposals to the Soviets that might lead to dangerous temptations to go even further should they be accepted.

So now he needed to be reassured that the U.S. government was not showing too much flexibility and could be counted on to be firm and unyielding in defending the Western position in Berlin. At their first meeting, Adenauer quickly noticed that Dulles was not well. When he later observed at lunch that the secretary was not eating, he ordered that some muesli be brought in. After a strong recommendation from the chancellor that this would be good for him, Dulles ate a few spoonfuls. He did not evidence great enjoyment, but Adenauer was obviously greatly concerned. After the meetings, when the *Columbine* was nearly ready to take off to return to the United States, a man ran up the runway with a large sack and announced that the chancellor had decided that the secretary needed a special diet until he recovered. Needless to say, the sack contained muesli.

Although in truth the chancellor obviously had Dulles's health very much in mind and perhaps modulated his criticisms and concerns more than he might otherwise have done, the various plenary and smaller meetings went off pretty much as we had hoped. Adenauer seemed to accept the secretary's assurances that the Western position would reflect unity and firmness and that our position in, and access to, West Berlin would be preserved. Dulles had also stressed that the United States would consult very intimately with the Federal Republic.

The chancellor was to need continuing reassurance during the following months that the West was not going astray, but Secretary Dulles would not be there to provide it. As the *Columbine* finally landed at Andrews Air Force Base outside Washington, Dulles steeled himself at the exit of the plane to shake hands and to say goodbye to the members of his party. I shall not forget his last words to me, stated with some irony: "I hope, Hillenbrand, that we were able to keep you amused on this trip." I was never to see him again. The next day he went to Bethesda Naval Hospital, where the diagnosis was of inoperable and terminal cancer. He submitted his resignation on March 30; the president accepted it on April 15. Meanwhile, Undersecretary Christian Herter had taken over as acting secretary of state.

The Herter Era Begins at State

It quickly became clear that, while an honorable and decent man, Christian Herter had neither the intellectual brilliance nor the gift of extemporaneous expression of John Foster Dulles. He preferred to be called "Governor," a position he had once held in Massachusetts. Aware of his own limitations, Herter placed great confidence in the counsel of his principal advisers. I was thus drawn into a small group of officers on whom he relied constantly for recommendations and action on the Berlin crisis. He suffered from crippling arthritis but bore his pain with admirable stoicism. With such people as Robert Murphy, Loy Henderson, and Livy Merchant at the top of the department, morale was high despite the heavy pressures of work. It was a happy time for the professional Foreign Service. The National Security Council staff had not yet begun to carve out a substantive role for itself. The president seemed content to let foreign affairs be handled by the foreign affairs agency, and he could generally be counted on to support the department in bureaucratic quarrels. The Congress also accepted the general soundness of American foreign policy. I came to admire the acting secretary, and we all hoped that, once Dulles had resigned, the president would appoint Herter as secretary of state. There were the usual Washington rumors that some other political figure was the front-runner, but we could think of no one better than the calm and supportive Governor Herter to take us through what promised to be a troubled time. We all welcomed the announcement in late April that the president had appointed Herter to succeed John Foster Dulles. Looking back, I can only conclude that our judgment was correct. Herter performed well both at Geneva and subsequently during a difficult twenty months.

A common mistake of researchers into the past is to attribute too much importance to the casual but recorded remarks of presidents or memorandums drafted by White House aides, as interesting and sometimes titillating as they may be. At least in those days, the State Department did the basic drafting of position papers in the foreign affairs field that, when approved by the secretary of state and the president, became national policy. Under current practice, however, and the institutionalization of presidential libraries, White House papers tend to become available more rapidly than the classified materials originating in State and its field posts. Yet much of the documentation thus quickly released will have had only marginally to do with the actual policy-making process as it worked itself out.

Macmillan Visits Moscow

The next important development came with the delivery in Moscow on February 16 of the French, British, and American replies to the Soviet note of January 10. The operative language stated that the three Western countries were prepared to participate in a conference of the foreign ministers of the USSR, France, Britain, and the United States at a date and place to be fixed by mutual agreement. The notes also "suggested that German advisers should be invited to the conference and should be consulted." In similar instructions, the three Western ambassadors were told to add orally, when delivering the notes to Gromyko, that their governments preferred Geneva or Vienna as site and about May 10 as date.[19]

Apart from the usual polemics and emphasis on a peace conference, the Soviet response of March 2 urged instead a meeting of heads of government but conceded that a conference of the foreign ministers of the USSR, the United States, the United Kingdom, France, Poland, and Czechoslovakia could be convoked to examine questions "concerning the peace treaty with Germany and concerning West Berlin" in the event that the Western powers were "not yet ready to take part in a summit conference." The note went on to suggest Vienna or Geneva as the site where such a meeting of foreign ministers might take place.[20]

Meanwhile, Prime Minister Macmillan had undertaken on his own a rather lengthy visit to the Soviet Union (February 24–March 3) to probe Khrushchev's intentions. In a prior message to Adenauer, Macmillan had described his purpose in going to Moscow as "to try to discover something of what [was] in the minds of the Soviet leaders" and not to negotiate. In all frankness, however, we shared the concern with both the Germans and the French that he might give the impression to Khrushchev of a greater willingness in the West to compromise on Berlin than we were able to accept. I do not doubt that the prime minister shared with most of us a commendable desire to avoid a head-on confrontation with the Soviets and to provide them with every opportunity to back away from their threat of unilateral action. It is interesting to note that, in his memoirs, Macmillan expressed his conviction that Dulles and Eisenhower had "complete confidence" in him.[21] This was more than a small exaggeration, but in the final analysis there was really no way that Macmillan's trip could be prevented, given his definition of its purposes. The memory of the "slippery slope" paper lingered on, and we shared the feeling that, of the four Western powers immediately concerned, the British were the most likely to seek the easy way out. In justice, one must add that, at no point, either before the Geneva Conference of Foreign Ministers or at the conference itself, did the British urge Western actions that would have jeopardized our basic position in Berlin. Foreign Secretary Selwyn Lloyd consistently sought the noncombative formulation and expressed a desire for compromise but not at an unacceptable cost.

After his return from Moscow, the prime minister had little positive to report about the Soviet position, but he did claim that the most important result of his visit was the proposal of the Soviet government contained in its note of March 2. During March he traveled to Bonn, Paris, and Washington to discuss his impressions and to withdraw his own preference for a summit meeting in favor of a foreign ministers' conference. The Western notes that went forward on March 26 proposed that the meeting of the foreign ministers of the USSR, the United States, the United Kingdom, and France convene in Geneva on May 11. The conference was to consider "questions relating to Germany, including a peace treaty with Germany and the question of Berlin." [22] In its quick reply by note on March 30, the Soviet Union expressed its agreement with the Western proposals regarding the agenda, date, and place of the conference but regretted that "full mutual understanding" had not been reached on the question of Czech and Polish participation. [23]

Preparatory Diplomacy

Following the receipt of the Soviet note of March 2, we and our allies felt reasonably certain that we were moving toward a high-level conference with the Soviet Union, and the Four-Power Working Group convened in Paris on March 9 for a two-week session (March 9–21, 1959) to get down to the serious business of preparing a Western negotiating position for such a conference. I headed the American delegation, which included Malcolm Toon from the Office of Soviet Affairs (he was later to become our ambassador in Moscow), Ted Lampson from the Office of German Affairs, and a number of others, including representatives from the Department of Defense. Again I note that it was still possible in 1959 for a medium-level State Department official who enjoyed the confidence of his superiors to be chief of delegation to a conference dealing with a subject of highest national interest. Such a thing would literally be impossible today in an era of swollen bureaucratic hierarchies and inflated titles. My opposite numbers in Paris, Patrick Hancock of the United Kingdom, Jean

Laloy of France, and Graf Baudissin of the Federal Republic, were senior Foreign Ministry officials. As diplomats are wont to do, the four of us quickly developed a certain rapport and, in informal meetings after plenary Working Group sessions, could sometimes resolve differences that had emerged. On the American side, before leaving Washington, we had worked out a detailed paper on the proposed elements of a Western position. I tabled it at an early plenary session of the group. Each of the other delegations also tabled papers dealing with various aspects of the problem, but none had the scope or comprehensiveness of the American plan. I think it fair to say that, despite many subsequent amendments and incorporation of other ideas, we had provided the basic framework for the Western Peace Plan proposal tabled at the Geneva Conference of Foreign Ministers on May 14 by Secretary Herter.

After two weeks of intensive and often prolonged sessions, the Working Group agreed on an overall paper for submission to governments. The American delegation had had little time to enjoy either the culinary or aesthetic delights of Paris, but we returned to Washington feeling that we had provided the primary impetus in the development of a Western position. My evaluation was that the final product of the Paris meeting was "better than it might have been." We knew, of course, that future Working Group meetings would be necessary, but first there would be a meeting of the four Western foreign ministers in Washington (March 31–April 4) to provide us with further guidance. Before this meeting, we had briefed Acting Secretary Herter, stressing that the Western plan was a comprehensive package that could not be picked apart. Underlying our position was the assumption that the West should not leave the initiative to the Soviet Union and that we should propose either a draft peace treaty or at least a statement of principles to govern a peace treaty. After considerable debate the foreign ministers finally agreed that the principles of a peace treaty should be put forward and a draft treaty only be tabled if the Soviets accepted those principles.

A premise uppermost in our minds during all these preparations was that the continuing support of public opinion during the crisis required not only firmness on the Western side but also a clear preference for diplomatic solutions and a willingness to negotiate. Hardly a day passed that the European and American press did not headline the gravity of the Berlin situation, the danger it presented of a major confrontation with the Soviet Union that could lead to war. Background briefings and sometimes overt statements by senior Pentagon officials about proposed or actual military deployments added to the atmosphere of crisis. Some harassments of American and British military traffic on the autobahn to Berlin took place, but none of these escalated to the point where the issue of using military force had to be directly faced. Through these turbulent months, the sober and calm approach of President Eisenhower kept the firebrands in Washington under control. While at one time (in January) he may have considered the possibility of forceful probing actions on the autobahn, as advocated by some in the Pentagon, he quickly concluded with Dulles that an attempt to send an armed convoy through to Berlin should only come if the Soviets substituted East German for Soviet officials. The British had from the outset of the crisis feared that the United States might take unilateral action to demonstrate force on the autobahn; the American press had been full of speculation along such lines. Macmillan showed obvious relief after Dulles told him in London that there would be no armed probes in the absence of a Soviet turnover of authority for processing Allied traffic to GDR officials.

Despite much bluster and threat, either in statements or in notes, it had become apparent that Khrushchev was now resigned, at least temporarily, to a diplomatic process. Acceptance of the May 11 date for the opening of the foreign ministers' conference meant that the May 27 expiration of the six-month ultimatum period no longer held, or at least so we chose to interpret it. Concern about the date had led the British particularly to emphasize the need to get the conference going earlier in May, and we experienced no difficulty in accepting the logic of such a chronology.

What had brought about this softening of the Soviet position? Was it the cumulative impact of various Western demonstrations of firmness or some other consideration that seemed important to Khrushchev? Reviewing the available literature on the subject (and there is not all that much), I am amazed at the assurance with which some historians attribute causality. Thus, for example, Professor Slusser writes that it was Macmillan's visit to Moscow, "more than any other factor, that produced Soviet agreement to participate in a foreign ministers' conference."[24] Macmillan, of course, believed this, but experience has taught me that, in highly complicated and tense crises, the precise factors leading to specific decisions are seldom possible to identify with certainty. One can conjecture and advance hypotheses, but the human decision-making process is usually too multicausal to reduce to a simple formula. In this case, whatever the factors that influenced Soviet thinking, we were glad on the Western side that diplomacy had an important, and perhaps decisive, role to play.

When German foreign minister Heinrich von Brentano arrived in Washington for the four-power meeting, we quickly learned that the Paris Working Group report had not pleased Chancellor Adenauer. When von Brentano arrived in New York after an ocean crossing on a steamer, he found a rocket from the chancellor awaiting him. The latter felt that the report went dangerously far in suggesting proposals that the Soviets might twist to their advantage or actually accept as a basis for negotiations that would arouse false hopes of reunification among the German public. The poor German foreign minister appeared visibly embarrassed at his first meeting with Secretary Herter and engaged in a good deal of figurative hand-wringing as he presented Adenauer's arguments. After all, he had presumably signed off on the report before sailing.

We did not accept such an assessment of dangers, of course. We thought that our plan for staged progression toward unification on the basis of free elections, accompanied by mutual troop withdrawals (along the lines of the 1955 Eden Plan but modifying it), and a solution of the Berlin problem within such a context would have maximum appeal to world public opinion. The terminal point was to be a peace treaty with a united Germany. We did not really expect the Soviets to accept such a Western proposal, but if by some reversal of policy they did, there would be real hope of achieving the kind of postwar settlement of the German problem that, in theory at least, we all desired.

It had become clear, in the light of German objections, that the Four-Power Working Group, which the foreign ministers agreed should next meet in London, would have to revise some portions of its report. We were determined, however, that the essential framework be preserved, and in a bilateral meeting with von Brentano on the margin of the NATO ministerial meeting in London (April 2–4, 1959), Acting Secretary Herter spoke frankly about the need to demonstrate flexibility and imagination in preparing the Western position if it was not to appear obdurate and unreasonable to public opinion. Von Brentano was again obviously ill at ease. He had strict orders from Adenauer with which he did not personally fully agree. He pleaded for understanding of his difficult position.

I was once again to head the American delegation to the London meeting of the Four-Power Working Group. The word had gotten around that there was where the action would now be on Berlin, and demands to join the delegation came from all sides. I was able to resist most of them, but the bureaucratic pressures built up to the point where we arrived in London with a swollen delegation that included a few prima donnas. One of my first tasks each day was to dream up activities for them that would keep them out of the hair of the rest of us. Some of the time, at least, it worked.

Given the problems with the Germans, we knew the London sessions would be difficult, if not acrimonious. Ambassador Grewe had been brought from Washington to lead the German delegation, and he was to play a continuing role as the German observer at the Geneva Conference of Foreign Ministers. He was a highly intelligent jurist who had adapted well to diplomacy. He never seemed entirely comfortable in Washington diplomatic society, but I had come to respect his fund of knowledge and ability to articulate German positions. I can recall lengthy conversations late into the evening that I had with him over the years in his study at the German embassy residence on Reservoir Road. I knew that he would be a formidable addition to the German delegation.

The Working Group met in London from April 13 through April 23. It was hard slogging, but we finally emerged with an agreed report to governments including the following documents: a revision of the "Phased Plan for German Reunification and European Security and a German Peace Settlement"; "Preliminary Draft Principles of a German Peace Settlement"; "Berlin"; "Tactics at the Foreign Ministers' Conference"; and "A Statement to the North Atlantic Council." There were also some recommendations for possible fallback positions in negotiations with the Soviets that, to avoid leaks, were classified even more highly than the documents noted. On the whole, the American side was pleased with the results, which, in truth, had exceeded our somewhat more pessimistic earlier expectations. The big question mark, of course, was Chancellor Adenauer's reaction to the package.

There is always a tendency for delegations to an important international conference to feel that what they are doing must captivate capitals and that full reporting of meetings, together with comment, is a necessity. We did not spare the cabled words in either Paris or London, partly recognizing, of course, that a harassed bureaucracy and senior officials in Washington could not really keep up with the flow of words and hence would be less likely to intrude with unwanted or irrelevant instructions. The experienced negotiator can resort to this tactic if he knows that he has the confidence of his principals and that what he agrees to will find their support. I do not recommend it, however, to anyone with a reputation for freewheeling.

In any event, we returned to Washington satisfied that we had done a good job and that our "Phased Plan" demonstrated the requisite qualities of imagination, flexibility, and public appeal. Our British and French colleagues felt the same, and, I believe, even Ambassador Grewe thought the report would not jolt Bonn. He had obviously been frequently on the line to his capital seeking instructions from von Brentano. Once again, however, the old German chancellor pulled the rug out from underneath his foreign minister. I could only recall von Brentano's painful embarrassment at his first meeting with Herter on the margin of the four-power Paris meeting of foreign ministers convened April 29–30 to review the report of the Working Group. Despite German acceptance of the report in London, the flushed and visibly overwrought von Brentano conveyed the bad news that, after all, his government could not accept the report without significant changes. It was not a great day for a foreign minister who had obviously once again been read the riot act by his chancellor.

Back in Bonn Adenauer could not resist making uncomplimentary remarks about a so-called working group that spoke for no one. He knew that I was the head of the American delegation, and he must have wondered whether his old friend had not gone off the deep end. To him our "Phased Plan," which he had undoubtedly been told was primarily an American initiative, must have seemed dangerously venturesome.

Our objective from the outset of the Four-Power Working Group sessions had been to arrive at a Western proposal aimed at the phased achievement of German reunification in the context of which the Berlin problem would also be solved. We had no illusions about the acceptability of such a proposal to the Soviets, embodying the principle of self-determination, but we hoped that it would meet the test of reasonableness before world opinion and thus put Khrushchev on the propaganda defensive. If, by some miracle, the Soviets reacted positively to our initiative, then we might together actually move toward a solution of the German problem in a manner consistent with both Western and reasonable (admittedly by our definition) Soviet security requirements.

What we did not sufficiently take into account was Chancellor Adenauer's obsessive concern about the gullibility of his own compatriots, not to speak of their allies, and the intensity of his reaction to our efforts. Some have argued that then, or earlier, he never really wanted a reunified Germany under any conditions, for this would have meant an eventual Social Democratic majority in an all-German legislature, but I found his motives to be much more complex than mere political expediency. He was, of course, the quintessential Rhinelander and could not help but consider the Saxons, and for that matter all Germans from the eastern parts of the former Reich, as of a lower order, nor did he have any great personal affection for the Berliners. Beyond these considerations, however, his hesitations reflected a deep pessimism about Germans as perpetually susceptible to the blandishments of the clever and the wicked. Who was to blame him after his personal experiences of the Nazi period? We tended to be less cynical, more believing in the possibility of attitudinal change and human improvement and that risks run can sometimes achieve gains and not inevitably result in ground lost.

In any event, the four foreign ministers finally agreed on the broad lines of the package to be presented to the Soviets at Geneva and directed the Working Group to redraft certain sections of its report. We were also to rework some of the language in our paper "Preliminary Draft Principles of a German Peace Treaty." All of this logomachy on the Western side is now buried in the mists of the past, but it seemed terribly important at the time. After his rather inglorious beginning in Paris, von Brentano had gone about as far as he dared (or perhaps a little beyond) in agreeing to the contents of the Western "Phased Plan." The Working Group would put the final touches on the documentation in Geneva, where we were to meet a few days before the foreign ministers assembled on May 11. We did not know we were to have some additional respite as the rather absurd dispute over how representatives of the two Germanies were to participate ran its course.

Contingency Planning

While all this diplomatic back and forth was going on, we were also engaged from the outset of the Berlin crisis in the preparation and revision of contingency plans for the event of unilateral action against our position in Berlin. There was little planning we could do for the worst-case hypothesis of a direct Soviet military attack on the French, British, and American garrisons in Berlin. The nuclear issue would arise almost immediately in the face of the overwhelming military force—twenty-one divisions—the Soviets could bring to bear. There were, however, many harassing or blocking actions short of that the Soviets could initiate, and it was these with which the contingency planners (who in the State Department were pretty much the same people working on the policy and negotiations side) had to deal.

The cynics among us were quick to point out that we seemed to have contingency plans for everything except that which actually happened. Sometimes it appeared that way: the nuances of harassment were more numerous than the plans we could tripartitely make on the Western side. Yet the exercise was necessary and, on balance, useful, for it made us understand our own weaknesses and strengths with greater clarity.

For obvious reasons, much of Berlin contingency planning remained highly classified. A primary focus during the pre–Geneva conference period was obviously the transfer to the East Germans of Soviet functions with respect to Allied access to Berlin—as Khrushchev had threatened to do. Tripartite talks (excluding the Germans) took place on the margin of the Paris foreign ministers' meeting in December 1958; again at the ambassadorial level in Washington during January; during Secretary Dulles's visit to Europe in early February; in tripartite talks in Washington later that month; in bilateral talks at Camp David between Eisenhower and Macmillan in March; and between the three foreign ministers in Washington on March 31. Needless to say, much drafting by subordinates provided the fuel for these discussions, and it is fair to note that most of the impetus as well as the paperwork came from the American side. As during the Kennedy stress on contingency planning in the fall of 1961, the British, and to a lesser degree the French, were reluctant to agree to any course of action that committed them in advance to an automatic response. Fortunately, the issue never rose in the concrete, and in practice I doubt that the American government would have acted in a crisis situation without a specific decision at the highest levels of government.

The Geneva Conference of Foreign Ministers

The Four-Power Working Group, to which I continued to head the American delegation, quickly put the finishing touches to the Western "Phased Plan" during its sessions in Geneva. We were searching for a good title when a British colleague, Bernard Ledwidge, blurted out "Western Peace Plan." It sounded like a good idea, and so it was called. We also agreed that Secretary of State Herter should introduce it at an appropriate early point in the conference.

Geneva was to experience a stifling hot summer in 1959, as was the rest of Western Europe. It made for an excellent vintage year but added to the doldrums of what was at best a tedious conference. When it began, we did not know, of course, that we were to spend three months in protracted and highly repetitious discussions, futile from the Western viewpoint except in one important respect. Geneva in 1959 was not a city that effervesced. The spirit of the failed League of Nations still hung over it, even in the atmosphere of its famous Bavaria café and restaurant. Farther into the past, the dour visage of John Calvin still seemed to dominate the old town and what passed for its old society. No one could deny the sheer physical beauty of the place at one end of Lake Geneva—itself certainly one of the loveliest natural lakes in the world—but the American delegation, housed in the Hotel du Rhone, was largely confined to a narrower visual perspective, dominated by paper, words, and the sort of artificial crisis atmosphere that conferences can generate. No one can be more inbred than the participants at a major conference, who, to liven up the dullness, no matter how adversarial their relationship, entertain one another at a constant round of so-called working lunches and dinners.

Always considerate and undoubtedly bored by the endless flow of words, Secretary Herter used Sundays to relax and to take members of his delegations for lunch at one of the fine restaurants in the Geneva–Lake Annecy area. A special favorite was the Auberge du Père Bise in Talloires, then at the height of its culinary glory.

Karl Marx was wrong in thinking that all great events and personalities reappear in history, the first time as tragedy, the second as farce. Some begin as farce, and that was the case with the Geneva Conference of Foreign Ministers. Before the substantive talks could start, the question of West and East German participation had to be resolved. A quadripartite liaison group (including Soviet representatives) had reached deadlock over the shape of the conference table, the Western powers favoring a square table and the Soviet Union a round table large enough to seat more than four delegations. We did not want the East Germans to end up as full participants at the conference. The next day the four foreign ministers had to postpone the scheduled opening of the conference until 6:00 P.M. while they wrestled with this weighty problem. Finally a compromise emerged: the four delegations would sit at a round table, but the representatives of the Federal Republic of Germany and the German Democratic Republic would sit at two separate square tables, not touching the round conference table but separated from it by six pencil widths. Much ingenuity obviously went into that solution. Why not eight pencil widths or four?

It was further agreed that, upon their request, the West and East German advisers could be given the right to speak, unless one of the four foreign ministers objected. Gromyko was given assurances that the Western side would not raise such objections unless the East German speaker abused his privilege. (As a matter of fact, despite some heated exchanges, neither the three Western nor the Soviet foreign ministers ever raised such a point of order.) To further underline its attitude toward the GDR the Western side from the outset decided that the standard reference would be to "the so-called GDR" and "the so-called GDR foreign minister," Lothar Bolz (who was the principal East German representative throughout the conference). Needless to say, this practice proved extremely galling to the Soviets and the East Germans, provoking Gromyko to occasional outbursts of sarcasm.

Logic can be a ruthless master, and what might seem like low-grade theater of the absurd in the 1990s seemed absolutely ineluctable in 1959. It was only with the change of position central to Willy Brandt's *Ostpolitik* of the early 1970s, including recognition of the GDR by the Western powers, that the rigidities of strict nonrecognition doctrine could be jettisoned.

I see no need to recount here the exhausting details of inconclusive and interminable discussions in Geneva that stretched into August. All the nonclassified speeches and documents appeared in a 603-page State Department publication released shortly after the conclusion of the conference.[25]

The classified documents and reports of numerous private conversations, I am able to say, add little to any judgment about the ultimate role of the conference and its final results. It was clearly a failure in terms of any movement toward settlement of the Berlin or larger German problem. It was a success in that threats of a six-month ultimatum ceased and the Soviets apparently accepted the need for continuing discussions with the Western powers about Berlin.

The American delegation quickly settled down to its own internal routines. As usual, there were many drones from other agencies, and the real work was done by a relatively few. Those of us from the delegation to the Four-Power Working Group sat together in a large room that quickly became known as the "bull pen." We drafted the reports, the memorandums, the position papers and fed them to Herter via Livy Merchant, who performed tirelessly. Air-conditioning did not exist in Geneva in those days, and both our office space in the U.S. mission building and the Palais des Nations of the old League, where plenary meetings took place, could become swelteringly hot.

This conference in Geneva proved to be among the first of the media circuses that have become standard phenomena on the margin of high-level conferences. The Berlin crisis had for more than six months been a center of press attention, and correspondents flocked by the many hundreds to Geneva to be near the source of news (the hordes of television personnel that are now routine were still in large part absent). In any event, the care and drinking of the press had highest priority, and each delegation tried to outdo itself with special arrangements. Perhaps the most elaborate, strangely enough, was the press room presided over by the chancellor's spokesman, Felix von Eckhardt. At least he had the best German wines. The life of a correspondent at a conference is a tedious one. He shops around for the tidbits of news that delegation spokesmen may let fall or, in triumph, arranges an interview with a senior official. He has to pound out his daily story and must often do it on the basis of rumors circulating in the press corps. There is a certain vicious circle in all of this. Members of delegations read the reports and wonder whether the correspondents have information that they do not. I know of cases where, in interviews, officials have passed on as solemn truth what started out as a rumor in the press corps. So are myths sometimes created.

Despite the emendations we were forced to make in the Working Group, we still felt that the Western Peace Plan was an imaginative and constructive approach to the German and Berlin problem. Our aim had been to provide a Western initiative that would seem reasonable and within whose framework the challenge to Berlin could be resolved. As I have said, we entertained no illusions about its acceptability to the Soviets, since we did not believe they wanted a reunified Germany under any conditions likely to be acceptable to us, but our plan would be there as a possible start to negotiations should that evaluation of Soviet intentions turn out to be wrong.

On May 14, Secretary Herter tabled the Western Peace Plan on behalf of the three governments, after explaining its purpose and contents. I can recall Gromyko's hesitant reaction; he obviously had not expected to receive something so all-embracing as this. It was clear he would require instructions from Moscow; so he limited his remarks to a brief defense of the GDR. By the next day he was ready and again put forward the Soviet draft of a German peace treaty containing forty-eight articles. This turned out to be the same text already presented to the Western powers with the Soviet note of January 10, 1959. The Soviet draft did not envisage a reunified Germany but a peace treaty with "the two existing German states." As far as our Peace Plan was concerned, he added, it was defective in that it proposed to lump together a series of complicated questions instead of trying to solve them separately, and moreover it attempted to substitute discussions on German reunification for discussion of a peace treaty. Although Foreign Minister Lloyd, Secretary Herter, and Foreign Minister Couve de Murville made a valiant effort in their subsequent statements to keep the Western Peace Plan alive, it was clear that the Soviets would have none of it. Had they had, in 1959, any real interest in German reunification, they could have probed how far we were prepared to go beyond the Peace Plan as such. Gromyko could have responded in more nuanced fashion. Berlin was obviously the focal point of Soviet concern at Geneva along with enhancing the status of the GDR.

As the end of May approached, the foreign ministers took a few days off to attend the funeral of John Foster Dulles in Washington (ironically enough Gromyko traveled as a passenger on Herter's Boeing 707 presidential jet). It had become evident that lengthy speeches at plenary sessions could not advance the discussion, and the emphasis now moved to private meetings, either bilateral or quadripartite. Plenary sessions continued, but more infrequently, sometimes mainly to give the West and East Germans, who were excluded from the private meetings, an opportunity to make speeches.

The Main Cast of Characters

I suppose there is no better way to get to know a group of foreign ministers than to observe them nearly every day for three months—at plenary sessions, at private meetings, and at so-called working lunches and dinners. The cumulative revelation of character, intelligence, and verbal skills created a fairly clear impression of the great men in all their weaknesses and strengths.

Foreign Minister Andrei Gromyko completely lived up to the reputation he enjoyed in the West. He was not without a sarcastic sense of humor, but never directed at himself. Although his English was fairly good, he always spoke in Russian at plenary sessions, requiring lengthy subsequent translations into English and French. While perhaps not quite in the same league as his predecessor as foreign minister, Vyacheslav Molotov (known not particularly affectionately as "Old Iron Pants"), Gromyko had the kind of *Sitzfleisch* that enabled him to endure and to participate in seemingly endless discussions. I was to observe this quality on many later occasions, but at Geneva it served him in particularly good stead. While Western foreign ministers became physically restless, he could drone on and on. His health seemed equally solid, but some could recall that, at the 1955 summit meeting at Geneva, he had lugubriously told some Western officials that he had cancer and that this might be the last international conference he could attend. Needless to say, he had been the victim of a false diagnosis.

While he could be hard and unbending as a negotiator, Gromyko did not rant and rave or simulate anger that he did not feel. Was he basically anti-American, or more generally anti-Western? Since over many years he was usually in an adversarial role as foreign minister with respect to the United States, it is easy to imagine that this would inevitably be reflected in his personal attitude. Yet I can recall few, if any, instances where he resorted to the jargon of Marxism-Leninism to attack Western positions. However, after Gorbachev took over as general secretary of the Communist Party, reports from Moscow indicated that Gromyko was among those in the Politburo advocating policies that were fundamentally anti-American.

The French foreign minister, Couve de Murville, came across initially as a pretty cold fish, and some would claim that this was the true man. In later meetings in Paris I found him considerably more human and relaxed. A Gaullist of Protestant family origins, tall and thin in stature, he loved to play with words in a melodious French. His spoken sentences were long and involved; one could almost see the interpreters sweat. Someone once described him as a linguistic dandy. Despite all the elegant circumlocutions, he accurately reflected the blunter view of President de Gaulle—a reality that was to cost us considerable grief in 1961 as Secretary Rusk pressed to undertake exploratory talks with the Soviets. One of the funnier sights in French politics at a later point must have been that of Couve campaigning for a seat in the National Assembly in the Faubourg Saint Germain quarter of Paris—an area of many convents as well as embassies. There was something incongruous about this pillar of French Protestantism knocking at convent doors to persuade the good sisters to vote for him.

The British foreign minister, Selwyn Lloyd, was an able lawyer-politician, articulate but not eloquent. He had good lines to read, supplied by Pat Hancock and a very strong British delegation. Lloyd seemed constantly to be searching for bases for compromise, sometimes emphasizing apparent verbal congruence when substantive agreement really did not exist. There was, for the reasons already indicated, lingering suspicion of ultimate British reliability, but we did not observe anything at Geneva that caused major concern. From everything we could see, this solid, unspectacular British official enjoyed the full confidence of Prime Minister Harold Macmillan as a leading and loyal member of his Conservative cabinet.

The foreign minister who was not there, lurking in the background but refusing to participate in plenary sessions along with the GDR's Lothar Bolz, was Heinrich von Brentano. The result was that Ambassador Grewe became the spokesman for the Federal Republic, while von Brentano drifted in and out of Geneva. He met occasionally with the Western foreign ministers to be briefed on their private meetings and to discuss strategy. I thought this put him in a humiliating situation, but we assumed the chancellor had simply vetoed his participation, separate table from Bolz notwithstanding. I had always liked von Brentano, dating from the days of the European Defense Community Treaty and the efforts to create a European Political Community. He was a lonely and cultured gentleman, a committed European with a clear anti-Nazi record, who always seemed to be living on the edge of his nerves and who, before we knew better about such things, was literally smoking himself to death. He died of lung cancer in 1964.

I need add little here to what I have already said about Secretary Herter. He was a true gentleman, able to rise above the constant pain of the arthritic condition that made him dependent on crutches to move around. If he lacked the gift of verbal improvisation, he could read with eloquence and conviction the statements and interventions that we composed and that Livy Merchant would pass on to him, sometimes with his own comments. He inevitably shared in the frustrations that such a wearisome conference imposed on all the Western participants—and perhaps on the Soviets as well—but maintained his good humor and sense of the ridiculous.

The End of the Conference and the Movement toward a Bilateral Summit at Camp David

While all this inconclusive talking was going on in Geneva, unilateral statements in capitals and direct exchanges between capitals were preparing the postconference phase of the Berlin crisis. Khrushchev injected himself into the diplomatic process by proclamations from Moscow, and it emerged with reasonable clarity that the Soviet leader badly wanted to meet with President Eisenhower. On July 11, the latter wrote to Khrushchev that it seemed useful to him to have an informal exchange of views with the Soviet secretary general and that Undersecretary Robert Murphy had conveyed some ideas on the subject to Soviet deputy premier Frol Kozlov, who had been on a visit to the United States. There may have been a certain irony in the use of Kozlov as a messenger of peace, since he came to be regarded by some as the leader of a hard-line faction in the Politburo pushing for no concessions on Berlin. In any event, Khrushchev, in a letter of July 22, eagerly accepted the president's proposal to meet with him informally in the United States in the summer and also welcomed the idea that Eisenhower might visit the Soviet Union in October.

If there had ever been any chance of progress at Geneva, this was presumably now ruled out by the prospective meeting of Eisenhower and Khrushchev. However, the summit meeting itself was placed in jeopardy by negative developments at Geneva. By one of those sudden transpositions not unknown to Soviet diplomacy, Gromyko had come more and more to emphasize the creation of an all-German committee to discuss the German problem, thus excluding the three Western powers from any further responsibility for the subject. Meanwhile, discussion of a possible interim Berlin settlement continued.

On June 16, and again on July 28, the Western foreign ministers had tabled proposals for an interim agreement on Berlin. These involved, inter alia, a ceiling on Allied troop levels in Berlin. The haggling over them and Soviet counterproposals consumed a month and a half with no real meeting of minds. A major sticking point was our insistence that Western rights in Berlin must remain intact after expiration of the interim agreement. Inaccurate leaks to the press about the Western proposals aroused considerable criticism, particularly in West Germany and West Berlin itself, on the ground that they made too many concessions to the Soviets. I do not think these concerns were justified, but the chancellor's reactive hyperbole seemed inevitable in a tension-laden situation.

In Eisenhower's mind, his willingness to invite Khrushchev to a summit meeting seemed at first largely to be conditioned by the extent of progress reached at Geneva. Yet as a result of talks in Moscow on the margin of Vice President Nixon's visit to that city in late July, the president now felt it possible to proceed with the Khrushchev visit, even though it was clear in his own mind that the Soviets had not basically altered their position at Geneva. He suggested a date sometime in September.

As a result of his private meeting with Gromyko on August 1, Secretary Herter came to the firm conclusion that the Soviet Union would not commit itself on the issue of continuing Western rights and that there was, therefore, no possibility of reaching an interim agreement on Berlin. In any event, Herter suggested, since Khrushchev now knew that he would be visiting the United States, there was no need for any Soviet concessions at Geneva.

The final plenary session (the twenty-fifth) of the Geneva Conference of Foreign Ministers took place on August 5. There were long speeches by the ministers intended largely for home consumption. The final communiqué was relatively brief but did not escape some of the usual platitudes that inevitably find their way into such documents.[26] Everyone knew where the action was shifting. Time had run out on us in Geneva, and we were all anxious to get home. There is a natural rhythm to negotiations. Some can continue much longer than three months if the prospect for success remains alive. We had obviously come to a dead end, and the futility of going through empty motions had become apparent to all, including the Soviet delegation. So we eagerly left Geneva to return to our respective capitals.

There were, however, a few aspects of those weary months that deserve at least brief comment. One of the stories going the rounds at Geneva in an effort to explain seeming American willingness to accept concessions, including eventually the summit meeting with Khrushchev, was that Eisenhower, the Pentagon, and Herter still believed in the existence of a "missile gap" between the Soviet Union and the United States. I do not know at precisely what point our U-2 flights over the Soviet Union provided us with the information that many of the apparently deployed Soviet missiles capable of reaching the United States were dummies and that American intercontinental ballistic missile strength remained adequate. The Eisenhower memoirs throw some light on the subject. Khrushchev obviously knew he was faking it. The hyperdramatic way he reacted to the U-2 revelation in the spring of 1960 may have been partly influenced by his recognition that the game was up (see the discussion below of the abortive 1960 Paris summit meeting).

In his memoirs, Eisenhower notes, "Though by early 1959 we knew the Soviet Union still led us in certain areas of missile research and production (especially high-powered boosters) we were also aware that our total defense capabilities were more than sufficient to deter Soviet aggression." Eisenhower went on to say that, by January 1960, new intelligence reports (presumably from U-2 overflights of the USSR) "narrowed almost to negligibility the extent of the Soviet lead in long-range and sea-launched missiles."[27]

A constant consideration affecting the Western negotiators at Geneva, and particularly the American side, was the effect that press reporting of the conference, sometimes highly inaccurate and speculative, would have on the morale of West Berlin. Those of us with experience in the city knew how mercurial the mood of both its population and its leaders could be. Under the kinds of pressure from Khrushchev that the Berliners felt directed at them, every seeming Western concession could immediately be interpreted as the beginning of a sellout. As early as June 25, Governing Mayor Brandt had aroused the level of anxiety with his statement that the Western proposals went to the limit of what was tolerable. As the Berlin expert on our delegation, I was caught between pressure from the U.S. mission in Berlin to do something to allay the concerns of Berliners and the U.S. delegation in Geneva, where resentment was building up among some members against what were regarded as Berlin importunities. A visit to the city by Secretary Herter scheduled for late July assumed an increasingly important role, as our mission reported that the outlook of Berlin's leaders had reached "the gloomiest level" since the beginning of the crisis in November 1958.

Visits by American leaders to West Berlin during the fifties and sixties generally turned into massive demonstrations of regard for the United States by the rank-and-file Berliners of that generation. Coming when it did on July 25–26, the Herter reception was so spontaneously enthusiastic that it electrified the secretary and his party. I can recall the pressure of the friendly crowds as the cortege proceeded from the airport to U.S. headquarters. Many tossed flowers as they waved and chanted. The local police estimated the people on the streets as more than one and a half million. The rejuvenating effect on Berlin morale (and incidentally on American morale) was what we had hoped it would be. Herter returned to Geneva feeling that his excursion had been eminently worthwhile. In Berlin, he had given the right reassurances, both privately to officials and publicly to the people of West Berlin.

I have lived through a number of these emotional experiences as prominent Americans came to West Berlin, most notably the climactic visit of President Kennedy in 1963. They served a useful, sometimes necessary, psychological function for both the Berliners and the visitors. One problem was that other presidents, knowing of the tumultuous welcome given to Kennedy, have wanted equal treatment. This became more and more difficult to promise as the older generation of Berliners, with memories of the airlift, died off and as our involvement in Vietnam and the changing mood of the times created a substantial anti-American element in the city. When Nixon visited Berlin in 1969, we had to make elaborate arrangements, including a visit to the Siemens plant, where the workforce could be counted on to cheer, to shield the president from hostile demonstrations and to provide at least a modicum of enthusiasm.

One of the ritualistic requirements for high-level visitors to Berlin was that, in one formula or another, they repeat the standard American strategic support of the city. When I was ambassador in Bonn, on visits to the city that received any publicity, I had to reiterate in various ways our commitment to the defense of West Berlin. Failure to do so would immediately have been interpreted as a watering down of that commitment.

Eisenhower Enters the Diplomatic Fray

There was to be little rest for the weary. President Eisenhower had decided that, before he met with Khrushchev in the United States, he should visit the principal European capitals to make sure that the line he proposed to take would have the full support of Allied governments. I was one of the small group of officials that accompanied the president on his almost new Boeing 707 jet. As someone who has observed the elephantiasis from which official parties accompanying successive presidents have suffered, I can only look back on those simpler days with nostalgia. Part of the process by which our presidency became bloated and imperial has been the proliferation of both White House staff and security types who insist on going along when presidents travel abroad or for that matter in the United States. Host governments cannot help but get the impression that the presidential court is vastly overmanned.

Because we were such a small group, the substantively competent among us had much more direct access to a traveling president than would be possible today. I had been warned that Eisenhower could be irascible if provoked, but I saw no direct evidence of this. He obviously liked the limelight and the applause, as do most great individuals who derive energy from fame and the affection of crowds. Who could deny that the record of Eisenhower warranted such fame and affection? He was clearly no intellectual and had little gift for verbal improvisation. He did not lack, however, in shrewdness and fundamental common sense. He had that instinctive urge of the good diplomat to avoid confrontations that were bound to prove excessively costly and to seek peaceful resolution of disputes. The tortured and convoluted sentences in which he sometimes spoke at press conferences were frequently the result of his search for a way to reflect all the nuances in complicated situations, but at times they could also have been deliberately intended to bamboozle a press corps for which he did not necessarily have the highest respect.

Our first stop was Bonn, where concern over Berlin and the steadfastness of the Allies remained at a high level. The only other stops were to be in London and Paris, but NATO officials and the Italian prime minister were also to meet with the president during his days in Paris. As we pointed out in our general position paper for the trip, the president's visit to Europe would serve an essential psychological function before his meeting with Khrushchev.

I can well recall Eisenhower's first private meeting with Adenauer. Apart from the German interpreter, I was the only other person present and afterward wrote up a detailed memorandum of conversation. The talk at this meeting and a following session with senior advisers, including Secretary Herter, also present, was in fairly general terms about the world situation. Adenauer did mention that he had received a letter from Khrushchev a few days earlier advocating economic cooperation between the Soviet Union and the Federal Republic and that his response would be reasonable and moderate in tone. The principal discussion about Germany and Berlin was to take place at a second private meeting to which I was supposed to accompany Eisenhower. I was, however, prevented from doing so when Adenauer quickly led the president into his office and closed the door in my face. The German interpreter, Heinz Weber, was, of course, already in the room. Perhaps the chancellor was still piqued at my role as chairman of the American delegation to the Four-Power Working Group, but I was not very happy to sit in the anteroom.

American presidents all too frequently have let themselves be manipulated into permitting so-called private meetings in which, apart from the principals, the only other person present is the foreign interpreter. Since presidents are not in the habit of taking notes or writing their own memorandums of conversation, the result is that the only record of such meetings is that provided by the foreign interpreter. We have no way of judging how accurate such records are or whether distortions or omissions of what is said creep in. I have known Heinz Weber, a most talented interpreter, for a long time, and I have no doubt that over the years he has been thoroughly honest in his reporting. Whether, busy with translating, he can note down or recall all of the nuances and the precise meaning of all statements is a legitimate question. I always found it demeaning to have to rely on a subsequent briefing by the interpreter, as well as on oral summary remarks by the president, to ascertain what transpired at such private sessions. One point the chancellor had stressed was to be extremely wary of Soviet trickery. How reassured he actually was is not clear. In any event, the U.S.-German communiqué of August 27 publicly reaffirmed the standard U.S. policy toward Berlin.[28]

Eisenhower's meetings with Prime Minister Macmillan in London and at Chequers, with Secretary Herter present, produced no surprises, nor for that matter did his subsequent meetings in Paris, with President de Gaulle.

The problem of Berlin played less of a role than one might have anticipated given the continuing media and governmental interest in the subject. The president reassured de Gaulle, as he had Adenauer and Macmillan, that he did not intend to make any proposals to Khrushchev or to start any negotiations with him and that all discussion of the subject must take place within the framework of our existing rights in Berlin.

As a necessary preliminary to his meeting with Khrushchev, the president's trip served an obviously useful purpose. The word "exploratory" as a description of the forthcoming talks seemed to reassure the Europeans that the United States would not go marching off on its own. "Exploratory" was a word destined to play an important descriptive role again in 1961 during a later phase of the Berlin crisis. American officials were well aware in 1959, of course, that during the postwar period Europeans were ambivalent about bilateral U.S.-Soviet relations. They wanted an easing of tensions between the superpowers, but whenever the two got together at the summit level, they became nervous about the possibility that their own interests might be discussed, and even disposed of, behind their backs. This syndrome continued to operate up to the collapse of the Soviet Union.

Khrushchev Comes to America

The Khrushchev visit to the United States, September 15–27, had elements of both drama and farce, beginning with farce. Heads of state normally receive a salute of twenty-one guns upon arrival. What should Khrushchev receive as secretary general of the Communist Party in the Soviet Union and chairman of the Council of Ministers? The State Department division was sorely troubled; there were no real precedents. Our embassy in Moscow was instructed to make discreet inquiries. The response came quickly without equivocation: treat him as head of state. So he received a twenty-one-gun salute. The Soviet leader would have the opportunity to see such diverse parts of the country as an Iowa farm, the Golden Gate, and the Los Angeles freeway system. Despite all the uneasiness on the part of conservatives about the Khrushchev visit, there was considerable competition among politicians urging that his itinerary include their home state or city.

At a preliminary meeting on September 16, Gromyko and Herter agreed that the basic substantive talks would take place at Camp David, the favorite resort of successive presidents in the hills of Maryland, after Khrushchev's tour of the country. Khrushchev's days as sightseer went off reasonably well as he flew about the country in Eisenhower's presidential jet. The only real contretemps came in California after the chairman had expressed a desire to visit Disneyland. Both the Soviet and American security people had reacted negatively and vetoed the request on security grounds. Unfortunately, but perhaps understandably as an exercise in bureaucratic buck-passing, the Soviet officials blamed the refusal on the American side. Khrushchev bridled, attributing it all to American discourtesy, and on several occasions expressed his resentment. Thus even Mickey Mouse became politicized.

Once he had arrived at Camp David, after a restful evening, Khrushchev met with the president on the morning of September 26 with advisers present. I was seated directly behind Eisenhower on the assumption that I could whisper into his ear when required. He had his usual three-by-five-inch file cards containing briefings in the left front pocket of his jacket. The standard prescription was one subject per card, pica type, elite type not permitted. One could not get much information on a three-by-five card, but that was the way the president liked it. I once wrote a skit (fortunately never performed) about an imaginary meeting between Eisenhower and de Gaulle. Each had his own three-by-five briefing cards in his front left coat pocket (unfair to de Gaulle, who never required that sort of jog to memory), and at their initial meeting, as they bowed courteously to each other, all their cards fell on the floor. Both presidents then got on their knees to retrieve the appropriate cards, but the mess was hopeless. After frantically groping around, the great men called in their advisers, told them to pick up and sort out the cards and then exchange them so that there would be no need for further discussion.

In any event, Eisenhower had a clear idea of what he wanted to say to Khrushchev. The gist of his opening statement was that if an honorable way could be found to ease tension over Berlin, progress could be made on other questions affecting the two countries. During the earlier preliminary meeting in Washington on September 15, the president had said that he agreed with Khrushchev that the situation in Berlin was abnormal but that the Soviet Union should refrain from unilateral action against Berlin until the United States was able to discharge its obligation to the German people. Whether the president's language qualified as the most felicitous possible, no one could argue that the situation of Berlin—an exclave one hundred miles behind the Iron Curtain—was normal.

The exchanges that morning between Eisenhower and Khrushchev, while generally civil, really did not add much to the lines of argument pursued by both sides so exhaustively at Geneva. The Soviet leader played on the abnormality of the situation of Berlin and stressed the necessity of concluding a peace treaty with Germany. He did concede, however, that some period of time would be required to take the edge off the Berlin question so that the prestige of the United States might not be injured.

The afternoon session considerably raised the level of tension. Khrushchev reacted negatively to an American working paper that had been handed to him, charging that the only thing the paper provided for was a Soviet commitment not to sign a peace treaty with Germany. He added that the paper confirmed reports circulating before his arrival that the United States expected to impress him with its wealth and power so as to change the Soviet position on Germany and Berlin. Eisenhower tried to be conciliatory but stressed that he would have to resign as president if he ever accepted a time limit after which the United States would have to withdraw from Berlin.

That evening Eisenhower and Khrushchev took a walk in the woods; no complete record of their conversation apparently exists on the American side. I can recall seeing the two of them strolling down a path accompanied only by a Soviet interpreter. Eisenhower was not a tall man, but he towered over Khrushchev. In any event, the morning session of September 27 resulted in agreement that a brief joint communiqué should be drafted. Eisenhower summarized what he believed to be the understanding reached with Khrushchev: that the United States would not try to perpetuate the situation in Berlin and that the Soviet Union would not force the Western powers out of Berlin. Khrushchev accepted this formulation subject to the proviso that the statement with respect to Berlin should not be interpreted to mean that the two countries favored prolonging the occupation status of the city.[29]

At a subsequent internal meeting of the U.S. delegation, the president remarked, according to the memorandum describing the meeting, that there was "no choice but to resume negotiations so long as we in fact do not see a perpetuation of the situation in Berlin; clearly we did not contemplate 50 years in occupation there."[30] This was a variant of a theme that frequently appeared in Eisenhower's thinking about the abnormality of the postwar situation with sizable American forces still on the Continent.

The agreed communiqué released on September 27 contained the following language: "With respect to the specific question of Berlin, an understanding was reached, subject to the approval of the other parties directly concerned, that negotiations would be reopened with a view to achieving a solution which would be in accordance with the interests of all concerned and in the interest of the maintenance of peace."

This was not particularly elegant and, from the Western point of view, not entirely satisfactory. Eisenhower had held out for the inclusion of wording that would clearly avoid any implication of deadline, and when

Khrushchev at the last minute said he could not accept putting in the communiqué any suggestion of excluding a time limit within which he would move to sign a peace treaty with the GDR—a concession to which he previously, if reluctantly, agreed—the president objected that then he would go neither to a summit nor to Russia. Khrushchev quickly intervened, with a thought that might have seemed strange to anyone assuming he exercised absolute power, saying that he had to explain to the Politburo the reasons that led to his decision before he could make a public statement along the lines desired. He asked that the president wait until Tuesday morning before making the point publicly. Then he would confirm its accuracy in Moscow.

So it went. Eisenhower in a news conference on September 28 stated, inter alia, that the negotiations referred to in the communiqué "should not be prolonged indefinitely but there could be no fixed time limit on them." In turn, on September 29, Khrushchev confirmed "that talks on the Berlin question should be resumed, that no time limit whatsoever [was] to be established for them, but that they also should not be dragged out for an indefinite time." [31]

My impressions of Khrushchev, admittedly not as a direct interlocutor, were mixed. The man obviously had talent as a ham actor; he could turn on the anger or the charm seemingly at will. He displayed an underlying shrewdness and appeared determined not to be overly awed with what he saw in the United States; yet some of his remarks indicated that certain positive features of the country had sunk in. Nothing he said threw much new light on his underlying motives with respect to West Berlin. He clearly wanted us out, but why he was prepared to incur the risks that his unilateral challenge to the Western position obviously involved never emerged beyond the stereotyped arguments he repeated. He did, at least, modify the ultimatum that had been a part of the Soviet position in late 1958. Clearly burdened with heavy suspicion of American intentions, he did not seem to appreciate that his own behavior would inevitably arouse suspicions on the other side.

Physically he was not very impressive, short and roly-poly, though the Italian tailor who, it was reported, now fashioned his suits had weaned him away from the bell-bottom trousers and ill-fitting jackets that had been a characteristic of so many postwar Soviet officials. He stubbornly refused to wear anything but a presumably noncapitalist dark suit to the White House state dinner, which then presented the anomaly of Americans in white tie and tails contrasted with Soviet business suits. We were to see another and more frightening side of Khrushchev in Paris the following year.

By mutual agreement, the supposed return visit to Moscow of President Eisenhower was put off to the spring of 1960, to be followed by a four-power summit meeting. The visit to Moscow was, in fact, never to take place. Eisenhower's thinking moved toward favoring an initial summit meeting with the French and British present. For those of us concerned with the Berlin problem in Washington, the lifting of the time limit for Soviet unilateral action brought an enormous sense of relief. We had been working under great tension for nearly a year, facing the possibility of a confrontation over Berlin. While obviously we could not now relax, the next phase of our activities could be more deliberate and less ultimatum-linked. They began, however, at once. I can remember sending forward a memorandum on September 30, raising the question of whether the United States was now actively prepared to go to the summit, and if so, whether there should be a prior meeting of foreign ministers. On the substantive side, I asked whether we should be thinking in terms of a standstill agreement on Berlin along the lines of the Western proposals at Geneva of July 28 or whether our approach should now be more fundamental, aiming at an arrangement for Berlin that would last until reunification (I could not know that it would be more than a decade later that we would, in the Quadripartite Agreement of 1971, achieve the latter).

The Abortive Summit of May 1960

The rest of 1959 involved largely Western inter-Allied consultations. On October 9 letters went forward from the president to Macmillan, de Gaulle, and Adenauer arguing that the Camp David talks had removed many of the objections to a summit conference because the appearance of threat and duress had been sufficiently altered. Although Eisenhower did not use the expression himself then or later, the so-called Spirit of Camp David, to which Khrushchev and Soviet propaganda were to make frequent allusion, did seem to have provided a somewhat different psychological setting for consideration of the Berlin problem. He suggested that an East-West summit might take place early in December prior to the regular NATO ministerial meeting scheduled for December 15. This proposed timetable quickly proved unrealistic.

The Allied response varied. While Macmillan quickly accepted the proposal for a summit meeting, as one might have expected, and Adenauer was cautious but approving in principle, de Gaulle wanted to wait and observe Soviet behavior for a further period. A second message from Eisenhower sent on October 16 reiterated his arguments for moving toward an East-West summit. In the face of strong continuing objections from de Gaulle to any such early summit meeting (an attitude of reservation toward talking with the Soviets that was to create major difficulties with the United States in 1961), Eisenhower proposed an early four-power Western summit meeting to which the French president agreed, but (still thinking in terms of the triumvirate he really wanted) suggested a three-power summit, permitting Mr. Adenauer to join them when they discussed Germany. He also allowed that, if Khrushchev's behavior so warranted, one could think of inviting him to a summit conference, possibly toward April 1960.

Needless to say, we were immediately caught up in preparations for the Western summit now set to be held in Paris on December 19. The memorandums flew back and forth, exploring possible positions not only for the December meeting but for eventual use with the Soviets. Bilateral U.S. exchanges with the British and the Germans, as well as four-power preparatory meetings in Washington, filled November and early December. It seemed like no sooner had I drafted one memorandum than I was faced with demands for another. Although there was little specific guidance as to what new ideas might be theoretically acceptable, I knew pretty well what the limits of the possible and the desirable were. The working diplomat must operate within the frame of reference that events, personalities, and precedents impose if he is not to lose credibility and the willingness of his principals to accept his advice.

So it was that I found myself once again headed for Europe in mid-December to accompany Secretary Herter to the NATO ministerial meeting in Brussels, and from there to proceed to Paris for the Western summit (December 19–21). It was a strenuous week but on the whole satisfactory in terms of our objectives. We emerged with French agreement to meet at the summit with Khrushchev, with the reaffirmed resolve of the four governments that the West must not do anything that would result in West Berlin's falling into the hands of the Soviet Union, and with confirmation of the continuing validity of the positions taken by the Western foreign ministers at Geneva. As host chairman, President de Gaulle did a masterful job, at a final plenary session, of summarizing the range of agreement reached and the dangers as well as opportunities that the current situation seemed to involve.

I had met de Gaulle before, most recently during the Eisenhower visit to Paris in September, but had not witnessed him perform at his magisterial best. With his formidable presence and confident manner of speech, he dominated the plenary discussions. He seemed indeed to reflect the enormous tradition and historical grandeur of the France he felt himself to symbolize. He had already acquired that additional corpulence the high-calorie cuisine of the Élysée Palace imposed upon him, but with his height he carried it off reasonably well. So many have written so much about this man, about his strengths and weaknesses, apart from his own memoirs, that seemingly little remains to be said. I saw him generally at his most formidable, master of the situation as host and dominant inter-locutor, but one could discern as well a huge stubbornness, an unwilling-ness to bend when some flexibility would have advanced his purposes more, and a disdain for those who, for whatever reason, could not accept the logic of arguments that seemed to him impeccable.

Macmillan came across, on this occasion as on others, just about as one would expect: a polished, upper-class Englishman, a bit of an intellec-tual, and a consummate politician. His diction was generally excellent but sometimes punctuated by those hesitations and mannerisms that English people of his class and educational background seem to feel it necessary to impose upon themselves. He was entirely sincere, I believe, in his quest for peace in the shadow of the nuclear holocaust that he feared might result from a confrontation over Berlin.[32]

Adenauer was, as usual, cautious but interposed no real objections to the course of action so clearly favored by Eisenhower. He stressed the need for careful preparations for the meeting with Khrushchev, from which he would, of course, be excluded, reflecting his continuing fear (not specifi-cally articulated on this occasion) that, somehow or other, the Western side might be tempted to make unacceptable concessions.

The upshot of the exchanges with Khrushchev that followed the West-ern summit was agreement on May 16, 1960, as the starting date for the four-power East-West summit meeting to be held in Paris. The months before, we knew, would be exhaustingly busy for those of us who would be doing the preparatory work for what we assumed would be a meeting of major historical significance.

As any experienced Washington bureaucrat could foretell, the prospect of a four-power summit with the Soviets involving the president would inevitably generate even more than the usual amount of paper and pre-paratory meetings. Even though the White House staff had not yet as-sumed its present elephantine proportions, the pressures of hierarchy assured intensive months of work for the State Department. The agreed timetable was that a four-power Working Group report should be ready for review by the four Allied foreign ministers at a special meeting to be held in Washington April 12–14.

Although I could not fully articulate my reasons—since they were partly hunch—I was not particularly sanguine that the forthcoming sum-mit would produce any real solution to the Berlin crisis. There were not many new ideas floating around that would advance the discussion much beyond the intensive Working Group and ministerial deliberations of

1959. In a memorandum dated January 15, somewhat grandiloquently entitled "A Study of the Possible Consequences of the Western Powers' Failure to Reach Agreement with the Soviet Union on Berlin," I expressed the view that the time had come "when there must be a closer connection between the quadripartite development of a negotiating position on Berlin on the one hand and tripartite contingency planning on the other." One of my points was that the West Germans should be brought more into Allied contingency planning, partly because the economic sanctions that they could impose on the GDR were likely to be among our most effective countermeasures.[33]

The Four-Power Working Group report reached completion in time for the meeting of foreign ministers. The section on tactics had an important place, and the foreign ministers approved its basic approach, agreeing that the Western powers should be ready to table a proposal for a plebiscite in all of Germany on the Soviet and Western concepts of a German peace treaty. The report also contained a possible proposal for the reunification of Berlin. The foreign ministers directed the Working Group to prepare some standby papers that would be available for presentation at the summit if it seemed desirable. None of these, as it turned out, were ever to be used, but in any event the Working Group, after concentrated meetings in Washington, completed its revised report. We had streamlined, inter alia, the so-called Solution C of the April 1959 London Working Group report. This had been recommended as an ultimate fallback position but was, of course, never used. It provided a sophisticated but nonexplicit version of the old agency theory, which had caused such a storm when first articulated by Secretary Dulles. It would have had the effect of freezing existing procedures for Allied traffic no matter who executed them.

In mid-March (March 14–17), Chancellor Adenauer visited Washington. He seemed less perturbed about Allied preparations for discussions on Berlin at the summit than he had been the previous year. He was to become much more upset by proposals that General Lauris Norstad, the Supreme Allied Commander Europe, had advanced for a European inspection zone (usually referred to as the Norstad Plan). Norstad, who was also the commander of Live Oak, the special military headquarters that had been set up in Europe to deal with the Berlin crisis, had put forward some ideas for possible discussion at the summit. These would have involved mobile ground inspection in as large an area as practical between the Atlantic and the Urals, aerial inspection over a somewhat lesser area, and overlapping radar stations on the Western and Eastern perimeters of inspection aimed at avoiding surprise surface attack.

Although Adenauer and de Gaulle (with somewhat less vehemence) both opposed the Norstad Plan, which was never put to the Soviets, ideas of this kind had continuing viability and some actual implementation in the post-Helsinki period. In 1960, however, they did not have much prospect in the face of the chancellor's adamant opposition. He simply did not want any Soviet inspectors wandering around the Federal Republic.

Both Macmillan and de Gaulle followed the chancellor on visits to Washington. They did not add anything significantly new to the discussion of Berlin, although the French president was able to report on the conversation he had had with Khrushchev during the latter's visit to France in March 1960.

Early May brought a number of meetings of foreign ministers and the Working Group intended to lead up to the summit. The four-power and NATO ministerial sessions in Istanbul (May 1–4) took place under highly dramatic and unusual circumstances. Turkey was aflame with domestic unrest, and Prime Minister Adnan Menderes had declared martial law on April 29. As we rode from the airport to the Istanbul Hilton Hotel, where most of the delegations were quartered, the atmosphere of the city reflected tension and foreboding of worse to come. Tanks and soldiers appeared in mass formations, but the rioting and demonstrations that had precipitated the declaration of martial law seemed to have been put down, at least for the time being. The government insisted on proceeding with the NATO conference, including the various social events that had been scheduled.

The four Western foreign ministers had their usual prior meeting in the Hilton Hotel. As expected, they asked the Working Group to prepare some new language to take account of their discussion and particularly some points raised by von Brentano. The ministers could not decide whether the summit should avoid the details of a Berlin arrangement, limiting itself to a directive to a subordinate body to work out the specifics, or whether it should aim at an agreement on Berlin. The ministers agreed to meet again in Paris on the eve of the summit. Moving to a nearby suite in the hotel, the Working Group engaged in a lengthy, somewhat unreal discussion with members sitting on beds and documents scattered over coffee tables. We finally agreed on compromise language that, we hoped, would capture the not entirely clear intent of the ministers.

Meanwhile, the situation in Istanbul, and elsewhere in the country, had further deteriorated. On the morning of May 2, the various NATO delegations proceeded by car through tank- and troop-lined streets to the site of the meeting, an imposing palace. We were to go through the same experience before and after each session; whatever the turbulence in other parts of the city, the government had effectively sealed off the NATO meeting with an impressive display of force. But even the most insensitive diplomat could not help but feel the electricity in the atmosphere, the lurking threat of violence in the streets. That evening, despite the curfew, we all moved through eerily deserted streets under intensive guard, from the hotel to the enormous Dolmabaczi Palace, where the Turkish hosts offered a spectacular buffet followed by dancing. They had even thought to provide dancing partners for the largely male NATO delegates—young Foreign Ministry employees flown in from Ankara. I can recall dancing with one rather handsome young lady who spent an entire fox trot assuring me that her presence and that of her colleagues should not be mistaken as a sign of support for the government. The whole evening was surely one of the most bizarre that any of us had ever experienced, but the government had decided to carry on. It was not to carry on much longer.

On the following evening Foreign Minister Zorlu hosted a grand dinner, again for all members of all delegations, in the ballroom of the Hilton Hotel. He made the usual toast and pro-NATO remarks, but his heart was obviously not in it. He knew much better than any of his guests how serious the situation had become. A military coup, some days after we had all disbanded back to our respective countries, put both Menderes and Zorlu behind bars. They were executed by hanging shortly thereafter.

Meanwhile, Soviet propaganda had not relaxed in the spirit of Camp David. The abuse particularly singled out the Federal Republic and Adenauer, but it also repeated Khrushchev's previous threat to sign a separate peace treaty with the GDR. This was apparently the Soviet leader's way of softening up the West as part of his presummit tactics. Secretary Herter and Undersecretary of State Douglas C. Dillon made speeches in response stressing that the Allies would not bow to threats. One could hardly describe the atmosphere, and the prospects for May 16, as propitious. Less than a week before that date, the Soviets made a proposal to the Western powers, the main feature of which stipulated that the end of any temporary agreement on Berlin along the lines discussed at Geneva would be a peace treaty and the transformation of West Berlin into a free city. It was hard to describe this as anything but a step backward. Instructed by the foreign ministers, the Four-Power Working Group sprang into action on May 14 in Paris to produce a paper entitled "Western Critique of New Soviet Proposals on Berlin to Be Put Forward If Soviet Proposals Are Released for Publication."

An even more serious shadow hung over the summit. On May 1 Soviet defenses brought down an American U-2 high-altitude reconnaissance plane near the city of Sverdlovsk, setting in motion a chain of causation that led to the collapse of the Paris summit. In his memoirs, President Eisenhower describes in detail the whole U-2 episode, including his ultimate and unprecedented acknowledgment of responsibility for espionage activity, after a cover story concocted in the State Department lost all persuasiveness. Suffice it to say here that, on May 5, Khrushchev went public announcing that an American had been shot down over the Soviet Union.[34] Before he reached Paris, the Soviet leader engaged in a rising crescendo of invective. We had reports in Washington that he was under pressure to scuttle the forthcoming meeting, and when he called on de Gaulle during the morning of May 15, he left a memorandum detailing conditions that would have to be met before he would attend a summit conference. In essence, these called for an undertaking by the United States not to violate Soviet frontiers by plane flights, to condemn such "provocative acts committed in the past," and to promise to punish "those responsible for such actions."

Although some advised him not to proceed to Paris under the circumstances, the president refused to accept the onus for torpedoing the conference. He arrived in Paris on May 15 and that evening met with de Gaulle and Macmillan. Although they foresaw trouble, no one really had any idea what Khrushchev would do or say. When the three met with Khrushchev the following morning, the latter read a vituperative statement, withdrew the invitation to Eisenhower to visit Moscow, and proposed that the summit conference be postponed for approximately six to eight months (obviously meaning after the American president was no longer in office). After a further inconclusive exchange between Eisenhower and Khrushchev, which the latter described as unsatisfactory, and futile interventions by Macmillan and de Gaulle, Khrushchev and his delegation stalked out of the Élysée Palace. He had previously made the point that he did not consider the morning session a summit conference but merely a preliminary meeting dealing with procedural matters. Thus the session (if it could be called that) ended in somewhat of a shambles. I can remember Eisenhower shaking his head and muttering as he passed through the front door of the Élysée, "This is the damndest conference I've ever attended."[35]

On the following day, de Gaulle tried to reconvene the four-power meeting, but Khrushchev did not show up. He sent several messages to the effect that, while he would attend a preliminary meeting to ascertain if conditions would permit a summit conference, he was not prepared as the situation stood to attend such a conference. While still in Paris, he turned on the histrionics full blast at a press conference. After considerable bluster and threat, he made the point that the existing situation with respect to Berlin would "apparently have to be preserved till the heads of government meeting, which, . . . [he] hoped, [would] take place in six or eight months."[36]

Speculation about the motives behind Khrushchev's behavior in Paris is endlessly fascinating, at least for diplomatic historians. The Western foreign ministers meeting on the margin of the nonexistent summit came to the conclusion that the Soviet Union had wanted to wreck the conference and that the U-2 incident was merely a pretext. I am not absolutely sure, although this was the conventional wisdom at the time. Khrushchev in his memoirs says little on the subject that would throw any additional light on his behavior; his resentment toward Eisenhower, expressed in more general but unflattering terms, does emerge.

Certainly the abortive Paris summit was one of the more curious episodes in modern diplomacy. One might ask whether any possible middle ground existed that would fall between Eisenhower's full acceptance of responsibility for the U-2 fiasco and the admission of ignorance by President Reagan in the Irangate affair. The president felt fully justified in what he did, arguing that criticism of the wisdom of the U-2 flights failed to take account of the valuable information they had provided. There did seem to be a genuine element of personal affront in Khrushchev's rage, and perhaps his angry words also reflected chagrin that his elaborate shell game with dummy missiles in silos had been exposed. He demonstrated in Paris once again that he was a consummate ham, and one could never be sure what his underlying level of emotion really was.

The American delegation to the summit that never took place returned to Washington in a state of puzzlement and some anxiety. We did not know, of course, precisely what Khrushchev had in mind, whether he really meant nothing would happen to change the status quo in Berlin before another summit meeting. His vitriolic attacks on the Western position hardly suggested a willingness simply to wait while doing nothing. The Soviet leader actually meant what he said, but this did not mean that the rest of 1960 proved relatively tranquil in and about Berlin. The East Germans, obviously disappointed by Khrushchev's unwillingness to move immediately, were allowed as consolation to step up harassment of civilian access to and from Berlin. Given Western uncertainty about Khrushchev's real intentions, the immediate emphasis shifted to contingency planning for the eventuality of Soviet unilateral action. Meeting in Paris on May 18, the Western foreign ministers asked for a review of existing plans to be presented to the three heads of government. We produced such a paper within a few hours. Whether it consoled either the ministers or their principals I would very much doubt. The fear was that Khrushchev, stopping off in East Berlin on his way back to Moscow, would use the opportunity to launch his long-threatened unilateral action. Actually, the tone of his speech in that city was not particularly inflammatory, and he repeated his willingness to wait for the expected East-West summit to be held in six to eight months to find a solution to the problem of a peace treaty with the two German states.

In this uneasy atmosphere, we waited out the remaining months of 1960. It was clear to those of us working on the Berlin problem that the absence of Soviet pressure against our basic position would only be temporary and that the best we could do was to hold the line during the declining days of the Eisenhower administration.

We had long since concluded that denunciation by the West Germans of the Interzonal Trade Agreement between the Federal Republic and the GDR represented the single most effective economic sanction that the West had available. The Bonn government itself doubted this as well as the British and the French, but when, in late August and September, East Germany began a series of harassments of civilian access to Berlin, which lasted through the fall months, the West Germans finally took action along the lines we favored. This quickly led to East German concessions that permitted an understanding on December 29 to restore the Interzonal Trade Agreement effective January 1, 1961. We felt satisfied that the outcome vindicated our confidence in the effectiveness of economic sanctions against the GDR, given the very favorable terms extended to the East Germans by the Interzonal Trade Agreement.

In a conversation with me on the margin of the NATO ministerial meeting in Paris (December 16–18, 1960), German foreign minister van Brentano acknowledged that the apparent effectiveness of the West German denunciation of the Interzonal Trade Agreement had surprised him personally. His government had not appreciated what a potent weapon it possessed.

There were further difficulties with the East Germans extending into early 1961 that made the Western powers reluctant to resume the issuance of temporary travel documents to East Germans, but these too were resolved by March 1961.

Other problems also arose in the last months of 1960 that made the Khrushchev lull a fairly turbulent period. They generated much paper and inter-Allied discussion as well as some consideration of possible proposals to be made in 1961, but the impending change of regime in the United States made all this activity inconclusive.

6 Kennedy and the Berlin Crisis

· ·

State Department officials in Washington are bound to be uneasy when administrations change, particularly when a new party takes over. The desire to sweep out the old with a new broom, to write off existing officials and the policies they represent as irrevocably tainted by their past associations, has occurred all too frequently. We did not know what to expect when, after the turn of the year, Kennedy appointees began to turn up in the State Department building to prepare for the transition later in January. The new secretary of state designate, Dean Rusk, occupied an office on the ground floor normally part of the international conference area of the department. A few days after his arrival he asked me to come and see him to discuss the Berlin situation. I quickly learned that he knew how to ask the right questions. He shared the natural skepticism of the incoming new team about the possible foibles of the old, but this was a highly intelligent man prepared to listen and to revise any preconceived ideas he might have brought with him. Before leaving I told him that I was preparing some detailed memorandums on the Berlin crisis that I hoped would be useful to the new administration.

Thomas Schoenbaum's fine biography of Dean Rusk, published in 1988, does justice to his subject, a man whom I came to admire for his courage, shrewdness, eloquence, and quality of mind. Rusk's own later book, *As I Saw It*, confirmed that this was a man of character and ability.[1] He was an outstanding public servant, and one can hope that the historical judgment of his general performance will not overly stress his role in the Vietnam tragedy. Nor should it base itself on the sometimes negative appraisals of the man in superficial quickie outpourings by members of the Kennedy White House. Their books, in my view, reflected the bias of White House staffers whose actual position and influence on policy were somewhat less than they described and contained numerous factual errors about subjects concerning which I had intimate personal knowledge.

We learned early on that Foy Kohler, who had taken over from Livy Merchant as assistant secretary of state for European affairs in 1960, and I would remain in our positions to preserve some continuity and expertise. Kohler was a wizened little man, sharp as a whip, with much resolve and diplomatic skill. As a Soviet expert, he knew a great deal about the USSR, a country to which he was later to become ambassador. With my knowledge of things German, I thought we made an excellent team, and I was glad to know he would be there to help fight the inevitable bureaucratic battles.

One of the realities that emerged quickly enough was that a number of new people in the White House, and some in the State Department, did not have a high regard for the handling of the Berlin problem by the Eisenhower administration. They felt the U.S. position had been far too inflexible and that it should be possible to clear away the whole business by a proper approach to negotiations. None of these officials had any operational responsibility for Berlin, and as a matter of fact, while able to raise a considerable hue and cry during the spring and summer of 1961, they had little effective impact on the way the Kennedy administration's Berlin policy eventually developed. Since these were some of the same officials who rushed into print with books shortly after leaving office, their version of events has tended to create a number of false impressions.[2]

Khrushchev did not wait very long for the new administration to settle in before once again taking the offensive on Berlin. An aide-mémoire addressed to the German Federal Republic on February 17 (obviously also intended for reading in Washington) reiterated the standard Soviet position on Berlin and maintained that any interim arrangement for West Berlin would have to be for a strictly limited time and that at the expiry of this period, if no peace treaty with the two German states had been concluded, the Soviet Union would sign a peace treaty with the GDR. This would mean "ending the occupation regime in West Berlin with all the attending consequences," particularly with regard to communications "by land, water, and air."[3] Without setting a specific deadline, the aide-mémoire came fairly close to being another ultimatum, and Khrushchev referred to it as stating the Soviet position in a discussion with U.S. ambassador Llewellyn Thompson on March 9. Thompson used the occasion to give the Soviet leader a letter from the president expressing the hope that the two could meet soon for an informal exchange of views.[4]

In April, the Kennedy administration ran into the totally distracting quagmire of the Bay of Pigs. It was a colossal fiasco. How much effect it had on Khrushchev's evaluation of the new president we do not precisely know, but it cannot have raised his assessment of the quality of American leadership or its handling of a crisis situation. In this way, it could well have influenced his evaluation of Kennedy's resolve and, hence, his tactics at the Vienna meeting that he was to have with the president a few months later. Those of us laboring in the vineyard of Berlin affairs had ample reason to think that our overall position had been weakened.

Meanwhile, we in the State Department were trying to bring our knowledge of the period since the original Khrushchev challenge of November 1958 into an educative process that the White House had itself encouraged by a specific request from McGeorge Bundy, special assistant to the president for national security affairs. I wrote a lengthy memorandum entitled "The Problem of Berlin," which we sent forward.[5] In it, I attempted to pull together what I believed to be the main elements of the situation as it had developed and what we might expect in the future. One never knows with certainty how much impact on thinking such an attempt at comprehensive analysis may have, but I believe it helped to bring a certain measure of realism, about both possibilities and limitations, to those who read it.

President Kennedy had also asked former secretary of state Dean Acheson to examine the Berlin problem and to make appropriate recommendations. Acheson submitted the first version of his report on April 3; it was to cause waves. During the visit to Washington in early April of Prime Minister Macmillan, Kennedy requested Acheson to make an initial presentation at a meeting on April 5. Although the latter's views were still somewhat tentative, they did not have a particularly soothing effect on the British, who did agree, however, that Berlin contingency planning required urgent review.[6] British skittishness about any prior commitment to a preordained course of action in the event of serious harassment of Allied access to Berlin was to be a continuing feature of contingency planning during the Kennedy presidency, as it had been during the Eisenhower period. While some inveighed against what to them seemed like excessive timidity, I always viewed the British position as responsible. In the nuclear age, no government could accept being bound by an iron-clad formula for action without opportunity for review at the highest levels.

The stream of foreign visitors next brought Chancellor Adenauer to Washington (April 12–13). The visit provided a study in contrasts. The shrewd, old German leader (then eighty-five) had to deal with a president half his age and did not know quite what to expect. He could not help harking back to the good old days, particularly his close relationship with John Foster Dulles. It became clear very quickly to those of us at the initial meeting that he and Kennedy were not going to hit it off very well. Adenauer could speak with clarity and authority, but his concerns seemed to the bright younger man to be excessive and those of someone grown too old in office. The peculiar strength and staying power of the chancellor did not come across to a group of Kennedyites largely ignorant of German postwar history. Only Dean Rusk, disagree as he might on certain points, recognized and acknowledged the authority of the man. It was an ironic chronological detail that Adenauer resigned from the chancellorship on October 16, 1963, little more than a month before the assassination of President Kennedy on November 22, 1963.

The discussion of Berlin during the Adenauer visit added little new to the subject. Foreign Minister von Brentano stressed German fears that harassment of access to Berlin would begin with civilian rather than Allied military traffic, but this did not really jibe with what we believed to be the more likely scenario, particularly after the way the GDR had been brought to heel late in 1960 by West German economic sanctions.[7] The chancellor was cordial enough to me personally. Perhaps he had forgiven me for my role in the Four-Power Working Group, or perhaps he now considered Kohler and me as elements of stability in the midst of all these bright, young Kennedy men who wanted to find an easy way out of the Berlin crisis.

My first trip abroad with Secretary Rusk took us to Oslo for the spring meeting of NATO foreign ministers. Oslo did not prove to be as melodramatic a setting as Istanbul had been a year earlier. We arrived fairly late on May 7, 1960, and I can recall that the first concern of the American delegation was to find something to eat. Norwegian labor laws being what they were, our hotel's kitchen had long since closed, and the very idea of late-night room service had become repugnant. After much prowling around, the hungry Americans were finally able to arouse some help that eventually produced a platter of sandwiches and bottles of beer. Our hunger thus assuaged, we were able to turn in with strength for the morrow. The three Western ministers, without the Germans, had also met earlier that evening. While others foraged for food, I made notes of what turned out to be a rather desultory discussion of Soviet intentions with respect to Germany and Berlin.

Khrushchev had injected himself into the discussion in a speech on May 2. He stated that the problem of Berlin and of a separate peace treaty would be solved during 1961. He was prepared to wait no longer than after the West German elections in September and the Soviet party congress in October. The meeting of the quadripartite foreign ministers on May 8 took note of this statement but agreed that there appeared to be little basis for any Western initiative leading to negotiations with the Soviets. As note taker at the meeting, which wandered off to a lengthy discussion of Laos, I felt that Secretary Rusk had demonstrated his skills as a discussion leader but that no one on the Western side had any really new ideas as to how to deal with the Berlin problem.[8] The NATO foreign ministers' meeting that followed on May 8–9 likewise added nothing significantly novel to discussion of the subject; the initiative remained clearly with Khrushchev. That was not at all strange, given the fact that the Western side was quite satisfied with the Berlin status quo.

In any event, Khrushchev had invited Kennedy to meet with him in Vienna in early June, and, contrary to Rusk's advice, the president agreed to such a summit meeting on June 3–4. The White House also quickly made arrangements for a stopover in Paris en route. Needless to say, President de Gaulle felt this was entirely appropriate and proper; he decided to put on a grand spectacle, including a state dinner in the Hall of Mirrors at Versailles. We, of course, do not have anything comparable in Washington, and since the British still have their royal family occupying palaces, neither do they. One of the unanticipated benefits of the French Revolution was to provide the elected governments of France incomparable settings for state dinners and other functions. As a member of the American delegation, I received invitations to the social functions. One could not help but enjoy the combination of spectacle and cuisine at Versailles. The Hall of Mirrors in candlelight is a shimmering kaleidoscope of reflected brilliance, and the service by numerous liveried waiters seemed to have come straight out of the Sun King's times. I have sometimes found the menus at French state dinners a bit on the heavy side. A big slab of paté de foie gras, no matter how delicious, accompanied by a vintage sauterne, served as sort of an interlude, weighs heavily on body and soul. No wonder affluent Frenchmen so often complained of *crise de foie*, once almost an occupational disease among certain classes in France.

A French official whom I knew passed on to me a story so revelatory of the persistence of monarchist values in France that, despite its possible apocryphal nature, is worth repeating. The VIP suite in the Quai d'Orsay palace, generally reserved for heads of state, boasts among its fixtures a gilded bathtub on a marble dais. In making a last-minute inspection of the facilities before the arrival of the Kennedys, a protocol officer noticed to his horror that there was a ring around the bathtub. In some agitation, he summoned one of the cleaning women and pointed to the ring. "Why yes, I saw it," she responded, "but it was left there by the Queen of England" (who had been a recent visitor to Paris) "and I thought the Kennedys would be honored to know they were using the same bathtub as the queen."

The actual discussion of Berlin in Paris did not get much beyond a reiteration by de Gaulle of the need to stand firm and of the futility of discussing the subject with Khrushchev. If the Soviets moved unilaterally on Berlin, general war would result.[9] This was a line to which de Gaulle and his foreign minister, Couve de Murville, would adhere in the months to come.

I enjoyed one of the more bizarre traveling experiences of my life in getting from Paris to Vienna. Secretary Rusk had thought I should be in Vienna the day before the president arrived, and arrangements were made for me to ride on the military transport plane used to move Kennedy's armor-plated limousine. There were always two of these available on presidential trips to more than one country so that there could always be one awaiting him upon arrival. Whether this constituted a prudent use of taxpayers' money is at least a debatable question, but the prescribed dictates of security override all such considerations, despite the fact that, of all Western states, we have probably the poorest record of protecting our chief executives from injury or death. In any event, upon boarding the plane, I quickly discovered that the only comfortable seat other than those of the crew was in the strapped-down Cadillac, the door of which was fortunately open. I climbed in and then rode in vicarious style until our landing in Vienna. One can really stretch out in a stretch limousine. I can recommend it for those rare individuals likely to have the opportunity to sit in one on a plane.

Vienna is one of those cities that either charms or repels. A whole group of American sentimentalists assigned to Vienna in early postwar years never forgot those glory days of youthful adventure amid the monuments of empire. As aficionados, they could reminisce endlessly about the subject. I came to know the city well only relatively late, when it provided a place of occasional weekend refuge during my Budapest days. If I have always found it a bit schmaltzy, it also exercises a certain fascination and charm both as a relic of bygone glory and as a contributor to some of the main intellectual currents of our time. The wines and the great music are always there to provide relaxation and aesthetic satisfaction.

The Vienna Encounter of Kennedy and Khrushchev

Many have written much about the confrontation between Kennedy and Khrushchev in Vienna. The Soviet leader obviously came there thinking he could rough up the president, perhaps after having drawn the wrong conclusion about his character from the Bay of Pigs fiasco, and, by threatening him on the Berlin issue, force concessions from a bullied young man. I think it is clear that Kennedy did not expect the verbal fusillade that he received. While the briefing materials prepared for him anticipated no softening of the basic Soviet position, they understated the vehemence with which Khrushchev would make his case.

The first day of the meeting, June 3, went off about as expected, dedicated as it was to the general state of Soviet-American relations and to such specific topics as Laos, Cuba, and China. Khrushchev did not lose the opportunity to ridicule Kennedy over the Bay of Pigs, but he did not signal the aggressive stance he would take on the morning of June 4, when Germany and Berlin would be the topic.

As Austria's chief of state, President Anton Raab had insisted on being the host that evening at a grand dinner in the Schoenbrun Palace. It was not quite Versailles, but the past splendors of the Austro-Hungarian Empire, abetted by modern floodlights that bathed the gardens in magnificent illumination, were grand enough. Apart from the two delegations, seemingly all of Austria's political and economic elite had crowded in. The trouble was that the imperial kitchens had long since fallen into disuse, and Vienna's leading caterer had to bring in all the food and drink. It became clear with the soup course that something had gone dramatically wrong. It was stone cold. From my vantage point just below the head table, I could literally see Raab's face getting red from the neck up. There were whispered and agitated discussions with liveried flunkies. Then real disaster struck. The meat course was also stone cold. With flushed face, Raab scolded whoever was within range while at the same time apologizing profusely to Kennedy and Khrushchev. When the time came for toasts, he had calmed down and joked, "At least the white wine was supposed to be cold." He did not add that this was just another example of Austrian *Schlamperei*. The caterer tried to explain it all in the Vienna morning press of June 4: the problem, he claimed, was that there were no warming facilities at Schoenbrun, and without them, it had proved impossible to keep the food from cooling off. I doubt that the Austrian government used his services again.

Khrushchev began on June 4 by stating that a line had to be drawn under World War II and a peace treaty signed. If the United States and the Federal Republic refused to participate in this process, the Soviet Union would sign a peace treaty with the GDR alone. This would end the state of war, and all commitments stemming from the German surrender would lose their validity. This would apply, he went on, to institutions, occupation rights, and access to Berlin, including the air corridors. A free city of West Berlin would then be established.

There was nothing really new in all this. He had made the same points on other occasions. His bullying tone and explicit threats in the private discussion that followed after lunch could, however, only shock the president. Observing Kennedy's reaction when he came out of the improvised conference room in the American ambassador's residence, I could not help but think back to those early days in the Allied Control Commission for Germany when aggressive and bullying Soviet military officials also managed completely to turn around previously well-disposed Americans like General Clay. Referring to the possibility of an interim agreement, Khrushchev indicated that the USSR was prepared to wait six months while the two German states negotiated but could not accept further delay and would probably sign a peace treaty, with all its consequences, at the end of the year. In response to the president's specific question as to whether the treaty would result in blockage of Allied access, Khrushchev answered that the GDR would then have complete control over access rights, and if the United States wanted war that would be its problem. Kennedy observed in conclusion that it would be "a cold winter." [10]

One obviously had to take the Soviet leader seriously, although he had canceled previous ultimatums on Berlin. The young president did not like what he had heard and temperamentally was bound to react somewhat differently than the vastly more experienced President Eisenhower (the Supreme Allied Commander of the victorious Western forces in World War II, he had had much background in the evaluation and exercise of power). There was certainly high drama involved at Vienna, and the fact that the president had brought with him to Washington a group of highly intelligent but also highly excitable young men from Cambridge, Massachusetts, guaranteed an almost immediate effusion of evocative description and instant opinion. This did not mean that the experienced professionals who were also present at Vienna did not share the president's concern. We were somewhat less emotional and likely to argue that careful analysis, as well as full consultation with our allies, should precede any public taking of positions. We had not reached the conclusion, later expressed by de Gaulle, that Khrushchev was basically bluffing, and no one supposed that the Soviet challenge did not portend a serious crisis over Berlin. In any event, we all knew that the period ahead would be one of many meetings, intense discussion, and a demand for new approaches, sometimes from those who had never really understood the old approaches.

I well remember how a small group of us waited in somber mood outside the door of the room where Kennedy and Khrushchev were meeting. A grim-faced president finally emerged and repeated something to the effect that it would be a long cold winter. Khrushchev had handed the president an aide-mémoire detailing the Soviet position. [11] It added nothing significantly new to what he had said orally, but it constituted the formal diplomatic document to which a response would have to be made. The

Soviet ambassadors in London and Paris delivered similar documents to the British and French governments so that careful tripartite coordination of replies would be essential—a nicety seemingly lost on some of the White House wordsmiths. On his way back from Vienna the president did stop over on June 5 in London to discuss the Vienna meeting with Prime Minister Macmillan and Foreign Secretary Sir Alec Douglas-Home. In his television and radio report to the nation on June 6, Kennedy said that he had spent two very somber days in talking to Khrushchev and that their "most somber talks were on the subject of Germany and Berlin."[12]

A Turbulent Post-Vienna Period

A threefold task faced those of us working on the Berlin problem: to prepare a reply to the Soviet aide-mémoire, to review our contingency planning, and to reexamine our basic negotiating position on Germany and Berlin to be ready for possible eventual discussions with the Soviets. Achieving these desiderata was to prove more complicated, and at times more frustrating, than any of us had envisaged.

The handling of the reply to the Soviet aide-mémoire quickly became a somewhat farcical operation because of White House sloppiness; however, it was the State Department that had to bear the onus for the delay in our response. The accounts in Schoenbaum's biography of Dean Rusk and in Rusk's *As I Saw It* are essentially correct as far as they go,[13] but given the number of highly inaccurate versions that have received general acceptance ever since the early accounts of "the one thousand days" before the president's assassination, some review here of what actually happened may make at least a small further contribution to the cause of historical accuracy.

On June 10, the Soviet Union made public the text of its aide-mémoire of June 4, thus confirming to the world its hard position on Berlin. This was followed by a series of pronouncements during June and July by Khrushchev reaffirming that a peace treaty with Germany must come "this year" with all of the consequences for access to Berlin that this would entail.[14] These not only kept the Berlin problem on the front pages of the world press but also heightened Kennedy's impatience at what seemed to him to be State Department dilatoriness in getting a response ready to the aide-mémoire. Rumors circulated around Washington that disarray in the Western camp and lack of American determination were causing the delay.

We had actually prepared a draft reply refuting the aide-mémoire point by point as early as June 7. Although a number of changes were obviously made along the way, its basic approach and argumentation survived into the final text. Unfortunately for us, the president seemed to be unaware of this. He was also unaware that we had sent our original draft over to the White House for comment shortly after it was prepared.[15] It was greeted with complete silence, and our efforts to obtain an initial reaction elicited only vague responses. What had actually happened, we later learned, was that our draft had ended up in the safe of Ralph Dungan, a presidential assistant, to which only he had the combination. He then went off on a two-week holiday.

In order to speed up the coordinating process, despite the absence of any White House comment, we held tripartite and quadripartite meetings in Washington on June 14–17 designed to obtain an agreed position on the reply to the document that all three governments had received. The Four-Power Working Group on Germany and Berlin continued its work of analysis in Washington and on June 30 agreed, at the insistence of the French, that three separate communications with identical operative language be sent. On the same day the State Department sent a new draft to the White House. We had already sent over a second copy of the original version when it became clear that the White House could not locate the document resting in Dungan's safe, but once again the second copy was misplaced for some days. We were without effective White House input during our discussions with the British, French, and Germans. Needless to say, no one in the White House whispered a word of this fiasco to Kennedy, and the president was left with the impression that the State Department was solely responsible for the delay.

The White House reaction to our June 30 draft came quickly enough. The president and his speechwriters apparently did not like its formal tone and legal arguments. Moreover, it did not propose a clear negotiating position. What they wanted was new language and creative new ideas. In practice, of course, being creative in the White House meant little more than indulging in fulsome rhetoric, and Ted Sorensen produced precisely that in what was supposed to be a shorter and simpler version. Our reaction in the department was clearly one of horror. Sending a diplomatic instrument couched in that kind of flamboyant phraseology would have made us a laughing stock among our colleagues, and the British and French would never accept modifying their texts to incorporate such language. The inexperienced White House staffers obviously could not distinguish between a formal diplomatic communication intended for the historical record and a political speech. They likewise seemed to forget, as they did subsequently, that we were in this together with the British and the French as tripartite occupying powers in Berlin and that we could not be singing out loud to a different tune. When this point finally sank in, if only temporarily, Kennedy recognized that the note, as it had evolved, could not be significantly changed without risking protracted further delay. Final coordination with the British and French and a delay of a few days to permit a German memorandum in response to an earlier memorandum from the USSR to be delivered, as agreed, ahead of ours all required another two weeks—but on July 17 the American, British, and French notes went forward for delivery in Moscow. The president insisted, however, that a truncated version of the Sorensen draft be issued as a separate U.S. statement. This appeared on July 19, and Kennedy read a portion of it during his press conference the same day.[16]

I have devoted some space to this episode because it provides such a classic example of how historical myths come into being and perpetuate themselves, in this case because of unwillingness in the White House to accept the responsibility for an amazingly sloppy review procedure. This was obviously not a world-shattering matter, but was not without its consequences. Kennedy's generally negative attitude toward the State Department derived to a large extent from his presumed experience with the reply to the Soviet aide-mémoire. The president did ask for a chronology covering the handling of our reply, which we quickly produced, but if it reached him, we saw no evidence that its implications had sunk in.

The Second Acheson Memorandum and Its Aftermath

As part of the process of review prompted by the Vienna confrontation, Kennedy asked Acheson (housed in a State Department office) to bring his earlier memorandum up to date and to make further recommendations. We knew pretty much where they would end up and that their seeming belligerency would again shock those in the White House and the State Department who sought a solution in negotiations. Despite his Harvard Law School connection, Acheson was quintessentially the Yale man. I could never be entirely sure whether his apparent bloody-mindedness was partly an attempt to *épater* (flabbergast) *les clercs harvardiens* or essentially a negotiating tactic vis-à-vis those whom he regarded as the "softies" in the administration, in the hope that what would finally emerge was a position that made sense and did not fall into the trap of negotiating away West Berlin. Later during 1961–63 he invited me to have lunch alone with him a number of times at the Metropolitan Club. He continued to have much curiosity about what we were doing with respect to Berlin, but it was clear that (apart from the period of the Cuban missile crisis) he no longer enjoyed direct and frequent access to the White House.

In any event, Acheson submitted his report to the president on June 28. It set off the anticipated alarm bells and became an important initial part of the intensive process of unilateral, and subsequently multilateral, review and policy making that filled the month of July. Those of us caught up directly in that process worked to the point of exhaustion late into the night. I can recall my good wife coming down to the department during the evenings with much appreciated hot food.

A number of books have discussed the contents of the Acheson report with reasonable accuracy.[17] In essence, what it argued was that Khrushchev had precipitated the Berlin crisis not in order to achieve local desiderata but to test the general American will to resist. Hence any effort to negotiate would be taken as a sign of weakness. Strong action was necessary to demonstrate our resolve to defend the status quo in Berlin. To threaten nuclear action would not be credible; we should accordingly demonstrate American resolve by substantially increasing our forces in West Germany and in the United States. Should Khrushchev carry out his threats to take unilateral action resulting in interruption of U.S. access to Berlin, we should launch an airlift and, if this failed, a ground probe involving two divisions. The latter would demonstrate our preparedness to escalate, if required, to a nuclear exchange. Once we had, in effect, succeeded in proving our resolve, we should then offer Khrushchev a face-saving formula.

It was perhaps natural that many of those who have written about this period, or provided comments for oral history projects, should describe the bureaucratic tug-of-war that followed as between hard-liners and soft-liners (the terms "hawks" and "doves" had not yet come into common usage). I thought then, and think now, that such a dichotomy distorted the actual spectrum of views. Kennedy and the White House contingent, supported by Abe Chayes, Roger Hilsman, and George McGhee in the State Department, wanted "creative negotiations" to be the essence of our response to Khrushchev. It is true that some of the Kennedyites felt that anyone who did not wholly agree with them must necessarily be against the idea of any negotiations at the present stage, as Acheson clearly seemed to be. They reacted strongly to any course of action that might lead to a nuclear confrontation over Berlin, if Khrushchev was to be taken literally. I believe that Dean Rusk, Foy Kohler, and I could all agree that nuclear war over Berlin would be the ultimate irrationality. Moreover, we knew that the British and the French would never agree in advance to a course of action that might involve a two-division probe into the GDR without consideration at the highest level when the time actually came.

Both Acheson and the proponents of substantive negotiations forgot that a third option existed between refusing negotiations and trying to achieve a negotiated settlement at any cost. This was an option already demonstrated to be effective in 1959—the option of discussions for the purpose of delay to give Khrushchev an excuse for not doing unilaterally what he had threatened to do but, in the final analysis, did not really want to do. Of the Kennedy people, Dean Rusk was seemingly the only one to grasp this quickly. Another thing the White House appeared to forget was the need to keep German-American relations from collapsing over the Berlin issue. Although by 1961 his authority had somewhat waned, Adenauer was still chancellor, and those of us who had lived through the 1959–60 period had not forgotten how difficult he could be if he felt that we were prepared to give away what he considered to be the vital interests of the Federal Republic. We also knew well enough that a substantive basis for comprehensive agreement did not exist in 1961, but we agreed that talk and more talk was preferable to calling Khrushchev's bluff and perhaps forcing him into irrational action.

Two significant organizational developments took place in the post-Vienna period that would affect me personally. Plans to create an Operations Center on the seventh floor of the State Department came to fruition. It was meant to bring together experts in one place to deal with crisis situations and to provide them with office space, staff, good communications, and, if required, even sleeping facilities. Berlin obviously was a real crisis, and so it was decided that I would move to the seventh floor to head the group of officers who would accompany me. My deputy in the Office of German Affairs, Bob Brandin, would take over the day-to-day handling of German affairs other than Berlin.

The National Security Council met on June 29 and took decisions calling for a comprehensive review and specific recommendations to be discussed at a July 13 meeting of the council. National Security Action Memorandum No. 58 of June 30, 1961, gave the secretary of state general responsibility for coordinating the various studies called for by the NSC and for developing an "integrated time table" intended to achieve maximum deterrent effect with respect to the Soviet Union as well as the agreement and maximum cooperation of our allies. The instrument for this purpose would be the existing Interdepartmental Coordinating Group on Germany and Berlin. It would be chaired by Secretary Rusk or a representative designated by him.[18]

One problem that quickly arose was how to revive a body that had largely become moribund during the first five months of the Kennedy administration. In fact, the parallel Interdepartmental Group on Berlin Contingency Planning had not met as such since December 1960. It met for the first time in June to receive a report on what had happened in the interim from Assistant Secretary of State Foy Kohler. After the hectically intensive work of July, this formidably named and combined bureaucratic apparatus was to become the Berlin Task Force with Foy Kohler as its effective head and me as his deputy, frequently called upon to chair meetings of the group in his absence. In retrospect, one can find things to criticize in the way we organized our work during the Kennedy phase of the Berlin crisis, but, by the standards of a less than perfect world, the task force provided a reasonably effective coordinating and educative mechanism. As members from the various agencies got to know one another better, the quality of debate and our ability to find mutually acceptable solutions notably improved. If important decisions were sometimes made elsewhere, the task force found itself more and more in a position to affect the substance of final agreement at the four-power level on Berlin contingency planning. On the other hand, the State Department members of the task force and the White House pretty much reserved for themselves the preparation of positions for possible discussions with the Soviets.

One is easily tempted to scoff at problems of bureaucratic organization. They often seem petty and self-serving. But they can also make a great difference in the effectiveness of a government faced with a major crisis. I have little doubt that the innovations of the post-Vienna period made a real contribution to such effectiveness, given the much more massive involvement in the Berlin crisis of American officials with little or no substantive competence than was the case during the Eisenhower years.

America Prepares to Arm and to Talk

While all this was going on, a working group of the Interdepartmental Coordinating Group operated around the clock (sometimes literally) to complete a report for the meeting of the National Security Council on July 13. The final document and attachments proved a formidable one: a "Summary of Development of the Course of Action," a section entitled "Imminent Decisions," followed by ten annexes containing recommendations and specific studies by the relevant government agencies. The impact on National Security Council members who presumably had to familiarize themselves with the contents was bound to be overwhelming. Experience had taught us that only the secretaries of state and defense would really master the subject matter. We had not deliberately set out to drown the recipients of our report in a mass of paper, but we were dealing with a complicated problem requiring a multifaceted treatment. One theme that began to emerge in our thinking, stimulated by an argument advanced orally by Herman Kahn, was that the threat of an arms race, pitting the industrially superior United States against the Soviet Union, might in itself constitute an effective deterrent against continuing Soviet pressure on Berlin. Acheson himself had not made this point specifically, but it seemed to some of us a logical by-product of the sort of military preparations he had advocated. Indeed, it might obviate the need to execute the major steps of such a military buildup.

A lengthy discussion of the report in the National Security Council led to further instructions from the president "to prepare evaluations of alternative courses of actions and specific recommendations for the implementation of such actions," to be discussed at a National Security Council meeting on July 19. National Security Council Action Memorandum No. 59, dated July 14, 1961, passed out the specific assignments.[19] The already exhausted Interdepartmental Working Group did not receive this new directive with enthusiasm. To produce what had been requested in five days seemed an impossible task, bearing in mind that the same handful of State Department officers were also trying to complete the final phases of getting off a response to the Soviet aide-mémoire. That we met the deadline was a tribute to the stamina, experience, and knowledge of those working on this second, mammoth report. There were some unsung heroes in the Interdepartmental Working Group. It is a pity that colleagues who toil arduously in the diplomatic vineyard seldom obtain the recognition due them; some of their names may not even appear on the official papers eventually included in the published *Foreign Relations of the United States*.

Another important document that Secretary Rusk, Foy Kohler, and I put together during those hectic days we called an "Outline on Germany and Berlin."[20] In it we tried to provide in compressed, but not oversimplified, form the essentials of our position on Berlin and Germany as a whole. It helped us, as we were drafting it, to sharpen our own thinking on the subject, and we subsequently drew on it conceptually in the Rusk-Gromyko discussions of 1961–62 and in defining our own behavior in the face of Soviet threats and actions. We also hoped that it would be helpful in restoring some measure of order in White House thinking.

The paper began by specifying the relevant vital interests of the United States as we saw them:

1. The presence and security of the Western forces in West Berlin
2. The security and viability of West Berlin
3. Physical access to West Berlin
4. The security of the Federal Republic against attacks from the East

The paper went on to note that, apart from these vital interests, the United States also had important but still unrealized political goals in Germany, such as the application to all of Germany of the principle of self-determination and the intimate association of a unified Germany with the West. Some aspects of the situation with regard to Berlin and Germany were not politically acceptable, we acknowledged, and unlikely to be changed in the near future. Among these, which provided no occasion for a resort to force by the West, were the de facto division of Germany and the de facto absorption of East Berlin into East Germany. Cutting across all these issues was the major U.S. interest in maintaining Allied unity and strengthening NATO. The memorandum then went on to analyze Soviet objectives. It did not minimize the danger, but neither did it imply that, without major concessions on our part, the situation would inevitably be the prelude to Armageddon.

The attempt to define our vital interests in Germany and Berlin was not an innovation, although we had never put the four together in precisely this way. Our note of December 21, 1958, had already spoken of the unchallengeable right of the three Western powers to maintain garrisons in their sectors of Berlin and to have free access thereto.[21] At a later point the note had emphasized the right and responsibility of the three powers to protect the freedom and security of West Berlin. In his second memorandum, Acheson had also spelled out "three essentials" with respect to West Berlin. I note all of this here because, at a later point, during the period of recriminations in the West that followed the construction of the Berlin Wall, our failure to include what happened in East Berlin as a vital interest was criticized as an invitation to the Soviets to do anything they wanted in that sector of the city.

Our memorandum concluded with recommendations for necessary consultations with our allies once we had made up our minds on our preferred course of action. We did not want the tendency toward unilateralism on the part of some officials to lead to a disruptive crisis with our allies.

The July 19 meeting of the National Security Council again had an enormous packet of papers before it discussing options and making recommendations. The council discussed a number of possibilities related to the decisions that President Kennedy was to make public on July 25 in his Report to the Nation on the Berlin Crisis. The rhetoric of his speech was good, firm yet nonbelligerent, offering to consider any arrangement in Germany consistent with peace and freedom. But the main purpose of the address was to announce that the president would request of the Congress an additional appropriation of $3.247 billion for the armed forces to be added to a supplementary request for $3 billion made earlier; an increase in the total authorized strength of the army from 875,000 to 1,000,000; an increase in the strength of the navy of 29,000 men and 69,000 men in the air force; and authority to call to active duty certain reserve units and individual reservists. The president went on to say that, under the requested authority, he would order to active duty a number of air transport squadrons and National Guard tactical air squadrons to provide airlift capacity and air protection. He added that planes and ships once destined for retirement would be retained or reactivated and that half of the new money requested would be used for procurement of nonnuclear weapons, ammunition, and equipment.[22]

This was a formidable package, calculated to impress on the Soviets the seriousness of our purpose and the danger of launching an arms race with the economically superior United States. Needless to say, Kennedy's speech did not come as a surprise to our allies. The president had sent personal messages to Macmillan, de Gaulle, and Adenauer on July 20 summarizing the decisions reached at the National Security Council meeting on July 19. A memorandum handed by Secretary Rusk to representatives of the British, French, and German embassies on July 21 contained a fuller account of the measures to be announced in the president's speech, and American ambassadors in all NATO countries received instructions to convey essentially the same information to their respective governments.[23] Taking over the procedural suggestions of our "Outline on Germany and Berlin," the memorandums proposed that four-power consultations at the senior officer level take place in Paris for a week beginning July 28, to be followed by a meeting in Paris of the four Western foreign ministers, who would subsequently report to NATO. The three countries quickly accepted this suggested schedule.

As I look back over the years at those tense National Security Council meetings, I cannot say that they constituted an impressive example of orderly decision making. Most of the principals had obviously not digested the mass of materials thrown at them by the Interdepartmental Working Group, and they had little, if anything, to say. The president was not really a very good or orderly chairman, and points of difference did not always seem to get resolved even in his own mind. It would have been fair to say that the council sometimes resembled more a consultative than a decision-making body. The principle of order was actually provided by McGeorge Bundy, special assistant for national security affairs, who, at the direction of the president, drafted the Records of Actions and Action Memoranda intended as instructions to the various agencies of government. Through Bundy's skill in putting words down on paper, Kennedy could exercise his prerogative to make decisions, even when they did not quite convey the sense of what had seemingly been agreed, or at least discussed, during the NSC session. Although the recipients of minutes and Action Memoranda may at times have been jolted by the clarity of what had been unclear, there was no real element of dishonesty in this. It was, after all, presumably the way the president wanted it.

Persuading the Allies

The preparations for our meetings in Paris proceeded at a high level of emotional intensity. We were bone tired after the round-the-clock weeks before the July 19 National Security Council meeting and the days of turbulent drafting that followed. In a few days we would be off to Paris for the Four-Power Working Group session to begin July 28. What the press labels "hectic diplomatic activity" becomes for the participants a test of physical and intellectual endurance. It is easy to understand how, under similar circumstances, exhausted diplomats and statesmen have in the past made seemingly egregious mistakes of judgment. I have always valued as colleagues those officials who do not flap, no matter how serious the crisis and how overwhelming the demands on their time. We were fortunate, in those early days of what was to become the Berlin Task Force, to have assembled a small group of dedicated and highly competent Foreign Service officers who possessed the ability to do sustained work of high quality under intense pressure. It was a difficult period of testing, but my colleagues came through it, I believe, with a superior level of performance. Yet who will remember them for what they accomplished that summer? Their names lie buried in the sheer mass of accumulated archives.

There were, we thought, some distinct advantages to having the quadripartite meetings in Paris. To begin with, the choice of location might flatter de Gaulle and make him a little less difficult (an illusion, we soon discovered). It would also get us out of the direct line of fire of the nervous Nellies in the White House and State Department who could not seem to appreciate that negotiations purely on Soviet terms would only sacrifice both our position in Berlin and our relationship with the Federal Republic of Germany. As the department's legal adviser, Abe Chayes had a legitimate claim to be a member of the U.S. delegation, and his behavior in Paris generally proved to be constructive, if somewhat out of the main stream of activity.

We drove ourselves hard preparing for the foreign ministers' meeting to come and for what we hoped would be a general endorsement of the American position (outlined in the president's speech of July 25) both on military preparations and on the need for negotiations that we saw as a necessary adjunct to the proposed military measures. While we anticipated some problems with the French, we frankly did not foresee the buzz saw into which Secretary Rusk was to run, nor were we forewarned that de Gaulle was as stubbornly opposed to any negotiations with the Soviets as he proved to be. I should add that, contrary to the illusions entertained by some journalists and academics, diplomats at conferences in the midst of crises work long hours under intense pressure. There was little time in Paris for leisurely dining at great French restaurants or anything more than fleeting interludes at museums. By the summer of 1961, I had long since lost count of the numerous trips I had made to Europe in connection with the Berlin crisis.

A tripartite meeting of foreign ministers (without the Germans) held earlier on August 5 foreshadowed the disagreement on the tactical approach to negotiations. The sessions at the quadripartite foreign ministers meeting on August 5–6 proved to be both protracted and acrimonious. The British foreign secretary, then still Lord Home, generally supported Rusk but left most of the argumentation to the secretary of state. Foreign Minister von Brentano was cautiously supportive, but he had been sand-bagged by the chancellor in 1959 and would not get far out in front. As it turned out, when Secretary Rusk visited Adenauer at his vacation home in Cadenabbia, Italy, after the Paris meetings, he found the chancellor willing to accept negotiations that did not compromise basic rights. The French foreign minister Couve de Murville was both long winded and sarcastic. Any idea of negotiating with the Soviets would not have French agreement, he repeated in various ways, and he was unwilling to accept even our compromise formula of "exploratory talks to determine whether a basis for negotiations exist[ed]." He was getting his brief directly from President de Gaulle, of course, with the great man operating on the assumption that "Khrushchev makes a lot of noise, but he doesn't do anything."

I could note that Rusk's patience was wearing thin as hour followed hour of fruitless debate. He knew that, if a confrontation over Berlin took place, it was the United States that would have to assume the ultimate nuclear risk. He could not understand how we could rationally proceed without attempting to negotiate with the Soviets. The secretary argued at the meeting that the Soviet Union had put proposals before the world and that there would have to be negotiations at some point. Couve de Murville simply could not agree.

As the American rapporteur of this seemingly endless session, I knew I would be working late into the night to get off a detailed reporting telegram to Washington. Every experienced Foreign Service officer cast frequently in the role of rapporteur develops his own system of abbreviations to assist his memory. I was confident that I could reconstruct protracted conversations with reasonable accuracy at any length that the subject required, and this seemed to be a case where a report as close as possible to verbatim would be desirable. The result was one of the longest telegrams that I have ever produced. At a staff meeting the following morning, Rusk could only recommend that my telegram be read carefully if one really wanted to know what happened at yesterday's meeting. I took it as a compliment. My facility at reconstructing discussions in detail was to get an extensive workout during the year that followed the outset of the Cuban missile crisis.[24]

I should add that, despite the hassle over negotiations, the Paris meetings did result in other agreements on how to deal with the Berlin issue. The foreign ministers approved our Four-Power Working Group reports entitled "Substantive Political Questions" and "Information" without much discussion, and Couve finally even agreed to let the Washington Four-Power Ambassadorial Group work out possible positions for negotiations to be conducted at the level of foreign ministers. Left outstanding were the conditions under which and when such negotiations should be sought.[25]

The Berlin Wall

After our return to Washington, I quickly took off with my family for what I hoped would be a ten-day holiday on Tybee Island off the coast of Georgia. We were aware, of course, that the increasing flow of refugees from East Germany mainly through Berlin (stimulated by the psychological phenomenon of *Torschlusspanik*—panic over the possibility that the gate would be slammed shut) was putting the GDR regime and the Soviets under heavy pressure to do something. Such intelligence reports as we had received indicated that the most probable action would be to impose strict controls on movement into East Berlin from the rest of the GDR. I had seen none that predicted what actually happened on August 13. In a July 22 comment, however, on Ambassador Walter Dowling's analysis of the growing unrest in East Germany, we in the department expressed the view that of various contingencies the most likely was that the GDR regime would take measures to control the refugee flow. It could do this either by tightening controls over travel from the Soviet zone to East Berlin or by severely restricting travel from East Berlin to West Berlin. We were wrong, however, in thinking that it was Soviet policy, at least for the moment, to tolerate the flow of refugees while pressing toward a decision on Berlin.

Prior to that date, the Soviets had kept up a fusillade of threats to sign a separate peace treaty with all of the already stated consequences. Khrushchev's reaction to Kennedy's speech of July 25, as expressed to John

McCloy, the president's special adviser on disarmament, at his summer residence on the Black Sea on July 27, was particularly blustery. He said he had no other choice but to treat Kennedy's speech as an ultimatum and that he would proceed to sign a peace treaty and prepare for war. Both the United States and the Soviet Union would survive a nuclear war, but America's allies in Europe would be annihilated, and hundreds of millions of people would die and many more be contaminated. The Soviet reply to the three Western notes of July 17 came on August 3 and promptly became the subject of an analysis by the Four-Power Working Group still meeting in Paris.[26] The group concluded that the Soviet reply contained nothing really new, although it did not specify a time limit for signing a peace treaty as the Soviet aide-mémoire of June 4 and subsequent speeches by Khrushchev had done. It repeated the point that the only objective of negotiations would be the early conclusion of a peace treaty with the two German states. In two speeches on August 7 and August 11, Khrushchev stressed the danger of nuclear war with the aim, it seemed, of frightening the European allies of the United States. He warned that if war came, it would not end until both sides had used all their weapons "including the most destructive ones." He added that the Soviet Union had at its disposal the means "not only for striking a crushing blow at the territorial United States" but also "to render harmless the aggressor's allies and destroy American military bases throughout the world."

Khrushchev made no reference in any of his speeches to the growing refugee flow from East Germany or the need to do something about it. Ironically enough, his own threats of dire things to come added to the unrest in the GDR. The hemorrhaging of the able-bodied population was not, however, purely a phenomenon of the summer of 1961. We had reasonably reliable registration figures for refugees assembled by the West German authorities since 1949. The number of refugees increased from 129,245 in that year to 331,390 in 1953 (the year of the crushed East German uprising). With a few exceptions the refugee flow in subsequent years hovered around 200,000. In 1957 the Ullbricht regime tightened controls on interzonal travel by East Germans, and thereafter the bulk of the refugees came through West Berlin. In July 1961 the total of refugees was more than 30,000, and by August 9 the daily flow had risen to nearly 2,000. Not only were the numbers startling, but in the first six months of 1961, some 61.8 percent of the refugees were in the category of gainfully employed. When the West German minister for all-German affairs, Ernst Lemmer, announced on August 11 that, if the refugee flow continued at the current rate, the figure of 200,000 (the total for the entire year 1960) would be reached by the end of the summer, it was obvious that the

GDR would take desperate measures of some sort lest the whole country implode.[27]

Many books and articles have attempted to describe the events of August 13 and the days that followed. I see little point in repeating all the details here. The basic facts were that, during the early morning hours of August 13 (a Sunday when Allied officials were least likely to be on duty), members of the *Volkspolizei* and the East German army began to seal off the border between the three Western sectors of Berlin and the Soviet sector of the city. They erected barbed wire barriers, dug trenches, and tore up the pavements. The pretext, according to a GDR decree published on August 13, was to "establish an order on the border of West Berlin which [would] seriously block the way to the subversive activity against the socialist camp countries, so that reliable safeguards and effective control [could] be established around the whole territory of West Berlin, including its border with democratic Berlin." Under an accompanying decree, East Berliners and East Germans would require special permits to enter West Berlin, but West Berliners could continue to enter East Berlin upon showing proper identity, as could foreign nationals and diplomats.

The East Germans gradually strengthened the temporary barriers erected on August 13, and on August 18 they began to construct a six-foot-high concrete block wall topped by barbed wire. They also tightened up controls on the movement of West Berliners to East Berlin and reduced the number of crossing points to seven, one of which was specifically reserved for foreign nationals, including diplomats and members of the three Allied armed forces. The well-known and oft-pictured Checkpoint Charlie on the Allied side of the wall thus came into existence.

Many commentators criticized what they regarded as inadequate and overly cautious Allied reaction to the border closing. Some argued that we should simply have brought bulldozers and tanks up to the wire barriers and knocked them down, presumably on the assumption that this would not have precipitated a counteraction by the Soviets with their enormously superior tank forces in East Germany or would not simply have resulted in new barriers being erected a hundred feet or so farther into East Berlin, thus requiring a literal invasion by Allied forces of the Soviet sector of the city. Apart from the fact that the British and the French would never have gone along with any such action, an incursion into East Berlin by meager Allied forces with relatively few tanks could quickly have turned into a militarily suicidal operation. Our contingency planning for various eventualities in East Berlin never contemplated military penetration into the Soviet sector.

We, of course, made all the usual protests for the record, starting with

Secretary Rusk's statement on August 13. A letter of protest from the three Western commandants to the Soviet commandant in East Berlin followed on August 15, and on August 17 the three Western governments handed over notes of protest to the Soviet Foreign Ministry in Moscow.[28] The main thrust of all of these was that the action taken in East Berlin violated the four-power status of the city. It was clear, however, from a discussion in the U.S. Steering Group on Berlin held August 15 (which I missed as an absentee from Washington) that the United States intended, as Rusk put it, to "keep shooting issues and non-shooting issues separate" and that the closing of the East Berlin border was not a shooting issue.[29]

I had been on Tybee Island only a few days when I received an urgent telephone call from Assistant Secretary Kohler requesting that I return to Washington as rapidly as possible. Somewhat out of touch with the dramatic events of August 13, I quickly realized from what Kohler told me that we would have a major crisis on our hands. The volatility of Berlin sentiment, either in the direction of courage or panic, has frequently caught the Western powers by surprise, and this was to provide another good example. Even Chancellor Adenauer greatly underestimated the degree of shock that the Berliners would suffer or, for that matter, the strength of reaction in the Federal Republic itself. Criticism of the Allied response mounted as the "sense of outrage" grew in the city and in West Germany. The realization also quickly grew in Washington that, despite the logic of our position in terms of our definition of vital interests in Berlin, we needed to take some more demonstrative actions beyond protests that merely underlined our impotence in the face of the Wall. The fact that the Federal Republic was in the last weeks of a national electoral campaign that pitted Berlin's governing mayor Willy Brandt, the SPD chancellor candidate, against Konrad Adenauer, once again the chancellor candidate of the CDU, could only add to the atmosphere of recrimination and inflated rhetoric. Brandt, as spokesman for West Berlin, criticized what he described as Allied inactivity and urged that the occupying powers take a number of steps to demonstrate their resolve. Some of these seemed counterproductive or otherwise undesirable, but a few became the basis for subsequent Allied action.

There is little doubt that what Brandt regarded as inadequate Allied reaction to the Wall was for him a deeply disillusioning experience that affected his subsequent attitude toward the Western powers. He was aware, of course, that President Kennedy, in his speech of July 25, had publicly limited our vital interests in Berlin to the Western sectors of the city and access thereto, and in fact, he and his aide Egon Bahr had adversely commented on the implications of such a limitation. Somehow, perhaps, he had still thought that in a pinch we would use military force to prevent the kind of formal division of the city that the Wall represented.

In any event, Washington quickly accepted that West Berlin was suffering from a "crisis of confidence," as Ambassador Dowling had put it in a telegram, and that some symbolic actions beyond protests needed to be taken. On August 18, the United States announced that it would dispatch a battle group of fifteen hundred men to reinforce the garrison in West Berlin. The British also took action to strengthen their forces in the city. President Kennedy then decided to send Vice President Lyndon Johnson as his personal representative to Bonn and Berlin, accompanied by General Clay. The visit to Berlin, as had Secretary of State Herter's in 1959, elicited a typical demonstration of great popular enthusiasm. Observers were able to note an almost immediate improvement in Berlin morale, which was further augmented by the arrival of the American battle group and by actions taken against the East German presence in West Berlin. Troops were also deployed on the Western side of the Wall in defiance of a GDR warning to keep a distance of one hundred meters on each side of the sector border.

The vice presidential visit was not without its farcical aspects. Johnson had a well-known penchant for collecting china during his travels abroad. The fact that it was a Sunday and all the stores were closed did not matter to the vice president, who pushed Brandt hard to make the necessary arrangements. When Johnson left Berlin early Monday morning, he carried with him a twenty-four-person coffee service from the Berliner Porzellanfabrik.

So the Wall came into being—an aesthetic and moral monstrosity but crudely effective in achieving its purposes. Individual Germans would still heroically, and often ingeniously, escape to the West or die in the attempt. Time institutionalizes most things, and, until the Wall came down in 1989, twenty-eight years after it first went up, I could only marvel once again at the durability of the provisional. The Wall became a major tourist attraction for visitors to West Berlin and a source of repeated empty rhetoric for Western leaders.

The Kennedy administration's attitude toward the Wall was bound to be ambivalent. Apart from ineffective protests for the record against East German military activities in East Berlin and the insistence on free movement of official Allied personnel into and out of East Berlin, the Western powers had long since given up any claim to authority in the Soviet sector of the city. While the ever increasing flow of refugees from the German Democratic Republic was a telling demonstration of massive unhappiness with the East German regime, and thus an expression of the human desire for freedom, the regime necessarily must have felt that the survival of the GDR was at stake and that some sort of drastic action to stop the hemorrhaging of people was required. We did not know, of course, precisely how much of Khrushchev's emotional animus on the Berlin issue came from the refugee crisis, but it was not illogical to suppose that the Wall might reduce the urgency with which he felt the Western presence in Berlin, and the conduit provided thereby, had to be eliminated.

The Berlin Crisis Continues

Any idea, however, that the Berlin crisis was now for all practical purposes over, as some seemed to hope, was just plain wrong. We did not think so in the State Department, although we could see that some of the pressure on Khrushchev to make specific ultimative threats might now be relieved. He was too far out on a limb simply to give up on Berlin, so we expected more bluster and threat as well as possible physical harassment of our position in Berlin or on the access routes. Apart from talking with the Soviets, which we felt to be indispensable, our emphasis during the autumn within the Berlin Task Force and the Washington Ambassadorial Group was on the refinement of Allied contingency planning.

At the end of August, President Kennedy took an action that frankly did not inspire much enthusiasm in the State Department. He appointed General Lucius Clay as his personal representative, with the rank of ambassador, on temporary assignment to Berlin. Clay was to communicate directly with the secretary of state and the president but was not to become part of the regular military chain of command or to derogate from the responsibilities of Ambassador Dowling as chief of mission in Berlin. Anyone familiar with the headstrong and self-confident General Clay could safely predict that the president's instructions, contained in a letter to Clay, suffered from an inherent contradiction that would quickly become apparent. Clay was to arrive in Berlin by mid-September.

On the organizational front in Washington, we proceeded to formalize what had already developed as an operational entity on the American side. Secretary of State Rusk and Secretary of Defense McNamara agreed on the creation of the Berlin Task Force to coordinate Berlin planning within the U.S. government. Among representatives from other departments—and the desire to join was manifold—were Assistant Secretary of Defense for International Security Affairs Paul Nitze and Major General David Gray of the staff of the Joint Chiefs of Staff. The basic membership of the task force, which was physically to function in the Operations Center of the State Department, came from the Office of German Affairs. The Berlin Task Force held its first meeting under the new rubric on August 17; it quickly became the operational center for the discussion of American contingency planning and other matters relating to Berlin.

At the four-power level, the Four-Power Ambassadorial Steering Group, chaired by Foy Kohler, with the British, French, and German ambassadors representing their respective countries, became the focal point of coordination on Berlin. Created by the four foreign ministers during this August meeting in Paris, it took over the essential functions of the old Quadripartite Working Group on Berlin. Without delay, it established several subgroups: a political subgroup later to become the Contingency Coordinating Group (which I chaired), a military subgroup, an economic subgroup, and an East German subgroup. We were now in a position, we thought, to deal adequately with the heavy pressures that we anticipated during the autumn months within the U.S. government, from our allies, and from the domestic and international press, to which the Berlin situation had continued to be the hottest news item around. There are those who scorn the minutiae of organizational patterns, but anyone with the kind of experience we had knew that getting the machinery right made an enormous difference as to how effectively problems could be handled. This was a lesson that some subsequent administrations never seemed to learn. Institutional memory within the U.S. government tends to suffer from periodic blackouts.

The Clay Episode

The drama of General Clay's days in Berlin produced both its pathetic and alarming moments. Our forebodings in the State Department turned out to be all too correct. This was a man with an almost overriding sense of mission, a disregard for orderly procedures, and no real sense of the caution that the nuclear age necessarily imposed on responsible leaders. No one could deny his sincerity of purpose, his personal willingness to take risks, or his scorn for those more reticent to confront the Soviets with what they could only regard as unnecessary challenges. One may criticize diplomats for excessive prudence, but prudence supported by determination on essentials has started few, if any, wars. Sound policy does not require empty gestures no matter how exhilarating at the moment.

In any event, Clay arrived in Berlin during September. Apart from the inevitable jurisdictional confusion that his writ created from the outset, he was not there very long before he launched his first initiative, which was not without its comic opera aspects. Access to the exclave of Steinstuecken had been a source of difficulty over the years. The East Germans never missed an opportunity to take advantage of the geographical isolation of the exclave and, as part of the Wall-building process, had erected barbed-wire barriers around Steinstuecken with its some 180 inhabitants. When Clay attempted to order two infantry companies to break through to Steinstuecken, U.S. Army Europe (USAREUR) commander general Bruce Clarke (who happened to be visiting Berlin at the time) countermanded his instructions and in effect told Clay to take his "cotton-picking fingers" off Clarke's troops. Instead, Clay then flew to Steinstuecken by army helicopter, a perfectly legal operation, since the flight took place within the Berlin Control Zone. Despite the inevitable GDR protests, such flights subsequently became routine, and eventually a single roadway was reopened. Years later, the roadway from West Berlin to Steinstuecken became a tourist attraction with the access road surrounded by walls on both sides. Clay's boldness had in this instance paid off, and visitors to Berlin were able to experience the vicarious thrill of penetrating hostile territory.

The altercation with General Clarke was symptomatic of the inevitable conflict of authority that Clay's insertion into the picture would bring about. Major General Albert Watson, the commandant, was the senior American military figure in Berlin subject only politically to Ambassador Walter Dowling in Bonn, who exercised the residual powers of the former American high commissioner for Germany. In his military capacity, Watson reported to General Clarke in Heidelberg, who, in turn, reported to General Lauris Norstad, U.S. commander in chief for Europe and Supreme Allied Commander Europe wearing his NATO hat. As commander of Live Oak (the special headquarters created tripartitely to handle Berlin-related military contingencies), Norstad also had special responsibilities to the U.S., French, and British governments. No general likes to have his command responsibility usurped, and Clay's attempt to give orders to the Berlin commandant could only raise hackles in Heidelberg and Paris. In the nuclear age responsible senior officers are extremely sensitive to any use of force that could escalate out of control, a sense of restraint that frankly General Clay did not seem to share.

This, then, was the still somewhat confused command situation that permitted Clay to precipitate the tank confrontation with the Soviets at the Friedrichstrasse crossing point (Checkpoint Charlie)—an incident that quickly became a worldwide media sensation. Berlin morale required a periodic infusion of heroics, and Clay was able to provide that. He could not, however, persuade either Clarke or Norstad that what he was doing was either prudent or militarily tolerable.

After the flap over Steinstuecken, the Berlin scene during October seemed relatively quiet. The Wall had achieved its essential purpose of stopping the massive flow of refugees from the GDR, and the three Allies had accepted that their entry into and exit from East Berlin would be limited to the Friedrichstrasse crossing. The actual checkpoint procedures differed somewhat among the three: the British, for example, saw no problem in showing their passports for identification, whereas the Americans did not show any personal identification other than the uniforms on soldiers and the official license tags on State Department vehicles.

On October 22, a Sunday, Minister Allan Lightner (head of the permanent State Department mission in West Berlin) and his wife were on their way to the opera in East Berlin. After clearing through Checkpoint Charlie, Lightner drove his blue Volkswagen toward the East German guards (if he had driven a Cadillac, he might have passed through unmolested). They demanded identification, which Lightner refused to show. This began a psychological tug-of-war at the checkpoint that ended when Lightner, flanked by a squad of U.S. Military Police with loaded rifles at the ready, twice entered East Berlin. The following day the GDR boss, Walter Ullbricht, issued a decree stating that all Allied civilians would have to identify themselves before entering East Berlin.

Two days later armed patrols again accompanied American officials past the checkpoint, and Clay requested General Watson to place U.S. forces in Berlin on alert and to deploy tanks near Checkpoint Charlie. Needless to say, Washington reacted with concern and instructed Ambassador Thompson to see Gromyko. That concern increased considerably when Marshal Koniev, the Soviet commander in the GDR, began to move tanks into East Berlin. Clay then ordered the American tanks to move up to the demarcation line at Checkpoint Charlie. Six Soviet tanks appeared and lined up some one hundred yards from the American tanks. As the tension mounted, Clay claimed that he had proved his point that the Soviets were responsible for the maintenance of Allied rights in Berlin. Khrushchev, who had been tied up with the Twenty-second Communist Party Congress, quickly got back into the act, and, sixteen hours after their arrival, the Soviet tanks disappeared. Shortly thereafter the American tanks pulled back into West Berlin.[30]

This was the beginning of the end for Clay, although he did not know it at the time. He had made his point, but the day after the tank confrontation ended, East German guards again turned back civilian officials who refused to show identification papers. The order went out for American civilian officials no longer to enter East Berlin by car; they could still go on foot or by subway, for which mode of access they were already authorized to show their passports. British and French civilian officials continued to enter by car, showing their passports as they had already been authorized to do. We could not afford to win many symbolic victories of this kind. No one knows, of course, what would have happened if the confronting tanks had begun to fire on each other and the fighting thereafter had escalated. What seemed particularly intolerable to Generals Clarke and Norstad was Clay's intrusion into their command channels in a matter involving alerting of troops and deployment of tanks and their crews. Both of them expressed themselves vociferously on the subject. It seemed like a classic case of picking the wrong issue for a show of determination.

After the tank confrontation at Checkpoint Charlie, White House and State Department concerns about Clay began to grow. We who had always been doubtful in State about the wisdom of sending him to Berlin recognized that the president had a political problem in that Clay was a prominent Republican and could not simply be dumped. Gradually, however, he began to appreciate that more and more he was being cut out of the essential policy-making process, and by early 1962 he left Berlin and returned to the United States without creating any particular fuss. He behaved as a gentleman in his departure and caused no real problem for the president.

Any assessment of the Clay episode in Berlin must start with the psychological fact that boldness in the face of harassment tends to evoke cheers. Many will react by saying "Bravo! At least he showed spunk." Seemingly overly cautious officials who do not like to take chances get little sympathy. It has always been thus. In dealing with Berlin issues, it was particularly difficult, given the emotion-laden situation of the city, to hold to the essentials, the so-called vital interests, and not to let secondary matters assume overwhelming importance. It was true enough that one could not appear supine or uncaring lest that be interpreted as also involving an unwillingness to defend vital interests. The existence of nuclear weapons had introduced a new element of caution into Soviet-American relations, and certainly the judgments that we made evolved within an automatic reluctance to do anything that might escalate out of control. I fear that General Clay temperamentally lacked that measure of self-imposed discipline and that while he did indeed have a stimulating effect on Berlin morale at a time when it needed uplifting, his mission proved ultimately to have been a failure in the sense that it left little to influence the subsequent development of events, the practices followed, or indeed the ultimate resolution of the Berlin problem provided ten years later by the Quadripartite Agreement on Berlin. In any event, no one could complain that he had not livened things up.

A Diplomatic Tour de Force

Genuine diplomatic tours de force do not come frequently, but Dean Rusk was to embark in September 1961 on a year of "exploratory talks" with Soviet foreign minister Gromyko in New York and Geneva that truly earned such a description. I accompanied the secretary to all these meetings, doing the preparatory paperwork and sometimes writing the reports. We were aware that the French still essentially disapproved, but they realistically knew that there was nothing they could do to keep a determined American secretary of state from exploring whether a basis for negotiations existed (which was the formula we used). Hence, in late August they agreed to exploratory talks to be conducted by Secretary Rusk within an agreed framework. The distinction between exploratory talks and actual negotiations may appear rather thin, but we were careful to avoid any talk of negotiations. Our objective was twofold: to ascertain whether there was any real basis for meaningful four-power discussions with the Soviets on Berlin and, in any event, to keep the Soviets engaged in a process that experience had shown provided whatever pretext they seemed to require for lifting, postponing, or abstaining from ultimatums.

On August 21, the White House had already intervened in a way that we could only regard as less than helpful. The president had sent a memorandum to Rusk stating: "I want to take a stronger lead on the Berlin negotiations."[31] He asked for a "clear paper" on an "agreed position" along the guidelines specified in the memorandum. In essence, they said we should not insist on the maintenance of occupation rights in Berlin if other strong guarantees could be designed; we should consider the option of proposing parallel peace treaties; our first presentation should be as appealing and persuasive as possible and not too far removed from our fallback position; and finally the framework of our proposals was to be as fresh as possible and not look like warmed-over stuff from 1959—in other words not a rehash of the Western Peace Plan.

Rusk agreed fully with our reaction that this was a formula not only for giving away the store to the Soviets but one certain to provoke the strong opposition of all our allies, even the British. The secretary went to see the president in an effort to persuade him that this simply would not do and that he needed an essentially free hand in his exploratory talks. Those in the White House who encouraged Kennedy to send his memorandum must have been furious at this intervention.

Between September 21 and October 6, 1961, Rusk met with Soviet foreign minister Gromyko three times in New York on the margin of the UN General Assembly session. Gromyko also came down to Washington once to meet with the president. The foreign minister proposed a German peace conference or, if the United States would not participate, a separate U.S.-Soviet agreement resulting in free-city status for West Berlin and a unilateral peace treaty between the Soviet Union and the GDR. In seemingly interminable talks, either in the tower apartment of the Waldorf-Astoria or in the headquarters of the Soviet mission to the United Nations, he and Rusk sparred verbally while I came close to developing writer's cramp. The secretary's basic line was that the Allies were in Berlin by right of conquest and not owing to the Soviets. The Soviets therefore could not take away what they did not have. We were obviously getting nowhere, but we were talking.[32] On October 17, Khrushchev in an address to the Twenty-second Congress of the Communist Party withdrew the December 31, 1961, deadline for a German peace treaty, indicating that settling the Berlin question was the main thing to do and that a specific date was no longer important. The exploratory talks were working as we had hoped.

I was never quite clear in my own mind whether Gromyko knew, in effect, that he was being used. He seemed quite willing to participate in what hard-liners in Moscow might have interpreted as essentially a diplomatic charade. One sidelight that we did note was that, during meetings at the Soviet mission to the United Nations, the secretary was always seated on a sofa under a picture of Lenin. The Soviet note taking always seemed more casual on such occasions, and we could only assume that a hidden recording device—perhaps behind Lenin—was providing a complete record of Rusk's words.

Since in the normal course of events, Gromyko would not be coming to New York again until September 1962, we had to find some other method of continuing the exploratory talks. It would not have seemed appropriate for Rusk to go to Moscow. The obvious solution was to have our much esteemed ambassador in Moscow, Llewellyn Thompson (the principal U.S. negotiator of the Austrian Peace Treaty), carry on the dialogue with Gromyko. Thompson began a series of meetings with the Soviet foreign minister in January. My task was to draft detailed instructions for each session that Rusk would review before telegraphic dispatch. The secretary and I were so in tune on Berlin that few revisions were necessary. Despite lengthy sessions and our attempt to spice up our position with a proposal for an international access authority to govern access to and from Berlin by land, water, and air, but without prejudice to our occupation rights in Berlin, the Soviets summarily rejected the idea, as we had expected. They kept coming back to Thompson with essentially the same line Gromyko had taken with Rusk in New York.[33]

The Soviets had meanwhile cooked up a new and serious threat to the Allied position in Berlin. They had made some ominous protests in September about what they alleged to be Allied misuse of the three designated air corridors to Berlin, but had done nothing further at the time. Now without warning, on February 8, 9, and 12, the Soviet authorities in the Berlin Air Safety Center (one of the few remaining four-power entities still operating to assure prompt availability of Allied civilian and military flights to East Germany) attempted to reserve the use of a number of flight levels in the Berlin air corridors during a specified time normally used by Allied planes. We had decided to reject this attempt to preempt the corridors by continuing our flights. The crux, of course, was the willingness of Pan Am, British European Airways, and Air France to continue their civilian flight schedules regardless of the implicit threat in the Soviet action. All three Western airlines responded positively and, so far as we were aware, in full recognition of the risk.

Then on February 14, Soviet aircraft on three occasions flew dangerously close to American aircraft in the North Corridor. Needless to say, the United States promptly protested what we could only regard as a serious and dangerous violation of established procedures and Allied rights to access by air.[34] Worse was yet to come. The Soviets began dropping metal chaff in the corridors calculated to disrupt Western navigation equipment. One of the peculiarities of winter weather in north Germany is a superabundance of fog and low cloud cover. Since our planes did not fly above ten thousand feet in the corridors, this meant that visual flying was a rarity.[35] Nevertheless, both civilian and military traffic continued. There were no accidents, but if there had been, one could easily imagine the buildup of emotional pressure and tension that would have resulted. The Soviets were truly flirting with danger.

In mid-March, while this was still going on, Secretary Rusk went to Geneva to head the American delegation to the Eighteen-Nation Disarmament Conference. I was inevitably a part of his entourage, since we expected that the occasion would provide him with an opportunity to continue his exploratory talks on Berlin with Gromyko. The first order of business was obviously to protest vigorously to the Soviet foreign minister and to stress that there could be no progress on Berlin as long as the air harassments continued. We had contingency plans to fly fighter escorts in the corridors if necessary (which we did not tell Gromyko), but it was not particularly clear what good they would do in face of the chaff problem.

In any event, the Soviet harassments ceased, and we were never able to tell whether this occurred because of Gromyko's intervention or because the Soviet leadership decided it was simply a losing game. Certainly the courage of our civilian pilots in continuing to fly into and out of Berlin played an important part in this, for the Soviets, rather inglorious denouement.

Apart from the usual circular exchange of incompatible positions, the Rusk-Gromyko meetings in Geneva did result in an exchange of what we called nonpapers. Actually both of them used the word "Principles" (the Soviet document was simply headed "Principles" and ours "Confidential Draft Principles"). Secretary Rusk handed the U.S. paper to Gromyko on March 22. We had felt that the time had come to put something in writing to test whether there was any flexibility in the Soviet position and indeed whether any basis for negotiations existed. As I can recall, I was personally not very sanguine that we could put together a package that would elicit a positive Soviet response without sacrificing some of the essentials of the Western position. The trick was to find some new elements while maintaining our basic position in a context that would not cause a storm in Bonn or Paris.

Our "Principles" paper envisaged an agreement between the USSR and the United States on certain general principles such as that West Berlin should be free to choose its own way of life, that its viability should be maintained, and that access should remain free and unhindered. It proposed that a committee of foreign ministers' deputies should in negotiations deal with proposals to improve the situation in Berlin consistent with those principles and the vital interests of both sides. As an interim step, the two countries should agree that "long established access procedures should remain in effect." We also included some general principles and reference to future negotiations, interim steps with respect to German reunification, diffusion of nuclear weapons, and abstention from the use of force to change "existing frontiers or demarcation lines in Europe" or "for any other aggressive purposes." [36]

The new German foreign minister, Gerhard Schroeder, had come to Geneva for the disarmament conference and met with Secretary Rusk in a hotel on the shore of Lake Geneva. I was to get to know him much better after my assignment to Bonn in 1963, but he was clearly a man of considerable intelligence and eloquence. We knew that he saw himself as a future chancellor of the Federal Republic, and if a later illness (probably a stroke) had not impaired his energy and his articulateness, he might well have achieved his ambition. I came to like him as a basically decent and honest man of considerable ability. After reading a copy of our "Principles" paper, he paused. It was clear that he saw some problems in our draft. He swallowed hard but finally, somewhat hesitantly, said the secretary might try it out on Gromyko. I could see that he had the possible reaction of Chancellor Adenauer in mind, but frankly, it did not seem to me that we had provided an indigestible stew. Ultra-right-wingers in the Federal Republic might object to the implicit recognition of the Oder-Neisse line, but this point should not have caused any problems for Adenauer.

Needless to say, Gromyko's "Principles" nonpaper contained no marked deviations from established Soviet positions. It called for the end of the occupation regime, the creation of a "free demilitarized" city of West Berlin, and the replacement of the American, British, and French garrisons by neutral or UN contingents. Access to West Berlin would be unrestricted "in accordance with generally accepted standards of international law and subject to the normal rules applicable to transit" across the territory of sovereign states. An international access authority might act as an arbiter in the case of difficulties, but with no power to control traffic "in the territory of the GDR."

After this exchange of so-called nonpapers and further fruitless restatements of positions by Rusk and Gromyko, the two returned to their capitals. Both made rather lengthy public statements explaining the positions they had taken in Geneva, but neither made reference to any exchange of written proposals.[37] We revised our "Principles" (now called "Draft Principles Procedures and Interim Steps") paper to incorporate the idea of an international access authority—something we had already separately and publicly proposed in a statement by the Department of State on March 3. The intention was to hand this over at the beginning of talks in Washington between Rusk and Soviet ambassador Anatoly Dobrynin.[38]

Meanwhile, the pot was boiling over in Bonn. Foreign Minister Schroeder had had a hard time when he returned from Geneva, and when we sent him the revised draft for clearance, the inevitable leak to the press occurred, the work of an unhappy group of conservative Foreign Office officials. An agitated German press and an agitated chancellor created another of the many crises of confidence that have littered postwar German-American relations (though none of them ever came to the point of permanent impairment). Adenauer particularly did not like the idea of an international access authority, but there had been no explosive reaction to the March 3 public statement on the subject. We could only conclude that we were faced with the kind of emotional reaction to an entire package similar to that caused by earlier drafts of what became the Western Peace Plan.[39] I frankly could not see anything in our "Principles" that would work contrary to basic German interests in the very unlikely event that the Soviets would ever accept them as a basis of negotiations. We intended them essentially as a probe in line with the entire concept of the exploratory talks in which Rusk was engaged.

In any event, we prepared still another version of our paper (no longer a nonpaper) that went forward to the secretary on April 24. We had tried to take account of some of the objections raised to the language of our previous revision, but the essentials remained. We knew Rusk was irritated at the Germans but felt he had no option but to go on talking to Dobrynin.[40] He never gave the further revised paper to the Soviets, nor for that matter to the Germans. His last meeting with Dobrynin in this series took place on May 30, and the dialogue continued to go round in circles. Meanwhile Rusk had made a quick trip to Europe to consult with our allies. As usual, I went along. There were no surprises in the various views expressed at the various stops.

The next round in this seemingly endless but still essential process of talking the issue to death came in Geneva on July 22 when Rusk again met with Gromyko on the margin of the disarmament conference. I can recall the weary repetition of old arguments on both sides, as well as our somewhat reluctant realization that the process must probably go on, either once again with Dobrynin in Washington or with Gromyko on the margin of the UN General Assembly session scheduled to begin September 17.[41]

One should not think that, while all this was happening, the Soviets and East Germans were doing nothing that would help keep the Berlin situation at a boil. There were brutal incidents along the West and East Berlin Wall aimed at attempted escapees, and the continuation of threats to sign the peace treaty and general bluster—although nothing of the gravity of the air corridor harassments earlier in the year. In a memorandum that I wrote dated August 7, "Handling the Impasse on Berlin," I tried to review for the secretary the negotiating history of the Berlin crisis and to suggest some possible new twists that we might give to our position in the event of certain contingencies such as signature of a peace treaty between the USSR and the GDR.[42] What happened, of course, is that the Berlin crisis became temporarily submerged in the more immediately explosive Cuban missile crisis.

The Cuban Missile Crisis

If one tried to put into the cabinet room of the White House everybody who has claimed some connection with the Executive Committee—the high-level group created by President Kennedy to assist him in handling the Cuban missile crisis—they simply would not fit. My role was admittedly less exalted. First, I served as a decoy, a ruse, to fool the press. I was also a member of a subgroup of the Executive Committee, meeting in the

White House, set up on the common assumption that the Soviets would inevitably react in Berlin, where we were physically weakest, in retaliation for what we might do with respect to Cuba. We were kept fully briefed as the decision-making process moved ahead in the Executive Committee.[43]

So many people have written so much about the Cuban missile crisis that I see little point in going over all the details once again. The excellent book by James Blight and David Welch, *On the Brink: Americans and Soviets Reexamine the Cuban Missile Crisis*, incorporates the best available information from both the Soviet and the American side.[44] Of all the crises with the Soviet Union during the postwar period, it provides perhaps the best concentrated case study of Soviet-American confrontation on an important issue that could theoretically have involved the use of nuclear weapons. The Berlin crisis was obviously more protracted, and perhaps in essence more fundamental, but not in chronological compactness or in the intensity of official attention.

The basic facts as revealed by U-2 aerial photography were disturbingly simple. The Soviets, whatever their ultimate motives, had begun to deploy medium-range missiles in Cuba with the obvious intention of achieving a strategic advantage over those considerable portions of the United States that those missiles could reach. In his memoirs, Khrushchev seems to argue that his two primary motives for putting missiles in Cuba were to "restrain the United States from precipitous military action against Castro's government" and to equalize "what the West like[d] to call 'the balance of power.'"[45] In *On the Brink*, Professors Blight and Welch list eight hypotheses, including the two motives stressed by Khrushchev, purporting to explain why he did what he did. One of them they call the "Berlin gambit," that Khrushchev, having been frustrated in his effort to force the Allies out of Berlin, deployed missiles in Cuba to create a situation that could lead to a satisfactory resolution of the Berlin situation from the Soviet point of view.[46] As I remember it, no one at the time, from the president on down, really had a clear idea of what Khrushchev's motives were, although the obvious hypotheses could not help but occur to all of us. An overriding consideration was bound to be that those missiles could reach vital portions of the United States.

My first exposure to the emerging crisis came during the visit of Gromyko to Washington on October 18. He called on the president and was received in the oval office. There was perfunctory discussion of Berlin, but then Kennedy raised the question of Soviet arms shipments to Cuba. In his response, Gromyko emphasized the defensive nature of those shipments. After listening, and in the light of what he already knew, the president then read his September 4 statement warning against the deployment of offensive weapons in Cuba. With a straight face, Gromyko did not rise to the bait. Kennedy gave him several opportunities to say something about the Soviet deployments, but the foreign minister added nothing.

When the two-hour session ended and Gromyko had left, the president said to me that he wanted as detailed an account of the conversation relating to Cuba as I could provide. This created no particular problem. My notes were complete, my memory good, and I quickly dictated the required portion. Given the direction of Kennedy's remarks, I did not need to be told why a special record of the meeting was important.[47] Although I have not had access to my memorandum, my best recollection of what took place that day in the Oval Office is that Gromyko had ample opportunity, if his instructions had so allowed, to tell the truth—or at least a portion of it—about what was happening in Cuba. Kennedy and Rusk clearly felt that he had been lying through his teeth.

I should note, however, that, in his memoirs, Gromyko claims that "Kennedy did not once directly raise the presence of Soviet medium-range missiles in Cuba" and that as a result there was no occasion to provide any answer on whether or not such weapons were in Cuba.[48] I find this casuistical. Gromyko was much too smart not to perceive what the president was getting at.

With that peculiar symbiosis of White House and virtually resident members of the White House press corps, correspondents obviously knew that something important was afoot. The anxious faces, the lights burning late into the night, the general atmosphere of tension—all conveyed this impression. The president wanted to bide his own time and personally announce what was happening to the American people and what course of action he proposed to follow. Members of the Executive Committee entered the White House unobserved via a basement tunnel from the adjacent Treasury Department building. My assigned task was to enter the White House, rather ostentatiously, through the main front door, where I could clearly be observed. The press, of course, knew of my long association with the Berlin crisis and would immediately jump to the conclusion that something was brewing in that much headlined city.

Needless to say, we did think something might very well happen in or about Berlin as the Cuban situation developed. Nearly four years of Soviet bluster and threat had sensitized us to the precarious geographical and military situation of West Berlin. If Khrushchev felt that he had to take some action in response to what we might do with respect to Cuba, then Berlin seemed the logical place for him to do it. We had all sorts of contingency plans to respond to various types of Soviet harassment directed at the Allied position in the city, or our access thereto, but it was obvious that, if overall deterrence failed, there was little we could do against a massive Soviet attack on the city. Our garrison of roughly twelve thousand American, British, and French troops could only hold out for a limited time, and the Allied leaders—particularly the president of the United States—would be faced with a rapid need to make momentous decisions.

In the event, as we know, Berlin remained quiet for the duration of the missile crisis. Our fears proved groundless, but we did not know that they would until it was all over. So our subgroup on Berlin worked feverishly in the White House while receiving current information about the development of the crisis. We were, of course, completely caught up in the intense emotional atmosphere of the place. It appeared as if a nuclear confrontation might occur, and it was natural that we would be concerned about the welfare of our families. We could not say all that we knew at home, but we could indicate what seemed like a rising level of danger. Once the president had made his public statement of October 22, the missile crisis obviously became a matter of concentrated media attention as a feeling of alarm and anxiety spread throughout the country.

I had never been impressed with the realism of emergency planning that envisaged the evacuation of designated government officials to a presumably immune hideout created deep beneath the Blue Ridge mountains in Virginia. As a participant in a so-called evacuation exercise that had us helicoptered to the entrance of the underground headquarters, I could only wonder at the enormous network of tunnels, work spaces, sleeping quarters, and storage areas that had been dug into the mountain. Huge black doors closed after us, and we were briefed on the impressive array of communications equipment and supplies that had been assembled to provide a command headquarters in the event of a nuclear attack on the Washington area. Even assuming that adequate warning was available so that we could get to the hideout, the idea that we would simply abandon our families to let them shift for themselves always struck me as lacking credibility. As the crisis developed, I prepared my family for a speedy departure from Chevy Chase into the distant countryside should I give the signal to go to a prearranged place. Only then would one even begin to be satisfied to become part of the official evacuation.

As noted, President Kennedy went public in a televised speech during the early evening of October 22, and within less than a week of intense drama and national concern the Cuban missile crisis was essentially over. On October 28, Khrushchev's message stated: "The Soviet Government, in addition to earlier instructions on the discontinuance of further work on construction sites, has given a new order to dismantle the weapons, which you describe as offensive, and to crate them and return them to the Soviet Union." [49]

It was by any measure a success for the president, who, in my view then and now, made the right basic decision on which of the possible options to choose in pressing the Soviets to remove their missiles from Cuba. Although the various channels of communication used between Washington and Moscow may have sometimes seemed confused, and liable to lead to further confusion, the end result at least appeared to validate the means used. Officials were working under intense personal strain. The possibility of nuclear war hovered in the background, even though we knew that our intercontinental ballistic missiles considerably outnumbered those of the Soviets.

Once it was all over, the inevitable process of holding postmortems began in earnest. In the State Department, and I would suppose elsewhere in the government, the participants broke down into two categories: those who thought that, in the aftermath of the crisis, golden opportunities would open up to move ahead on arms control, and generally to improve relations with the Soviet Union, and those who argued that the failure in Cuba would inevitably lead the Soviet government and military establishment to make every effort to build up its strategic missile force so as never again to be put in the kind of humiliating situation that developed in the missile crisis. Walt Rostow, Department of State counselor and head of the Policy Planning Staff, strongly supported the first assumption, while Soviet experts like Mose Harvey insisted on the second. We all know that Harvey and those who thought like him were essentially correct.

When one is caught up in a crisis working under enormous pressure to produce what the president, the secretary of state, and the developing situation itself demand, one does not have time to think of everything or to anticipate every possible move. Looking back, one can, of course, identify the imperfections of logic and planning—as scholars are wont to do. Although we had all sorts of contingency plans for Berlin, we, not surprisingly, had none prior to the missile crisis that specifically linked Berlin to what might happen in and about Cuba.

Perceptions of Continuing Berlin Crisis

Some commentators on the Berlin crisis have, in effect, terminated it with the end of the Cuban missile crisis. It may well be that the danger of Soviet unilateral action, in signing a peace treaty with the GDR purporting to end all our rights in Berlin, had diminished. But this was not, of course, what the Soviets were saying, and periodic threats and protests continued to come from Moscow. The four-power apparatus in Washington along with the Berlin Task Force continued to function at more or less full speed.

In his speech of December 12, 1962, to the Supreme Soviet of the USSR, Khrushchev stressed that "the urgency of concluding a German peace treaty and normalizing the situation in West Berlin on this basis had become even more obvious" in the current circumstances. He added that "the troops in West Berlin should not represent NATO countries" and that the United Nations should "undertake certain international obligations and functions there." Then, in an address in East Berlin on January 16, 1963, Khrushchev repeated the Soviet proposal of free-city status for West Berlin after signature of a peace treaty with the two German states or with one of them. However, he set no new deadline. One could perhaps detect a slightly milder tone in all of this, but no matter how the threat to Berlin in 1963 may appear in hindsight, we could not assume that the outcome in Cuba had ended the Berlin crisis.[50]

As 1963 began, I was becoming more and more restless. After more than four years of drafting many hundreds of thousands of words in telegrams, memorandums, and briefing papers, of attending and sometimes chairing countless meetings, of making crucial decisions or recommendations for decisions, of constant travel, I was psychologically and physically ready for a change. Foy Kohler had already left in the spring of 1962 to take over as ambassador in Moscow, and I had become director of the Berlin Task Force. William R. Tyler, an experienced and articulate officer, succeeded Kohler as assistant secretary of state for European affairs. Rumors were floating around Washington in the late fall of 1962 that the president intended to name me as ambassador to Vienna, but whatever their validity, others felt that I could not yet be released from Berlin crisis management. By the spring of 1963, however, as Undersecretary of State for Political Affairs George C. McGhee was named ambassador to Bonn to succeed Walter (Red) Dowling, the secretary and Undersecretary George Ball saw a need for me to go to Bonn as minister and deputy chief of mission. If this was not exactly what I had hoped for, I could see the logic behind such an assignment.

Summing Up the Berlin Crisis

By mid-May I had arrived in Bonn, and Soviet harassment of Allied traffic on the autobahn continued into the autumn. This seems, however, like an opportune point to sum up my perceptions and the conclusions at which I had arrived during those years of intimate involvement in the Berlin crisis. Scholars trying to piece together the various elements of that crisis have been handicapped by the uneven pace at which classified materials have become available. White House papers typically are released, or at least used, at an earlier point as they become part of collections at presidential libraries.

I have already said (in the preceding chapter) that no completely satisfactory explanation for Khrushchev's decision to precipitate the crisis in November 1958 is yet available. The idea that Berlin was essentially a sideshow for the Soviet leader, a tail to be yanked whenever the imperialistic powers misbehaved, as Fyodor Burlatsky (former speechwriter for Khrushchev) and Sergei Mikoyan (son of former Soviet first deputy premier Anastas I. Mikoyan) seemed to imply in their discussions with the Harvard Group, simply does not strike me as plausible.[51] Khrushchev obviously knew that, given the geographical situation of West Berlin, he could control the level of violence in and around Berlin. Perhaps when he began to issue his series of ultimatums and threats of unilateral action, he believed he could bluff the Allies out of Berlin. But surely he was not so foolish and uncomprehending as to be unaware that, once his initial efforts had failed, there was no issue that could so consolidate Western resolve and stimulate NATO unity as a prolonged Berlin crisis and that continuation of the crisis was having precisely that effect. If Berlin were only a means rather than an important objective in itself, why did he never during those weary years offer any sort of a deal to obtain what he allegedly really wanted, for example, a Western guarantee of no nuclear arms for the West Germans in exchange for relaxation of pressure on Berlin? The investment of Soviet time and energy on the Berlin crisis, including that of Chairman Khrushchev himself, was enormous.

During the early sixties I used to have lunch from time to time at the Hay-Adams House with the Soviet political counselor Georgi Kornienko. He seemed to prefer the dark wood paneling and dim lighting of this hotel restaurant to any other. I always thought it was because he did not want to be spotted having lunch with a State Department official. He was a squat little man with a shrewd intelligence and relentless pursuit of subject matter (he was later to become a senior deputy foreign minister in Moscow). Our talks were long and circular; both of us knew all the right national answers. If there was any one of my points that I believe sank in (and, I trust, was duly reported to Moscow), it was that our position in West Berlin represented a matter of grave national interest and that we would not be bullied out of the city.

Unless some unknown documents still buried in Russian archives come to light one day revealing Khrushchev's true motives, I fear that we shall never know with any degree of certainty what impelled him to take the action that he did in November 1958 and the years that followed. My own view is that, while his motives and the pressures on him may well have been mixed, an overriding objective was to end the Allied occupation in West Berlin and gradually thereafter to absorb the entire city in the German Democratic Republic. Having made the colossal blunder of thinking he could threaten the Allies out of West Berlin, he became the victim of his own logic and the great amount of prestige he had invested in a successful outcome of his venture. Even after the Wall ended the demographic drain from East Germany, he could still not escape the investment of prestige and effort already made and the pressures to succeed that it had generated within the Soviet Communist hierarchy and within the Communist world.

It may well also be that Khrushchev was essentially more bluster than performance. De Gaulle had apparently come to this conclusion after the abortive summit of May 1960 at which Khrushchev had put on a fiery performance. Some of his ministers heard him say: "Khrushchev makes a lot of noise, but he doesn't do anything. If you want to be a Hitler, you must make war. Khrushchev won't make war, and everybody knows it, beginning with Khrushchev." [52]

Looking back from the American side, one might now well conclude some thirty-five years after the crisis that at least some of Khrushchev's threats amounted to little more than bluff. But those of us dealing with the Berlin problem at the time could not be sure, even if we had occasional doubts. In the nuclear age, prudence dictated that we take him at his word. It is the nature of diplomacy that one must allow for the possibility, perhaps the reality, of a worst-case hypothesis. We could not be unmindful of overwhelming Soviet military superiority around Berlin, a basically indefensible exclave one hundred miles removed from the nearest border of the Federal Republic of Germany.

Despite the actual comparative relationship of nuclear forces during the 1958–62 period, this was also a time of public debate about the reality of deterrence precipitated by such writings as "The Delicate Balance of Terror" by Albert Wohlstetter (in the January 1959 issue of *Foreign Affairs*) and Herman Kahn's books *On Thermonuclear War* (1960) and *Thinking about the Unthinkable* (1962). The dread possibility of nuclear war was always in the background of my thinking, and if at times I advocated caution in situations where more gung ho types wanted action, no matter how risky, it was because I could only follow the logic of my own concept of nuclear deterrence as it evolved during the crisis. Years later I tried to summarize this in an article that appeared in *International Security* from which I quote:

> In assessing the present balance . . . one has to ask how the deterrent operates in our time. If one looks for absolute assurance and certainty, one will always be fearful that we have somehow fallen

short of perfection. Likewise, from the Soviet point of view, to be deterred does not require absolute certainty that an attack on the West would inevitably escalate into a strategic nuclear exchange. What is required is a sufficient degree of uncertainty about the potential development so that the ultimate risk of a strategic nuclear exchange simply cannot be taken. I have found it helpful in this context to think of the logic of Pascal's famous wager. Although he devised his argument for an entirely different purpose, it derived from a deep understanding of the infinitesimal calculus and the calculus of probability which he discovered. When the possible result of one's action is infinite in its negative implications (in this case not infinite but certainly beyond human conception in the direction of incalculability), then even one chance in many thousands, even millions, that an infinite result for practical purposes will be achieved, should, for the rational person, act as a deterrent. I do not want to suggest that the Soviet leadership thinks in terms of the calculus of probability, but some rudimentary application of this highly sophisticated logic must lie in the minds of any rational leadership, including an anxious Soviet leadership.[53]

This was all well and good, but what if the leadership was not rational in the sense that Hitler was not rational in his last months? That ultimately was our concern about Khrushchev. Could we be sure? As it turned out, Khrushchev took no action in the Berlin context that ran the risk of escalating to nuclear war that he could not ultimately control. His obvious agitation over the tank confrontation at Checkpoint Charlie was proof of this, and no matter how potentially dangerous Soviet actions in the Berlin air corridors early in 1962 might have proved to be, he probably still believed he could keep escalation under control. Looking back, one can agree with McGeorge Bundy in his 1988 book that, during the Berlin crisis, "the decisive nuclear reality for both sides was a risk of such enormous shared catastrophe that by comparison no numerical advantage or disadvantage could in the end count for much."[54]

This harsh logic imposed by nuclear weapons helps to explain why, contrary to our fears, Khrushchev did not take advantage of his geographically superior position with respect to Berlin to exercise counterpressures there during the Cuban missile crisis. The Blight book throws little light on this aspect of the crisis, but one may hypothesize that the intensity of confrontation over his missile deployment in Cuba may, in the mind of the Soviet leader, have argued against any compounding of the emotional issues directly involved at the time. The quality of Western deterrence, however that might specifically be defined, kept him from taking action against West Berlin, despite all the bluster, threats, and ultimatums. His frustration over Berlin may actually have provided part of the motivation for his Cuban venture.

Anyone who participated in the handling of the Berlin crisis during both the Eisenhower and Kennedy administrations could not help but note a considerable contrast in operating styles. President Eisenhower, after all, had been the commander in chief of the victorious Western forces in Europe and then, after the war, Supreme Allied Commander Europe. He had to make fateful decisions as well as to moderate between temperamental leaders, both American and Allied. He had been president six years when Khrushchev launched his November offensive against the Western powers in Berlin. While not a man of outstanding intelligence or depth of historical knowledge, he had both great common sense and enormous experience in the exercise of power on which to draw. He also insisted on orderly governmental processes, did not believe in surrounding himself with a swollen personal staff in the White House, and had confidence in the competence of the State Department, to which he left the day-to-day operational responsibility of dealing with the crisis. He did not underestimate the gravity of Khrushchev's challenge but reflected calmness and confidence in his analysis and behavior at meetings.

President Kennedy, we all knew, was not a well man. Apart from a chronic back problem that required a board-hard bed wherever he went, Kennedy also suffered from Addison's disease. I recall one visit to his White House bedroom during the morning when he was unable to get up but wanted to discuss an aspect of the Berlin problem. His fairly large bedside table resembled the assembly table in a busy pharmacy. It must have held forty or fifty bottles of medicine or containers of pills. I could only think that this was either a hypochondriac or, much more likely, a man who required frequent medication of all sorts just to keep going. On the other hand, President Eisenhower had suffered a serious heart attack before Khrushchev launched his offensive against Berlin in November 1958. In neither his nor Kennedy's case, however, did I ever detect anything that would lead to the conclusion that physical disability hampered their capacity to deal personally with the Berlin crisis at points of high tension.

Not surprisingly, the Kennedy White House operated in a more turbulent environment than Eisenhower's. The president, of course, lacked the depth of experience and the managerial skills of his predecessor, and he did not provide himself with the kind of staff that would bring order into an essentially disorderly process of decision making and follow-up. Although one could criticize the overly bureaucratic approach of the old Operations Coordination Board (OCB), which Kennedy abolished at the outset, it did provide a reasonably succinct and accurate record of what happened at meetings of the National Security Council or subcommittees thereof. If it had not been for the extraordinary ability of McGeorge Bundy to synthesize cabinet room discussions, and to get the president to sign off on skillfully drafted action memorandums, confusion might well have reigned. Kennedy was not a particularly effective chairman; one could not always be sure what he wanted or what he expected. In a White House populated by excitable and inexperienced young men, the level of intensity quickly rose in times of crisis, and a flood of lateral memorandums automatically followed that could only confuse the president.

One related problem was that meetings in the cabinet room of those with operational responsibility for Berlin usually drew a gaggle of staff onlookers sitting in chairs along the west wall. A few of these who committed their evenings to the Georgetown cocktail circuit were unable to conceal their importance and tended to talk far too much about had happened at meetings earlier in the day. This naturally created reluctance on the part of some participants, including Secretary Rusk, to speak up freely on particularly sensitive subjects.

Despite these disabilities, with Rusk able to see the president privately when necessary, and with the president's willingness to deal directly with relevant State Department officials, the end result was usually better than the method of arriving there. I can recall one instance when Bill Tyler and I were hailed over to the White House and ushered into the Oval Office to see Kennedy alone. We recommended that we go ahead with the action proposed on the autobahn despite Soviet protests. The president said he would take our advice, but he added that if things went wrong, our heads would be on the platter. Fortunately they did not go wrong.

Those of us who lived with the Berlin crisis during two administrations were not always right, and in 1961 we had to adjust to a basically different operating style. In my view, however, the general course of policy and actions taken in both administrations was substantially correct, and we emerged with our position in Berlin intact. That, I believe, will be the ultimate judgment of history.

7

Bonn and Budapest

· ·

My assignment to Bonn as minister and deputy chief of mission, after my having expected to go to Vienna as ambassador and after years of dealing with the Berlin crisis, was bound to seem somewhat anticlimactic. I certainly needed a lowering of stress, and I could always rationalize that, after all, Bonn was by any measure a more important post than Vienna. Moreover, as far as we knew at the time, the Soviets had not abandoned their threat to our basic position in Berlin (and we might well face another attempt to assert their geographical advantage by one form of harassment or another). We also knew that President Kennedy's scheduled visit to the Federal Republic would take place a few weeks after our arrival and would immediately engulf us in all the furor and hubbub of presidential travel. I had participated often enough as a member of presidential parties abroad to know what a strain summitry can put on receiving posts, but this was to be my first experience as part of an embassy apparatus faced with an imminent presidential visit.

West Germany Twenty Years after the War

As someone who had spent the immediate postwar years amid the ruins of the German Reich, then two years during the second half of the fifties in Berlin, and subsequently had worked intensively for nearly five years in Washington on the Berlin crisis, I could not help being impressed once again by the enormous changes that had taken place in West Germany during the twenty years after the end of World War II. Although there were still a few scattered vestiges of the ruins left by World War II, in some cases deliberately preserved (like the Gedaechtniskirche in West Berlin) as memorials, German assiduity had cleaned up the cities and constructed new office buildings and apartment houses. Some of these seemed jerry-built, and nearly all suffered from the Bauhaus influence ("stripped-down Bauhaus" I called them). But people were again housed, and office space was available for the management of a relatively booming German industry.

Coming out of the low-calorie, semistarvation diet of the immediate postwar years, the Germans had gone through their period of compensatory gluttony (the so-called *Schlagsahneepoche*—whipped cream era). In the midst of all this growing affluence, a significant portion of the German intellectual community, as in so many other European countries, strongly criticized or completely rejected the society around them, a society that they accused of attempting to restore some of the worst aspects of old Germany. Prominent and gifted novelists like Heinrich Böll and Magnus Enzenberger wrote book after book attacking the materialism and built-in hypocrisy of the Federal Republic. Some writers even suggested that the theoretically more egalitarian East Germany provided a better model, although the Berlin Wall should have served as a constant reminder that a goodly portion of the population of the GDR, if given a choice, would vote with their feet by departing for the West. Intellectual critics of their milieu served a useful purpose in noting imperfections and malpractices, but their influence on the actual behavior of the masses was small. They did, however, contribute to the atmosphere of discontent among a portion of the young in the late sixties and early seventies, a phenomenon not only in Germany, of course, but in most advanced industrial societies.

My predecessor as minister in Bonn, Brewster Morris, an old friend and colleague, left a few days after my arrival. As a dubious reward for four hard years in Bonn, he was appointed ambassador to Chad. Like the disciplined officer he was, he took it without a murmur. He briefed me as fully as he could before his departure. Toward the end of one session, he pulled some ragged scraps of paper from his pocket. Somewhat apologetically, he said, "There is not much really useful that I can leave you, but you will find these invaluable. They are the secret exits from all the hotel salons and other public places where national day receptions are held." He was right. The information proved invaluable. One would go to the same 150 national day receptions in Bonn (a nearly obligatory duty), shake the hand of the host ambassador, murmur congratulations, grab a glass of champagne from a nearby waiter, disappear into the crowd, and, after a decent interval, depart from the scene. Sometimes this meant ducking out through the kitchen to the astonishment of hotel staff. Years later, when I returned to Bonn as ambassador, I continued to find my knowledge of exits to be useful. One of the great illusions perpetrated by some commentators is that serious business can be transacted at diplomatic receptions. This may have been the case in the past, when diplomatic corps were smaller, but my experience has been that the decibel rating mounts so rapidly that, after five or ten minutes, everybody is shouting to make himself or herself heard at all. Escape under these circumstances is the best form of diplomacy. If there is a hot item of news or scandal, the gossips among the corps will get it spread around quickly in the early minutes.

The Kennedy Visit

As a visitor, I had heard the complaints of my foreign service colleagues about the overriding demands of White House representatives preparing for a presidential arrival. Yet exposure at first hand came as a shock. Membership in the White House staff, no matter in what capacity, apparently breeds a unique kind of arrogance that seems to assume that the glory and might of the office have rubbed off on everybody who comes anywhere near the president. During the postwar period, the U.S. government has suffered from creeping bureaucratic elephantiasis. The White House staff, with its ability to borrow personnel from other branches of the government without debiting its own budget, has grown and grown. The White House advance party that came in 1963 to prepare for the Kennedy visit descended on Bonn like a swarm of locusts. Administrative types acted as if they knew all there was to know about Germany and Bonn and immediately began to tell German officials how the program was to go. The Secret Service cohort displayed a take-charge attitude that indicated small respect for German security practices and an overweening confidence in their own ability to provide complete protection in a foreign country. The inevitable tug-of-war arose between proud German security officials and peremptory Secret Service representatives. I do not recall a single presidential visit to Western Europe, with which I was involved, when this kind of arrogant behavior did not embitter local government officials. As a matter of fact, the conduct of White House personnel, since there were more of them each time (there was sometimes even an advance advance party that preceded the regular advance party), seemed to become progressively more obtrusive. When sufficiently provoked, European officials would sometimes bitterly remark that, after all, it was American presidents, and not European leaders, who got shot at, and sometimes assassinated.

We had hardly moved into the minister's house (one of the nicest in the entire Foreign Service) when the advance party told us we would have to move out again. Much to the unhappiness of the also newly arrived ambassador, George C. McGhee, who protested in vain that the president should stay at his residence, the Secret Service had decided that the president would be safer in our house, set back as it was from the street with a long approaching driveway that could be blocked with barriers. We were to vacate the premises twenty-four hours before the president's arrival but were also to take care of a few command arrangements. One of them was to have sitting on a table in Kennedy's bedroom a chocolate cake, with one slice out, under a bell jar cover. We were never able to figure out why this was important, symbolically or dietarily, but the cake was there when the president arrived. We were unable to ascertain, in the face of the conspiracy of silence that his staff wrapped around him, whether Kennedy actually ate any of the cake.

Years later, I was to learn from Secretary of State William Rogers how a chance request could develop into a rigid requirement. On his first trip abroad, Rogers had indicated vaguely he would like some Chivas Regal before going to bed. A bottle awaited him in his quarters on his first stop. He said thanks. The word then flashed around, and at every subsequent stop a bottle of Chivas Regal appeared in his quarters. His protest that this was not really necessary, and that he didn't require scotch at every stop, fell on deaf ears. On each subsequent trip the bottle automatically appeared as a tribute to bureaucratic memory and imperviousness to change. My own experience as ambassador confirmed the need for rigorous self-discipline in making offhand requests.

For some decades, American presidents have traveled with a bevy of Filipino naval enlisted men who serve as personal servants. They are reasonably efficient and make it possible for the normal household staff, frightened into immobility by the entourage of the guest, conveniently to disappear. That meant every emergency, whether locating the crockery or the liquor supply, had to be referred for solution to the minister or his wife. Given the recentness of our own arrival in Bonn, we could not always respond with alacrity as to where things could be found. This brought down invectives from an assortment of flunkies who acted as if they spoke with the full authority of the presidency.

The visit of President Kennedy to West Germany proved to be a smash hit. The young president could do nothing wrong for a German public and press ready to applaud his every word and ceremonial act. It was clearly a high point in German-American relations, and every president who followed found himself burdened with the self-conceived need to receive similar plaudits and to turn out similarly large crowds. This they could not achieve, but the effort to emulate led to some peculiar improvisations and contortions of protocol. Kennedy had a remarkable public presence, a seeming combination of youth and vigor, and he spoke in a confident manner that sounded impressive even to Germans who did not understand a word he said. There to translate was the very able Foreign Office interpreter, Heinz Weber, who for more than thirty years provided eloquence in both English and German for presidents, chancellors, and foreign ministers, even to those who did not possess it. We had competent interpreters in the State Department, but successive presidents chose to rely on Weber's elegant phrasing, and at times rephrasing. He could make even an inept sentence sound good.

As an official spectator and participant in all this, I could not be a completely detached observer. We knew what was happening behind the scenes, and yet the genuineness of the president's popular reception, the evocation of true regard for the country he represented, could only impress the embassy staff as well as the reporting press. As official visits go, this was indeed a success not only in the flaccid phraseology of communiqués but as a real reflection of a mood and of fortuitous timing.

Presidential visits are never without their ludicrous aspects. Before the dinner to be given in the evening by the president for Chancellor Adenauer at the American Club (the chancellor had given his banquet for the president the previous evening at the Villa Hammerschmidt), we received urgent information that Princess Radziwill (Jacqueline Kennedy's sister, who was part of the official party) needed her hair done. German hairdressers normally close down on Mondays, but finally a resourceful member of the embassy staff found one open in Düsseldorf—about seventy-five miles from Bonn. Fortunately, presidential visits produce marine and army helicopters in quantity, so the princess was dispatched by helicopter to Düsseldorf for her hairdo. Never mind the expense or the pretense! When presidents travel, nothing is impossible for members of their entourage, and the Foreign Service once again had demonstrated its capacity for improvisation.

Wherever Kennedy went, enormous and enthusiastic crowds turned out. The shadow of Vietnam had not yet begun to darken the American image, and the young people of Germany joined in applauding the young American president. His formal speech to a distinguished audience in Frankfurt's historic Paulskirche impressed with its nobility of language and sentiment. He then went on to Berlin, where he made his famous address from the balcony of the city hall (Schöneberg *Rathaus*) to more than 250,000 Berliners assembled in the square before it. His attempt at German, "Ich bin ein Berliner" (I am a Berliner), while phonetically somewhat deficient, brought a roar of approval from the crowd, and the ever reliable Weber was there at his side to translate the president's German into German for those who needed it. The usual shuffling for position to be near

Kennedy took place on the balcony, with Adenauer and Brandt trying to be closest. Others found their place in accordance with their skills at maneuver and fast footwork. Over the years I have noted that some officials display a positive genius for moving to the front, to be near the great men, when photographers are present.

Life in Bonn and the Last Gasp of the Berlin Crisis

The Kennedy visit over and the media plaudits replaced by emphasis on the vacation season—almost as sacrosanct in Germany as in France—we could settle into our new routine in Bonn. The Berlin situation seemed relatively quiet; the Soviet *nomenklatura* (the Communist upper class in army, party, and government) also cherished their summer holidays. Among the largest American embassies in the world, despite the absence of any aid mission to swell personnel totals, our establishment in Bonn required considerable supervision and some rejuvenation.

George McGhee was a Texan, a Rhodes scholar, and a geologist who had made a small fortune in oil. He had served as ambassador to Turkey under President Truman and as head of the Policy Planning Staff and undersecretary of state for political affairs under Kennedy. He obviously knew his way around the bureaucracy; however, he was new to Germany and did not speak the language. I found that he wanted his conversations with German officials reported in meticulous detail, and the flow of recommendations from the embassy was heavy, if not always appreciated in Washington. George was a strong ambassador. We did not always agree, but he took my advice seriously.

It quickly became clear that McGhee intended to leave the management of the overly large embassy primarily to me. I also worked out with the ambassador that I would devote as much time as possible to seeing the many political and economic contacts I already had in the German government and legislature and report to Washington on broader German issues. I usually accompanied him in his meetings with the chancellor and other German leaders and sometimes found myself in the dual role of scribe and interpreter. All in all, we made a good team. He had seemingly limitless energy. I had the experience.

The embassy in Bonn was not only overstaffed. It already showed the kind of imbalance between State Department personnel and representatives of myriad other U.S. governmental agencies that was to become more and more the pattern. Everybody wanted to get into the act, and Washington agencies with fatter budgets than the traditionally starved State Department could afford to send their people abroad in profusion. The result was colossal embassies, sometimes larger in staff than the entire Foreign Ministry of the government to which they were accredited. We were a world power, but the value of output to bodies involved, in my view, added up to a bad investment. Sporadic efforts by Washington to decrease foreign representation usually ended up with the State Department faithfully carrying out the prescribed cuts while other agencies were skillfully wriggling out of compliance. The result was even more structural imbalance. I doubt that this is no longer the case.

Both the residences of the minister and the ambassador, from different vantage points, enjoyed spectacular views of the Rhine and the Siebengebirge (Seven Hills) on the east bank. The Rhine Valley near Bonn was a central area for German mythology and for many of the Wagnerian operas. On a misty morning, and they were frequent enough, one could see the Seven Hills seemingly rising out of the broad river and imagine the Rhine maidens disporting below, observed by Alberich the dwarf. Or imagine on the Drachenfels, the last of the hills to the south, Fafner the dragon guarding the Rheingold, to be slain there eventually by Siegfried. These were not great hills by any absolute measure, perhaps a little more than one thousand feet in height, but they reared right out of the river plain. Such things are relative. To the flatland Dutch who come in droves for weekends, they seemed like mountains. Both as minister and later as ambassador, for a total of nearly nine years, I found the ever changing view (with the fluctuation of seasons and atmospheric conditions) a constant source of aesthetic stimulation. To cross the river by ferry (a bridge was never built from Bad Godesberg to Koenigswinter) and to walk in the well-kept forest trails of the Siebengebirge brought special pleasure and some understanding of that peculiar German affinity for the forest that is so characteristic of the country's literature and general culture. The *Waldsterben* (dying of the forest) of our time was bound to evoke strong emotional reactions even in a largely industrialized and urbanized West Germany.

That summer I began to suffer from temple pains, and at night I would see colored halos around street lamps. By chance, I came across an article about glaucoma in a German newspaper and immediately jumped to the conclusion that that was what I had. Self-diagnosis can sometimes be hazardous, but in this case it proved correct. I finally made an appointment in late September with Professor Dr. Reiser, reputedly the best eye specialist in the area. It was high time. The pressure in my left eye measured out to be 48 (more than double the acceptable pressure), in my right eye 34. The good doctor insisted that I enter the Johanniter Krankenhaus (hospital) the next day, where he was the chief ophthalmologist. His diagnosis was that I had a fairly rare case of pigmentary glaucoma in both eyes and that the first priority was to bring the pressure down by trying various available medicaments. Almost immediately after my entry into the hospital, he and other doctors began putting drops into my eyes and repeatedly measuring the pressure.

With the ambassador on holiday, I was chargé d'affaires. A constant stream of officers from the embassy flowed into my hospital room for the first days with incoming cables to discuss and outgoing messages to approve. With all the medicaments in my eyes, I could not read well but I could listen and speak.

Reviewing my journal entries during those troubled days, scribbled in a wavering hand, I find much emphasis on the shock of having an eye disease that, if not brought under control, could lead to blindness. Apart from the imminence of death, nothing so wonderfully concentrates the mind as the prospect of blindness. My anxiety level would inevitably fluctuate between measurements of pressure, depending on whether the last measurement had been high and new medication was therefore obviously needed. Hospital tales can be very boring, especially if there are no Septembrinis and Napthas among the other patients. Suffice it to say that my twenty-four days in the Johanniter Krankenhaus did not pass quickly. I did not experience the peculiar timelessness of sanitorium existence on top of a mountain in Switzerland, noted by Thomas Mann in his *The Magic Mountain*. Despite my uncertain prognosis, I was very much in touch with the outside world.

Ambassador McGhee returned to Bonn to be confronted with what proved to be the last gasp of the Berlin crisis. For some critics, including at times President Kennedy, the issue seemed trivial, if not ludicrous. It quickly became known as the "tailgate" crisis, but for those Americans involved on the spot an important principle seemed to be at stake. In October the East German checkpoint guards at Marienborn (the western end of the central autobahn traversing the GDR from the Federal Republic of Berlin) twice held up American military truck convoys. They demanded that the tailgates of the vehicles be lowered so that the number of American military personnel could be counted and that, if there were more than thirty, they dismount to be counted. The American officer in charge refused, arguing that established procedures permitted only inspection of trucks from the outside and that the tailgate was only to be lowered if it was too high to permit visual inspection.

The inevitable escalation happened. In the face of an American ultimatum that the convoy would proceed after a certain time, the East Germans first raised their barrier. But on a later occasion, after the American ultimatum had been issued, they blocked the road with two armored personnel carriers. Protests in Moscow to the Soviets, who had previously argued that this was entirely an East German matter, finally resulted in the passage of the convoy. Both sides repeated the same scenario a few days later except that the East Germans refused to permit passage. We brought up additional convoys that allowed themselves to be halted. The resulting traffic jam at the GDR checkpoint stopped all traffic on the autobahn, and the East Germans finally capitulated. Fortunately, despite the posturing on both sides, no one started firing. Our position on principle was somewhat weakened by the British practice of lowering tailgates on demand.[1]

While there were a few more minor East German attempts at harassment, these ceased during November. The assumption was that Moscow had given the signal to call the whole thing off. Khrushchev's role in all this was somewhat ambiguous. One theory was that the initiative to let the East Germans make their demands had come from the Soviet military commanders in the GDR but that Moscow felt it subsequently necessary to back them up. President Kennedy himself was never comfortable with the American position and issued orders that the ultimatum procedure should not be used again without his personal approval.

It is fair to describe the tailgate controversy as the last act in the great Berlin crisis that had endured, in one form or another, for some five years. Thinking about the confrontation at the autobahn checkpoint in my hospital room, I could only be impressed by how adherence to what seemed like an important principle to the participants could have led to tragic results. If there had been an escalating firefight, no one could be sure where it might end. On the other hand, acceptance of the original East German demands might have led to escalating further demands on their part to the point where our access to West Berlin might have been seriously compromised. In its sometimes seemingly confused way, the tailgate issue mirrored so many aspects of the prolonged confrontation over Berlin. What were acceptable and nonacceptable changes in procedure? How did such changes affect our vital interests in Berlin as we had defined them? If we could not answer these questions with precision, at least we could be assured that, in its final outcome, the Berlin crisis had been essentially a victory for Western resolve and tactics.

I emerged from the hospital with a distinctly unfavorable prognosis. The pressure in both eyes was under temporary control, but Professor Reiser predicted (accurately it turned out) that surgery would eventually be necessary as I developed a tolerance for the various available drugs. In any event, putting drops in my eyes would be a lifelong necessity. There are many forms of expertise, but I had never thought of becoming an expert with the eye-dropper. Over the years, I have developed a technique for getting medicine in my eyes no matter how shaky and jiggly the environment.

A Changing Cast of Characters at the Top

As 1963 began to draw to a close, it became clear that, after more than fourteen years as head of government, Konrad Adenauer's days as chancellor were coming to an end. He was now eighty-seven years old, and while he was far from a man with failing powers, the rigidities of analysis and practice almost inevitable in such a long term of office, added to the natural impatience of his putative successor and those who hoped to move into high office with him, gradually undermined Adenauer's position. Many could not believe that this man, who had become so much an institution in postwar Germany, would ever really be replaced. The story had been going the rounds in Bonn that, at an office party to celebrate the chancellor's eighty-seventh birthday, the staff had presented him with a gold watch that only required to be wound every ten years. In thanking his aides for the gift, Adenauer said that he was touched by their thoughtfulness but that he was saddened by the consideration that, when he next had to wind the watch, some of those present would no longer be there.

Adenauer clearly did not think highly of Economics Minister Ludwig Erhard, who was waiting in the wings to succeed him. In fact, the CDU Bundestag *Fraktion* had already, in April, nominated Erhard as chancellor candidate to succeed Adenauer, presumably for the next elections. The old chancellor missed few opportunities to belittle the man. There was obviously a large difference in personalities, but there was also a perceptible difference in cultural outlook. Adenauer was, after all, the consummate Rhinelander with a strong orientation to Western Europe, particularly France. A staunch Catholic and a man of culture, he was steeped in the traditions of that part of Europe that had once been Roman. He did not like Germans from the east and the north, and his experience during the Nazi period had only confirmed his prejudices. On visits to his house on a hill in Rhoendorf, across the river slightly to the south of Bonn, I had been impressed by his collection of Gothic and other art, as well as his fine library. One reason, I suppose, why we hit it off so well when I was still a consul in Bremen (with an interest in the medieval era) was that I could identify the period and place of origin of some of his Gothic collection.

Erhard, on the other hand, was a somewhat rotund, often jovial man lacking the natural dignity and impressive mien of an Adenauer. His club foot required a special shoe. As head of the Bizonal Economic Administration in 1948, he presided on the German side over the successful monetary reform of that year. Although the major push actually came from within the American military government organization, Erhard showed considerable personal courage in carrying out a difficult, at times almost traumatic, writing down of old reichsmark values. Then, as economics minister during the long Adenauer chancellorship, he guided the German economy through a period of rapid and transforming growth on the basis of free-market principles that he had absorbed from the Swiss professor Wilhelm Roepke, whose intellectual influence was strong in postwar Germany. The designation "father of the German economic miracle" that others applied to him was not undeserved.

To Adenauer, however, he was a north German lacking sufficient commitment to the ideal of a unifying Western Europe that had become a major cause for the chancellor. In the light of my own experience before 1963 and subsequently, I could not deny the basic verisimilitude of Adenauer's perception. With some notable exceptions, most politicians from north Germany, oriented more toward Britain and North America rather than toward the Continent, did not have the driving zeal to build a new Europe that moved those with the geographical and cultural commitment of an Adenauer. One of life's little ironies was that just as Adenauer never became fluent in French, Erhard never acquired much English.

The political scene in the Federal Republic as Erhard took over the chancellorship late in 1963 did not seem burdened with major internal problems. The Berlin crisis had clearly reached its denouement, and while the elections of 1961 had resulted in significant CDU losses (down to 45.4 percent of the total vote) compared with those of 1957 (when Adenauer's party won 50.2 percent of the total vote and a clear majority in the Bundestag), both the extremist left-wing and right-wing parties were completely wiped out and, under the 5 percent minimum clause, captured no seats in the Bundestag. The FDP had won 12.8 percent of the total vote and sixty-seven seats in the Bundestag (actually the best national result it was ever to gain in the entire postwar period up to the present) and had demanded its due share of cabinet positions. An exasperated Adenauer was heard to exclaim, "Lieber zwei Wahlkämpfe als eine Kabinettsbilding" (Better two electoral campaigns than one cabinet formation). But the government finally was formed, and only the desire for a change at the top and the feeling that the old chancellor had served his full period of usefulness brought about his replacement.

One cannot overstate the historical importance of Konrad Adenauer, despite his prejudices and occasional pettiness toward individuals. He was to live until April 19, 1967, and never relented in his sniping at his successor in office. When a ruined and already divided nation needed a calm, effective leader with a vision of the future both for Germany and for Europe, Adenauer took over the direction of his country, beginning in 1948 with the Parliamentary Council that drafted the German Basic Law (constitution). Americans sometimes found his hesitations and concerns frustrating. They derived from a deep distrust of his own compatriots, but he was a man of his word and when he made a commitment always expended his best effort to carry it out. The men closest to him in the Chancellery admired him and were personally loyal to him. There were no kiss-and-tell books written by disgruntled former aides. Ambassador Horst Oster-held, who became my close friend while assigned as political counselor to the German embassy in Washington and who served for many years as Adenauer's foreign policy assistant, in his writings and in conversations, has always shown a deep admiration for the old chancellor and his *Leistungsfähigheit* (ability to produce) while in office.[2]

Ludwig Erhard, on the other hand, was clearly no Adenauer in temperament or political grasp. He had the courage to make difficult decisions but came across as a rather colorless economist with a consistent dedication to the free market. He lacked the historical grasp of an Adenauer nurtured in the tradition of Catholic social teachings, but recognized that a market economy could be politically tolerable only if combined with a measure of social justice. The CDU-sponsored term "*Sociale Marktwirtschaft*" (social market economy) thus caused him no conceptual problem. His weaknesses as a political leader were to lead to his downfall three years later. They also provided Adenauer with grist for his critical mill.

On November 22 Ambassador McGhee and Cele McGhee were celebrating their twenty-fifth wedding anniversary with a white-tie dance. They had invited friends from a number of countries as well as Germany itself. We were preparing to attend when a telephone call conveyed the tragic news that President Kennedy had been assassinated. We rushed over in full evening garb to the ambassador's residence to see if we could be helpful. The dance was obviously canceled, but there was some consolation in company. We all realized that the course of history had shifted, that America would never be psychologically quite the same again. We hung on the news reports as they came in, and received the condolences that came by telephone and sometimes in person. Finally, late that night we silently went home.

The next few days witnessed an outburst of mourning in the Federal Republic. The young president, after his triumphal visit to West Germany and Berlin earlier in the year, had achieved a remarkable degree of continuing popularity, even affection, with the German public. All weaknesses and reservations are forgotten in death. As is practically the universal diplomatic practice when a chief of state or head of government dies while in office, we put out a book for condolences—this time at the ambassador's residence rather than at the entrance of the towering and overwhelming chancery of the embassy. From Erhard and Adenauer on down, hundreds of officials, businessmen, and just everyday Germans came to sign the book and to express their sorrow. This was not just a matter of routine or protocol; the emotions were genuine. The young president, now come to such a tragic and untimely end, had achieved almost mythical status with his dynamism and charisma.

The Kennedy-Adenauer Heritage of Problems

The new chancellor had inherited three unresolved problems bearing on German-American relations: the implications of developing Franco-German closeness, and particularly the Franco-German Treaty of Friendship and Cooperation, on the Atlantic alliance; the future of the multilateral force (MLF) proposal; and the extension of offset arrangements between the Federal Republic and the United States. It was the last of these, nearly three years later, that made a major contribution to Erhard's downfall.

It was no secret that Konrad Adenauer was a strong proponent of Franco-German rapprochement. Whatever his precise motives after rejection of his proposal for a triumvirate of France, Britain, and the United States, and the subsequent rejection by the European Economic Community of his two Fouchet Plans for greater European political consultation, Charles de Gaulle made signature of an agreement with the Federal Republic a priority. He also undoubtedly wanted to take advantage of Adenauer's continuance in office at a time when most observers expected the chancellor to resign before the end of the year (as he had committed himself to do). The Franco-German Treaty of Friendship and Cooperation, signed in Paris by the two leaders on January 22, 1963, came as a surprise to most American officials, indeed to some as a major shock. A week earlier, at a press conference on January 14, de Gaulle announced that France rejected Kennedy's modified version of the multilateral force offer and that his country would take its own path as a nuclear power. Signature of the treaty was followed a week later by de Gaulle's veto of British entry into the European Economic Community. It could not but seem as if Adenauer was endorsing France's unilateral course. I was, of course, still in Washington dealing with other matters, but it struck me that the semihysterical reaction of some American officials was overblown. We knew de Gaulle had little love for the Anglo-Saxons, whom he regarded as basically opposed to the kind of Europe he envisaged. The outcome of the confused December meeting in Nassau between Prime Minister Macmillan and President Kennedy was bound to confirm in de Gaulle's mind that the Anglo-Saxons were up to it again with their special relationship and that the subsequent offer to him of Polaris missiles was patronizing, if not downright insulting. The great man was undoubtedly irritating, and at times impossible, but we showed little skill in handling him and in avoiding actions that were bound to raise his hackles.[3]

On the German side, there had been some debate within the cabinet as to whether the treaty should be signed in the aftermath of de Gaulle's press conference. Adenauer proved persuasive, however, and in the final analysis only Erhard continued to oppose the treaty. The sentiment in the Bundestag, whose consent was necessary for ratification, was less positive, particularly given the public criticism from the United States and other NATO countries that enveloped the document. After a prolonged debate, the Bundestag on May 16 approved the treaty after adding a preamble stressing the necessity for a close partnership between the United States and Europe and the entry of Great Britain and other states into the European Economic Community and the importance of the common defense within the NATO alliance.

It quickly became clear that, apart from its symbolic value, the Franco-German treaty would not change any of the fundaments governing the American relationship with Europe or the workings of the alliance. Adenauer was, after all, in his last year as chancellor, and even he, if forced to make a choice, could only have opted for the institutional web that had provided basic security for the Federal Republic. Some years later (in 1967), de Gaulle was indeed to eject NATO from France as his frustrations mounted, but this was neither to prove the disaster that many had feared it would nor to achieve any of de Gaulle's overriding objectives for Europe and France's role in it.

This was not a case of much ado about nothing, but it demonstrated the ease with which excited officials can create an atmosphere of crisis even when the basic causal and conditioning factors remain unchanged. We were all bound to be affected by that atmosphere, yet to react calmly, even while seething a bit inside, is the mark of a good diplomat. There were people in the White House and the State Department who tended to flap whenever something unexpected, not to say outrageous, happened. I had seen enough of that sort of thing in the Berlin context.

By the summer of 1963, it had become fairly obvious that extremist interpretations of the Franco-German treaty had little relevance to the drift of events. A standard German history of the period, written by Professor Hans-Peter Schwarz, discusses the events of that year under the heading "Das Scheitern des Deutsch-Franzoesischen Zweibundes" (The Breakdown of the German-French Dual Alliance).[4] When, however, Erhard took over as chancellor, despite his own clear record of opposition to Adenauer on the treaty issue, he felt it necessary to give us assurances that his basic loyalty was to NATO and to ties with the United States. This became a frequent theme in his discussions with us.

The Multilateral Force: Chimera or Good Idea Frustrated?

Every now and then, official American psychological processes go through a peculiar cycle. We perceive a need, itself largely psychological, on the part of our European allies for some new weapons deployment. We then devise some way to fill this need and offer it to the Europeans. Their response may be muted, but gradually the American side builds up a head of steam and begins to employ the hard sell. In the end, what started out as a favor becomes an American cause and a test of European loyalty to the alliance.

We went through this cycle during the later 1970s and early 1980s on the issue of cruise missile and Pershing II deployments in Europe. Twenty years earlier it was the multilateral force. In the late Eisenhower years, U.S. officials became concerned about what they perceived to be restiveness on the part of the nonnuclear European powers about American nuclear predominance in the alliance and, as a corollary, a desire somehow to have a finger on the nuclear trigger.

In December 1960 Secretary of State Herter made a proposal (which became known as the Herter Plan) at the NATO ministerial meeting. The idea was to make NATO a fourth atomic power (presumably the United States, France, and Britain were the other three) by creating a force of 5 submarines carrying a total of 80 Polaris missiles with nuclear warheads, this to be supplemented by 180 additional land-based missiles. The NATO Supreme Allied Commander, General Lauris Norstad, had been pushing such a proposal, which quickly obtained the support of German defense minister Franz Josef Strauss. During the somewhat confused early period of the Kennedy administration, engulfed in the Berlin crisis and attempting to develop a new military strategy for Berlin contingency planning, the proposal lingered in a bureaucratic limbo despite Kennedy's statement in 1961 that the MLF represented a step in the U.S. willingness to share nuclear responsibility with a united Europe. The intertwining of NATO involvement in Berlin contingency planning and the development of NATO's strategy of flexible response has, to my knowledge, never been adequately researched.

It was only during 1962–63 that conditions began to mature in Washington for a revival, in considerably new form, of the Herter Plan. For one thing, members of the Kennedy White House began to accept the importance of our relationship with the Federal Republic and that we could not unilaterally formulate policy affecting German interests without damage to that relationship. In the State Department itself a group of Europeanists led by Undersecretary George Ball began to increase their influence on overall policy. The first tangible evidence of this was the president's speech in Philadelphia on July 4, 1962, in which he foresaw an Atlantic partnership comprising a uniting Europe and the United States.[5]

By early 1963 this so-called Grand Design, if it ever had any real substance, had pretty much collapsed in the face of de Gaulle's actions. My own view was that it never amounted to anything more than rhetoric; it was only a prelude at best to the thoughtful formulation of a policy for the long-term relationship of the United States to Europe.[6] We had the alliance, of course, and the formula with respect to the European Economic Community that entailed acceptance of the economic disadvantages of progressive European integration because of the greater political advantages that this would bring with it. But the possibility of change over time, and the need to distinguish permanent from ephemeral American interests in our European relationship, were simply not taken into account. The cold war assumptions, as valid as they may have been for their time, became frozen into all our planning. In that sense, as futile as his efforts to be the spokesman for the West in an East-West dialogue were doomed to be, de Gaulle was perhaps more farsighted than our leaders.

Although I regretted the tendency in Washington, or in European capitals, to overreact to one another's blunders or the pursuit of interests not fully explained to one another, I shared in the prevailing tendency to deal with problems as they arose and to hope that new ones would not arise. One could argue, of course, that such limited pragmatism was far better than devising a grand strategy based on misunderstanding of present reality or flawed assumptions about the future.

In any event, the Europeanists in the State Department focused on the multilateral force as the initiative with most promise after the developments of early 1963. Although in his memoirs Undersecretary of State George Ball says that he was never a fervent believer in the MLF, as leader of the Europeanists, he was commonly thought to be pushing the project.[7] Other names that come to mind are Robert Schaetzel (deputy assistant secretary of state for Atlantic political affairs, later to be U.S. ambassador to the European Economic Community); Thomas Finletter (U.S. permanent representative to NATO); Henry Owen (a senior member of the Policy Planning Staff, later to be its director); and three former officials brought back as special advisers: Gerard Smith (formerly director of the Policy Planning Staff), Robert Bowie (formerly assistant secretary for policy planning), and Livingston Merchant (formerly assistant secretary for European affairs and undersecretary of state for political affairs). Dean Acheson also added his voice from time to time.

They constituted a pretty high-powered group. A regular cavalcade of officials from Washington visited European posts during 1963–64 to extol the merits of the MLF. They all came to Bonn, of course, for despite all the talk about the European urge to have a finger on the nuclear trigger, it was the West Germans who were the focus of concern. The package they were selling was quite different from the old Herter Plan. The missiles had moved completely to sea. The Polaris missiles were to be deployed on a fleet of surface ships (presumably old Victory ships from World War II brought out of mothballs).

I do not use the term "Europeanist" in a pejorative sense. I was, after all, a Europeanist myself by postwar experience and strong personal commitment. Having arrived in Bonn, however, I was perhaps in a better position to detect the nuances of German official and public opinion and to register real sentiments. The forced departure in 1962 of Franz Josef Strauss from the Ministry of Defense, and his replacement by Kai-Uwe von Hassel, removed one strong and sometimes unpredictable voice from the government, but of course not from public life. The combination of von Hassel and Foreign Minister Schroeder seemed generally supportive of the MLF idea, some would say supportive to the point of getting way out on a limb.

To Offset or Not to Offset

Every student of postwar economic history knows that for the first fifteen years or so after the war, as Western Europe was reconstructing itself, the United States seemed to be an inexhaustible source of dollars that we were prepared to feed to a dollar-hungry world. But at some point difficult to define with precision, the tide began to change. We were still far and away the richest country in the world by any conceivable economic measurement, but our international economy had begun to show signs of strain. By the late 1950s we were running what, by the standards of the day, seemed like alarmingly high balance of payments deficits (owing largely to outward capital flows rather than deficits on current account), principally with Western Europe. In December 1960, Secretary of the Treasury Robert Anderson and Undersecretary of State for Economic Affairs C. Douglas Dillon traveled to Bonn to request that the Federal Republic make an annual contribution of six hundred million dollars to help offset the dollar costs (dollars converted into deutschemarks for local use and thus a balance of payments drain) of U.S. forces stationed in West Germany. I can recall our feeling in the Office of German Affairs that the timing was somewhat peculiar, with the Republicans defeated in the 1960 elections and the Kennedy administration poised to take over.

Against the background of postwar history, the Anderson-Dillon request was more explosive than the casual observer might have thought. To the Germans it smacked of an attempt, using new nomenclature, to revive the old payments of occupation costs that had ceased with Germany's admission to NATO in 1955. The problem passed to the Kennedy administration, in which Secretary of Defense McNamara was to become its avid and hard-driving custodian. The offset agreement (this became the accepted designation) reached in 1961 provided essentially for major purchases for the German military forces of American equipment and weapons.

This was the beginning of a ritualistic negotiation every two years or so. One could almost hear the sighs of anxiety in Bonn every time a McNamara visit was announced. The Germans knew he would lean hard on them on both offset and strategic issues.

. . . .

I have discussed each of these problem areas separately for purposes of coherence, but they obviously all interacted in the sense that they, along with American handling of the Berlin crisis, contributed to the atmosphere of discord within the alliance that led some commentators to describe the 1962–63 period as a low point in American-European, and particularly American-German, relations. This despite the triumphant Kennedy visit to Germany in the spring of 1963. Looking back, it is easy to conclude that those of us who were concerned with the worsening atmosphere, and the seeming loss of mutual confidence in the alliance, overrated the irritations of the moment and underrated the binding ties of common interest between the United States and its allies. It has always been thus during the frequent so-called crises of confidence in the alliance. The problems and doubts of the moment seem to dominate, reinforced, of course, by media concentration on them. It is only when the binding ties of common interest lose substance that one, in theory at least, if not in practice, should be concerned.

During the three years of the Erhard chancellorship we, of course, had to deal with other serious problems, such as the completion of negotiations in the Kennedy round of trade talks and the signature and ratification of the Nuclear Non-Proliferation Treaty. All of this plus observing and reporting on the changing West German political scene, and in my case administering the embassy, kept us busy. I shall have more to say about these at a later point as well as the growing social burden imposed on senior American diplomats by an ever growing diplomatic corps in an important capital such as Bonn.

Erhard Takes Over as Chancellor

Adenauer was not wrong in judging that his successor had many deficiencies as a political leader. He came into office surrounded by the aura of economic success and considerable personal popularity. It was hard to dislike the man, but his years as chancellor, particularly after the successful elections of 1965, were marked by a growing sense of futility. In various meetings with him both in Bonn and at his vacation home on the Starmbergersee in Bavaria, I was always impressed by his good will and absence of pretension, but also by a certain lack of stature and authority. He sometimes behaved more like a professor of economics than the political leader of his country. He was basically a decent man in over his head.

He was not surrounded by incompetents. He brought into the Chancellery as minister of state Ludger Westrick, for many years Erhard's right-hand man as state secretary in the Economics Ministry—someone whose economic advice was generally sound. At times he seemed a little bewildered by the political fusillades aimed at the chancellor, but he was a strong member of the remarkably small personal staff with which Erhard worked. The key ministries, Foreign Affairs and Defense, remained under the same leadership, and the corps of state secretaries required only a few shifts throughout the government. Osterheld remained on in the Chancellery as Erhard's principal foreign affairs adviser and link with the working levels of the Foreign Ministry.

One lesson I had previously learned was that, while I could only deal directly with most ministers (there were a few exceptions in the cases of those I knew well) when I was chargé d'affaires, the state secretaries at the level immediately below ministers were generally repositories of knowledge and information. They were frequently better briefed than cabinet members. I cultivated them carefully as deputy chief of mission, and when in 1972 I returned to Bonn as ambassador, I continued to see the state secretaries in the Foreign, Defense, Finance, and Economics Ministries as well as their superiors. During the period up to the end of 1966, Karl Carstens (later to become president of the Federal Republic) was the senior state secretary in the Foreign Ministry. Rolf Lahr held the other state secretary position in the same ministry, primarily charged with economic matters. Another valuable contact was Ludger Westrick, whom I saw regularly.

One of life's pleasures, only infrequently experienced by the itinerant diplomat, is to meet old friends again in the cycle of time and place allotted to us. General Paul Freeman, commander of U.S. Army Europe, with headquarters in Heidelberg, we had known well twenty-one years earlier in India, where he was one of a group of bright young Chinese-speaking colonels assigned the thankless job, under General Stilwell, of training Chinese army troops. We spent some pleasant weekends with them in Heidelberg. Generally speaking, Ambassador McGhee did an excellent job of cultivating the American military commanders in Germany. I met many of them at his residence, but Paul and Mary Anne Freeman were special friends.

By the spring of 1964 it had become clear that my left eye was again out of control and that it could develop a tolerance quickly for any medication Professor Reiser could devise. The required surgery went off without incident. The next few days were worse. This was still the era when hospitals put your head between sand bags to prevent any motion that could cause a hemorrhage. It is amazing how many itches the human frame can develop under such circumstances. When I emerged from the Johanniter Krankenhaus some weeks later, I knew I would have to apply drops to both eyes four times a day or so, as well as have ocular pressure measured at regular intervals, for the rest of my life. If sufficiently motivated (and I had every reason to be), one can readily adapt to such a routine and not let it interfere with normal living or work. So much for my medical history, otherwise singularly uninteresting.

Shifts in German Thinking

Once back at the embassy I continued to broaden my contacts both in the government and in the legislature. Rainer Barzel, the CDU Fraktion leader in the Bundestag (the equivalent of our House majority leader), and I became good friends. Still relatively young (in his early forties), Barzel was a shrewd political operator but more than merely a clever manipulator. He could deliver the votes on government bills, but he also had a vision for the future of his party and his country that went beyond parliamentary activities. A man of moderate physical stature, he exuded confidence at this stage of his political life. I always found him honest in his analysis and an excellent source of information about the West German political scene. His subsequent career proved checkered. At one point he almost made it as chancellor, but thereafter it was all downhill.

Although *Ostpolitik* (Eastern policy) is properly associated with the name of Willy Brandt and entered its flowering stage only after he became chancellor in 1969, there were glimmerings of change away from the rigidities of the fifties even during the final years of the Adenauer chancellorship. When Gerhart Schroeder took over as foreign minister from von Brentano in 1961, his approach to relations with the Soviet Union and Eastern Europe seemed more open to the possibility of movement. We had noted such flexibility in his reaction to our "Principles" nonpaper in 1962, but after his experience that spring he knew he had to act cautiously lest he be undercut by Adenauer. It was clear from conversations with him that he was unhappy about the frozen situation that he had inherited.

With the advent to power of Erhard, he felt he had more *Bewegungsfreiheit* (freedom of movement), and he initiated some tentative efforts at improvements of relations with the East. The fact that the Berlin crisis had effectively ended, of course, made this easier. To Erhard and Westrick this was pretty much virgin territory, but they had confidence in Schroeder and soon themselves began to think in terms of a policy of movement.

The origins of *Ostpolitik* on the SPD side are interesting to trace. I knew from my time in Berlin, before Khrushchev precipitated the crisis over the city in November 1958, that Governing Mayor Brandt was restive under the restrictions placed on him by the Western military governments, particularly the banning of his proposed meeting with the Soviet ambassador in East Berlin. He had not become less restive during the long years of crisis over Berlin, and his negative reaction to the Allied response to the Berlin Wall in August 1961 was no secret. At his side was Egon Bahr, ever fruitful of ideas. He was known to some Americans from the early days as a hard-line, anti-Soviet commentator on RIAS (Radio in American Sector—the official American radio station), but his views had obviously mellowed. Over the years I had many encounters with Bahr in a variety of capacities. I found him uniformly intelligent and imaginative, frequently ingenious in his formulations. I also had the impression that he told one only as much as he wanted one to know and that what he withheld was sometimes important to forming a complete picture. Others were to accuse him directly of duplicity, but his contribution to the theoretical formulation of *Ostpolitik*, as well as its execution, was of major importance. My subsequent experience with him during the Nixon administration was less than exemplary.

By 1963 Bahr had coined the expression "*Wandel durch Annaehrung*" (change through rapprochement). Another expression that his fertile mind worked out was "*Politik der kleinen Schritten*" (the policy of small steps). Although Brandt had become leader of the Social Democratic Party and Bahr had a senior position in SPD headquarters (the so-called *Barracken* [barracks], a singularly ugly building located, ironically enough, on the street later to be named the Konrad Adenauer Allee), they were still in the mid-sixties on the march to political power, a time when their influence was largely limited to phrase making and planning for the future of their party.[8]

The issue of German national unification played a major role in postwar German history, even if the prospects of its realization never seemed very great and were at times totally out of the question in the foreseeable future. I have already mentioned the controversy over alleged lost opportunities in 1952–53, but in the early 1960s the situation appeared frozen. The Berlin crisis had produced the Western Peace Plan of 1959, although most of us shared the common assumption of the time that the Soviets would never permit the reunification of Germany, even a neutralized Germany completely detached from the Western alliance systems. I began to use the formula that reunification could only take place when and if the Soviet Union were to make a fundamental revision of its basic security requirements, concluding that it no longer required control over its satellite empire of Eastern Europe as a protective glacis. I would add that I could conceive of this happening only in the distant future and that therefore sound present policy might aim at some improvement of relations between East and West and any amelioration of internal conditions in Eastern Europe that this might permit. I quickly lost count of the number of interlocutors, official and otherwise, to whom I advanced such a diagnosis and prescription. What no one could foresee, of course, was under what conditions a process of change in the Soviet Union and Eastern Europe might take place that would open up new possibilities. In the 1960s no observers, to my knowledge, predicted the emergence of a Gorbachev or the sudden disintegration of the Soviet and Eastern European Communist regimes, although their economic and other imperfections even then were apparent enough.

There was always an inherent ambivalence in the attitudes of successive West German governments toward the reunification issue. It will be recalled that, fearing they would seem to be accepting the division of their country, the founding fathers of the Federal Republic refused to call their drafting body a constituent assembly but rather a *Parlamentarischer Rat* (Parliamentary Council) and their product not a constitution but rather a *Grundgesetz* (Basic Law). They wrote into the latter the claim to represent all Germans in the four zones of occupation. As a logical consequence of this claim, Walter Hallstein, the state secretary in the Foreign Ministry, gave his name to what became known as the Hallstein Doctrine—that the Federal Republic would sever diplomatic relations with any country that recognized the German Democratic Republic as an independent and sovereign nation. At the same time, Adenauer was in the forefront of those statesmen working for an integrated Western Europe and the various institutions that were established (or those that failed to be established such as the European Defense Community) as part of the process of integration. Some Social Democratic and other critics of the chancellor stressed the seeming illogic of tying the Federal Republic into Western Europe and NATO while a part of Germany drifted further and further away from the

West as a member of the Communist bloc. The chancellor's response was that only by building positions of military and economic strength in the West could one hope, at some distant point in the future, to again achieve German national unity. Some argued that Adenauer really did not want German reunification because the Social Democrats would have an assured majority in a united Germany and that, in any case, his whole record evidenced a deep distrust of historical Prussia and the eastern provinces. Looking back, we can now see that the seemingly obdurate old chancellor had sounder instincts than some of his critics and that the policy he advocated was ultimately part of the formula for success.

The verbal battle over the reunification issue was doomed to be inconclusive. There never was an offer from the Soviet Union that explicitly, or even implicitly, accepted the idea of free elections in all of Germany, and West German politicians of all parties were able to pay frequent lip service to the goal of reunification while proceeding with the immediate task at hand of rebuilding the economic and political structure of the Federal Republic and moving ahead with its foreign policy commitments. No German politician who had continuing career ambitions could publicly state that reunification was a totally impractical goal and should be abandoned once and for all. In 1974 the federal supreme court handed down a decision which, inter alia, reaffirmed the language of the Basic Law by cautioning all public officials that they were constitutionally obligated to do all they could to promote German reunification and to do nothing that would hinder it. German public opinion continued to favor the goal of national unity in principle, but as the years went on, more and more came to accept the status quo as the best attainable under the circumstances. Germany's new allies in NATO and the European institutions, needless to say, had no great interest in the achievement of an even greater and stronger Germany. While the three Western former occupying powers also gave formal commitment to the objective of reunification in the revised Convention on Relations (Deutschland Vertrag) of 1954, and many subsequent NATO communiqués committed the whole alliance for the same goal, all this seemed safe enough under what appeared to be indefinitely frozen circumstances.[9] Such was the situation when Erhard took over the chancellorship in 1963.

As officials with primarily an economic outlook, Erhard and his strong right hand, Ludger Westrick, began to think in terms of loosening up East-West relations by providing economic incentives. I can recall my surprise one day when Westrick told me in confidence, after a conversation on other business in his office, that the chancellor and he had been discussing among themselves the possibility of improving the Federal Republic's relations with the Soviet Union (and perhaps even making a contribution to eventual reunification) by offering the latter an economic aid package of some fifty billion deutschemarks to be paid in ten annual installments. This would be justified as partial reparations for the damage done to the Soviet economy by Hitler's armies. Westrick did not seem to be concerned about raising the money or committing future governments to continue payments. My reaction was muted. The Berlin crisis seemed over, and the economy of the Soviet Union certainly needed all the help it could get, but I wondered what tangible effect such an offer would have on basic Soviet policy. Westrick cautioned that these were only preliminary thoughts, and nothing might come of them. He was right on the last point. Although we discussed the idea on a few subsequent occasions, other issues loomed as more important. As far as I am aware, Erhard's and Westrick's thinking never became the subject of public discussion.

Erhard's Bumpy Road

It was not long before Erhard's weaknesses as a political leader began to emerge. He had been a successful and esteemed minister of economics, for many the father of German economic recovery. He was a man of good will and generally good nature, but he lacked the shrewdness and the hard-headedness of an Adenauer, as well as the ability to discipline errant members of his party and even of his cabinet. He enjoyed, however, a great measure of popular support, and the CDU counted on him to be the party's *Wahllokomotive* (electoral locomotive) in the federal elections that would come in 1965. He seemed, therefore, firmly planted in office for at least a few years.

That proved chronologically to be the case, but one began to hear references to him in Bonn as the *Gummi Loewe* (rubber lion). As a north German Protestant (the only non-Catholic to head a CDU-led government in postwar Germany) he did not know how best to appeal to restive Bavarians and Rhinelanders. Even an impressive victory for his party in the federal elections of September 1965 did not suffice. He indeed proved to be an electoral locomotive (the CDU/CSU captured 47.6 percent of the total vote and won 245 seats out of 496 in the Bundestag); his coalition partner, the FDP, won 9.5 percent of the votes cast and 49 seats in the Bundestag. Electoral victory, however, brought only temporary surcease from hostile political pressures, and by early 1966—so soon after electoral success—the attacks on his performance as chancellor resumed. The FDP became increasingly restive after a difficult period of cabinet formation.

Meanwhile, developments in German-American relations had not added to the chancellor's political strength. Despite the best efforts of visiting Americans—sometimes in teams headed by senior officials—to persuade the Germans to accept the MLF as a great and innovative idea, their response lacked genuine enthusiasm. However, the Erhard government, and Foreign Minister Schroeder specifically, finally accepted the scheme in principle and defended it publicly. I supported our position dutifully and at first even with some conviction, but by 1964 it had become reasonably clear that much of the steam had gone out of the proposal despite the best efforts of the Europeanists in the State Department to keep the issue at the top of the agenda.

Somewhat to my surprise, one day in mid-September 1964 I received a telephone call from Washington to come back to head a special study group being created by Undersecretary George Ball to evaluate the MLF. I reported to Washington within a few days. Ball told me he wanted an impartial and realistic assessment of just where the project stood, together with recommendations as to future U.S. policy. My group was impressively manned both from within the State Department and from the outside. I can recall that Henry Rowen (later to become assistant secretary of defense) and Arthur Hartman (later to become ambassador to France and the Soviet Union) were two of the members. We worked long hours to produce what I thought was a balanced and frank evaluation. So did George Ball. We concluded that, despite certain appealing aspects of the MLF proposal, it obviously had failed to attract the required European support and that the American policy of pushing it should be reconsidered. We cautioned, however, that any change of policy should be handled carefully in such a way as not to harm those European officials who had lent it their support.

I was never specifically informed what effect, if any, our report had on the president, who was now more and more obsessed with Vietnam. We knew that Secretary of State Rusk had lacked enthusiasm for the MLF.[10] In any event the whole project seemed to be withering on the vine in the absence of any significant European pressure (apart from the Germans) to move ahead with it. In December 1964, President Johnson formally withdrew the entire proposal.[11]

We had persuaded the Germans, more than any of the other NATO allies, to support the MLF strongly. Both Erhard and Foreign Minister Schroeder had given it their blessing, and even the SPD leadership, influenced principally by Fritz Erler (who was to die of leukemia the following year) and Helmut Schmidt, ended up by endorsing the MLF. The embarrassment and resentment of both CDU and SPD leaders was profound when the American action came seemingly almost without warning. Erhard and Schroeder were caught way out on a limb, their prestige shattered, and the SPD leadership lost a great deal of confidence in the reliability of the United States. As Helmut Schmidt put it more than a decade later: "Those of us who had put our prestige on the line to back a plan of strategic importance to the United States felt we had been duped and had lost respect at home. That was when I understood for the first time that it is domestically risky to commit oneself to a policy advocated by the ruling power if that power cannot be relied on to stick to its guns."[12]

Given the growing American involvement in Vietnam and the inability of MLF supporters in Washington to generate much enthusiasm for the project in other NATO countries, could this whole unfortunate episode have had a better denouement? Obviously yes. The arrogance of Washington and its disregard as the capital of a superpower for the sensitivities of allies has frequently made the task of American diplomats more difficult. The MLF episode was an egregious example of a behavior pattern that could only infuriate its victims. If the MLF was intrinsically a bad idea, as many came to believe, we could have found a more delicate and responsible way to withdraw, along with the Germans, from a project for which we had pushed so hard over a number of years.

In a more recent case—the deployment of INF (intermediate nuclear force) weapons in Europe during the early Reagan years—what started out as reluctant American response to what we felt to be a European psychological requirement gradually turned into an American cause, as we conjured up all sorts of arguments to justify what we were urging the Europeans to accept. Their willingness to go along then also became in our minds a test of loyalty to the alliance. All subtleties and nuances were swept aside as irrelevant. The problem for MLF supporters was that they could not persuade the president. His mistake was simply to brush the whole business into the dustbin without regard to commitments made and reputations at stake.

From the outset of his period in office as chancellor, Erhard attempted to reassure us that the German-American relationship was paramount and that, while the rapprochement with France after the war was important, it could not be allowed to disturb this primary relationship.[13] I do not know what de Gaulle's impressions were of the roly-poly German chancellor, but I have no reason to think that they could have been very positive. More different personality types in high office would have been difficult to find. Two of the great shocks that de Gaulle perpetrated on Europe during the 1960s—the expulsion of NATO headquarters and all NATO bases from France to take place no later than April 1, 1967, along with the withdrawal of all French troops from the integrated NATO command, and on May 16, 1966, the second French veto of British entry into the

European Economic Community (the first came on January 29, 1963)—occurred during Erhard's chancellorship. There is little evidence that the effect these actions might have on French-German relations played any important role in de Gaulle's decisions. They obviously troubled the chancellor a great deal, as he told us on numerous occasions, but he never pretended to have any influence over the course of French policy.

Of all the troublesome foreign policy issues the one that did the most political damage to Erhard was undoubtedly the continuing tug-of-war with the United States over offset payments to be made by the West Germans to compensate, at least in part, for the foreign exchange costs of the American troop presence in the Federal Republic. The battle over the payments to be made in 1964 proved to be particularly acrimonious. Whatever his virtues as secretary of defense—and they were not inconsiderable—Robert McNamara, to whom President Johnson had entrusted the matter, was not the most adept and flexible of negotiators. In the end, however, the United States got much of what it wanted.

The discussions of a new offset arrangement during the summer of 1966 proved to be particularly difficult. An apprehensive Erhard, fearful of the treatment he would get on this issue, had thought seriously of canceling his planned trip to Washington before finally deciding to go through with it. The developing issue during two days of hard negotiations (mainly between McNamara and Defense Minister Kai-Uwe von Hassel) was whether the Germans could buy medium-term U.S. treasury bonds rather than pay cash for military equipment and services. The climax came in a so-called *unter vier Augen* (under four eyes) meeting between Johnson and Erhard in the White House and then in a visit to the ranch in Texas. The president gave the somewhat bewildered German chancellor the "Johnson treatment," and the overwhelmed Erhard agreed that the final communiqué would commit the Federal Republic to meet all of its payments by mid-1967.

Erhard returned to Bonn a shattered man, to use the rhetoric of the time. The poor chancellor had been manhandled, and the German media minced no words in reporting his, from their viewpoint, inglorious treatment and abnegation. He was not to remain in power much longer, and there can be little doubt that the reports of his performance in the United States, added to the other domestic budgetary, business cycle, and leadership problems he was encountering, led to the collapse of his government on October 27, 1966, when the FDP ministers handed in their resignations. Without the FDP he no longer had a majority in the Bundestag, and his replacement inevitably followed a month later.

Although his direct involvement as a member of government was only to come later, Helmut Schmidt seems (in his *Men and Powers*) to attribute major responsibility to the treatment given Erhard by Johnson.[14] The former SPD chancellor would be the first to deny monocausality in a complicated political situation. Other important factors contributed to Erhard's downfall, but the image painted in the German media of a weak chancellor meekly submitting to a browbeating by the American president and returning to Germany in an obvious state of psychological shock certainly played a role in the disintegration of his government.

For complicated reasons that are well described in Ambassador McGhee's book *At the Making of a New Germany*, the formation of a so-called Grand Coalition between the CDU and the SPD became inevitable.[15] Kurt-Georg Kiesinger took over as chancellor and Willy Brandt as deputy chancellor and foreign minister. Ironically enough, the FDP, headed at the time by Erich Mende, remained out in the cold as the sole opposition party.[16] Over the years I had, of course, come to know Brandt much better than Kiesinger, who had left Bonn in 1958 to become minister president of Baden-Wurtemberg, but I had had some contact with the new chancellor prior to 1958 when he was a prominent parliamentarian specializing in foreign affairs. He came across as stately and eloquent with a good record as an executive. His early Nazi associations, while attacked both in the Federal Republic and the United States, were brushed aside as the inconsequential mistakes of a young man. He was of a generation that had one chronological foot in the Nazi era, and of those who remained in Germany there were relatively few who enjoyed the clear unblemished record of an Adenauer. The denazification procedures of the military government period had identified and punished the most egregiously involved. Kiesinger was obviously not among them.

During the fall of 1966 I received a telephone call from John Leddy, assistant secretary of state for European affairs, during which he noted that the United States was considering sending an ambassador to our diplomatic mission in Hungary for the first time (since the failed revolution of 1956 it had been under a chargé d'affaires and prior to that time a legation in charge of a minister). He asked whether I would be interested. I had been nearly three and a half years in Bonn and frankly was looking for a change. Recurrent rumors that I was being considered for the embassy in Vienna, as during an earlier period, had proved to be without substance. My response to Leddy was in the affirmative.

One of the problems with President Johnson was his overreaction to press leaks. Many presidential appointments had either died or been indefinitely postponed because someone, presumably in the White House or State Department, could not resist the temptation to show off his access to personnel secrets or perhaps had wanted to kill an assignment. The Periscope section of *Newsweek* was a particular bête noire for the president. And so the inevitable happened in my case. Early in 1967 the rumor of my forthcoming appointment as the first American ambassador to Hungary appeared in Periscope, and the whole move immediately went on ice for an indefinite period. It took six months to thaw the appointment out.

The Death of Adenauer

Konrad Adenauer died on April 19, 1967, in his ninety-second year. He had been troubled for many winters with a lingering case of flu that he found difficult to shake but always had—sometimes gathering strength at the villa he had come to love in Cadenabbia on Lake Como. This time he gradually weakened unto death. Even his political enemies had to acknowledge that a great man had passed away—one of those epic figures who emerge from relative obscurity to shape the course of history. The government delayed the state funeral long enough to permit the leaders of most countries, or their representatives, to come to the Federal Republic. The ceremony would involve a solemn requiem mass in the cathedral of Cologne, where he had served as mayor for so many years, and a slow march with honor guard down to the Rhine, where the casket would be placed on the deck of a German river patrol boat to proceed slowly upstream to Bad Honnef. Interment would take place near his hillside home.

We in the U.S. embassy were glad to hear that President Johnson would attend the funeral mass, but we also knew that we were in for a rough few days as the White House hordes descended upon us. The advance party appeared the day after Adenauer's death and began to issue demands. Despite Ambassador McGhee's objections, the Secret Service decided once again that our house within its own large compound provided better security. We had lived through the Kennedy visit, but this was a different president with a different staff that would inevitably want different things. Indeed, the president's minions pulled a number of real surprises out of their collective hat.

The master bedroom, in which Johnson would sleep, was a very large corner room ringed on both window sides with built-in bookshelves that we had filled with books. I can still remember the disgust on the face of a White House administrator when he first saw the room. "You can't expect the president to wake up in the morning and look at books." So he issued the order to have the bookshelves completely covered with plasterboard to be painted the same color as the walls of the room. We were reasonably sure the president would not have minded waking up to the sight of books, but there was no arguing with this proposed vandalism. The embassy carried out the order.

There was more to come. Our bathroom had a handsome marble floor, but this, according to the voice of the White House, needed immediate covering with a thick green carpet. The shower was too low, he also decided, and ordered it raised a foot. After a test, he decided that the water pressure was too weak for a presidential shower and ordered that a special pump be installed for the whole house. The embassy engineer warned that the piping, supplied in 1950 when the house was built, might not take the additional pressure, but this was waved aside cavalierly. We held our collective breath during the visit, but the pipes held. The day after the president's departure, with the pump already off, the overloaded system began to develop extensive leaks that required emergency repairs at considerable expense to the U.S. government.

We received orders to stock the refrigerators and bar with an extensive list of fine food and drink. We knew from past experience that the president would consume little, if any, of this himself, but it would all be gone by the end of the visit, either eaten and drunk by the houseboys and aides or stowed away on Air Force One or Two for return to the United States. The fine linens and glassware purchased for the occasion would also largely disappear. With the sense of arrogant privilege that proximity to the president seemed to bring with it, nothing was too good for White House staff members, no matter how humble in the pecking order.

The funeral mass in the magnificent Cologne cathedral went off with solemn dignity, attended by the leaders of many countries. The very visible pew completely filled with American Secret Service officials immediately behind President Johnson and his party provided perhaps the only incongruous note. None of the other dignitaries present felt the need for such conspicuous protection, including President de Gaulle with all his predilection for grandeur and despite the threat to his personal security that his Algerian policy had created.

After the requiem mass, the leaders marched slowly down to the Rhine behind the honor guard and casket, to the solemn beat of drums—President Johnson again surrounded by his protective squad. Slowly the patrol boat bearing the casket left the shore and proceeded upstream. We returned by car to Bad Godesberg, where once again we were able to see the boat with the casket on deck making its way slowly toward Bad Honnef. Some ceremonial attempts at dignity fall flat, but this seemed like both a moving and highly appropriate way to let the many thousands who lined the riverbank say goodbye to such a consummate Rhinelander. Interment took place privately near his home, a site the state has preserved as a national memorial.

That day brought back many personal memories of our early meetings in Cologne after the war, of the mutual friendship that grew between a young American and an old German politician who was to become the leader of a reviving Federal Republic, of the differences that developed between us during the Berlin crisis, and of his final acceptance that I had not gone off the deep end but was still a responsible American diplomat. Although other German leaders of the postwar era have brought high qualities of talent and intelligence to their tasks, none has possessed the same combination of integrity, shrewdness, devotion to duty, and high standards of personal behavior as Adenauer.

A Diplomatic Tug-of-War over Nuclear Nonproliferation

While I waited hopefully during the first half of 1967 for a revival of my appointment to Budapest, I found myself engaged in what seemed like an endless round of debate and arm-twisting over an issue that aroused surprising emotion on the German side, or at least among those officials and parliamentarians personally involved. As in the case of so many teapot tempests, a diplomat, his own foreign ministry, and the government with which he must deal can generate an intensity of indignation largely unreflected in the public opinion of their respective countries. The subject was the proposed Nuclear Nonproliferation Treaty (not actually open for signature until July 1, 1968, and signed by the Federal Republic only in November 1969), intended to prevent the spread of nuclear weapons beyond the five powers (the United States, the Soviet Union, Great Britain, France, and China) already possessing such weapons.

The two major nuclear powers, the United States and the Soviet Union, had an overriding common interest in preventing the further spread of nuclear weapons. The old antagonisms of the cold war era were, of course, still largely present despite the cessation of major Soviet threats to Berlin and the first glimmerings of détente, but we shared the desire to avoid increasing the danger of nuclear war through misperception or technical error that the multiplication of states possessing nuclear weapons would inevitably involve.

I did not believe then and do not believe now that German officials, with a few possible exceptions, seriously wanted to preserve the option of going nuclear at some distant point in the future. They were all aware that Adenauer in 1954 had renounced the production or use of so-called ABC (atomic, bacteriological, and chemical) weapons and that their NATO allies, not to speak of the Soviet Union, would never within the foreseeable future accept German manufacture of nuclear weapons. The principal German concern seemed to be that the treaty would preclude any future European nuclear force that might result from European political integration. Our position was that, should Europe ever achieve a degree of integration that would permit unified political control over a shared nuclear weaponry (presumably French and British by origin), the nonproliferation treaty would not preclude such a development.

My old friend from Washington days, political counselor Swidbert Schnippenkoetter at the German embassy, was now the coordinator for disarmament affairs with the rank of ambassador in the German Foreign Ministry. A brilliant diplomat and polemicist, Swidbert became strongly emotionally involved in what he felt was a legitimate defense of German and European interests. Our many and sometime lengthy personal discussions were mutually unpersuasive.

Another issue that emerged, raised principally by Gerhard Stoltenberg, minister for scientific research, was that the advanced nonnuclear powers of the West would be exposed to industrial espionage through the inspection procedures provided for by the treaty. We, of course, argued that this would not be the case.

The debate went on after I had left Bonn, but the Germans finally signed and ratified the treaty. I think it is fair to say that none of their fears have materialized. Nor is it likely, if Europe one day were to achieve that degree of political integration requisite for a unified military structure and command, that the nonproliferation treaty would prove a hindrance to any transfer of remaining French and British nuclear weapons to such a command. Once again the diplomatic issues of yesteryear, seemingly so important at the moment, have faded with the onrush of time, the change of alignments, and the emergence of new concerns. The content of politics forever fluctuates, and, apart from those basic principles to which people of honor must adhere, the responsible diplomat must be prepared to adapt to the reality of change. The issue in 1995 became renewal of the treaty after twenty-five years as called for in the text. This was accomplished.

Poor Swidbert! My friend died of cancer within a relatively short time— a great loss to the German Foreign Service and to my wife and me.

On to Budapest

In the late spring of 1967 John Leddy called again from Washington to say that the department now hoped to revive my appointment to Budapest and, barring further leaks or other mishaps, I should seriously begin planning to leave Bonn soon. There would, of course, be the usual formalities of hearings before the Senate Foreign Relations Committee required as part of the confirmation process for ambassadorial appointments.

This time the proceedings in Washington were to go off as planned, but none of us had any idea of the melodramatics still to come before I would actually arrive in Budapest. There were no leaks. Before leaving Bonn, I had to make the usual round of farewells calling on officials from the foreign minister on down as well as many of my diplomatic colleagues. The saying has it that when a senior diplomat leaves his post, he has to eat and drink his way out of town. The farewell dinners and receptions, mostly well meant and sincerely offered, become an enormous burden and drain on one's energy and dwindling time. Yet one has a natural reluctance to turn down the proffered hospitality of colleagues. One survives, and I know of no case where a diplomat collapsed unto death at a farewell dinner party. The full blow of enforced attendance and reciprocal hospitality, I was aware, comes at the ambassadorial level. I had observed Ambassador McGhee seemingly caught in an endless round of entertainments and counterentertainments and had respected his stamina.

Back in Washington after some leave, I appeared before the Senate Foreign Relations Committee anticipating no trouble. My testimony went off without mishap followed by committee approval and confirmation by the Senate. I spent the intervening time boning up on Hungary, reading the cables and talking to the desk officer and other officials. Then came the day for my appointment with the president to receive his charges and to provide what is called a "photo opportunity." Meanwhile, Faith was beginning the arrangements for a representative collection of modern American art to display in our residence.

Before I went to the White House, people warned me that I would find a president obsessed with Vietnam and that I could not expect more than ten minutes or so with him. They were right about the obsession but unaware about the vagaries of the Oval Office. When I appeared in the West Wing suitably identified, the keeper of the president's door warned me solemnly that the president was a very busy man and that I could only expect a few minutes with him. I said I fully understood and was then ushered into the Oval Office. My first impression was one of disorder, if not total chaos. Three large television sets occupied a prominent place, each, as I was quickly to learn, tuned in to one of the three major networks. A ticker tape spewed white streams of paper onto the carpet. The president rose to greet me and then motioned to me to sit down on the sofa and dashed over to the ticker presumably to see if any hot new item about Vietnam had come in. He was to repeat this performance several times interspersed with trips to the television sets. In between he asked me about Hungary and noted that Cardinal Mindszenty was a guest of the embassy. Suddenly Okimoto, the president's personal photographer, appeared out of nowhere to start snapping pictures. The president and I stood up for a more formal shot, and I have in my possession a colored photo of a beaming, avuncular Lyndon Johnson looking at me as if I were a long-lost nephew. Meanwhile, I could see through the partially open door that the keeper of the gate was getting more and more restive, looking conspicuously at his watch and gesturing that I should get out. One does not, however, walk out on one's president, especially when, admittedly with interruptions, he seemed interested in talking. Finally, the time came to leave, and as I passed through the outer office, all I got was a frown and another demonstrative look at the gatekeeper's watch.

A Melodramatic Entrée

So I departed from Washington to return briefly to Germany and then to proceed to Budapest via Vienna. I had expected to spend the night of Tuesday, October 17, 1967, at the Hilton Hotel in Vienna and then on Wednesday to move on to Budapest—a four-hour drive by car. While in Washington I had, of course, seen the cable traffic from Dick Tims, our chargé d'affaires in Budapest, indicating that, unless safe conduct to Austria could be arranged, Cardinal Mindszenty (our guest in the embassy since the failed revolution of 1956) was considering walking out before I arrived as a gesture of protest against what he regarded as both an unwarranted improvement of relations with an iniquitous regime and a personal affront. No one, however, anticipated the cliff-hanger that ensued. The international press quickly got hold of the story and bombarded me with telephone calls and attempted interviews the moment I arrived at the hotel in Vienna. Budapest reported that camera crews for the major U.S. television networks had arrived in the city. I refused comment and relied on our embassy in Vienna to keep me supplied with the mounting cable traffic between Washington, Budapest, Vienna, and Rome.

On October 18 the *New York Times* and other newspapers carried a report from Budapest by David Binder that the cardinal had indicated his intention to leave the embassy within a few days and that Cardinal Koenig, archbishop of Vienna, had flown to Budapest from Rome.[17] The last thing in the world my government wanted, I knew, was to have the cardinal walk out of the embassy as I was entering it for the first time—a sentiment I could heartily share. So I stayed holed up in my hotel room through Thursday, avoiding the press and awaiting the results of Koenig's intervention. We knew that if Mindszenty simply walked out of the embassy, he would immediately be arrested by the some twenty uniformed and plainclothes policemen who were keeping watch around the building[18] and that the conditions he was stipulating for his acceptance of a safe-conduct to the Austrian border were unlikely to be approved by the Hungarian government.

After my arrival in Budapest during the afternoon of October 20, I approached the entrance to the embassy—a rather forbidding dark stone six-story building on Szabadsag Ter (Freedom Square)—with considerable trepidation. None of us on the outside could be sure that as I entered he would not step out. Fortunately nothing of the sort happened. The desire of the pope that he stay put if safe passage could not be arranged had prevailed, at least temporarily.

Although I could feel much relief now that I was in and he was still in, I quickly found out that the cardinal had not firmly made up his mind to stay in the embassy. I thought it better during my first few days not to take the initiative in seeing Mindszenty unless he asked to see me, but on the morning of October 23 I sent word through Dick Tims that, while I did not wish to put the cardinal in a position that he might find difficult or embarrassing, I would be happy to call on him at his convenience. He indicated his willingness to see me without delay, so I knocked on his door and entered. He greeted me in a friendly fashion and did not seem unduly agitated. We spoke in German.

My first impression was of a slight, elderly gentleman of ascetic appearance, soft voice, and unassuming manner. This was a man who had suffered much: nine years in prison during the oppressive Rakosi regime, subjected to torture and a humiliating show trial. Then after a short period of freedom during the glory days in 1956 of the Hungarian Revolution, he had sought sanctuary in the American embassy as Soviet tanks crushed the Freedom Fighters. Now he had spent eleven more years, not tortured or imprisoned but certainly confined in his movements, unable to venture outside the embassy building. One might have expected someone more personally bitter over this long hiatus in his life as head of the primatial see of Hungary, but he seemed to reserve his bitterness for the Communist regime that he despised and for those who collaborated with it.

The cardinal began our conversation by saying he was sorry that he was causing such difficulties but that issues of principle were involved. He wanted me to know that there was nothing personal in all this. He was, however, in a very difficult situation. The Vatican was discussing his future with the Hungarian authorities, but the latter as atheists had absolutely no respect for the Vatican. I replied that as far as my government or I personally was concerned, as had already frequently been stated to him, we saw nothing in my appointment or arrival that need have any effect on his position. We would continue as before to extend the facilities of the embassy as a place of refuge. Mindszenty referred again to principles that he believed were involved but gave no indication of his intentions. While taking leave I noted that I would be available at any time if he wished to confer with me.

Later that day a member of the embassy staff went into the cardinal's quarters to deliver some periodicals. Mindszenty raised again the question of inviting his relatives living in Budapest to pay farewell calls on him. In commenting on the events of the day in my reporting telegram to Washington, I said it seemed fairly obvious that the cardinal's continuing sense of urgency, though not linked explicitly to any idea of a "walkout" prior to further word from Rome on the progress of negotiations, involved a basic misunderstanding between him and Cardinal Koenig on the time that might be required by the Vatican to complete its negotiations with the Hungarian authorities either to secure safe-conduct for him or to reach total impasse.[19]

On the following day Mindszenty continued to make remarks to embassy officers indicating he believed the Vatican-Hungarian negotiations might soon be completed and that he might be leaving the embassy in the near future. As time went by, however, and nothing happened, the cardinal gradually lost hope that a safe-conduct would be achievable, and he came to accept that my coming as ambassador really had not affected his personal position or raised issues of fundamental principle. He resumed his old routines, which included an evening walk after office hours in the dingy inner court of the embassy building. An embassy officer always accompanied him. If the weather was bad, he would pace up and down the long hallway on the same floor as his quarters.

My interaction and conversations with this remarkable man provided a steady supply of interesting insights. Nothing that followed, however, was to match the melodrama surrounding my arrival.

The first days of a new ambassador at his post, and in this case the first American ambassador ever to Hungary, are filled with briefings, preparatory activities, and getting to know his staff and their dependents. He assumes charge by telegram to Washington as his first official act, and thereafter all embassy cables while he is in the country go out under his name. Joined by his wife, he also has to concern himself about the state of the official residence, in this case located in the Buda hills near the end of a street named Zugligeti Ut. Until he has presented his credentials to the titular head of state, he cannot, however, function officially as the principal representative of his government or begin the frequently tedious round of calls that he must make on major officials and his diplomatic colleagues.

In Western capitals the presentation of credentials is usually a relatively simple, if formal, occasion, without much, if any, military fanfare. In the Communist capitals of Eastern Europe, however, the military review played a much larger role. And so it was in Budapest. After ascending the large ceremonial staircase of the huge late-nineteenth-century parliament building (many postcards of the city show the impressive facade of the building fronting on the left bank of the Danube, although the principal entrance is from the square on the opposite side), the chief of protocol ushered me and my principal officers of the embassy into a wood-paneled anteroom and then without delay into a larger, ornately furnished room where the deputy president of the Presidential Council awaited me. I made my remarks, mainly pious expressions of hope for improved relations, and handed over my letter of credence. He responded with similar platitudes. A waiter appeared with small glasses of Tokay wine—standard fare along with a minuscule cup of strong Turkish coffee as the inevitable culmination of every call on a senior official. We then proceeded down the grand staircase to the steps in front of the building, where we received the march-by of an obviously highly trained elite corps. I had to take the salute of the commanding officer, acknowledge the presentation of his sword, and then shout out in Hungarian the appropriate words of thanks and commendation (which I have long since forgotten). That was it. I was now a fully functioning ambassador and could begin my round of official calls. Actually I had seen the foreign minister, János Peter, the preceding day at his request.

It would be an exaggeration to claim that I found many issues of high policy on my plate. There were many problems to be discussed, some seemingly insoluble, within the limits prescribed by the reality that Hungary was a single-party, Communist state. The real power resided not in the formal governmental structure but in the Hungarian Socialist Workers Party, led by János Kádár, who had returned to Budapest to assume control in 1956 almost literally on the back of a Soviet tank. The party had an internal structure duplicating the major branches of government, as in the Soviet Union and other Eastern European countries. This did not mean that the principal ministries resembled purely hollow shells, since they had the burden of administrative responsibility across the broad field of government. It quickly became apparent that the Foreign Ministry, for example, if not the largely figurehead foreign minister, enjoyed considerable status and some independence of action, although all important decisions obviously had to be referred to the rather modern light brown stone-faced party headquarters building (I would not vouch for its present color after more than twenty-five years of further exposure to the brown coal pollution of Pest).

I did not expect much significant discussion during my first official call on the foreign minister (a former Protestant clergyman), and I was neither surprised nor disappointed. Peter was a dignified, heavyset man. He revealed nothing by his manner or remarks as to how he—a former churchman—felt about working for a Communist regime. He was cordial enough, as were nearly all Hungarian officials, but following his brief, he made a point I was to hear ad nauseam from practically every Hungarian official: that there was some scope for improvement of Hungarian-American relations but that there were clearly major differences of policy that placed limits on any real betterment of our relations.[20]

Needless to say, this came as no great shock to me. I knew what the built-in restrictions were, but the diplomat is ever hopeful of making some progress if only on the margins. The bitternesses of the cold war period had pretty well faded at least as far as Hungary was concerned, and if that country was still planted firmly in the Communist camp, we also knew that, in some respects, it wanted to look toward the West. Of all the Eastern European countries Hungary had gone the furthest in accepting the lure of consumer goods, whether or not they were capitalist in origin. The stores on the Vaczi Utca—Budapest's main shopping street—were far and away the best stocked in the Communist bloc. Fortunately for its population, Hungary had an exportable surplus of foodstuffs, and the average Hungarian could eat bountifully. Khrushchev rather scornfully referred to the system as "goulash communism." One thing we learned quickly enough, however, is that while there were many colorful restaurants in the city, the quality of cuisine was generally mediocre. What had once been a fairly distinguished, if heavy, cuisine had, in the absence of the profit motive on the part of restaurateurs, lost its inspiration while retaining its heaviness. But compared with Moscow, Bucharest, or Warsaw, Budapest was the liveliest city of Eastern Europe. Another thing I quickly learned, I may add, was that the Hungarians did not like to be called Eastern Europeans; they considered themselves a part of Central Europe.

Proceeding with my introductory calls, I saw the prime minister, the president of the council, the minister of the interior, and others. It quickly became evident that a principal interlocutor for the discussion of substantive business would be Deputy Foreign Minister Istvan Szilagyi—an experienced and highly intelligent diplomat whom I could count on to report accurately what I said and convey accurately to me the views of his government. He was a man of modest size and wiry build. When angry he seemed like a too tightly wound watch, but he always contained himself. We had numerous meetings during my period in Budapest, and I developed the kind of respect for him that one can for an able diplomatic adversary.

The prime minister, Jeno Fock, a small, thin man with a friendly smile and a good sense of humor, was known as an economic reformer. After the usual exchange of comments that we both hoped to improve relations between the United States and Hungary but that there were issues on which our governments basically differed, he indicated that he would refrain today from raising the question of Vietnam. We devoted the bulk of our conversation to the New Economic Mechanism (a reform program supposed to introduce more flexibility into the economy) due to go into effect on January 1, 1968, of which he was one of the conceptual fathers. He admitted that reforms intended to shake up the economy and bring about psychological and social adjustments would cause difficulties for many Hungarians, but he was optimistic about the eventual outcome.

In commenting to the department on our meeting I noted that Fock's involvement in the New Economic Mechanism was very heavy and that its failure would seriously jeopardize his own political position.[21] Looking back as I write this, at a time when Hungary is still grappling with the problems of economic transition under a post-Communist regime, I can only be impressed with the slowness and the difficulty of systemic change. The economic reformers in Hungary during the years that the Hungarian Socialist Workers Party dominated the political scene had a series of ups and downs depending on whether the Communist Party boss, János Kádár, gave them a green light or withdrew his favor. More than thirty years have gone by since the New Economic Mechanism had its inception. The difficult issues that inevitably arose in the attempt to move toward a market-oriented economy and could not effectively be addressed by a Communist state remain, in one form or another. One may hope, however, that in the end a democratic regime can better succeed in revitalizing an economy with considerable potential but still bearing the heavy burden of the past.

Of all my initial calls, the most interesting was undoubtedly the rather lengthy session I had with János Kádár, head of the Hungarian Socialist Workers Party and literally the boss of the country.[22] (I may note parenthetically that Hungarian proper names are actually inverted so that in Hungary he would be called Kádár János.) As I entered his Mussolini-size office in party headquarters, he greeted me cordially and offered the usual strong Turkish coffee and a tiny glass of Tokay wine (normally this came at the end of a conversation).

My first impression was of a florid, slightly puffy-faced individual of solid proportions but not fat. As we talked, I could only conclude that this was not a man at ease with his role in history. He did not specifically refer to the events of 1956, but his rather lengthy opening remarks seemed to be an elaborate indirect justification of his action in coming back with the Soviet tanks that crushed the Hungarian Freedom Fighters and then assuming power. It also quickly became clear that he had a sense of humor.

The subject of Cardinal Mindszenty inevitably came up, but Kádár did not make the usual official pitch that the cardinal's presence in the embassy placed an insurmountable burden on Hungarian-American relations. Instead he told of a visit to Moscow while Khrushchev was still in power there. The Soviet leader invited him to attend a football match (soccer to Americans) featuring the Moscow Dynamos, then a world-class team. During the halftime break, Khrushchev invited him to visit the inevitable VIP lounge beneath the stands. As he entered with Khrushchev, he noticed a rather tall man standing in a corner. Khrushchev beckoned him over and introduced him (via interpreter, of course) as Averill Harriman, who happened to be in Moscow at the time on some sort of official mission.

Kádár said he jokingly added that he had something for which to be equally thankful to both Khrushchev and Harriman. Khrushchev bridled and with some indignation asked what could the Hungarian leader be equally thankful for to both Harriman and himself. According to Kádár, he laughed and explained that he was thankful to Khrushchev for having taken Matyas Rakosi (the bloody-minded Hungarian Communist Party chief who was forced into exile in the Soviet Union by the 1956 Hungarian Revolution) off his hands, and thankful to Mr. Harriman because his government had taken Cardinal Mindszenty off his hands. He concluded his story by adding with another laugh that Khrushchev didn't think this attempt at humor was funny.

Kádár went to some lengths to explain that the recent shooting of a Hungarian attempting to escape over the Austrian frontier was a mistake and not worthy of a civilized country. He indicated that the Hungarian authorities would issue orders to border guards that would prevent any repetition of this unfortunate occurrence.

As far as Hungarian-American relations were concerned, we went through the usual exchange of comments about our mutual desire for their improvement but realistic acceptance of the fact that there were significant differences of view that would limit such improvement.

I left this encounter with mixed feelings. The man was more personally sympathetic than I had expected, yet as the Communist Party boss he represented a system that was basically repugnant to democratic values. Human beings can be a complicated mixture of good and bad qualities, of clear vision and blind self-deception. Coming from relatively humble origins, Kádár obviously fancied himself as a man of the people. As I quickly learned, one of his favorite ways to spend an evening was to have dinner with his wife at the Matyas Pince (Matthew's Cellar) restaurant, where they would sit at an inconspicuous corner table eating and listening to the inevitable gypsy orchestra. There was no particular fuss about his being there with at least a seeming absence of protective goons. His behavior during the turbulent spring of 1968 and in other contexts during my time in Budapest definitely placed him on the side of those favoring reforms within Communism, but as became ever more clear, the price he had to pay for latitude to move ahead with "goulash communism" in the economic area was unswerving support of Soviet foreign policy goals. The crushing of the Prague Spring, however, created for him a painfully insoluble dilemma.

After I had completed my round of calls on officials and most ambassadors of the diplomatic corps, the routine of the embassy took over. We knew, of course, that our telephone wires were tapped and listening devices planted in our homes and in the embassy wherever foreign nationals had access. We found once that the secret police had lowered a sensitive microphone from the roof down the chimney of the fireplace in Cardinal Mindszenty's library–sitting room. Given the technology for listening at a distance available to the Ministry of the Interior, located at the other side of Szabadsag Ter (Freedom Square) across from our Chancery, the only room in the building in which we could feel secure electronically was the safe room found in every American embassy. Most of our staff lived with this reality of constant surveillance in good style, but a few found it beyond their capacity to adjust and had to be transferred out before their normal tours. We knew that the Hungarian authorities provided household servants on the assumption that they would regularly report what we were saying and doing. One day we found a listening device under the arm of a statue of Eros in our garden. Even the time-tried method of going for a stroll outside when one wanted not to be overheard had lost its efficacy.

Owing to the efforts of my wife working with the State Department's Art in Embassies program, we assembled a very good and representative collection of modern American painting and sculptures at our official residence. The residence itself was a stately old-style villa in the hills of Buda with a large terraced garden on a number of levels. We quickly found that Hungarian artists, condemned to conform to the dictates of Communist realism or not be displayed, were desperately hungry for exposure to nonrepresentational art, and we tried to include them from time to time in parties that we gave. One of the attractions of the residence in its heyday had been an impressive paneled entrance hall with a number of Rubenesque murals as a part of the decor. We noted that the breasts of the nymphs had required patching. Further inquiries disclosed that Soviet officers had occupied the house at the end of the war and, presumably fueled by vodka, had practiced their marksmanship with pistols by using the breasts as targets.

One thing we learned quickly was that Hungarian government and party officials only attended lunches and dinners given by the American ambassador if they had been cleared in advance by the Ministry of the Interior, and even when they accepted invitations, they sometimes simply did not show up. There were, however, several hundred musicians, opera singers, and ballet dancers—designated by the Western diplomatic corps as "trained seals"—who could accept invitations at the drop of a hat. This ensured lively parties and full consumption of any food provided. A teeming buffet table would quickly cease to teem as Hungarian guests descended like a horde of locusts on the platters of food. And who could blame them? We were able to provide a bountiful supply of food and drink not normally available.

A Routine and Not-So-Routine Ambassadorship

An ambassador has to do many things, some pleasant, some onerous, and some just boring. The cable and other traffic in and out keeps him, his staff, and in return the Department of State reasonably well informed. We provided a constant flow of reporting messages to Washington and to relevant U.S. embassies, some of which I drafted myself. It would be unrealistic to suggest that events in Hungary, except on a few special occasions, were the center of attention in Washington (with the exception of the Hungarian desk officer). This is a lesson that ambassadors to other than the major posts sometimes find difficult to accept.

It would be equally futile in this memoir to attempt an account of all the problems we had to deal with in Budapest or of all the people we met or the experiences we had. There were, however, a number of developments that transcended the purely local and that provided insights into the nature of the Hungarian Communist regime or about individuals who came within the embassy orbit.

During my time in Budapest, for example, the Soviet Union's effort to have the People's Republic of China read out of the world Communist movement reached its peak. The process was to involve an international conference of Communist and workers' parties. To show their support of Soviet foreign policy, the leaders of the Hungarian Socialist Workers' Party took the initiative in moving toward this conference. A preparatory consultative party meeting in Budapest took place in late February 1968.

We quickly learned that the best sources of information about the preparatory meetings were the Romanian and Italian embassies. One might wonder why the Italian ambassador Alessandro Barratieri was so well informed. Therein lay an early insight into the nature of the Italian Communist Party that was to evidence itself years afterward in the phenomenon of Eurocommunism. Presumably with the concurrence of the Foreign Ministry in Rome, the ambassador gave a dinner party for the Italian Communist delegation after its leader, upon his arrival in Budapest, had made a formal courtesy call at the embassy to pay his respects to the ambassador. The delegation seemed to have no qualms about keeping Barratieri fully briefed on a day-to-day basis, nor did he have any qualms about passing on to us what he had learned.

In our assessment of what proved to be only the first of three such consultative meetings, we described it as a mixed success. The Soviet delegation could return home with general agreement that the desired international Communist conference would be held soon, soured somewhat by a Romanian walkout from the meeting and by the absence of some country representatives. Hungarian press reports, as one might have expected, claimed the results were better than anticipated and showed "inspiring unanimity."[23]

In late September 1968, delegates from fifty-eight countries convened in Budapest for a second preparatory committee session. Once again the Romanian and Italian embassies provided essential information. And once again the preparatory committee could not conclude its work but found it necessary to hold another session in Budapest beginning November 17.

The November meeting finally agreed to call the international conference of Communist and workers' parties for Moscow in May 1969, with the agenda as adopted by the consultative conference. According to our Italian source, the reason why the Italian and other Western European Communist Parties had in the end accepted a communiqué fixing the Moscow conference was that they had received specific commitments from the Soviets that freedom of dissent would be allowed at the conference for individual national party delegations. On the other hand, Hungarian party circles interpreted the communiqué as reflecting a substantial victory for the Soviet and Hungarian parties.

Needless to say, our ability to observe this internal Communist tug-of-war so close at hand and with such inside information available provided some fascinating insights. Whatever the role of ideology—and it appeared to be much less important than old-fashioned diplomatic maneuver—what we saw was essentially a series of power plays between those delegations determined to accept the Soviet line without qualification and those that refused to go along without reservations. Owing at least in part to skillful Hungarian manipulation, the three preparatory meetings held in Budapest finally concluded with a result acceptable to the Soviet Union, but only after a six-month delay of the final world conference. Kádár had proved his loyalty and could now proceed with economic reform, if not with Soviet blessing then at least with Soviet tolerance. The manager of the Gellert Hotel (Budapest's classical hotel famed for the artificial wave machine of its swimming pool) could now relax after having had three times to tell all guests that they must abandon their rooms to make way for the various national Communist Party delegations.

Life with the Cardinal

Life with Cardinal Mindszenty in the embassy went on without high drama. His health was precarious, we knew, but during my time in Budapest never reached such a critical stage that we seriously had to consider the possibility of his hospitalization. Regular visits from the State Department regional doctor stationed in Vienna at least kept us apprised of any potentially threatening developments. We knew, of course, that a serious illness requiring hospitalization in Budapest would abruptly end the cardinal's sojourn in the embassy. Once in Hungarian official hands, he would never be allowed to return to American diplomatic refuge. One of the decision-making burdens that an ambassador would necessarily bear, as I well knew, was whether or not to call on the Hungarian authorities for medical help in the event of a sudden dramatic decline in the cardinal's condition.

After the initial strain in our personal relationship resulting from the circumstances surrounding my arrival had disappeared, we got along quite well. Frequently he would knock on my door connecting directly with his quarters, or I on his, when either of us had something to discuss. He never complained about the inevitable vicissitudes of a life as confining as his had to be. Only the sight of Stalin's statue in Freedom Square, which he could not help but observe every time he looked out his window, seemed to irritate him. He obviously enjoyed his daily evening walk after office hours, always accompanied by an American officer, and particularly looked forward to his Sunday mass for the Catholic members of the embassy staff held in the large open space outside the entrance to the ambassador's office. Although his spoken English was heavy with accent and frequent error, he did not hesitate to preach, sometimes at considerable length, to his small congregation and to say mass in English on an impromptu altar. His sermons were nearly always devotional in content. On Christmas and Easter we would permit members of the diplomatic corps to attend mass, and the cardinal would sometimes use those occasions to inject criticisms of the Communist regime into his sermons. Despite the nonecclesiastical embassy decor, these were rather solemn and elevating liturgical experiences to which many diplomats came.

Here was a man who by 1968 had already spent more than twenty years behind walls with the exception of three weeks of freedom during the failed revolution of 1956. Much less would have broken the spirit of most people, but at eighty he continued to hope and to display at times even a fiery outlook. It was never entirely clear why the Hungarian authorities seemed to fear him so much, although his position as cardinal primate of Esztergom, under the old Hungarian constitution, made him chief of state in the absence of a regent. Perhaps they worried about his symbolic importance in a country of deep but now largely repressed Catholic tradition.

Prior to his becoming a bishop, he had served for twenty-five years as a country priest. Much of his constricted outlook came from the limiting experiences of rural life, imprisonment, and then confinement in the embassy. He had little sense of the practical and felt strongly that American policy was far too accommodating toward the Soviet Union specifically, and more generally, toward the Communist governments of Eastern Europe.

Most of the time, however, we did not discuss political subjects. He diligently followed provincial developments in Hungary. Once, I can recall, when we needed information for the U.S. Department of Agriculture about crop conditions in a remote part of the country, he was able to provide useful information based on his careful auditing of provincial radio broadcasts.

Representing only a small part of seemingly thousands of pages of notes and writings that the cardinal had amassed, his memoirs (published in English in 1974) proved to be a considerable disappointment.[24] They told little of the inner turmoil that this remarkable man must have suffered in an ultimately frustrating life sustained only by a deep faith. There are two conflicting interpretations of the tragedy that his life involved: one that he was really a martyr manqué who would have been much happier if he had not taken refuge in our embassy but instead had stood up to the triumphant Soviet leadership in 1956, prepared to suffer whatever hardships events would decree; the other that he sought refuge in the embassy because he would not face the prospect of further mistreatment given his experience of imprisonment and torture. As is so often the case in human affairs, the truth, I suspect, lay somewhere in the middle of these two extremes. The cardinal was prepared to suffer and die if this would serve a purpose, but in the chaos of a collapsing revolution to seek shelter where it was available came as a natural instinct.

Although every chief of mission in Budapest during Mindszenty's more than fifteen years in the embassy undoubtedly hoped that some compromise could be worked out that would permit his safe passage to the West, it was not because his presence provided undue hardship, either physical or psychological, for the American staff. The possible burden of ultimate decision should his health suddenly collapse was always there in the background, but day-to-day life in the embassy went off smoothly enough once the near trauma of my arrival had faded. His needs were simple and his requests few. His austere meals, prepared in the basement snack bar of the embassy, caused no problem. With his supper the cardinal normally permitted himself a portion of a small bottle of beer. I found it amusing to hear expressions of sympathy so frequently from diplomatic colleagues, at times with slightly malicious overtones, over the undoubted hardships and inconveniences that Mindszenty's presence in the embassy must inevitably involve. As a matter of fact, he was generally very little trouble and provided a certain panache for our establishment that we all enjoyed. A few years later, when I was assistant secretary of state for European affairs, I was able to play a small role from the Washington end in the negotiations that led to his safe-conduct from Hungary to Austria in 1971.

The Crushing of the Prague Spring

Certainly the most dramatic and tragic event of my time in Budapest occurred not in Hungary but in neighboring Czechoslovakia with the crushing of the Prague Spring in 1968. However, the Hungarian authorities and Kádár personally became intimately involved in both the preliminaries and reluctant implementation of the Brezhnev Doctrine (which in effect stipulated that the Soviet Union had a right to crush any movement that threatened to overthrow an existing Communist government in Eastern Europe). All our information indicated that Kádár did his best to prevent forceful intervention against the Dubček regime but finally failed.

As we watched the drama developing in Czechoslovakia, we could not help but note the frenetic efforts of Hungarian officials to counsel both prudence on the part of Prague and patience on the part of Moscow. Czech embassy officials in Budapest who sympathized with the Dubček reforms were delighted when, in a radio and television interview, Prime Minister Jeno Fock clearly expressed sympathy for the attempt to introduce democratic measures in socialist Czechoslovakia. Hungarian officials including Kádár made several trips to Moscow to try to avoid Soviet military intervention and attempted in private statements to give the impression that such intervention was unlikely and that a tragic repetition of the Hungarian experience of 1956 would be avoided.

As the reform movement in Czechoslovakia moved into the summer months, however, the mood began perceptibly to change. Budapest was full of rumors about the possibility of Soviet military action and of Kádár's growing pessimism about the eventual outcome of reforms with which he was supposed to be basically sympathetic. The tension kept building up as August came and as Dubček refused to attend a meeting in Warsaw called by the Soviets for July 15. The entire Soviet Politburo visited Prague on July 22, and Soviet troops began to mass on the Czech frontier.

Faith and I went to Lake Balaton—a main resort area of Hungary—for the weekend of August 19–20. On Sunday evening as we were driving back to Budapest, we were suddenly forced to get off the road by Hungarian police. Soon the beginnings of what turned out to be an entire Soviet division started passing by, heading north as we watched from a fortunately broad shoulder of the road. The rolling stock of a Soviet unit, obviously not mechanized, did not impress us. It seemed to consist largely of commandeered Hungarian trucks. Finally the troops had passed, and we were able to resume our trip back to Budapest. It required no powers of prophecy to conclude that the Soviet division was headed for Czechoslovakia. Back in Budapest I found my military attaché and staff in the embassy assembling reports on Soviet and other troop movements all seemingly related to the Czechoslovakia crisis.

We know that some 200,000 Soviet and satellite troops (with only Romania abstaining) entered Czechoslovakia in a first wave later to be increased to some 650,000 in the face of large-scale Czech demonstrations. Hungarian troops participating in the invasion took up positions in Slovakia to the south of Prague. We reported all we were able to observe and to pick up in Budapest, where both the popular and private official mood was one of dismay. The controlled press and media, in attempting to justify the action taken, sounded more forced than ever, and it was clear that, Kádár's efforts to avert military action having failed, the Communist leadership of the country had concluded it had no other option but to participate and to try to put the best public face possible on the whole mess. In the final analysis, Hungary, too, was no better than a satellite of the Soviet Union.

I quickly received instructions to convey to the Hungarian government a copy of President Johnson's statement on Czechoslovakia and to say that the United States took a most serious view of the situation. Like most such ex post facto expressions of official displeasure, this was essentially an exercise in futility, but it did give my Foreign Office interlocutor an opportunity visually, if not orally, to indicate his unhappiness with events. He could only refer to a Hungarian News Agency expression of hope that within a short time the situation in Czechoslovakia would have cleared up to a point where a satisfactory resolution could be reached.

Reports began to circulate that the initial Hungarian units entering Czechoslovakia had to be replaced quickly. Stationed in the Hungarian-speaking portion of Slovakia, they had displayed too much sympathy with the population. A current joke circulating in Budapest asked the question: What are the five armies doing in Czechoslovakia? Answer: They're trying to find the fellow who invited them. The local rumor mill also had Kádár in trouble with Communist hard-liners for endorsing the Dubček reforms and only converting at the last minute; that he was in real trouble turned out to be essentially false.

We all know what subsequently happened: the Soviets forced abandonment of reforms and gradually made Dubček (in April 1969), along with other liberals, leave the Central Committee to be replaced by hard-liners. Thus ended a valiant but doomed effort at reform from within. The warning was clear to the other satellites: go slow with systemic change or the Brezhnev Doctrine will be invoked.

I was not able to determine with any precision how far the shock of Czechoslovakia slowed up Hungarian attempts at reform. The leadership had endorsed the New Economic Mechanism, which, of course, in its scope fell far short of the broader reforms identified with Dubček, and there was little overt evidence that the Hungarian economic reformers were being reined in. As far as relations with the United States and other Western countries were concerned, realistic Hungarians recognized that their participation in the military invasion of Czechoslovakia was bound to slow up the improvement for which the government seemed to hope.

Hungarian Miscellany

An ambassador in Communist Eastern Europe had to deal with a multiplicity of problems, some seemingly important at the time but soon overtaken by events, others seemingly routine but crucial to an individual or a group. Among the latter were the American claims against the Hungarian government for properties expropriated after the Communist takeover in 1947 and the encashment into forints of American Social Security checks by beneficiaries living in Hungary at a reasonable rate of exchange. The Hungarian authorities knew very well that, until they were willing to make what we would consider a reasonable settlement of the claims issue, economic relations with the United States could never become normal, yet for reasons of principle and foreign exchange scarcity they could not accept the claims as made. I do not know how many times I raised this question in meetings with Szilagyi and other officials knowing in advance what their responses would be.

In fact both Szilagyi and I had a whole list of issues that we routinely felt compelled to raise whenever we met. After a number of such occasions when we were visibly boring each other, we agreed to number our various arguments and thereafter merely to say, "Today I want to make points 1, 3, 4, and 6," or whatever. The practice made our meetings somewhat snappier.

After considerable haggling, I am glad to say, we were able to work out an improvement in the exchange rate accorded to American Social Security beneficiaries. I was surprised to learn when the subject first came to my attention how many such beneficiaries actually had come back to Hungary to retire. There were several thousand of them, and their dollar checks provided a not inconsiderable amount of hard currency for the Hungarian government.

Another not historically momentous problem, but important to the Hungarian economic authorities, was the certification of their slaughterhouses as meeting minimum U.S. Department of Agriculture sanitary requirements so that Hungarian canned ham could be exported to the United States. The Hungarians had somewhat enviously observed Polish success in selling canned ham to the large Polish ethnic communities in the United States and thought the Hungarian communities in such cities as Cleveland—ironically enough greatly augmented by the post-1956 emigration from Hungary—would make a similar ethnically stimulated market. And if the hams could obtain entry, perhaps Hungarian salami—admittedly among the best in the world—could follow. In any event, after much discussion and cable traffic with Washington, we were finally able to have a Department of Agriculture inspection team come to Hungary and take a look at some selected abattoirs. The inspectors certified two as meeting our standards, and shortly thereafter the flow of hams to America began. I cannot vouch for the figure, but after I had left Hungary, I was told that the value of ham exports to the United States from that country had reached some fifty million dollars.

One of the most difficult periods of my time in Budapest involved the deep freeze that followed the defection in the United States of the political counselor of the Hungarian embassy in Washington, János Radvanyi. The Foreign Ministry hailed me in, and Szilagyi greeted me with stony visage and harsh words. The defection of a highly valued diplomat had obviously come as a major blow to pride, and the implication of the official protest was that somehow or other the U.S. government must have entrapped him. There was nothing much I could say except to note that he had come over entirely of his free will and that it was entirely consistent with long-standing American practice to provide asylum for political refugees. It took months before the Radvanyi case became history rather than a current emotional issue.

Our engagement in Vietnam was another topic that provided fodder for Hungarian official lectures to the American ambassador. As the war escalated in the closing year of the Johnson administration, the Hungarian government felt constrained to join in the rash of staged demonstrations in front of American embassies in Eastern Europe. These were obviously highly contrived affairs never threatening to get out of control. We would receive prior warning from the Foreign Ministry that a demonstration was in the offing and would arrive at the embassy at such and such a time. The announced timing was usually highly accurate. When the demonstrators seemed unusually aroused, they would throw rocks at the embassy, but we noted that their accuracy was remarkable in breaking only windows on the ground floor, although the next floor windows would have been highly vulnerable. The Foreign Ministry paid for any damage done with admirable promptness. There was obviously something bordering on the farcical in these "spontaneous" protests against American iniquity, and like some other aspects of Communist Hungary the synthetic and the phony could not help but emerge.

As 1969 began and the newly elected Nixon administration took office, I started to hear rumors that a personal change of status was in the offing. Then a cable came requesting that I return at once to Washington for consultation. When I arrived at the State Department, I was quickly ushered in to see the new secretary of state, William Rogers. He said he wanted me to take over as assistant secretary of state for European affairs, adding that Bob Murphy, who was helping him and the president choose people for senior positions in the department, had recommended the appointment.

Although I had hoped to stay on in Budapest for another year or two, this was the kind of assignment one could hardly refuse. Rogers said he wanted me to report as soon as possible but agreed that I could return to Hungary for a week to make the usual diplomatic farewells. So I flew back for a hectic few days of calls on officials and diplomatic colleagues. Given the time pressures, I could avoid most of the normal process of eating and drinking one's way out of town as local officials and friends offer seemingly endless rounds of farewell lunches, dinners, and receptions. Poor Faith! She would have the burden of overseeing the packing of effects and coping with the inevitable unexpected contingencies that arise as one departs from a foreign post again.

Some Final Thoughts on Hungary

An ambassador in Communist Eastern Europe could not be a missionary. If he was to conduct business effectively with Communist officials, he could not engage them constantly in ideological debate but had to accept them realistically for what they were and try his best to understand their thought processes. He had to be exemplary in his personal life and example so as not to give occasion for scorn (directed at just another example of Western hypocrisy). They would in any case have planted listening devices and servant spies in his residence so that they would know a great deal about his lifestyle and, if he had any pronounced weaknesses, they would try to exploit them.

This sense of being constantly under observation could weigh heavily on one, and a few members of the embassy staff cracked up under the strain and had to be transferred out. I simply assumed that anything said indoors, either at home or in the embassy building (with the exception of the electronically secured safe room), could be overheard, and I do not think this reflected hypersensitivity on my part. Our first cook, a Mr. Repasci, had the reputation of being one of the best in the country. He certainly was an expert with pot and skillet; his strudel melted in your mouth. His marketing bills were exorbitant and showed as much creativity as his cooking. We were sorry to lose him after a year when a heart attack forced him to retire. We had no doubt that the reports on the Hillenbrands that he submitted to the secret police made interesting reading if they displayed the same inventiveness that went into his accounts.

Another colorful employee at the residence was Fritz, our butler. An ancient man with shaky hands, he claimed as a youth to have worked in Vienna for the emperor Franz Josef. He had a good sense of humor and provided much conversational material for house guests and the Hillenbrand family. On particularly shaky days the crockery would clatter vigorously as he served at table. One day we discovered a large bottle into which he systematically dumped the leftovers from unfinished drinks of guests to make a personal cocktail of many potions and colors—a mixture only an old toper could find drinkable.

One question that puzzled me during our stay in Budapest was the depth of conviction on the part of Communist officials and party members. My conclusion was that Marxism-Leninism as a basic philosophy of life, a sort of quasi religion that made its adherents willing to sacrifice everything, even life, for the cause, had largely lost its credibility. What remained was essentially a frozen power structure within which the *nomenklatura* enjoyed luxuries and perquisites denied to the rest of the population—a power structure that it was in their obvious interest to preserve. There were some true believers, of course, but what I came to call the waning of ideological fervor was an observable phenomenon even in the late 1960s. I have little doubt that this dwindling sense of deeper purpose beyond expediency, and the related loss of any sense of legitimacy, explain at least in part the crumbling in 1989 of Eastern European regimes in the face of massive popular demonstrations, without any real attempt to use the still formidable military and paramilitary internal security forces available to them.

I was also not impressed with the genuineness of the Marxism professed by those members of the economics faculty of the Karl Marx University that I met. In private some of them sounded more like Keynesians. My time in Hungary saw the origins of economic reform in the country. A group of reformers within the Hungarian Socialist Workers Party, apparently encouraged by Kádár, began to introduce elements of change into the economy. Their initial effort was to enliven the state-owned factories by giving more autonomy to their managers, even permitting them to deal directly with non-Hungarian enterprises. The reforms, of course, were intended to break away somewhat from the dead hand of the central planning apparatus that had become an inevitable part of all Communist states. The term "market-oriented economy," so much employed among Eastern European reformers in the late 1980s and early 1990s, had not yet become fashionable, but in some inchoate and confused way, they were trying to move in such a direction.

The course of Hungarian economic reform since my time in the country became long and checkered. Opposition would arise periodically among conservatives in the Communist Party, and Kádár would withdraw his blessing as the reformers retreated into temporary obscurity, only later to reemerge. If one could learn any lesson from the Hungarian experience, it was that piecemeal attempts at economic reform within Communist systems could not bring about the kind of fundamental changes required. Only after the peaceful revolutions of 1989–90 could reformers hope to move ahead along a broad front, but even then only learning from sad experience how difficult and painful the transition from a centrally planned economy to a market-oriented economy must inevitably be.

We at the embassy did not appreciate how unreliable the cooked official statistics were. The liberation of Eastern Europe countries in 1989–90 revealed how useless the inherited data base turned out to be, and Gorbachev himself expressed puzzlement over the untrustworthiness of Soviet statistics. When the West Germans began the difficult process in 1990 of absorbing the former East German economy, they also found that such elementary data as gross national product (GNP) figures for the German

Democratic Republic or the profitability of state-owned enterprises were either greatly inflated or totally lacking in meaningful cost accounting.

As a result, but also because cold war psychology tended to favor statistical inflation, there was in the West a fundamental tendency to overestimate the economic strength and performance of the Soviet Union and the Communist countries of Eastern Europe. Phony statistics taken for granted as reliable led to a whole host of faulty judgments about the economic potential and competitiveness with the West of the centrally planned economies.

There were, of course, some underlying realities provided by the basic Hungarian character, which is a confused mixture of the ebulliently romantic and the sadly realistic. Conquered several times by invaders from the east or south and finally incorporated into the Austro-Hungarian Empire, the country has experienced a troubled history, but the Magyar sense of unique identity, bolstered by a singularly difficult agglutinative language, has survived lengthy Mongol and Turkish occupations. Yet the very unrelatedness of its language to the Indo-European languages of Europe has condemned a rich literature to remain relatively unknown elsewhere.

Recognizing their faults and excesses, one could not help but develop a deep affection for these emotional and fundamentally sad people—a sadness reflected in their literature and their music. Hungarian folk music is either frenetically lively or profoundly pathetic, varying from the czardas to numerous laments for lost loves. As in the Vienna of the old Austro-Hungarian Empire, even the gaiety has a note of unreality mixed with a sense of mortality and evanescence. Like the heath areas of north Germany and England, the Hungarian Puszta (the central plain of the country) is a sad and lonely landscape inspiring the solitary wanderer to think of human transience and the relative permanence of nature. Much Hungarian folk music reflects the mood of the Puszta.

Budapest, like Vienna, was a city overflowing with music. Two opera houses, a symphony orchestra, and numerous other facilities provided a constant array of musical performances, and state-subsidized tickets were cheap. As in other European countries, the whole musical enterprise depended on the generous flow of subsidies. Faith and I attended many performances and found the standards generally very high. As already noted, ballet dancers, singers, and musicians were always available to fill out guest lists for receptions and dinners. Most of them stayed strictly away from political subjects, but a few showed no hesitation or fear in openly criticizing the government. The level of tolerance for free speech was probably higher in Hungary than in any other Eastern European capital, and the Hungarians seemed infinitely creative in making jokes about their own regime and those of other Communist countries, particularly the Soviet Union. Acceptance of all this was at the psychological level the counterpart of what Khrushchev had called "goulash communism."

We enjoyed the restaurant life of Budapest, although the quality of food was sometimes uneven and the so-called gypsy orchestras ubiquitous. One restaurant with only a zither player was a special favorite. Faith and I had nothing against musicians playing Hungarian folk music, but one sometimes preferred to dine without orchestral din. The lead violin player would also inevitably come near to play a sad and often lovely melody close to the ears of the ladies at one's table. In any event, by the time we left Budapest, we looked forward to quiet dinners in Washington restaurants. I might add that, despite the deterioration in state-owned restaurants from the level of what had been an excellent Hungarian national cuisine, the food was still far better than in any other Eastern European country, and especially the Soviet Union. Budapest was, not without justification, known as the Paris of Eastern Europe, as long as one did not attempt a point-by-point comparison with the real Paris.

One of the advantages of an Iron Curtain post during the late sixties was the absence of the social whirl so characteristic of Western European cities. We had our diplomatic lunches, dinners, and receptions, of course, and official visitors dribbled in and out but on a modest scale. The level of obligatory entertaining or being entertained remained tolerable. The big Fourth of July reception that an American ambassador of that era was expected to stage annually for the local American community, the diplomatic corps, and government officials fortunately could take place, the weather permitting, in the large garden of the residence. The weather permitted in 1968, and who should turn up unexpectedly among the guests but Ed Sullivan of the Ed Sullivan television show, apparently in Budapest to scout Hungarian talent. As at all such national day receptions, which can be an awful bore, diplomatic colleagues and representatives from the Foreign and other ministries turn up dutifully but anticipating no great time.

My period in Budapest was too short to achieve any real mastery of Hungarian, although I made a serious effort to learn it. I could at least appreciate the intricacies of that very difficult Finno-Ugaritic language and why every educated Hungarian is ipso facto a linguist. That meant fortunately that nearly every official with whom I had to deal spoke either German, French, or English, and in some cases all three. By the time I left the country, I could at least read the newspapers and carry on a modest social conversation. As the years thereafter went by, however, I found to my regret that total disuse had made what knowledge I had, except for a few common expressions, sink deep into my subconscious.

8
Washington: The First Nixon Years

. . . .

Neither Faith nor I was very enthusiastic about our return to Washington. Apart from the physical dislocation after only eighteen months in Budapest, it meant the loss of allowances and servants
as well as a house hunt in an overheated real estate market. No wonder
the average Foreign Service officer tries to avoid Washington assignments.
Fortunately, we found a nice house in Georgetown at a reasonable rental,
and were quickly engulfed in the Washington official whirl.

My attitude toward the new Nixon administration was complex. I knew
the president's personal reputation, of course, and that provided little consolation. On the other hand, I had felt that Johnson had gone off the deep
end on Vietnam and there was some hope that the new administration
might adopt a more realistic policy. As a career diplomat I was prepared
to render loyal service to a new American president and his secretary of
state, but the fact that I saw no undesirable changes on the horizon in our
European policy provided some reassurance.

Once, in the mid-1960s, when I was chargé d'affaires in Bonn, Richard
Nixon came to Europe in a private capacity. I invited him for lunch and
was frankly impressed by his grasp of foreign affairs. He had already formulated in his mind many of the ideas for policy that he implemented
during his first term as president. I never believed, therefore, that they had
all emanated from the fertile mind of his national security adviser, as so
many seemed to think, particularly after the disgrace of Watergate, when
it became difficult within the Beltway and in academia to accept that anything good could have originated with Nixon himself.

Secretary of State William Rogers, a highly successful lawyer and former attorney general of the United States under President Eisenhower, impressed me from the start as a man of shrewd integrity, sharp mind, and
much practical wisdom. He did not know very much about Europe or the

conduct of diplomacy but had all the qualities of a quick learner. I concluded that it would be a pleasure working under him and that he would allow much latitude for individual initiative.

An assistant secretary of state heading a regional bureau in those days had considerable authority. Defined as a subcabinet position, the job represented both a reward for experience and an expression of confidence in a senior Foreign Service officer. On the negative side, it was known as a killer job involving long hours, considerable travel, and necessary involvement in the diplomatic social whirl of Washington. The Bureau of European Affairs enjoyed the reputation, deservedly so I thought, of being the elite bureau in the department, attractive for both its foreign posts and at home some of the ablest officers in the Foreign Service. Nothing in my three and a half years in charge made me change that assessment. I quickly decided to keep on my principal deputy, George Springsteen, a tough and able Foreign Service reserve officer, whom I had come to know earlier when he was the personal assistant of Undersecretary of State George Ball.

One of the first things I learned in Washington was that, shortly after taking office, Nixon had issued an order transferring the chairmanship of major interagency committees to the White House, which meant to Henry Kissinger as national security adviser. Previously these so-called undersecretary committees had been chaired by the senior State Department undersecretary. This was obviously a blatant power grab inflicted on Rogers, who, in his inexperience, had accepted the shift of authority. Knowledgeable members of the Washington press corps immediately caught on to what had happened. I could see all sorts of problems in the offing and that I would be going to frequent meetings in the White House.

I had hardly arrived when Secretary Rogers told me that the president had decided to make a trip to Europe in February. As was so often the case with Nixonian initiatives, one could never be sure at the outset whether it was primarily a public relations stunt or a calculated action intended to achieve an important result. There was certainly no crying need for an immediate presidential visit to Europe, but the rationale for the trip was that it would provide a badly needed reaffirmation of our commitment to partnership with Europe. The assumption, not entirely without justification, was that the United States had largely acted unilaterally in the past and we needed to show the Europeans that we intended from now on to consult them in advance.

The first stop was Brussels. Addressing the NATO Permanent Council, Nixon laid it on thickly but not inaccurately: "The nations of NATO are rich in physical resources—but they are even richer in their accumulated wisdom and their experience of the world today. In fashioning America's policies, we need the benefit of that wisdom and that experience."[1]

In his elongated memoirs, Henry Kissinger devotes some thirty-eight pages of packed type to the first European trip. He writes about the malaise of the Western alliance and describes NATO as in disarray.[2] This was, of course, a thesis he had emphasized in his 1965 book *The Troubled Alliance*. Prophets of doom were always seeing the alliance as in a state of crisis—a theme periodically stressed by journalists and the uninitiated within governments. In my experience, NATO was usually alleged to be passing from one crisis to another. What the naysayers did not realize was that, as long as a Soviet military threat seemed to exist, the glue that held the alliance together was far stronger than the centrifugal forces working within it. Certainly American leaders had to say the right things and to provide the needed assurances, but self-interest in the continuation of a common defense regularly overrode the discontents with American unilateralism and emerging economic weakness.

The next stop was London. Prime Minister Harold Wilson obviously wanted to put on a good show for the president. As leader of the Labour Party, he knew that a considerable ideological gulf separated his government from the Nixon administration that even frequent references to the "special relationship" between Britain and the United States could not conceal. He was also undoubtedly aware of his reputation for wiliness, some would say slipperiness. Apart from all the substantive talks that did not really open up any new vistas, the real tour de force took place in the cabinet room at 10 Downing Street. Wilson had all the stars of his cabinet present, for example, Roy Jenkins, Michael Stewart, Richard Crossman, Anthony Crosland, Dennis Healey, Barbara Castle, and others. He asked each of them to explain his or her responsibilities briefly. Such a concentration of articulateness and grasp of subject would be hard to duplicate. Certainly no American cabinet that I have seen in action could even come close. The most dyed-in-the-wool Nixonian could not help being impressed, which, of course, was precisely what Wilson intended.

Over the years, both as an official and later as a consultant accompanying American institutional investors to Europe, I have been impressed by the way the British system turns out politicians, and frequently businesspeople and bankers, with an ability to express themselves eloquently and grammatically. The British class structure that funnels its future governing elites into public schools and thereafter into Oxford or Cambridge obviously contributes to this along with the kind of education they receive. The verbal bumbler will not get very far in the House of Commons.

Considering the amount of attention it received, the most important issue in Germany, our next stop, was how to ensure an adequate popular welcome for the visiting president, particularly in West Berlin (no American president could be in the Federal Republic without an obligatory stopover in the city). All subsequent presidential visits unfortunately had to take place in the shadow of the tumultuous and enthusiastic reception accorded President Kennedy in 1963. Given the situation in Vietnam and the rebellious mood of the late 1960s among the young, there was no way the Nixon party could expect to duplicate the crowds and the spirit of 1963. Someone had the bright idea in Berlin, however, to have the president visit the sprawling Siemens plant in the Siemensstadt area of the city and to have him address an assembly of the workforce (still in the neighborhood of thirty thousand). It was one of the ironies of the time that the real workers of Berlin, as contrasted with the intellectuals and the students, still recognized the American role in providing security for the Western sectors and could be counted on to cheer enthusiastically. Since the meeting took place in a huge metal shed, the decibel rating in response to Nixonian rhetoric about the importance of the city quickly reached a satisfactory high. Thus was comparative honor saved.

In Bonn itself, the Nixon party approached its talks with Chancellor Kurt Kiesinger's Grand Coalition government with the same unbalanced evaluation of German-American relations as it had in Brussels with respect to European-American relations. Once again, as perhaps was only natural for a new Republican government following eight years of Democratic presidents, the thinking was in terms of crisis. Those who had observed German-American relations over the entire postwar period and had lived through the inevitable ups and downs that occur in the relations of all states shared a more relaxed attitude. They were aware of the proclivity of German visitors to Washington overly to dramatize the situation and to downplay the binding ties and common interests that we shared.

No one knew, of course, that elections in September 1969 would bring the Grand Coalition to an end, but it was clear that Vice Chancellor and Foreign Minister Willy Brandt felt restive with his place in the government and very much wanted the top position for himself. The role that the smaller Liberal Party would play in the autumn was still obscure, since that would depend on the electoral results.

I need say little about our next stop—Rome. The Italian political scene has generally been a mystery to senior American officials. Prime ministers and their cabinets came and went as the governing class played a game of musical chairs, and more or less the same faces kept turning up, if in different ministerial posts. Individual politicians might have sage advice to give, but the prime minister, in taking any position, had to remember that his government was an uneasy coalition of four or five parties each of which insisted on its prerogatives.[3]

Any American presidential visit to Rome must include an obligatory call on the pope, in this case Paul VI. Since the regular Rome stop was fully scheduled, it required a quick flight back to Rome after the Paris visit before Nixon's return to the United States. After a short private meeting between the pope and president, the rest of us trooped into the ornate meeting room. The pope—a small man in stature—impressed me as a gentle person somewhat weighed down by the problems with which he had to deal. American political exigencies not only require that a president coming to Italy must call on the pope, but Lyndon Johnson, that consummate politician but not consummate diplomat, once wanted to stop over in Italy during a trip abroad, see the pope, but completely skip the Italian government. When our experienced and able ambassador in Rome, J. Frederick Reinhardt, objected that this would be impossible in protocol terms because there was no way the president could get to the Vatican City without landing on Italian soil, Johnson became extremely irritated. Reinhardt stuck to his guns, and Johnson finally reluctantly agreed. He never forgave Reinhardt, who shortly thereafter was relieved of his post—admittedly after having served nearly seven years in Rome.

A primary goal of the whole trip, according to the White House, with Paris as perhaps the most important stop, was to improve our relationship with President de Gaulle of France by showing him that we respected his views and would henceforth seek them. There seemed to be little understanding in Washington that the French leader had never really recovered his poise and confidence after the tumultuous challenges to his regime in 1968. No one could predict, of course, that by staking his willingness to stay in office on a rather foolish plebiscite he would leave the French presidency within a few months.

President Nixon's strong negative views about modern abstract art were well known. The art in the American ambassador's residence, where Nixon would be staying while in Paris, was largely nonrepresentational, put there by Ambassador Robert Sargent Shriver Jr., a holdover from the Johnson administration who had not yet been replaced. The White House advance party, according to embassy sources, had a collective fit at the sight of all that modern stuff and ordered that it be replaced by something more congenial to the president's tastes. The artistic resources of the American embassy, while not qualitatively deep, were quantitatively sufficient to cover all the vacated residence walls. The most reactionary advocate in Moscow of socialist realism would have been happy at the result.

The talks on the first day produced few surprises but many platitudes as well as assurances that we now planned to take France more seriously. A grand state dinner at the Élysée Palace filled the evening and brought inevitable indigestion for those who let themselves go on the paté and other varieties of rich food and vintage wines. The toasts were lengthy and warm. Nixon was particularly good at this sort of thing; he had the gift of seeming to believe every word he said.

I do not recall that the second day's talks added very much. The White House delegation scarcely seemed to be aware that the principal enemy of the cause of European unity during the past decade had been President de Gaulle and that there was a basic incompatibility between good words for European unity and de Gaulle's vision of Europe.

The second evening, Nixon returned de Gaulle's hospitality with a dinner at the American ambassador's residence. Our present residence is in a former Rothschild mansion at 41 rue du Faubourg St. Honoré, but in 1967 it was still in the house acquired by Ambassador Gerard in the 1920s—a spacious mansion but hardly large enough for a presidential retinue, French guests, and all the others who had managed to wheedle invitations. Yehudi Menuhin was to provide the entertainment after dinner. After eating a mainly American (with a few flourishes) meal—some of the food and the wines had been flown in from the United States—we dutifully followed the two presidents into the largest of the salons, where folding chairs and an improvised little wooden stage provided the decor. Whether de Gaulle commented on the art that he saw I do not know.

Few would dispute Menuhin's reputation as a great violinist—at least at that period—but he had a captive audience and, before beginning to play, decided to say a few words in French. The few words grew into many words as he eloquently pleaded the cause of peace with the two presidents. I was sitting close enough to de Gaulle and Nixon to note their increasing restiveness. They had not come to dinner to be lectured by a violinist who had forgotten his concluding lines. Finally, he took up his violin and began to play. Everyone breathed a sigh of relief. It was really not such a bad speech. He had just picked the wrong time and place. Nixon, incidentally, could not understand a word, since his French was nonexistent. No postwar American president has demonstrated any noteworthy linguistic skills.

All in all, this early excursion to Europe served a useful purpose. It showed the new president cared, and generally he made a good impression. Summitry can prove hazardous, and professional diplomats are wary about the trail of misunderstandings or disappointed expectations that ill-conceived high-level meetings can leave behind them. As a realist, however, I had come to accept that the lure of presidential travel in Air Force One is strong and becomes stronger as the strains of life in Washington grow.

Comparing the Kennedy visits to Europe with which I had been involved and now the first Nixon visit, I could only conclude that the number of itinerant journalists and media types accompanying the president had progressively increased. It was now preordained that any such trip would turn into a media circus. The result was an enormous waste of talent and time as unhappy and frequently cynical correspondents sat around waiting for some nuggets of news to drop. A few favorites would have personal access to principals, much to the chagrin of the majority, who had to rely on corridor rumors and the periodic press briefings that usually left them restive and adversarial. Without having really absorbed the new lingo and "philosophy" during my few days in Washington before leaving for Europe, I found myself briefing the press largely on the basis of intuition and surmise. In any event, my hesitant generalizations were no worse than some of the other pap they were fed. The few essential points about the new Nixon approach were at least driven home ad nauseam.

When irritated by stupid questions or querulous complaints, I could not refrain from recalling (to myself of course) the little poem of Humbert Wolfe addressed to his fellow compatriots, but with broader application:

> You cannot hope
> to bribe or twist
> Thank God! the
> British journalist
>
> But, seeing what
> the man will do
> unbribed, there's
> no occasion to.

Under less harassing conditions, I tell myself with conviction that the free press is an essential ingredient of democracy and that a superfluity of journalists on presidential trips abroad (many of them bright and eager) is as much the fault of home offices that want their own in-house bylines as it is the result of the travel lust of frustrated press and media representatives who want to live it up on their firms' expense accounts. This whole question of how journalists can function effectively both on trips and in a Washington overcrowded with journalists, columnists, and broadcast media types is a troubling one, and I should be the first to admit that I have no definitive answers.

Back in Washington, I quickly found that, if power had shifted to the White House on those relatively few subjects in which Nixon and Kissinger were interested, the multitude of other subjects requiring attention, the daily flow of traffic in and out of the State Department, the visitors, diplomats, and journalists needing to be seen, ensured that the assistant secretary of state for European affairs could seldom get off his merry-go-round. In the evening there were receptions and dinners that Faith and I could not evade. Some were even pleasurable. A stream of high-level officials to Washington meant frequent state dinners in the White House.

We had an amusing experience of déjà vu at one of the early White House affairs. After our time in Budapest, Faith and I had had our fill—at least for a while—of gypsy orchestras. The president or one of his advisers decided to liven up the state dinners. Just after the guests had sat down, with an annunciatory fanfare, a group of instrumentalists—the so-called Strolling Strings of the Air Force—burst into the West Wing of the White House (which serves as the state dining room) dressed like gypsies and playing a familiar Hungarian melody. Faith and I were not seated near each other, but we immediately caught each other's eye and had the same thought: my God they've followed us all the way from Budapest. The Strolling Strings were Nixon's favorite and, as we were to experience, turned up frequently at state dinners.

Dinners on the diplomatic circuit generally produced fine, if too bountiful, food and sometimes interesting conversation. One practice I found tedious that was indulged in by a number of ambassadorial hosts was their proclivity to use either the occasion of the inevitable toast late in the meal or the preliminary "greeting" after the guests were seated to make lengthy remarks, always positive of course, about the guest of honor, if there was one, and then seriatim about all the other guests. If an ambassador was particularly wordy, and some indeed were, this process could stretch on and on—much to the dismay of the cook in the kitchen one could be sure.

Reinvigorating NATO and More Travel

The North Atlantic Treaty Organization was to hold its twentieth anniversary meeting in Washington in April. Practically from its inception in 1949, the spring sessions of semiannual NATO meetings of foreign ministers (sometimes boosted to the heads of governments level) have taken place on a rotating basis in capitals of member countries. The regular December meetings, on the other hand, have always been held at NATO headquarters when located in London, Paris, and finally Brussels.

The president clearly wanted to make the occasion memorable in line with his proclaimed goal of breathing new life into worthy old institutions. The idea that NATO suffered from a deep crisis persisted in the White House. This is the kind of situation that typically calls for dramatic new initiatives, so we were not surprised in the Bureau of European Affairs to receive from Secretary Rogers a White House instruction to produce the same. This was not an easy assignment. After all, NATO had fulfilled and was fulfilling its essential purpose of providing security for Western Europe and ultimately for the United States. Anything beyond that would amount to pure gravy. But well-trained diplomats can usually improvise to meet the needs of presidents and prime ministers. So it was that two ideas came to the White House that Nixon could use if he wished. He did wish and in his keynote speech to the opening public session of the NATO meeting proposed that, in addition to the semiannual meetings of NATO foreign ministers, there also be semiannual meetings of the undersecretaries of state or their equivalents (the number two men in foreign ministries).

The pièce de résistance, however, was the proposal for the establishment of a Committee on the Challenges of Modern Society. It provided something new and concrete that heads of government could endorse, although some undoubtedly thought that NATO was not the most appropriate organization for an initiative of this type. Expressions of displeasure from the Organization for Economic Cooperation and Development (OECD) in Paris quickly crossed the Atlantic, but the die was cast. I note that, in his memoirs, Kissinger claims these ideas either as his own (the undersecretaries' meetings) or having his presumably decisive endorsement (the committee proposal attributed to Pat Moynihan).[4] We minions in the State Department never knew what claims of origin went into National Security Council memorandums. If an idea was rejected, however, the fact that it came from the State Department was always underlined.

Whatever the claim to authorship, both of these proposals obviously smacked of gimmickry. After a few desultory sessions the meetings of undersecretaries on a regular basis died a natural death. The Committee on the Challenges of Modern Society (CCMS as it inevitably became known) acquired a bureaucratic life of its own within the NATO structure and in 1989 celebrated its twentieth anniversary. It undoubtedly did some good things, and no one can deny that its focus on environmental degradation relates to a basic problem of our time. To what degree its reports and recommendations actually influenced the actions of member governments, or whether the same work could not have been done better by an organization such as the OECD, which included Japan as a member, I do not pretend to know.

Another presidential trip abroad broke into the routines of a Washington summit. Nixon decided to include Romania as the last stop on a trip around the world focused mainly on Asia—the first visit by an American president to a Communist country in Eastern Europe. Part of the American press attacked the idea as unnecessarily provocative to the Soviet

Union; Nixon certainly was not averse to needling the Soviets. President Nicolae Ceauşescu—as he was later progressively to prove—provided no model of political or personal behavior, but he had shown some independence vis-à-vis the Soviet Union at a time when all the other so-called satellites stood firmly in line. He seemed like just the kind of hard-nosed ruler that Nixon might like.

My instructions were to join the presidential party in New Delhi and to be part of the official delegation in both New Delhi and Karachi, the next stops. So in late July I flew to India—a country in the midst of the monsoon season. There was considerable pomp and circumstance in both New Delhi and Karachi, but since I had no responsibility for the subcontinent, my role was essentially that of spectator at meetings and banquets. Romania, however, was part of my bailiwick, and on August 2 we arrived in Bucharest. After the usual military ceremonies at the airport, the party proceeded to the VIP guest quarters of Ceauşescu. The dictator had arranged for a large and enthusiastic crowd to greet Nixon en route, as he had for every appearance of our president in the country.

The guest quarters proved to be no austere motel-type arrangement as seemingly would befit a proletarian-oriented regime. Each member of the official party had his own suite with a luxurious green marble bathroom. When one opened a door leading from the bathroom, one stepped onto the side of a private swimming pool, also in green marble. These were undoubtedly the most luxurious guest quarters that I have ever occupied. They were an early sign of the pompous, overblown building mania that later afflicted the Romanian leader and led to the mammoth palace project nearly completed at the time of his deposition and summary execution in 1989.

The talks between the two presidents produced nothing sensational, but as Nixon indicated to members of his party, the toughness of Ceauşescu was an admirable trait. The photographs given much publicity of the two leaders joining peasants in a street dance were inherently ludicrous, particularly when one remembered that those smiling faces were ordered to be there by government edict.

White House Follies and Foibles

As we moved further into 1969, it also became clearer that the president and Henry Kissinger had small regard for the Department of State and intended to work around it whenever possible. I could sense hostility on the part of some White House staff members that, knowing the breed, I could only judge reflected the views of those above them. Objectively viewed, it was not a particularly impressive collection of individuals. The president, as I knew, had intelligence and sharp political awareness. Unfortunately, he also possessed less desirable qualities: deep resentments, a vindictive spirit, and almost paranoid suspicions of the press and, I fear, most of the Foreign Service, which he identified with the despised Eastern establishment. Even a cursory check of the data would have revealed broader ethnic and regional diversity in the Foreign Service than that of his own White House staff. I had seen enough of him to judge him a twisted man but sufficiently gifted so that, if he received good counsel to bring out the best in him, he had the imagination and creativity to achieve great things.

Some of Henry Kissinger's less endearing characteristics were not as evident as they were to become, but it was clear that his ego would permit no sharing of credit for success or acceptance of any responsibility for failure. The man was obviously intelligent and good at formulating ideas within an orderly conceptual framework. I could only regret that from the outset we seemed to be caught up in the White House–State Department frictions. I did not fully understand yet what a master of bureaucratic maneuver he would turn out to be.

Perhaps the most interesting member of the senior White House staff was Pat Moynihan. As a Democrat in a Republican stronghold, he seemed out of place, yet he undoubtedly saw the potential for good in the positive qualities of the president. When it came to putting thoughts into eloquent and expressive language, no one in the White House could equal him. His encomium to the president written and delivered to a group of senior officials assembled for the purpose some years into the first term struck me as sincere recognition of the achievements and the promise of a president who was later to become such a tragic failure.

I need say little about the rest of the White House staff. Watergate exposed the weaknesses and complicities of many. They were not without talent, but they mutually reinforced the atmosphere of intrigue and duplicity that more and more came to characterize the White House, including its handling of foreign affairs. Some of the president's own qualities of suspicion and vindictiveness inevitably became the accepted model of behavior. A large gap developed between the polite language of official and public discourse and the crude scatology of small private sessions with the president. I had noted on trips how, after an arduous day or two at an official stop, as the plane went up, the level of discourse between a relaxing Nixon and his closest cronies sharply descended.

The White House pomp and circumstance is pretty heady stuff. Whenever there is a band or orchestra around, the appearance of the president inevitably brings on "Hail to the Chief," and the military can provide musicians upon request. Some presidents obviously like the fanfare and the glory more than others; the Nixon team simply doted on it. The more or less routine procedure at state dinners held in the White House involved assembling the guests in the large East Room. The president would have the guest of honor and wife, the secretary of state and wife, and sometimes the assistant secretary of state for the appropriate region and wife for cocktails in the upstairs sitting room. Faith and I enjoyed these occasions, over which Nixon as host presided with some grace. At the appropriate moment, the orchestra would strike up "Hail to the Chief," and the president and guests of honor would descend the staircase in semiroyal fashion to enter the East Room and move to the head of the receiving line that protocol types had already set up. The guests would then shake the hands of the dignitaries and move on for drinks in the adjoining rooms before, on signal from protocol, they entered the state dining room in the West Wing.

I should note that all of this would have been preceded by the ritualistic initial reception on the White House grounds for the distinguished foreign visitor. No longer did the president have to go out to the airport—usually Andrews Air Force Base—to greet the new arrival. The carefully arranged invited guests plus a crowd of the curious allowed to view from the flanks would fill the space behind the White House facing south. With fanfare the limousines would draw up and discharge the visitors. After a handshake, Nixon would then lead the prime minister, president, or monarch to the raised platform equipped with numerous microphones, where Nixon would make appropriate welcoming remarks and the dignitary would then respond. After the playing of national anthems, a rather cramped march-by of special troop units took place, followed by a fife and drum corps dressed in U.S. Revolutionary War uniforms. That was it. Harm was seldom done, and what we knew in the trade as military honors were accorded. I always found the fife and drum corps somewhat ridiculous, but they too did no harm and added an additional bit of color.

So far as I am aware, this is still pretty much the standardized procedure for greeting heads of state and heads of governments. The whole ritual may seem to some as a relic of outmoded times, but it serves an ego-stroking function and fits into the image of an imperial presidency. All governments, democratic or otherwise, seem to operate on the assumption that a military display for the arriving high official and his or her "inspection" of the troops serves some functional, if forgotten, purpose.

The know-it-all attitude of the Nixon White House could lead to some real gaffes. One of these arose out of wishful thinking about the outcome of the German federal elections of late September 1969. Until then Chancellor Kurt Kiesinger had presided over a somewhat precarious, so-called

Grosse Coalition (Grand Coalition) between the two major parties, the CDU and the SPD, formed after the collapse of the Erhard government in 1966. The Nixon people liked Kiesinger and wanted him to win the elections and succeed himself in 1969. He was actually a suave, eloquent, and intelligent man who had performed a neat balancing act as head of the German government. With the usual Western European six-hour lead in time, the German electoral results began coming in to Washington during the late afternoon of September 29. The CDU and its Bavarian sister party, the CSU, lost only three seats (from 245 to 242) and still won 46.1 percent of the votes cast; the SPD gained 22 seats (from 202 to 224 with 42.7 percent of the votes cast); the small opposition party, the FDP, lost 10 seats (from 40 to 30 with 5.7 percent of the votes cast). To the naked eye it looked like a continuation of the Grand Coalition would follow as a matter of course. What the naked eye did not discern was the deeper political undercurrents that led to the formation of an SPD-FDP coalition government with the SPD leader Willy Brandt as chancellor (with a total of 254 seats in the Bundestag he had a working, if not impressive, majority).

As the returns came into Washington, the State Department cautioned the White House against any hasty assumptions about the shape of the new German government and to withhold the usual congratulatory message to the victorious head of government until we were sure who he would be. But not the White House! The wish was father to the thought, and some high official (we were never able to pin down the precise responsibility) authorized the dispatch of a congratulatory message to Kiesinger. Needless to say, the ensuing embarrassment when Brandt took over and Kiesinger went into opposition led to recrimination and finger-pointing, but this at least was one blunder the White House could not blame on the State Department, as it covertly tried to do in other cases of dubious judgments.

The height (or perhaps depth) of the ridiculous came early in 1970. British prime minister Harold Wilson was visiting Washington on January 27. Guests at the usual reception on the White House lawn, or arriving for the state dinner that evening, incredulously saw the presidential security force decked out in Graustarkian (the press preferred the term "ruritanian") new uniforms. Most of us could not repress a noticeable grin at this example of imagination run riot. The outfits consisted of double-breasted white tunics trimmed with gold braid, stiff plastic shakos decorated with the White House crest, and headgear resembling that worn by German traffic policemen or American drum majors. Needless to say, the Secret Service guards did not seem at ease in their new finery, but at least they provided the guests with a novel topic of conversation.

The press, of course, had a field day with this attempt to dress up White

House security. Even the *New York Times* had a short, critical editorial, quoting Portia in Shakespeare's *Merchant of Venice*: "I think he bought his doublet in Italy, his round hose in France, his bonnet in Germany." After a brief interval, the new uniforms simply disappeared into the recesses of the White House never to be worn again. The whole ridiculous business revealed an absence of taste and yearning for imperial trappings that could only startle a State Department official. What Harold Wilson thought he did not say. After all, he was accustomed to the finery of royal guards.

The Move from Confrontation to Negotiation

Without doubt the most positive international achievement of the Nixon administration was the American role, despite some strong initial negative White House reactions, in the complex of negotiations with the Soviet Union (and secondarily with Poland and the German Democratic Republic) that culminated in a number of important agreements and a triumphant Nixonian visit to Moscow in the late spring of 1972. When Willy Brandt became chancellor of the Federal Republic of Germany in the fall of 1969, he was in a position to push the opening to the East that became known as *Ostpolitik*.

During the 1960s, both as governing mayor of Berlin and then as foreign minister, Brandt had maintained contact with Soviet diplomats and developed the various concepts and formulations that went into his Eastern policy. He came to the conclusion that, in the aftermath of the extended Berlin crisis and the building of the Wall, the Soviets were prepared seriously to discuss arrangements aimed at stabilizing the situation in and around Berlin while obtaining a greater measure of recognition of the German Democratic Republic. Some of his ideas came from Peter Bender, a journalist with close ties to the Social Democratic Party, and others from his confidant Egon Bahr. The latter was to play an important role when Brandt took over as chancellor. Expressions such as *Kleine Schritte* (small steps) as a means of achieving *Wandlung durch Annäherung* (change through rapprochement) expressed the underlying philosophy of this new proposed approach. It reflected, of course, what at the time seemed a realistic acceptance of the fact that German unification was unachievable within the foreseeable future, if not for all time.

The drift of Brandt's thinking was not unwelcome in Lyndon Johnson's Washington, but as the president became progressively more obsessed by Vietnam, he could not provide the kind of sustained pressure required to get things moving. In any event, the crushing of the Prague Spring in 1968, just as Johnson was on the eve of departure for Moscow, effectively destroyed the possibility of any early initiative involving the Soviet Union.

Even before he became chancellor in October 1969, Brandt used his position as foreign minister to push negotiations with the Soviets on Berlin. One of the institutional spawnings of the Berlin crisis was the regular quadripartite dinner (France, Britain, the United States, and the Federal Republic) held the night before the beginning of semiannual NATO ministerial meetings to discuss matters relating to Berlin and Germany as a whole. Other NATO members were never happy about this custom, which, they felt, provided already agreed language on Germany and Berlin for the NATO communiqué and preempted substantive discussion of the subject at NATO sessions. They also knew that the four foreign ministers were discussing other subjects as well for which they did not have any claim to legal exclusivity.

At the quadripartite dinner held at Reykjavík in June 1968, Brandt had proposed that Berlin be raised during East-West discussions to ease tensions in Europe. I was, of course, still in Hungary, but this Brandt initiative lay on the table when I came to Washington early in 1969. During Nixon's February speech at the Siemensstadt in Berlin, he issued a call to the Soviets to end past tensions over Berlin. A bilateral exchange between Nixon and Aleksey Kosygin followed in the spring in which the president more specifically offered to negotiate on Berlin (without informing the other three interested countries, it may be noted). Meanwhile foreign ministers of the Warsaw Pact countries in a Budapest communiqué of March 17 again proposed the holding of a European security conference, and in their April 11 meeting in Washington the NATO foreign ministers "expressed their support for continuing efforts by the Three Powers to explore . . . possibilities for ordered and negotiated progress" with the object of achieving concrete measures aimed at improving the situation of Berlin with the Soviet Union.[5] Although the Soviet response dragged in a lot of old positional baggage, it clearly left open the way for eventual four-power talks on Berlin.

I had had enough experience with the White House of several preceding presidents to know that, despite sporadic and sometimes unpredictable White House involvement, the hard slogging, the sustained thinking and drafting of memorandums and instructions and participation in both intra- and multi-governmental meetings, would have to be handled by the Bureau of European Affairs. In a burst of foresight, shortly after coming to Washington, I had begun the process of bringing James Sutterlin, the embassy's political counselor in Bonn, a knowledgeable and imaginative officer, to take over direction of the Office of German Affairs. He was to prove an able source of ideas and well-drafted memorandums and telegrams.

In a speech on July 10, 1969, Soviet foreign minister Gromyko said that the Soviet Union would be willing to hold talks on West Berlin if the Western powers took into account the interests of Eastern security. President Nixon accepted our recommendation, which went to him in the form of a memorandum from Secretary Rogers, that we seek Western agreement to inform the Soviet government that we would study Gromyko's statement and that the Federal Republic would be prepared to discuss travel and communications problems with the German Democratic Republic. This led quickly enough to a tripartite diplomatic exchange, and a period of what the press calls "intensive diplomatic activity" followed. A memorandum drafted in the Bureau of European Affairs went forward in July from Secretary Rogers to the president proposing a course of action that could open the way to meaningful discussions on Berlin. After some delay to iron out procedural differences on the Western side, a tripartite note went forward on December 16 proposing, inter alia, that preparatory talks be held with a view to holding formal negotiations.

Although I was personally very much involved, I have not thought it necessary to record in detail here the diplomacy leading up to, and the actual negotiation of, the Quadripartite Agreement on Berlin. The fine book *Berlin: From Symbol of Confrontation to Keystone of Stability*, by James S. Sutterlin and David Klein, provides by far the most complete and accurate account of the diplomacy of those negotiations.[6] In a book that I edited and coauthored, *The Future of Berlin*, I also discuss in detail the political and legal implications of that agreement.[7] Suffice it to say here that, after further tripartite exchanges with the Soviets, the latter agreed in February 1970 to meet at the ambassadorial level in the former Allied Central Commission for Germany building in West Berlin. The European Affairs Bureau continued to do the basic drafting on the American side of follow-up documents that finally culminated with the formal beginning of negotiations on Berlin on March 26, 1970.

It had become clear that the Soviets wanted badly to have a conference on European security and were presumably prepared to pay some price to get it. Their motive in part was to enhance the status of the GDR as a full participant but primarily, through such a conference, to achieve, in effect, a substitute for that elusive peace treaty and thus collectively to ratify the de facto boundary settlements of the postwar period. Why the Soviet leaders, not always known for their high regard for legal commitments, should have placed such value on a process that would have produced essentially a legal document never became entirely apparent, but there was no doubt that they and their Warsaw Pact allies were hell-bent to have it. Little did they know at the time, of course, that the final Helsinki agreement that emerged at the end of the process would turn out to be such an effective propaganda weapon for the West in the late seventies and early eighties.

At the same time, the Brezhnev regime was sending out signals that it might be prepared to discuss the Berlin situation in a less threatening context than during the failed Khrushchev offensive against the basic position of the Western powers in the city. The Wall had stopped the hemorrhaging of population from the GDR, and from such information as we had, the men around Leonid Brezhnev were less venturesome and more committed to stability than the impetuous Khrushchev. In any event, Brandt, as chancellor, was all the more persuaded that the time had come to move ahead with his *Ostpolitik*. He and Bahr were prepared to extend the area of discussion beyond European security and Berlin and, in effect, to enlarge the web of linkages.

Starting with earlier days in Berlin, I had always found Willy Brandt to be a somewhat enigmatic personality. He had a prickly ego and a limited sense of humor but a great deal of charisma and, at his best, moving oratorical skills. He never seemed to be a man entirely at ease with himself, nor did he understand that negative personal behavior traits could make him the object of gossip and, on the part of his political opponents, ridicule. Yet on balance he had the capacity for distinguished leadership, if sometimes only in spurts. His personal views, to the extent that he would discuss them, were those of a moderate socialist with sincere, but not overly strong, ideological commitment to the traditions of his party. In other words, he could be an effective politician within the Bonn milieu, and now for the first time as head of government he could attempt to implement his ideas.

Egon Bahr had, in my experience, gone through a fairly radical personal transformation. As already noted, he began as a hard-line cold warrior in the early postwar years broadcasting on the U.S.-operated Radio in American Sector Berlin. By the 1960s he had become a source of new ideas on Eastern policy within the SPD, and when Brandt became foreign minister in 1965, he moved into the Foreign Ministry as head of its Policy Planning Staff. In that position his staff produced a memorandum, not made public until 1973 but the contents of which became known to the cognoscenti through leaks. It outlined three options for talks with the East, the most extreme of which would aim at a Central European security system with little or no role left for the United States. Many, especially CDU members, believed that Bahr personally favored such a goal, and their distrust of his motives continued through the years. I had no doubts about his intelligence or his ability to find adept language to justify his objectives, but after meeting with him, either alone or in a group, I was not always sure that he had been completely frank, or sometimes even clear, in what he had said.

Walter Scheel, the new FDP foreign minister, was a shrewd politician in his own right, but with Brandt in the Chancellery it was obvious that control of *Ostpolitik* would lie elsewhere than with Scheel. When in the early summer of 1972 I arrived in Bonn as ambassador, he was still foreign minister. I found him, as I had known him before as a rising politician, to be honest and reliable. He had a lively sense of humor and did not, like some of his political contemporaries, have a surplus of unbared sensitivities. As political leader of the small Liberal Party he could never hope to become chancellor but in 1974 became president of the Federal Republic with the support of the Social Democrats.

The Conduct of Negotiations: Back-Channel Messages and Other Deceits

At both the Washington and Bonn ends, the procedures for coordinating Western positions quickly fell into place. The Bonn group had for many years provided the institutional mechanism for four-power consultations in that capital. In Washington, we set up a European Interdepartmental Group as well as a restricted section of the long-existing Berlin Task Force, both of which I chaired. This permitted rapid interagency clearance when necessary, but I signed off most day-to-day instructions to the negotiators. Matters of basic policy went to Secretary Rogers for signature but in some cases were also referred to the White House for clearance. To iron out quadripartite differences that could not be settled in Bonn, I would meet at one of the four capitals at the so-called senior officials level with my British, French, and German counterparts—sessions that Egon Bahr also sometimes attended for the German side. This organizational pattern may seem a bit elaborate as described, but it worked reasonably well, taking account of the need for lateral clearances within governments as well as between governments. The White House role during the first phase of the negotiations was muted once we had obtained the president's approval for our proposed general negotiating approach. As a matter of fact, initial White House reaction to the whole business was distinctly unenthusiastic—a reaction that was to turn even more negative as other aspects of *Ostpolitik* unfolded.[8]

Our negotiator in Berlin, Ambassador Kenneth Rush, was not a trained diplomat. As a former senior corporate executive, he could drive hard toward an objective but became restive under the constraints that multilateral diplomacy inevitably imposed. A political appointee, he felt closer to officials like John Mitchell and others in the administration than to the secretary of state. However, assisted by able Foreign Service officers in Bonn and Berlin who had his confidence, he demonstrated during 1970–71 both considerable learning capacity and willingness to slog it out. He was directly involved in the White House cabal described below that complicated later phases of the negotiations.

The first phase of Berlin negotiations, which lasted until September 1970, resembled a stately minuet. The four ambassadors made sometimes lengthy speeches laying out the Western and Eastern positions, but there was no serious effort to resolve the many obvious differences that had emerged. One could say, however, that some idea of the range of subject matter to be covered gradually began to take shape, and at the sixth ambassadorial meeting the French ambassador, Jean Sauvagnargues, tabled a Western paper setting forth the contents of a possible agreement on Berlin.

As I have said, during this first phase of negotiations, the White House showed singularly little enthusiasm for the whole business. The president's and his national security adviser's suspicions of German motives and reliability became accentuated by the discussions launched early in 1970 between Egon Bahr and Soviet leaders that led to the Moscow Treaty of August 12, 1970, between the Federal Republic and the Soviet Union.

It was perhaps no wonder that a basically conservative White House (although Nixon sometimes showed surprising flexibility on economic and social policy) should find a socialist leader like Chancellor Willy Brandt ideologically suspect. His opening to the East, as realistic as one might have argued it to be after twenty-five years of frozen fronts between East and West, could only strike hard-line officials as unduly venturesome, if not downright treasonable. They saw no virtue in movement, if the movement was all seemingly in the wrong direction of concessions contrary to long-established German and Western positions.

We in the State Department who knew better the historical antecedents and the people involved were more pragmatic. If progress could be made in improving the situation of Berlin, the West might well be prepared to pay a price for Soviet concessions, particularly if that price essentially involved a change of German governmental positions on such matters as the Hallstein Doctrine, recognition of the GDR, or acceptance of the Oder-Neisse boundary, about all of which we had come to feel that more flexibility would be desirable.

It had become clear fairly quickly that Brandt and Bahr were prepared to move considerably farther and faster than any previous German government toward acceptance of the East German regime as a fact of life with which they had to deal directly. I recall an early quadripartite meeting in Bonn of senior officials at which Bahr appeared to announce that, with India on the verge of recognizing the GDR, the Hallstein Doctrine was for all practical purposes dead. He did not specifically say at the time that the federal government would as a result now itself be prepared to recognize the GDR, but this was in a sense the logical implication of the way he described the situation. I knew that this was bound to come as a shock to Washington, where the conditioned reflex of successive American governments had been to support German government pleas that we assist in strictly holding the line in support of the Hallstein Doctrine—no matter how much private grumbling there might be about the rigidities of Bonn. It was also a basic fact that strict nonrecognition was essentially a policy of the Federal Republic that we supported out of loyalty (as during the Berlin crisis of 1958–63) rather than deep conviction that this was the only possible road to take.

One of several myths that found wide acceptance, in this case on the German side, was that the State Department basically opposed negotiations on Berlin and frequently dragged its feet before and after the ambassadorial negotiations began. It was never completely clear to us why this should be the case, since we had done all the basic drafting recommending negotiations and preparing for them, but such is the elusiveness of truth. We were, of course, suspicious that, with its proclivity to play the bad cop–good cop game, the National Security Council staff had felt it desirable thus to pass the burden of responsibility for those delays built into the very complicated quadripartite negotiating process itself. Certainly we argued for the positions we thought wise, but in no case did we seek delay for the sake of delay or recommend the impossible in order to hamper the success of negotiations. Any examination of the detailed record will clearly prove this.[9]

Even at a fairly early stage, the groundwork was laid for a multiplication of channels that was bound at a later stage to cause confusion, just as it did in the SALT I negotiations. The irony was that this came at a time when the White House was still deeply suspicious of the German leaders and clearly thought they were going off the deep end during the summer and fall of 1970. As Kissinger wrote in his memoirs, it all began with the Germans in October 1969, when, at Brandt's request, the national security adviser met with Egon Bahr in Washington. Kissinger had agreed with Rogers (in what Kissinger termed a "compact") that he would not negotiate with Bahr and that I would sit in on the meetings. The first such meeting was ostensibly a lunch at the White House, which I attended and at which no matters of great moment were discussed. After lunch Bahr and I left, he through the front door. He then reentered it through the basement for a further talk with Kissinger while I returned to the State Department. Thus the way was opened for back-channel messages between the national security adviser and Bahr without the involvement of the State Department.[10] Washington being the kind of town it is, we quickly learned about this duplicity. We did not know, of course, that it was but the prelude to a whole host of so-called back-channel communications intended to freeze out Secretary Rogers.

Ambassador Rush had his own private channel to the White House via his friend Attorney General John Mitchell and conducted secret bilateral meetings with the Soviet ambassador in Bonn acting directly on White House instructions while Kissinger communicated with Moscow through the Soviet ambassador in Washington, Anatoly Dobrynin. As Sutterlin and Klein detail in their book, this tangled web of deceit accomplished nothing significant in the quadripartite negotiations that could not have been obtained in a more straightforward manner.[11] It was bound to lead to the puzzlement and frequent irritation of our French and British allies, who thought they were equal partners in the negotiations. They quickly deduced that the American side was engaged in shenanigans. Their indignation was understandable. They could hardly repress their sarcasm at meetings of the senior officials that I regularly attended. They knew there was nothing much that I or the State Department could do about a performance that they could only regard as irregular and disloyal. You had the rather absurd picture of a White House scheming with the Soviets and the Germans against the president's chosen secretary of state (as well as our British and French allies) in a way that could only humiliate Rogers and weaken the effectiveness of American diplomacy.

In fact, the whole White House treatment of Secretary Rogers was comprehensible only in terms of abnormal psychology. Here was a man who, as attorney general and principal adviser, had done much to save Nixon's political career in 1956 when Eisenhower was apparently prepared to dump him as vice president. One would have thought that he would have an especially close relationship to the president, who would seek his advice on a regular basis. However, it was not so. Whatever Nixon's personal aversion to the State Department, there was plenty of evidence to suggest that his national security adviser and staff did their best to diminish both Rogers and the department that he headed.

Linkages and More Linkages

We and the Germans knew that, no matter how much the Soviets wanted it, the mere prospect of a European security conference would not suffice to compensate them for the kind of agreement on Berlin that we sought. I doubt whether the White House appreciated this as we moved further into 1970.

Early in his administration, the president had made clear his dedication to the concept of linkage, presumably meaning that we would not rush into negotiations on one subject without making some progress on others that were of importance to us. One problem was the vagueness of the concept. What had to be linked with what? Did it mean that one must pass up targets of opportunity with the Soviets because we were not making desired progress in other areas? When foreign ambassadors, some of whom regularly called on me, asked me for an explanation, I would respond that linkage should not be understood in mechanistic terms. It was rather a psychological reality. If things were going well in the relations between the Soviet Union and the United States in a number of areas, we were obviously going to be positively affected in our willingness to move ahead with negotiations in other areas. I am not sure this formula made the White House completely happy, but I persisted with it.

Another problem with linkage is that two or more can play at the game, as we were to find out in the analogous case of playing the China card. We could make the Soviets nervous by seeming to improve our relations with the People's Republic of China, but the Soviets could make us nervous by seeming to improve their relations with China. The Chinese, too, found they could play their own card in reverse, alternatively with the Soviet Union or the United States.

In any event, we were faced in 1970 with a clear case of linkage by the Soviet Union. If we wanted a satisfactory agreement on Berlin, we would have to offer more. But at that point we and the French and British really had little more to offer. The Germans did. Here is where *Ostpolitik* really came in, much to the concern of the worrywarts in the White House who saw the initiative going elsewhere and in a direction that they identified with both a resurgent German nationalism and inherent Socialist weakness with respect to Communism.

During the late winter and spring of 1970, Egon Bahr was already in Moscow busily dealing with the Soviets and setting up the basis for the negotiation of a formal treaty between the Soviet Union and the Federal Republic of Germany. The essence of the treaty was West German recognition of the status quo in Eastern Europe, with existing borders regarded as inviolable and the German Democratic Republic as a reality to be dealt with directly. Although the treaty contained no specific language to that effect, it seemed to imply the renunciation of the goal of German reunification. Foreign Ministers Scheel and Gromyko conducted the final negotiations in Moscow, and Brandt and Kosygin (as chairman of the Soviet Council of Ministers and thus formal head of government) signed the treaty in the Kremlin on August 12, 1970.

Needless to say, such a treaty inevitably created a stormy reaction in the Federal Republic within the opposition parties. In an effort to placate the critics, the German government had delivered a letter to the Soviet government stating that it continued to endorse the "political objective" of German reunification in "free self-determination." Opposition lawyers quickly pointed out that such a letter was not legally binding.

In any event, the Moscow Treaty opened the way to eventually successful West German negotiations with the GDR, which, up to that point, had made little progress. Although the actual signature of agreements did not take place until 1971, and indeed until late 1972 in the case of the Treaty on the Basis of Relations between the Federal Republic and the GDR, the momentum was now clearly on the side of those seeking a comprehensive package of agreements of which the Quadripartite Agreement on Berlin would be one.

Thus as we moved into late 1970, the pieces began to fall together. The West wanted an agreement on Berlin and acceptance of MBFR (mutual and balanced force reduction) negotiations. The Soviets wanted a conference on security in Europe, recognition of the GDR, and a West German treaty with Moscow and with Poland (the last was signed December 7, 1970), and we both seemed to want an agreement on arms limitations (SALT I). This was mutual linkage on a grand scale.[12]

I was never quite certain at what precise point the White House decided to jump on the bandwagon and, while still emitting occasional murmurs of disapproval, move toward full acceptance of the political advantages to be gained. It had become quite clear that, willy-nilly, the Germans were going ahead with their *Ostpolitik* and that this was becoming an integral part of what we needed to achieve a satisfactory agreement on Berlin, even though the ambassadorial negotiations in that city were still short of making real progress. In any event, we in the State Department began to sense a different variety of signals coming out of the White House and began to feel that negotiations could now proceed on their merits rather than being entangled in a web of prejudices and confused indications.

I should say a word about negotiations to achieve mutual and balanced force reductions (MBFR), which became part of the package. I had never believed there was anything sacrosanct about the precise number of American troops in Europe, and specifically in West Germany, but I knew that any large-scale unilateral American force reduction with no compensating Soviet reductions would have serious negative consequences for

NATO and our relations with the Federal Republic. Each year Senator Mike Mansfield, the Democratic majority leader in the Senate, periodically called for major American force withdrawals from Europe and submitted what became known as Mansfield Amendments to relevant legislation to mandate such withdrawals. These never obtained a majority, but it was always a battle requiring appearances on the Hill (including my own) to hold our ground given the growing unpopularity of the war in Vietnam and the more generalized mood to which it gave rise that the boys should come back home.

Sophisticated Germans like Helmut Schmidt, at the time minister of defense, knew that our forces in Germany were some 20 percent under strength, with many experienced officers and noncommissioned officers sent to Vietnam along with troops that might otherwise have been in Germany. A few Germans like Rudolf Augstein, publisher of *Der Spiegel*, claimed that the primary motive for Brandt's *Ostpolitik* was the chancellor's conviction that the U.S. government might one day withdraw from Europe. I never thought this made much sense as a unitary explanation of a whole set of complicated motives moving the chancellor and Egon Bahr, but on the other hand, properly qualified, I could not judge it entirely implausible. I find nothing, however, in Brandt's memoirs, or in anything he ever said to me, to suggest that this played a major role in his thinking.[13]

In any event, the primary appeal of negotiations over mutual force reductions in 1970–71 was their possible use as an offset to congressional pressures for unilateral troop withdrawals from Europe. I recall an early conversation with Eliot Richardson, then as undersecretary of state the number two man in the department. After bemoaning Mansfieldism we agreed that, if we could engage the Soviets in discussions about mutual troop reductions, we would be in a strong position to argue that you did not give your principal negotiating counter away in advance by taking action unilaterally to reduce your forces.

Seemingly good ideas stimulate many claims to authorship. Henry Kissinger made no such claim. Although he wrote in his memoirs "that he had no objection to using MBFR as a break on unilateral Congressional acts," he continued to feel that NATO was in such a precarious state that the Soviets would use MBFR negotiations to unravel the alliance.[14] His chairmanship of White House meetings intended to arrive at an eventual U.S. position turned into an exercise in bureaucratic delay. He gave members of the Joint Chiefs' staff intricate tasks and tight deadlines that ensured they would work around the clock. As the State Department representative at these meetings, I could only wince and pity the poor staffers who would see little of their families in the weeks ahead. This was stalling on a grand scale, but we in State believed that the combined pressures from the U.S. Senate and our European allies would sooner or later necessitate MBFR negotiations.

My own view was that the White House once again exaggerated the crisis in NATO—if that was the proper term at all—and that, apart from the tactical usefulness of MBFR negotiations to ward off the Senator Mansfields, we could use such negotiations to achieve broader objectives. Our European allies wanted them, and it was excessively pessimistic to assume that we were bound to sacrifice some degree of Western security by engaging the Soviets in them. In any event, the NATO bid for MBFR negotiations eventually became a part of the interlocked package of Western and Soviet objectives. It would be hard to argue in the light of what actually happened that Kissinger's fears, and Nixon's to the extent that he shared them, proved well grounded. Mansfieldism faded away, and the MBFR negotiations, to which the Soviets finally agreed, began in October 1973 in Vienna. They dragged on and on for some thirteen years, finally to be replaced in 1989 by Negotiations on Conventional Armed Forces in Europe (CFE). White House concerns to the contrary notwithstanding, the West gave away nothing, the alliance remained firm, and all of this was, in any case, to be overtaken by the dramatic changes that Gorbachev introduced in the field of arms control.

Negotiations with the Soviets on Berlin Move toward a Climax

A visit to Washington on October 22, 1970, by Soviet foreign minister Gromyko brought a clear expression of support by President Nixon for an agreement on Berlin. The Soviets, too, seemed to be showing increasing interest in an agreement and were now telling the Germans that time was of the essence. Since the latter had linked ratification of the Moscow and Warsaw Treaties to completion of the negotiations on Berlin, they both logically wanted quick movement in the four-power negotiations. The Germans, particularly Bahr, carried on bilateral discussions with the Soviets about the specific content of a Berlin agreement, needless to say in complete disregard of the four-power status of the city. From a purely legal point of view, things had gotten out of hand, but this obviously fit into the web of surreptitious dealings with the Soviets and the Germans that the White House found so congenial.

We were aware of some of this, but not all of it all of the time. Although we knew we were being used as convenient whipping boys when reasonable Western negotiating positions ran into Soviet rejections, there was little we could do other than continue with the process as best we could while more and more persuaded that Soviet motives were strong for final acceptance of a satisfactory interim agreement on Berlin. No one was thinking in terms of any final settlement of the Berlin problem in the absence of that German unity that alone could make the city no longer a geographical exclave.

It would be interesting to speculate as to what the Soviets thought about all this. They obviously went along, for they could hardly lose from what they could only interpret as disarray within the U.S. government. They must have been bemused by the spectacle of the American national security adviser taking them and the SPD leaders into his confidence while, in effect, conspiring against officials of his own government not to speak of the allied British and French. It was a theater of the absurd in diplomacy.

Kissinger's attempted justification in his memoirs was essentially that all of this was necessary to break through inevitable bureaucratic rigidity. What we had here was a rather amateurish, conspiratorial concept of diplomacy. The paranoid atmosphere of the White House, of course, made it seem only natural that the unfriendly bureaucrats in the State Department had to be circumvented if the negotiations, once they had been accepted as at all desirable, were to succeed.

The reality was, of course, quite different. The final agreement contained nothing that could not have been reached by a more orderly approach to the negotiations. Perhaps some improvements might have been obtainable. As it turned out, any preconceived time pressures turned out to be illusory, since, by a peculiar inversion of linkage, the Soviets found it inexpedient formally to sign the agreement on Berlin after the four ambassadors in Berlin had reached agreement on a final text. They wanted to be certain that the Germans would ratify the Moscow and Warsaw Treaties first.

Frenetic negotiations filled the first eight months of 1971, as slowly but surely the constituent parts of an overall agreement emerged. Once the Soviets had accepted that the negotiations would not affect the rights of the three Western powers in their sectors of Berlin (as did a so-called Principles Paper tabled in December 1970 by Ambassador Pjotr Abrassimov, the Soviet negotiator in Berlin), the way seemed clear to an eventual interim agreement on Berlin that would, we hoped, provide a regime for the city that would remove it as the center of dangerous controversy between East and West while keeping open the possibility of a final settlement of the German and Berlin questions.

We sent numerous instructions, sometimes almost on a daily basis, and attended many meetings in Washington and in Europe. Not the least of my tasks was to placate the British and the French and to assure them, as best I could, that they were not the victims of a gigantic shell game with an unpredictable outcome. There were inevitable snags and confusions, but our confidence in a successful outcome grew. The White House was obviously unable to deal with all of the complicated details of a complex agreement but focused its attention on what it believed to be a few fundamental issues.

So on September 3, 1971, after some last-minute miscues and some slippery actions by the Soviets, the four ambassadors were able to sign the Quadripartite Agreement on Berlin. This did not, of course, put it automatically into effect. As noted, formal action by governments was still required, and this was not automatically forthcoming from the Soviets. The Soviets now delayed in the face of what they saw as growing opposition in the Federal Republic to ratification of the Moscow and Warsaw Treaties, which for them, after all, had been a necessary part of the quid pro quo for a Berlin settlement.

Other Concerns of an Assistant Secretary for Europe

By devoting so much space to what was, after all, an important and ultimately successful series of negotiations—and to which we shall have to return—one can easily give the impression that backstopping them (to use the popular bureaucratic expression of the era) was our all-consuming activity. This was far from the case. The assistant secretary of state for European affairs had to deal with a host of other problems. Apart from managing the Bureau of European Affairs, my days involved many appearances on the Hill to defend budgets and to testify on policy. There was also the care, feeding, and advising of the variegated stable of ambassadors serving in the many posts for which my bureau had responsibility. Since Europe had most of the prize posts sought by political appointees (largely major contributors to the Republican Party), we ended up with the usual collection of prima donnas, and in a few cases real lulus.

Sergent Shriver managed to hang on in Paris into 1970, but all the rest of the political appointees were brand new. They telephoned frequently, and I quickly became an expert at hand-holding by international hookup. I was to see some of them on visits to their posts with Secretary Rogers or alone, and all of them at the annual conferences of European ambassadors, East and West, over which I would preside. A few of them I found on the basis of experience to be outstandingly able, others mediocre at best, and a few complete disasters. The career officers, mainly assigned to Eastern European posts, were competent professionals and needed little beyond the normal flow of instructions.

It was the plethora of substantive problems, however, that consumed much of my time and energy. To recount all the details would merely bloat this memoir, but a few are worth noting both as illustrative and as of some intrinsic interest, even if only in the category of historical curiosities.

Malta and Mintoff

The case of Malta and Dom Mintoff, its difficult and erratic prime minister during the 1970s, provided a classic example of how an obstinate leader of a very small but strategically located island country can engage the concerned attention of great powers and a major alliance. Although the specific issue was the continuance of a British naval presence on the island, the United States, as was its wont, quickly became an important player in the effort to find some sort of compromise formula that both Mintoff and the British could accept. The NATO alliance had become quite comfortable with a succession of center-right governments on Malta, but the electoral victory of the Socialist Party headed by Mintoff in June 1971 brought forebodings of trouble to come.

The prickly little prime minister quickly began to make threats that if the British did not agree to pay much more for their naval base, he might have to turn to Libya or possibly the Soviet Union to substitute for them as a source of revenue. Even a casual look at a map, with Malta located only a relatively short distance from the southern coast of Sicily, would quickly bring home the strategic location of the island and the unacceptability of any significant Soviet or even Libyan influence there. The prospect shook NATO headquarters, and diplomatic exchanges multiplied between Brussels, Rome, Washington, and London. The British, however, were reluctant to raise the ante and at times seemed prepared to call what they regarded as Mintoff's bluff.

Needless to say, my bureau became very much involved in the whole, at times rather bizarre and even ridiculous, business. We sometimes admittedly felt that the man was beyond control to the point where he might actually carry out his threats. At other times the emerging scenario seemed to resemble nothing so much as low-grade opéra bouffe. A U.S. contribution to any final financial settlement, it quickly became clear, would be required given the low state of the British treasury.

The British base on Malta was not a product of World War II. It had existed for some 170 years; in 1971 there were some thirty-five hundred British personnel on the island plus some seven thousand dependents. During the months after the Socialist victory that brought Mintoff to power, the Heath government in London thought it had reached agreement with the Maltese. When this fell through, the British muttered that Mintoff was attempting blackmail. Finally, on December 29 they announced that they would withdraw all their forces from Malta. "Deadline Dom," as he was now called in London, then set a new deadline of January 15. The British ordered evacuation of dependents, a process that extended well into January, leaving in its wake some six thousand unemployed Maltese. We and the Italians were urging the British to try further and offered to put some money into a final package of thirty-five million dollars (Mintoff wanted forty-five million). The British reacted with some scorn, but finally Lord Carrington, the British defense minister, flew to Rome in January to meet with Mintoff. NATO secretary general Joseph Luns also participated in the discussions, since the offer was now being described as the NATO package. Mintoff announced the extension of his January deadline.

The negotiations continued, ending finally on March 26, 1972, with the announcement at Marlborough House in London of a seven-year agreement signed by Mintoff and Lord Carrington. Malta would receive some thirty-seven million dollars per year, a total, it might be noted, not far from the NATO compromise proposal. Britain was to pay a little more than one-third of thirty-seven billion dollars; the rest would come from other NATO countries, particularly the United States.

Dom Mintoff returned to Malta to receive a hero's welcome, at least from members of his own party. The British ended up by paying no more in cash than they had under the old arrangements. We provided most of the essential extra funding. What had seemed like a hopeless stalemate involving two intransigent negotiating partners who could not be farther apart evolved into an agreement that left all the principals relatively happy. I do not know what lessons in diplomatic technique could be drawn from the whole affair other than that money can serve as an essential lubricant and that, under certain circumstances, the use of deadlines or ultimatums (as Khrushchev found during the Berlin crisis) may serve a negotiational purpose. I do not know how many meetings I attended, how many incoming cables I read, how many outgoing telegrams I authorized—all on the subject of Malta—during 1971 and early 1972. After announcement of the agreement with the British, the island quickly sank from view. His nuisance value to the alliance largely gone, Mintoff remained in relatively quiet power until 1984.[15]

Trying to Penetrate Swiss Banking Secrecy

One of the more frustrating experiences of my three and a half years as assistant secretary of state was the protracted effort to obtain significant concessions from the Swiss authorities that would enable some penetration of their banking system in the case of American criminals who were laundering illegal assets in Swiss numbered accounts. The problem did not, of course, originate with the Nixon administration. The Department of Justice and particularly Robert M. Morgenthau, the U.S. district attorney in New York City, had been pushing for action. Some members of Congress led by Representative Wright Patman of Texas, chairman of the House Banking and Currency Committee, wanted a law that would regulate American dealings with foreign banks that refused to divulge information about deposits by Americans.

It came as no surprise, therefore, that fairly early in 1969 I was approached by the Department of Justice to undertake formal negotiations with the Swiss to achieve some relaxation of their banking secrecy code. Thus began a seemingly interminable series of talks with Swiss negotiators. Sometimes we thought we were making progress, but each time the door would slam shut. Meanwhile, I was learning a great deal about Swiss banking practices as well as the multifarious uses of numbered accounts to evade the application of American laws. As time went on, a harsh reality into which we ran was that tax cheating was not in violation of Swiss criminal law and that probably the most we could get was access into Swiss bank accounts in cases where that criminal law had clearly been broken. Only fraud, narcotics trading, and a few securities cases seemed to qualify. In vain we would expostulate that the Chicago gangster Al Capone, not known for his virtuous life, could only be sent to jail on income tax evasion charges. So the negotiations continued with occasional glimmerings of hope that we might, if only patient enough, achieve at least a minor breakthrough.

In December 1969, President Nixon fired U.S. attorney Morgenthau, a Democrat, and replaced him with Whitney North Seymour. Rumors quickly spread that this was due to Morgenthau's interest in dealings by the president's former law partner as well as several leading New York banks. However, Seymour indicated that he would continue to crack down on abuse of foreign banking laws, which he did within the limits imposed by the absence of any agreement with the Swiss government. At no time did I ever feel that the White House wanted us to cease pursuing an agreement on banking secrets with the Swiss.

Finally, after some three years of negotiations (intermittent it is true), we came close at the working level to hammering out a draft treaty. At that point, I was fully engaged in preparing for the Moscow summit and my departure as ambassador to Bonn. During August 1972, when already in Bonn, I would read with chagrin in the press that Swiss government spokespeople were saying that, in the light of objections being received from Swiss businesspeople and bankers, it was "practically excluded" that a final draft of the treaty would be ready for submission to parliament during 1972.

On May 25 of the following year, however, the United States and Switzerland did sign a treaty giving us at least a part of what we were asking for in the way of Swiss government aid in penetrating Swiss banking secrecy in certain types of criminal cases. I like to think that our efforts had laid an effective groundwork for the success of 1973.[16]

NATO Ministerial Meetings and the Inducement of Crisis

One of the things an American secretary of state and the foreign ministers of other NATO countries can count on, even in the 1990s, is the need to attend with seasonal regularity the semiannual meetings of NATO foreign ministers. The December session customarily takes place at NATO headquarters in Brussels, while the spring session is held on a rotating basis in the capitals of member countries. I had had considerable experience with these gatherings during the late Eisenhower and Kennedy administrations when the Berlin crisis dominated discussions with the peculiar sense of urgency that topic produced.

The first Nixon term was a less harried period in East-West terms, but there was always the need to keep Allies informed of ongoing negotiations with the Soviets. It would be foolish, however, to deny that Foreign Ministry staffs—and that included the Bureau of European Affairs in the State Department, which was responsible for NATO matters—had to face the common problem of stimulating the interest of their ministers prior to each of these high-level gatherings. Out of this need came a certain official hyperbole about the state of the alliance. As I wrote in an earlier article:

> American briefing papers, prepared in the State Department and usually under strong urging by the American NATO Delegation, have customarily exhorted the Secretary of State of the time to assert leadership to reassure our doubting Allies and to explain the American position on controversial issues. This buildup has partly reflected the factual situation, for NATO has ever been an imperfect organization. But it has also reflected the peculiar state of mind of bureaucrats as they prepared for ministerial meetings, a subtle realization that, at the psychological level, without the prodding that a mood of tension and crisis can give, governments and publics might lapse into dangerous torpor. The usual effect of ministerial meetings, and of the occasional NATO summit meetings, was one of catharsis, sometimes followed

by a temporary euphoria soon to be replaced by the gathering gloom of the next round.[17]

Traveling with Secretary Rogers was always a great pleasure. His interest, once aroused, led him to focus quickly on the main issues. He did not like long speeches, but his injections into the debate (Europeans like to call discussions of this sort a debate) were always precise and to the point and frequently provided outlets from the verbal morass into which others had led. Since no NATO ministerial meeting, at least of this era, could go by without every foreign minister present expressing his views, whether entirely relevant or not, this meant listening long hours to frequently rambling presentations.

Communiqué drafting was always a chore, especially for the officials chosen by each delegation to work (sit up) all night before the final day of the meeting in an effort to meld together the various drafts that some delegations had brought with them from capitals. Agreement by ministers on the final communiqué text was seldom a routine matter. In my observations, there is nothing a conclave of great men likes to do more than nitpick the language of communiqués, though, with some exceptions, these documents quickly lapse into the realm of the forgotten.

The regular high-level meetings did serve a useful purpose. Ministers got to know one another better, as did their staffs. A certain camaraderie inevitably developed, and we all recognized we were there to serve an essential common purpose. Despite the test of patience sometimes involved, I enjoyed these meetings and the exercise of primary responsibility for the participation of the secretary and the American delegation. There was, of course, a darker side to all this. As noted, ministers often bored the assembled dignitaries and staffs with platitudinous speeches obviously written by someone else. The haggling over words in communiqués often descended to sheer logomachy. One sometimes felt that if the defenses of NATO depended on the decision-making process of governments, all would be lost.

After each such meeting it became my lot to fly to Madrid to brief the Spanish government on the broad lines of what had taken place. Franco was clearly in physical decline, as we had observed during the Nixon visit to Madrid in 1970, but he still made the important decisions. The Spanish government consisted largely of technocrats who clearly saw themselves leading their country into a new post-Franco era. My visits would always begin with a private meeting with the foreign minister, Lopez Bravo, an intelligent and unusually handsome official who took over from Fernando Castiella. I was to know him even better years later when, as a banker, he became a member of the Board of Governors of the Atlantic Institute for International Affairs. He died tragically in an airplane accident.

After an hour or so with the foreign minister, I would then proceed to a large conference room filled, it seemed, with most of the cabinet and military general staff. Simultaneous translation was provided for my remarks and the question and answer period that followed. Spanish interest in NATO was obviously great, and while I do not claim prophetic powers, I could sense that, once the internal political situation had sufficiently changed, Spain would want to move toward membership in the alliance.

Spanish and Portuguese Base Negotiations

Regardless of the qualms some might have felt about the governments of Spain and Portugal, the U.S. Air Force and Navy clearly and strongly wanted to keep our bases in those countries as essential in the continuing cold war confrontation. I had been around the military long enough in Germany and elsewhere to know that the combination of good life and convenient operations in foreign bases could generate overwhelming arguments for their indispensability. Our orders, however, were to negotiate extension of the agreements covering four bases in Spain and one in the Portuguese Azores. The negotiations with Spain would inevitably be the most complicated, which is not to say that those with Portugal would be easy. What the whole process amounted to was to find some meeting point between the demands for aid from the two countries and what we were willing and able to pay—in other words a good old-fashioned haggle.

My bureau was to provide the research and paperwork for the negotiations with Spain that Undersecretary for Political Affairs U. Alexis Johnson would principally conduct, while I would handle the Azores negotiations directly with the Portuguese. Actually the agreement with Spain (the so-called Pact of Madrid), first signed in 1953 and renewed in 1958 and 1963, had expired in September 1968, but both sides agreed to take no action to close down the bases until it was clear that negotiations with the new Nixon administration had either failed or succeeded. Needless to say, many in Congress and the liberal press raised vociferous objections to dealing with a Spanish government still headed by President Franco.[18] Similar objections but less loudly expressed were launched against the Azores negotiations with the Marcello Caetano government.

I could appreciate the sincerity and indignation of the opposition but could only note that it did not address, except by implication, the crucial question of whether, in the still prevailing East-West confrontation, the bases served a valuable military purpose for which we should be prepared to pay a reasonable fee. No matter how overblown, the military had made essentially a good case.

The talks with Spain went on, mainly in Washington, for some seventeen months, culminating in an exchange of diplomatic notes on June 20, 1970, between Secretary Rogers and Foreign Minister Castiella (who had been intimately involved in the negotiations). The notes extended the basic agreement of September 1953 not for another five years but only until September 26, 1970. During the interim the two governments were "to determine the new relationship of cooperation between the two countries that would follow the present agreement." The price was a U.S. commitment to continue to provide military assistance "at an appropriate level" during the period of the extension plus thirty-five million dollars in Export-Import Bank credits for the purchase of military equipment in the United States.

Further intensive negotiations led to the signing on August 6, 1970, of a five-year extension of the basic agreement. We would keep our air bases at Torrejon (near Madrid), Saragossa, a naval base at Rota, and a standby air base at Morón. In exchange we made a broad pledge to support the defense system of Spain, to give Spain $60 million in military grants, and to make $120 million available in Export-Import Bank credits.

The U.S. Senate did not greet the pact with shouts of joy, partly because both it and the earlier temporary extensions were signed by Secretary Rogers and Foreign Minister Castiella as executive agreements and not as treaties requiring consent to ratification by the Senate. We had expected a rough time on the Hill, and we got it. As a disciplined member of the executive branch I, of course, defended the department's role in the negotiations and the final agreements, but as a political scientist I knew that, in our system with its separation of powers, tensions between the Congress and the departments of government were inevitable and indeed provided a kind of dynamic counterpoint that could lead either to a more balanced final product or to what it has now become fashionable to call gridlock. Executive agreements constituted an attempt to evade the latter, but it required no flight of imagination to conclude that Senator Fulbright and the Foreign Relations Committee that he chaired would not like it.

There was, of course, also the issue of doing business with a government that had the dubious antecedents of Franco Spain. The general approach of the Nixon administration, as was the case with all American governments of the cold war era, was to take our friends where we could find them. There was always the hope that such an attitude would encourage political and economic reform. While it would be presumptuous to claim that the democratization process that followed in both Spain and Portugal during the 1970s had a direct causal link to our base agreements, the aid involved and our willingness to deal with them as, in effect, partners did contribute something to a major historical process. Members of the Congress could afford the luxury of being purists full of indignation and criticism, but as is the case so often in life, the only choice open to those who must choose is the lesser of evils.

My negotiations with the Portuguese in both Lisbon and Washington were difficult enough but did not arouse comparable emotional reactions in the Congress or the press. They dragged on considerably longer, but finally on December 9, 1971, Secretary Rogers and the Portuguese foreign minister exchanged notes extending until February 4, 1974, the arrangement permitting peacetime stationing of U.S. forces at Lajos Field in the Azores. The exchange took place in Brussels on the margin of the semiannual NATO ministerial meeting and did not come cheaply. We agreed to a two-year Public Law 480 program amounting to fifteen million dollars per year, an Export-Import Bank commitment to provide approximately four hundred million dollars to finance U.S. goods for development projects in Portugal, plus some miscellaneous small items of assistance.

So much, then, for what were basically tedious and time-consuming negotiations. I like to think of them as a professional job well done by those of us involved. The Spanish and Portuguese officials with whom we had to deal were unfailingly polite and ultimately anxious to reach agreement. They knew the U.S. military wanted badly to keep the bases and believed that a rich America should be able to pay generously for the privilege. The Spanish were most interested in military aid, while the Portuguese stressed the development of their civilian economy. Contrary to the emotional all-out opposition of some members of Congress and the media, I thought then, and think even more so now, that it would have been a mistake to treat either the Spanish or the Portuguese as pariahs. We did not know what to expect, of course, but our discerning experts on the Iberian Peninsula could detect signs of change—a loosening up of societies and governments in a democratic direction.

A Miscellany of Subcabinet Activities

A constant stream of visitors from Western Europe flowed to Washington during the first Nixon term. My bureau had to receive them or, in the case of cabinet-level officials and above, handle the briefings and other paperwork. There particularly seemed to be a never-ending succession of German parliamentarians and senior officials all of whom, of course, wanted to see the president or, failing that, at least the secretary of state. Nixon actually proved to be obliging when it came to spending a few minutes to provide a photo opportunity with parliamentarians and others whom we had recommended for a meeting. We were the most powerful country in the alliance, and it was important for German politicians to be able to say on their return that they had had an *ernstes Gespräch* (serious conversation) with the president, not to speak of German press and media coverage. To be able to brag that one had had thirty or thirty-five minutes with Nixon rather than a perfunctory fifteen minutes represented a real coup.

We began to note a peculiar phenomenon. The time between when the visiting dignitary left the Oval Office and actually appeared at the White House entrance where the German television cameras and correspondents were waiting seemed to grow progressively longer. What was happening during those unaccounted-for minutes? Discreet inquiries revealed that they were being spent in the men's room. It required no psychic powers to conclude that the word had spread: you can ostensibly prolong your time with the president by an extended stay in the men's room. The members of the Freudian psychoanalytic confraternity, who during the war made sweeping judgments about the dominance of the anal personality type in the German national character, would have cited all this as further proof. The explanation was much simpler. Bragging rights upon return to the Federal Republic and enhanced status in the eyes of the German press and media came with more minutes with the president. Hence stays in the men's room grew longer and longer. Finally one day the secret was out, perhaps revealed by a talkative White House staffer. So another little deception of the German political class came to an end.

One of the organizational anomalies of the State Department up to the present is that Canada falls within the jurisdiction of the Bureau of European Affairs. Some supporters on the Hill and elsewhere of the Canadian connection (Canada is, after all, our principal trading partner in the world) have pressed for a more distinctive handling of Canadian affairs within State, and this led eventually to a relabeling of the bureau to become the Bureau of European and Canadian Affairs with a deputy assistant secretary of state specifically designated to deal with Canada. In my time, however, we were still simply the Bureau of European Affairs, but negotiations with Canada on such problems as cleaning up Lake Erie, boundary disputes, and fishing rights at the St. George Banks were not the least of my concerns.

At one point the possibility of moving Canada out of European Affairs into the Bureau of Inter-American Affairs came up, but the Canadians vigorously opposed being blanketed into Latin America. That ended the discussion. An underlying cause of sadness and apprehension for Canadian officials at this time was the danger, as they saw it, of Canada splitting in two as Quebec national demands became ever sharper. There was, of course, nothing very useful that we could do in such a highly charged contestation, although we had not thought that President de Gaulle's obvious meddling in the situation had been helpful. By the spring of 1969 he had left office, but Canada's problem remained as festering as ever.

Moving toward a Moscow Summit Meeting

German ratification of the Moscow Treaty, and secondarily of the treaty with Poland, was proving more difficult than many had expected. The White House, and so far as we could tell, Moscow, wanted a summit meeting between Nixon and Brezhnev as soon as possible, but this obviously could not be firmly in place until all of the German and European security-related agreements were sure to come into effect. Interest thus focused on the crucial internal German debate. There was deep irony in all this. After the pell-mell rush to get the Quadripartite Agreement on Berlin concluded, after all the back-channel messages, the whole process had now become entangled in the deliberations of the German Bundestag.

Apart from the fact that 1972 was an election year, I did not then think, nor do I now think, that the Nixon-Kissinger approach to Moscow was purely tactical or at bottom insincere. Even given their limitations of intelligence and vigor, I could also accept that the Soviet leadership saw advantage in improving relations with the United States. Whatever one may have concluded from American tactics in Vietnam, three years of command responsibility for our nuclear weaponry—a responsibility also borne by Brezhnev and the Politburo—had clearly impressed on the president the desirability of lowering the level of tension between the two countries. The overall nuclear capability of both countries that could lead to mutual total destruction could not but breed maximum caution.

Both Brandt and the White House had underestimated the intensity of opposition among a sizable segment of the CDU/CSU. The government majority of the combined SPD and FDP only amounted to eight. Though I thought them to be wrong, I did not doubt the sincerity of those deputies opposed to the Moscow and Warsaw Treaties. They deeply distrusted Bahr and Brandt, whom they considered capable of selling out German national aspirations for eventual unification, and they were frankly puzzled by what they believed was a misguided change of direction on the part of the American government. They saw *Ostpolitik* leading inexorably to the eventual neutralization of the Federal Republic and its withdrawal from NATO—an objective that they thought Bahr at least wanted to achieve.

In any event, my friend Rainer Barzel, who on October 14, 1971, became chairman of the CDU and chancellor candidate of his party while remaining head of the CDU *Fraktion* in the Bundestag, faced a formidable task. A moderate himself on the Eastern treaties who probably could have taken them pretty much as they were, he knew from the outset that the strong opposition to them of a significant segment of his party—not to speak of the Bavarian CSU—would make a more nuanced position necessary. In an effort to maintain a constructive posture toward *Ostpolitik*, he came up with the idea of endorsing the treaties but with improvements. I saw him in Washington a few months later, and he impressed me as a much troubled man anxious not to appear too negative but bound by the majority sentiment in the party he led.

The formal debate on the treaties in the Bundestag began February 23, 1972, with their first reading. Not entirely unexpectedly, Brandt's majority of eight began to erode with defectors both from the SPD and the FDP leaving their parties to join the CDU. The pressure began to build up until in April Barzel could conclude that the government majority no longer existed. Once this seemed clear, the logic of the situation called for resort to Article 67 of the German Basic Law, which provides that

> The Bundestag may express its lack of confidence in the Federal Chancellor only by electing, by the majority of its members, a successor and by submitting a request to the Federal President for the dismissal of the Federal Chancellor. The Federal President must comply with the request and approve the person elected.
>
> There must be an interval of forty-eight hours between the motion and the election.[19]

The so-called constructive vote of no confidence was put into the Basic Law to avoid frivolous votes against the government without any new chancellor in sight who could put together a new majority, as occurred so often during the Weimar Republic. It took place on April 27, the first time it had been used in the Federal Republic. The forty-eight hours preceding the vote were tense with emotion and last-minute parliamentary maneuvering. In order to guarantee absolute party discipline, the SPD party leadership permitted only a few reliable members to place their votes in the urn; the rest would abstain. The FDP did the same. The general expectation was that a thin majority would vote against Brandt and that Barzel would become the new chancellor. It was one of those historic moments profoundly affecting the fate of a major policy as well as individual lives.

The result of the vote came as a shock to Barzel and the CDU/CSU: 247 had voted yes, 10 no. Barzel had fallen short by 2 votes of the required majority of 249. He had obviously been betrayed by 2 or perhaps 3 members of his own party. As he himself later admitted, the mystery of their identity remains, although there was the likelihood of a successful SPD bribery attempt. This could not, however, be proved beyond dispute.

Ratification of the treaties by the Bundestag had, of course, not yet taken place. The SPD had no effective majority on which it could count. Having lost out in a process with which he had personally felt uncomfortable, Barzel now moved to achieve some sort of compromise that would, in effect, improve the Moscow Treaty and enable the majority of his own party to vote for it. Of course he had wanted to be chancellor, but when the constructive vote of no confidence failed, he seized on the device of an interpretative resolution that he hoped would suffice to win the support of his Bundestag *Fraktion* for the Moscow Treaty. After some heated intraparty debates, Barzel and Brandt finally agreed on a procedure that produced a draft declaration on the Eastern treaties. The opposition to the basic treaties on the part of leading CDU/CSU politicians continued strong and forced Barzel to give up the idea of an all-party vote in favor of the treaties. He then turned to the tactic of urging at least abstention for his party from the vote on ratification. Meanwhile, the Soviets, in negotiations concluded with their ambassador in Bonn, had accepted the idea of a Bundestag declaration. They obviously wanted ratification badly.

When the final vote came on May 17, 1972, a handful of CDU/CSU deputies broke party discipline and voted against the Moscow and Warsaw Treaties. The great majority, however, abstained, and thus the treaties were approved for ratification. It was not a glorious affirmation but sufficed to meet the parliamentary requirements. In the process Barzel had alienated important members of his party, who would not quickly forget his role in saving the Eastern treaties. He had realized at an early stage that all-out opposition to *Ostpolitik* did not add up to a viable policy, but he was never in a position publicly to articulate the logic of his position. He was never to achieve his ambition to be chancellor, but in that hectic winter and spring of 1972 he displayed much courage and a sense of responsibility that overrode purely personal and expediential considerations.[20]

One can only speculate as to what the next few years might have been like if Barzel had not been able to pull off his parliamentary legerdemain. He was later, of course, to pay a political price. The two superpowers were in a real sense dependent on what happened in Bonn for the improvement in their own relations that followed, without being able to exercise any decisive influence on the outcome. So history can be shaped in a secondary and indeterminate way.

It is worth noting that, in his *White House Years*, Kissinger makes no reference to the high political drama unfolding in Bonn except to report a conversation with Soviet ambassador Dobrynin on May 9, when he told the latter of an agreement between Barzel and Brandt that would lead to Bundestag ratification of the Eastern treaties.[21] The implication was that this information influenced the Soviets to react more mildly to our bombing of Hanoi and mining of Haiphong Harbor. The Soviets, of course, knew about the German situation directly from their able ambassador in Bonn, Valentin Falin, who had been negotiating with the Germans about the declaration and reporting fully on German political developments to Moscow.

For those who write history, the interpretation of memoirs must inevitably take into account the primary interests of those making policy. Nixon and Kissinger wanted Soviet help on Vietnam and hoped to deploy the apparent Soviet desire for a summit as a bargaining counter. Once again the White House used various channels of communication, some of which it hid from the State Department. It seemingly gave little attention to what was happening in Germany. Given my position and professional background, I could only follow the situation in Bonn with intense interest. It seemed obvious to me that if the Bundestag rejected the Eastern treaties, the whole package would fall apart and Brezhnev would find it impossible to receive Nixon in Moscow.

On the easy assumption that the summit would finally take place, the White House and the State Department had continued to press ahead with arrangements with the Soviets. It was to be a long summit—some eight days in Moscow—and Nixon and Brezhnev both wanted agreements ready for their signatures every day with accompanying hoopla and media coverage. The SALT I and Anti-Ballistic Missile (ABM) Treaties still being negotiated in Helsinki would be the centerpiece, but the European bureau was instructed to find, and if necessary negotiate, other agreements for these daily signing ceremonies.

It was a daunting task but perhaps not so difficult as it might have seemed to the uninitiated. There were, after all, always such standbys as environmental protection, medical science and public health, cooperation in space, science, and technology, and prevention of incidents at sea to which we could turn. The appropriate Soviet officials liked coming to Washington and were under obvious instructions to be flexible. The negotiations moved quickly to satisfactory, if routine, conclusions. As the time for the summit approached, with the exception of the talks in Helsinki, the agreements for daily signings were ready.

I was a little nonplussed, after concluding negotiations on the text of a new cultural exchange agreement with a senior Soviet official from Moscow, to learn that he expected we would both affix our personal seals in red wax on the final document. I had no personal seal, but a frantic search that night uncovered my Eagle Scout ring. So I was prepared and after initialing the agreement used my ring as a seal. It left a splendid impression, and there were no complaints. I have sometimes wondered what the KGB made of it all.

The Moscow Summit Meeting of May 22–30, 1972

The Moscow summit began only five days after Bundestag ratification of the Moscow and Warsaw Treaties. By any measure it seemed bound to be an important historical event. The clash of systems that had been the central cause of the cold war now appeared to be easing, and there was hope that the nuclear arms race that it had spawned could at least be capped. Moreover, the complex of linked agreements without which the summit could not have taken place offered the prospect of progress on a number of fronts. I suppose those caught up in seeming breakthroughs cannot help but think of themselves as playing a role in history. Experience had taught me that summits can turn out to be an enormous waste of time and energy—the scourge of professional diplomats—but this summit seemed fortuitous both in its timing and in its possible reflection of a real turning point in Soviet-American relations.

Anyway, here I was, a senior member of the American delegation. I had known for some time of my appointment to Bonn as ambassador to succeed Kenneth Rush, who had come home to be deputy secretary of defense. In fact, my confirmation by the Senate had already taken place. Secretary Rogers had asked me to stay on as assistant secretary through the summit and the subsequent formal signing in Berlin of the Quadripartite Agreement. It was a busy time for me, and I looked forward to taking over in Bonn when all the current hustle and bustle was over. I had frankly had my fill of dealing with a White House so paranoid that it frequently seemed to trust the Soviets more than its own State Department. Although I approved of the main lines of our policy in Europe, we could have achieved our goals, I thought, with a more direct approach to diplomacy rather than resorting to various so-called backchannels, some of them kept secret from the secretary of state and our ambassador in Moscow, Jacob Beam. I feared that what had happened before would happen again in Moscow: that the president in his private talks with Brezhnev would rely on the Soviet interpreter, Victor Sukhodrev, rather than bringing in our own, and that we on the American side would be left with no real record of the conversations. My fears were fully corroborated by events. We would also find out that Kissinger had worked out with the Soviets a communiqué and a so-called Basic Principles on Relations without telling anyone in the State Department. I assumed there would be more of this kind of hanky-panky during the course of the summit.

The Kremlin of the Tsars provided an awesome setting for the conference and the banqueting that went with it. Huge crystal chandeliers hung from the ceilings of every room, and St. Catherine's Hall, where the daily signing of agreements took place, added a degree of environmental splendor to the diplomats and officials in dark suits standing around while the principals signed documents. There was obviously something ironic about all this grandeur run by dark-suited Marxist-Leninists, who, in theory at least, were the heirs of a proletarian revolution. They had obviously learned to live comfortably with the heavy burden of imperial splendor. During one of the breaks between meetings, a self-appointed guide led some of us with some pride to view a private chapel near our conference room that the leadership had carefully preserved as an ecclesiastical jewel. I found it difficult, however, to envision Lenin, Stalin, or subsequent general secretaries sneaking off to the chapel for a moment of prayer.

The first plenary session of the summit—and all subsequent plenary sessions—took place in a large Kremlin conference room. As in seemingly every other room in the palace, a large crystal chandelier dominated the chamber. It hung directly over the center of the large elongated conference table. Seated on the American side were the president with Secretary Rogers on his right and Henry Kissinger on his left. Ambassador Beam was on Rogers's right and I next to him. On the Soviet side Brezhnev sat opposite the president with Kosygin on his right and Nikolai Podgorny on his left. Gromyko and Dobrynin were on Podgorny's left, and other Soviet officials present included Wassili Kuznetsov and Andrei Alexandrov.

I mention these details because they were relevant to a rather farcical contretemps that followed, when I noted that Nixon and Kissinger had spread their briefing papers out on the table. I glanced up at the chandelier and whispered to Rogers behind Beam's back that he might want to tell the president not to leave his papers so exposed. Rogers whispered to Nixon, who whispered to Kissinger. Both of the latter began to rearrange their papers somewhat conspicuously. Brezhnev looked on owlishly with no visible astonishment, but Gromyko, never known for his quick wit and generally regarded as dour, spoke up while glancing at the chandelier: "Not to worry. Photographic equipment was installed by the tsars. Takes very poor pictures." I thought this was funny and noted his words. Then the discussion proceeded.

I see little point here in detailing the long exchanges and negotiations of the following days. Others have amply written about them elsewhere, and by and large accurately.[22] A few observations, however, are perhaps worth making.

As we had feared, Nixon depended at times on the Soviet interpreter during his private talks with Brezhnev. The result was no adequate record on the American side. Other American presidents had occasionally followed the same unwise practice. It was almost as if they did not want an accurate record of what they said to be available within their own government while knowing, of course, that the Soviets would have such a complete record. One could only attribute this strange behavior either to lack of confidence in the abilities of his own officials to keep secrets, or to a desire to test proposals, no matter how outrageous, without facing the embarrassment of acknowledging that they were even being considered.

As the summit went on, we noted that Brezhnev and those with him sometimes abruptly terminated a session, or simply left us sitting there at the table, while they solemnly filed out. We learned that they had gone to consult with the Politburo waiting in an adjoining room. Brezhnev clearly was not Stalin or even a Khrushchev. He seemed to operate pretty much as if a collegium were running his country. He exhibited no inclination to dynamism, spoke relatively slowly, and walked deliberately. He did, however, seem in full possession of his faculties, unlike the impression he gave during his last years in office. I could not help but be impressed by the superior authority that the American president had to make decisions on the spot without involving any one in Washington.

The days of the summit went by almost in routine fashion. There were the expected Kremlin banquets and the inevitable *Swan Lake* ballet at the Bolshoi. During the latter I found myself sitting in a box next to one of the Soviet protocol directors. I noted quickly that his interest in the ballet—one magnificently in the best Bolshoi tradition—was minimal and that he was having a hard time staying awake. During the intermission I could not resist saying, "I suppose you have seen many performances of *Swan Lake* in your official capacity." With some spirit he responded, "I have sat through ninety performances of the ballet during my time as a protocol officer. I know the steps better than the dancers do."

One could not avoid feeling that, as a member of the American delegation, one was a part of history being made. I had attended many previous summits, but this one offered the hope of contributing in a real way to a lessening of tensions between the Soviet Union and the United States. In the nuclear confrontation of the cold war, any genuine move toward détente could only represent progress. So while I could not approve of the internal machinations that the White House seemed compelled to impose on parts of its own delegation, I could only applaud the general direction in which American policy appeared to be moving. It was just another of the frequent contradictions that approval of ends but not of means imposed upon loyal State Department officials.

Hectic days of maneuver and deception preceded the climactic signing on May 26 of the ABM and SALT I Treaties. I was thankfully not involved in any of this. One can find the best and at times highly indignant account in Gerard Smith's book *Doubletalk*.[23] Gerry, head of our negotiating delegation in Helsinki from the outset, was shabbily treated by the White House. It all boiled down, of course, to the latter's desire to get maximum credit and publicity for the accomplishment of the treaties. The White House culture, with its resort to double-talk, to duplicate and confusing negotiations in Moscow and Helsinki, had once again displayed its peculiar blindness to the means pursued in the achievement of what were basically laudable ends.

Despite all the criticism the two treaties received in Washington and elsewhere, they represented a step forward in an area where there had been little previous progress. At least we now for the first time had ceilings on missile launchers and on defensive systems that could be strategically unbalancing. Our delegation in Helsinki had done well and deserved better.

I have a blown-up color photograph provided by the United States Information Agency of the signing ceremony in St. Catherine's Hall. It shows the American delegation lined up behind or on the right side of the signers' table, while the still larger Soviet group of officials stood behind or to the left. Everyone wants to get into the act on such occasions, and I was as guilty as the rest. The photograph shows me standing next to Henry Kissinger.

Although one could argue now in the light of the Soviet collapse that the inability of President Nixon to deliver on the economic commitments to Brezhnev made in Moscow had diminished its historic importance, I could not accept such a rationalization. It would, of course, have been better if the United States had implemented Nixon's proposals and the plans behind them. Effective diplomacy is never served by the need to welch on commitments made and accepted in good faith.

Final Chores before Bonn

With the summit over, Secretary Rogers would now come into his own, for it was he, Soviet foreign minister Gromyko, the French foreign minister Maurice Schuman, and the British foreign minister Douglas-Home who on June 3, 1972, signed the Final Protocol to the Quadripartite

Agreement on Berlin that made it legally binding. I accompanied the secretary to Berlin for what I hoped would be my last official act as assistant secretary of state before taking over my new post as ambassador in Bonn. We flew from Moscow to Berlin in Rogers's plane. The signing ceremony in the former Allied High Commission building was simple and brief. All four foreign ministers avoided long speeches. Their mood was relaxed, and one could hope that, after so many years of crisis and dispute over Berlin, a compromise arrangement had now been reached for the city that would permit a new era of relaxed growth.

Our feeling at the time was that if the agreement held, with the Soviets willing to accept the bundle of compromises and admitted ambiguities embodied in it, then there would be no more Berlin crises of the kind that had periodically seemed to threaten the city and general peace. In truth, despite differences of interpretation about certain clauses of the agreement and despite a continuing Soviet reluctance to permit the development of closer ties between the Federal Republic and West Berlin, the Berlin problem was never again to play the enormously emotional and potentially explosive role in East-West relations that it had prior to 1972. Until German unification in 1990 the city continued to be, in its way, a thorn in the side of the GDR and Eastern Europe, but with the refugee flow long since blocked by the Wall, the city ceased to be a primary focal point of conflict. By the late 1970s those concerned about Berlin (including myself) began to worry about the provincialization of the city.

After the signing ceremony in Berlin and a meeting in Bonn with Chancellor Brandt and Foreign Minister Scheel to brief them on the Moscow summit, Secretary Rogers was supposed to fly to Madrid to do the same for the Spanish and Portuguese governments. I had hoped to stay on in Bonn, but it was not to be. The secretary was called back to Washington urgently, and he told me I would have to fill in for him.

It was another and the last of my many trips to Madrid—this time in a special air force plane. My audience in Madrid was more senior and numerous than ever, as might have been expected given the subject matter. As on previous briefing missions of this kind, the information imparted was probably less important than the fact that it was being made available by a special emissary. An experienced diplomat knows that information is gratifying to the recipient and may sometimes be useful but that at the psychological level its absence can lead to resentment and a sense of deep grievance. That is why what to the casual observer may seem like an endless and useless round of diplomatic exchanges, meetings, and intergovernmental communications is really part of the routine of diplomacy. Government leaders and their bureaucracies have an insatiable appetite for information that must be satisfied.

So finally, after all this, I was able to assume my post as ambassador to the Federal Republic of Germany. My three and a half years as assistant secretary of state had been both fascinating and in some respects frustrating. We had been able to accomplish much, but having to deal with a frequently hostile (and sometimes downright dishonest) White House made official life excessively difficult and unpredictable. Defending the bureaucratic interests of the State Department in a hostile environment had not been easy. It was not just another turf war but our sense that the orderly and proven processes of American government were at stake.

9

Ambassador in Bonn

. . . .

My return to Bonn as ambassador came as a welcome relief as well as a logical climax to a diplomatic career so dedicated to Europe in general and Germany in particular. Three and one-half years as assistant secretary of state had taken their toll. I was emotionally tired and ready for a change of venue. I saw, moreover, no real prospect of any improvement in the relations of the White House and the State Department. I knew all of the Federal Republic's leading political figures, many of them from their parliamentary origins. I could speak German and could look forward to a useful assignment.

As she had done for our residence in Budapest, Faith was able to put together a representative collection of modern American paintings and sculptures. From previous experience we knew that the security types would never allow the president, should he visit Bonn, to stay in the relatively exposed official residence in the Rolandstrasse but would insist that he stay at the more secluded house of the deputy chief of mission. That meant we would not incur presidential wrath over our presumed bad taste in art. The ambassador's residence in Bonn once belonged to a wealthy merchant. Perched on a rise above the Rhine with extensive gardens leading down to the river, the impressively large house with extensive terracing had a magnificent view of the Rhine and of the Siebengebirge (Seven Hills) on the opposite side. At every season of the year, the hills rising a thousand feet above the river provided an endless array of changing color and lighting—perhaps the most pleasantly sustained aesthetic experience of my life. Königswinter, a resort town along the other bank of the river, attracted numerous weekend visitors from the flatlands of Holland, so the Siebengebirge in popular parlance naturally became the Dutch Alps (Holländische Alpen).

Shortly after my official arrival at post, senior members of the embassy staff and I had to dust off our morning formals (our senior defense atta-chés simply had to polish their medals) for my presentation of credentials to federal president Gustav Heinemann. At least no military parade would be involved. We proceeded en masse to the Villa Hammerschmidt, the president's residence on the Rhine, to be greeted by the chief of protocol. Then President Heinemann appeared. We each made brief speeches and promised to do all we could to further good relations between our coun-tries. Then we toasted each other in champagne and ended with a bit of informal conversation. It is not a bad way to start an ambassadorship. It gives senior staff a sense of participation in a common enterprise about to begin. The problem, of course, is the contemporary multiplicity of coun-tries that, whether needed or not, establish diplomatic missions in major capitals (more than 130 at the time in Bonn). Since they all demand equal treatment, the burden on protocol staffs and presidents becomes heavy and time devouring.

Settling In

Settling in should have proved relatively easy. After all, we knew the place. The list of calls to be made, however, was formidable. When only major countries maintained diplomatic establishments in other capitals, the problem was manageable, but in a capital with so many embassies, the traditional custom of having a newly arrived ambassador call on all his colleagues seemed outmoded. Yet I knew that one could not be too selec-tive or sensitivities would be aroused. One simply had to ration the calls, perhaps one in the morning and one in the afternoon, starting with the ambassadors of major allies. In the old days, the custom also prevailed of receiving return calls from those on whom one had called, but fortunately only a relatively few still observed this practice in Bonn. Apart from dip-lomatic colleagues, there were also numerous calls to be made on cabinet ministers, senior government officials, party leaders, and important mem-bers of the Bundestag. By dogged discipline one got through these essen-tial formalities, but the continuing diplomatic and official social whirl re-mained for one's entire stay.

There were first of all, and perhaps worst of all, the national day recep-tions—on the average nearly one every third day. I still had my sketches of secret exits to the public places in which these affairs might be held, but a goodly number of ambassadors were now holding them in their resi-dences. A more useful setting is the small luncheon (sometimes with only two present) or dinner, but I have generally found office calls on officials to be the most efficacious. A highly practical instrument for exchange of information was the monthly quadripartite lunch (British, French, American ambassadors and the state secretary of the German Foreign Ministry) with the host rotating among the four. We intermittently used German, French, or English.

In fact the whole business of required ambassadorial representational activities in a major capital constitutes a burden that is frequently both time wasting and physically exhausting. You can't escape it and do your job, but there need to be some agreed distinctions between the essential and the nonessential. No one will deny that, when senior American officials visit a post like Bonn, one must provide the setting for lunches and dinners at which they can meet relevant German officials and that, when the government provides hospitality, the ambassador has to be present as a guest. He must also attend functions hosted by senior officials of government for distinguished visitors from other countries as well as lunches and dinners given by members of his staff who invite him. All of this is self-evident, and I see no reason to think it has changed much in recent years.

Then there were junketeering congressmen, although Bonn admittedly lacked the magnetism of Paris, Rome, or London. However, we were not neglected. Some were on serious fact-finding trips—as Washington parlance put it—and more power to them. But many came for entertainment, and an ambassador ultimately had to be concerned about their feeding, their sightseeing, and making sure that they had access to the PX and sales stores. A few played the role of bully using the implied power of the budgetary purse to demand special treatment of all sorts. Over the years I had generally enjoyed good working relations with most members of the Congress both in testifying before committees in Washington and in providing serious visitors with entrée to appropriate local officials. There were some real lulus, however, who brought little credit to the legislative branch of the U.S. government.

Another task that an ambassador must perform involves what is now called public diplomacy. In practical terms that meant making numerous speeches around the Federal Republic, some important statements of policy, others more trivial. I appeared at the opening of American exhibits at trade fairs or American libraries, at German universities, and at every other conceivable occasion where an appeal to an ambassador's sense of duty could successfully be made. I usually spoke in German and in the end enjoyed most of these appearances. Some encounters at universities turned out to be more than a challenge. American unpopularity over Vietnam was at its zenith among students. No matter what the subject of my remarks—and they were seldom voluntarily about Vietnam, which I had long come to consider an exercise in futility—as American ambassador I could usually count on a demonstration to greet me when I appeared on university grounds followed by noisy interruptions and occasionally a violent takeover of the hall and the podium. As they ushered me out a rear exit with many apologies, university officials would in the latter case express their helplessness in the face of student activism. I hope I was philosophic enough to leave without any display of offended dignity. In any case I would be ready to try again, perhaps at another university. The University of Erlangen, I found, provided the least hostile setting, and there I was able to give two undisturbed scholarly lectures—one on the American educational system and the other on the contribution of medieval natural law theory to international law.

The most active year when it came to speech making was 1976—the two hundredth anniversary of our Declaration of Independence. All over the Federal Republic local communities and city and state officials, in an outburst of sentimental gratitude for American friendship, sponsored commemorative events at which I made appropriate remarks. Now that we were out of Vietnam, even the universities had seemingly become more mellow. I did not keep a detailed record but by rough calculation must have made in the neighborhood of one hundred such appearances during the first six months of 1976.

I mention these things to show that the demands on an ambassador's time could indeed be formidable but not to imply that they were the most important duties he had. Representing my country in the multiplicity of diplomatic activities requiring my personal participation and providing, I would hope, wise leadership for an admittedly overblown embassy staff remained the core of my work. My time in Germany was a highly interesting period, and through the friendships that I had developed over the years with many senior German politicians, businessmen, and journalists, I could try to provide insights and analysis, perhaps not otherwise available. Nothing has happened in the intervening years since I left Bonn and the Foreign Service that would make an ambassador's personal involvement and judgments based on knowledge of the country and its leaders less important.

There was also Berlin. Until German unification came in 1990, the American ambassador in Bonn, along with his British and French colleagues (all of us chiefs of mission in Berlin), also exercised the residual powers of the Allied high commissioners to deal with matters relating to Berlin, the reunification of Germany, and an ultimate peace treaty. With splendid inconsistency considering the emphasis on total GDR sovereignty the Soviet ambassador in East Berlin exercised the same residual powers. In any event I found it necessary to spend five days or so per month in Berlin to demonstrate by physical presence and relevant pronouncements our continuing interest in the city. This involved no real hardship. The ambassador's residence in the city provided comfortable, in some respects elegant quarters, and it was always pleasant to settle in there for a few days and to be close to the incomparable music and theater of Berlin.

The German Political Scene

With *Ostpolitik* now clearly past its initial phase and so far a seeming success, the Social Democratic Party leadership might well have exhibited something akin to doctrinal triumphalism. I did not notice much of this in my contacts with Chancellor Brandt and other party dignitaries but rather a quiet and at times weary satisfaction. After all, getting this far had not been easy, and there was still no real assurance that the Soviets would carry out their part of the implicit bargain they had struck. By and large, it turned out that they pretty much did. Berlin had lost its explosiveness even though Soviet attempts continued to whittle down the ties between the city and the Federal Republic that had been one of the points left obscure in the final language of the Quadripartite Agreement.

Although federal elections were not required until 1973, Brandt had made up his mind that fall elections in 1972 would provide the best opportunity for SPD gains. Some additional electoral support was sure to come from the accomplishments of *Ostpolitik*, he calculated, and no one of stature in his party felt differently. He therefore took action to activate Article 68 of the Basic Law enabling President Heinemann to dissolve the Bundestag. General elections were set for November 19, 1972.

For Rainer Barzel the elections provided a make-or-break situation. His party was far from united. Some members resented the role he had played during the debate over ratification of the Eastern treaties, suspecting—as was probably true—that Barzel really favored ratification of the treaties and that his call for abstention in the decisive vote merely amounted to recognition that the majority of the CDU/CSU would under no circumstances vote in favor of them.

I saw both Brandt and Barzel as well as their close party associates as often as I could during the preelection period. I was determined that this election should not evoke any surprised reactions in the White House, and I reported fully along with the political section of the embassy on the campaign and trends in public opinion. The campaign quickly dissolved into an attempt by the SPD, successful at least in part, to portray Brandt as the experienced and noble statesman who had, in effect, reversed the course of history, while Barzel was nothing but a callow young upstart good only at intrigue and manipulation within his own parliamentary group. Since Brandt had become somewhat of an icon, the CDU/CSU was forced to waste time and energy in an effort to prove that Barzel was a bigger man than he was being portrayed.

Fortunately, the campaign as such lasted only two months (unlike our marathon presidential contests), but an experienced observer could detect a rising note of seemingly unprecedented emotion and bitterness. German politicians are far from above dirt slinging, and they went at it vigorously. The SPD was fortunate in having most intellectuals, writers, and artists on its side, and they joined in merrily with Günther Grass in the lead. I have never had any illusions about the dedication of intellectuals to balance and truth when they are emotionally involved in a cause. This campaign proved no exception.

For what they were worth, the polls indicated a continuing SPD-FDP electoral victory, but in most countries politicians seemingly destined to lose carry on to the bitter end, hoping perhaps that somehow the pollsters have got it wrong or that there will be a last-minute surge in their favor. So it was that on November 19 the SPD won 45.9 percent of the votes cast on the so-called second and determining ballot and 230 seats in the Bundestag; its coalition partner, the FDP, won 9.4 percent of the votes cast and 41 seats in the Bundestag, while the CDU/CSU won 44.8 percent of the votes cast and 225 seats in the Bundestag. It was the first time in the history of the Federal Republic that the SPD had more total votes than the CDU/CSU, and hence a larger *Fraktion*, in the Bundestag. With the 41 seats of the FDP, the Brandt government would now enjoy a comfortable working majority in the main branch of the German legislature. After the 1969 elections the two parties had only enjoyed a majority of 12 seats, and the close vote on the CDU/CSU's constructive vote of no confidence had shown to what extent that majority had eroded. In 1972, I should add, no other party came even close to reaching the 5 percent minimum requirement for representation in the Bundestag.

Although the immediate reaction of CDU/CSU leaders was to express continuing support for Barzel as party leader (even his archenemy, the Bavarian Franz Josef Strauss, joined in the chorus), discerning observers saw trouble ahead. Waiting in the wings were Helmut Kohl, minister president of Rheinland Pfalz, and also Franz Josef Strauss, who now saw himself, if he played his cards right, as the potential chancellor candidate of the CDU/CSU in 1976. The internal pressures against Barzel in his party began to build up. It took some six months for actual change to come, but after losing a large majority of his *Fraktion* on his motion for CDU abstention on the Bundestag vote to endorse simultaneous entry of the Federal Republic and the GDR into the United Nations, he resigned as *Fraktion* leader. A week later he announced that he would not run again for party chairman at the next party congress. On May 17, 1973, the

Fraktion elected Karl Carstens as its leader, and at an extraordinary party conference in June, a large majority of the delegates present chose Helmut Kohl as party leader although he was not a member of the Bundestag.

My personal reaction to all this was a mixture of fascination as an observer and sadness at the rapid demise of a politician whom I had come to know well over the years. He had impressed me both as a party tactician within the Bundestag and as a political leader with a realistic vision of the future. He had fought hard and lost. From a purely expediential point of view, I and hence the U.S. government were losing a good source of information about the inner workings of the legislature and his party. I did not know then, nor seemingly did any but a very few, that to ease the pain of his departure he had been promised a rather juicy consultancy with the Flick firm (this became public only ten years later).

As good fortune would have it, I had known Karl Carstens, the new CDU *Fraktion* leader, since the early postwar days when he served as an assistant to the revered SPD mayor Wilhelm Kaisen of Bremen. Carstens had never identified himself, however, with the SPD and had come to play a major role as a senior official of the German Foreign Ministry. I had dealt with him many times over the years. Somewhat to my surprise, he had then turned up as a CDU member of the Bundestag chosen on a party list, and now he had suddenly emerged as *Fraktion* leader and in effect principal parliamentary spokesman for his party. He was later to become president of the Federal Republic. He had always been an extremely friendly but cautious senior bureaucrat, and I knew that while he would be a valuable contact, he would not be as revealing and personally involved a source as Barzel had been. He was a man of the highest integrity who taught international law on the side at the University of Cologne but also adaptable enough to enter into the sometimes rough and frequently turbulent verbal give-and-take of the German legislature.

One might have supposed that the SPD leadership, flushed with victory in the elections, would have looked eagerly to a future of relatively unimpeded coalition control of the Bundestag. Some undoubtedly did, with the prospect of four unbroken years of SPD/FDP hegemony looming ahead. But at the very top of the SPD the mood paradoxically was one of psychological and physical exhaustion after four hard, slogging years of *Ostpolitik* and then a trying electoral campaign. To make matters worse Brandt now required an operation on his larynx—a fearful prospect for any professional politician. Putting the SPD/FDP cabinet together provided another source of strain. Skillful maneuvering obtained for the FDP more and better positions than its actual strength in the coalition warranted, including a commitment to support an FDP candidate for the federal presidency: Foreign Minister Walter Scheel.

Observing all this, I could not but begin to wonder about the ultimate durability of a government that seemed to be having so much trouble in getting its act together. Yet its majority was so large and so many careers depended on its remaining in power that it was difficult in 1972 to imagine any circumstances other than the ill health of the chancellor that would bring about major changes before the elections of 1976.[1]

Getting the Two German States into the United Nations

An unfinished item of business after the signing of the Final Protocol to the Quadripartite Agreement on Berlin was the conclusion of negotiations between the two German states of a so-called Basic Relations Treaty ordinating the relations between them. These ended successfully on November 7, 1972, thus opening the way for the contemplated entry into the United Nations of both the Federal Republic of Germany and the German Democratic Republic. I have already noted that this remained far from accepted doctrine in the CDU/CSU and led to Rainer Barzel's downfall. But Brandt had the necessary majority in the Bundestag to proceed.

An immediate and obvious issue for the three Western Allies had been how to achieve this in a way consistent with the provision in Annex IV of the Quadripartite Agreement that the Federal Republic "may represent the interests of the Western sectors of Berlin in international organizations and international conferences" without at the same time detracting from or doing damage to the rights and responsibilities of the four powers. "A lawyer's drafting problem," one might exclaim, "that should be relatively easy to solve." But it proved much more complicated than that owing once again to bilateral U.S.-Soviet dealings behind the backs of the British and the French.

In any event, the British, French, American, and Soviet ambassadors (Sir Nicholas Henderson, Jean Sauvagnargues, Martin Hillenbrand, and Yuri Yefremov) assembled in Berlin prior to the expected conclusion of negotiations between the two German states. Our task on the Western side was to draft an agreed four-power declaration that would say as much as possible about the preservation unchanged of four-power rights and responsibilities while not damaging any of the benefits gained for Berlin or the Federal Republic, both explicitly and implicitly, in the Quadripartite Agreement on Berlin. It was agreed that we would meet in the cavernous building formerly occupied by the Allied Control Council—an edifice of symbolic significance in German history both prewar and postwar.

As we gathered for our initial session, we were not strangers. We had all met before, including exchanges of calls with Yefremov, and we attempted to create an atmosphere of cordiality. Media interest in Berlin was intense. I had first run into Jean Sauvagnargues during the early 1950s when he was in the French Foreign Ministry. An accomplished diplomat, he had served some years in African exile after a run-in with President de Gaulle. Neither he nor I, I am sure, knew in 1972 that some years later he would become the French foreign minister. He had a sharp wit and like many French diplomats—it seems almost to be bred in them—a keen sensitivity to anything that might seem like a derogation of his personal position as the representative of France. I found him a good and friendly interlocutor, even when the behavior of the White House could only have been irritating.

Nicko Henderson came out of the typical class-structured British public school Oxbridge tradition of professional diplomacy. He was able and pleasant, with a realistic sense of his own country's relative decline in the postwar era. He reveled in looking disheveled. One had the impression that, after dressing carefully in typically expensive British clothes, he then deliberately disarranged his shirt and tie so that the two parts of the latter flew off in different directions. After his tour in Bonn, he went to Paris as ambassador. In retirement thereafter he caught the eye of Margaret Thatcher, who did the unprecedented thing of calling him out of retirement and sending him to Washington as ambassador.

Yuri Yefremov was normally jollier than the usual senior Soviet diplomat, some of whom specialized in looking dour. Small in stature, he enjoyed friendly talk. An engineer by training rather than a professional diplomat, he loved to tell stories about growing up in south Russia near the Volga River. He could remember when caviar was so plentiful that even young people could eat it out of a vat with large wooden spoons. What had ruined the supply, he claimed, was the construction of major dams on the Volga and Dnieper Rivers. Unfortunately, the sturgeon, a large and sluggish fish, could not master the fish ladders alongside the dams. Now the available caviar went largely into the export trade with a little left over for the Kremlin and for ambassadors to distribute as holiday gifts to local officials and diplomatic colleagues. Though genial in manner, he would show himself to be a skillful negotiator not hesitant to go back to Moscow for new instructions when we seemed to have reached an impasse.

With this cast of characters in place, we began our discussion. The quadripartite Bonn group had already worked out a draft statement that the three of us naturally tabled during the first session and awaited the Soviet reaction that Yefremov would obviously have to get from Moscow. We thought we could thus move expeditiously toward agreed language, since we knew the Soviets badly wanted to clear the way for GDR membership in the United Nations and the recognition that would come with it.

Yefremov quickly had his instructions from Moscow, and I received surprising instructions from Washington. What I did not know until I drew the logical conclusion was that, during an earlier visit to the White House of Foreign Minister Gromyko, he and Kissinger had already worked out the text for a four-power statement. It was not a very good draft, and parts of it read like a bad translation from the German.

The Gromyko-Kissinger text read as follows: "The governments of the Soviet Union, Great Britain, the United States and France have agreed to support the application for UN membership when submitted by the FRG and GDR and to affirm in this connection that such membership shall in no way affect or change the question of the Four Power rights and responsibilities, or the agreements, decisions, and practices that relate to them."[2]

My instructions were to table this text as a new U.S. proposal. I did so reluctantly. Yefremov responded quickly that it was acceptable to him. My British and French colleagues immediately jumped to the obvious conclusion that there had been Soviet-American collusion of the kind previously experienced during the negotiation of the Quadripartite Agreement itself. My embarrassment was as obvious as the irritation of Sauvagnargues and Henderson. There was simply no need or excuse for this sort of thing. Fortunately the French proved stubborn, and after several further sessions we finally emerged with a greatly improved text reading as follows:

> The Governments of the French Republic, the Union of Soviet Socialist Republics, the United Kingdom of Great Britain and Northern Ireland and the United States of America, having been represented by their Ambassadors, who held a series of meetings in the building formerly occupied by the Allied Control Council, are in agreement that they will support the applications of the Federal Republic of Germany and the German Democratic Republic, and affirm in this connection that this membership shall in no way affect the rights and responsibilities of the Four Powers and the corresponding related Quadripartite agreements, decisions, and practices.[3]

The improvements were not purely legal niceties but had the virtue of much greater clarity and precision in achieving our objective of ensuring that the Federal Republic would represent the interests of the Western sectors of Berlin in the United Nations without any derogation of the basic tripartite status and rights in those sectors. It had been an interesting and unnecessarily complicated exercise in diplomacy. I could not help being irked by the insensitivity of the White House once again to the fact that private deals with the Soviet Union on matters affecting French and British interests could only undermine the effective relationship based on trust and friendship of senior Allied diplomats at a post. They and their foreign ministries could not dismiss this sort of ill-concealed superpower collusion as just another example of White House tricks. Fortunately, both my British and French colleagues proved personally understanding, although the way the negotiations in Berlin had unfolded provided a continuing source of witticisms directed at me about how American policy was made. I could only wince and agree.

Making and Keeping Contacts

I don't always pick the winners, but something told me fairly early on that, despite criticisms of him as purely an ambitious politician with no depth, Minister President Helmut Kohl of Rheinland Pfalz would eventually play an important national role. A first visit to him in Mainz began what became a fruitful relationship involving lengthy private luncheon meetings in the *Ratskeller* restaurant and annual invitations to stand with him, his wife, and a few selected local dignitaries on the *Rathaus* balcony to view the Rose Monday Parade (Rosen Montag Zug). I quickly concluded that, while he was clearly not an intellectual or academic type, Kohl had all the right instincts and the required rapport with voters en masse to be a highly successful politician. He seemed to draw strength from the cheering crowds as they marched by the *Rathaus* waving at him and shouting "Helmut, Helmut."

I have known all sorts of political leaders. Some are cynical. Some find the whole business of appealing to the masses a colossal bore, but they are stuck with it. For a select few, however—and they win election after election—their empathy with the voters provides real pleasure. Kohl was clearly among them. I should note, however, that Adenauer's earlier electoral magic was not based on personal delight in conducting a campaign; his sense of earnestness and deep-seated probity as well as his understanding of popular fears and concerns provided his principal attraction to the German voter of his era.

With the fall of Barzel, Kohl became CDU party chairman but as a non-Bundestag member could not become chairman of the CDU *Fraktion*. He saw little to be gained at that point by attempting a move to Bonn, where the CDU, under the new secretary general Kurt Biedenkopf, was in the process of organizing itself more effectively in its new headquarters building.

On the SPD side, other than the chancellor, Finance Minister Helmut Schmidt, and Egon Bahr, now minister for special tasks, my principal contacts were the new defense minister Georg Leber, *Fraktion* leader Herbert Wehner, and a number of other parliamentarians. I was aware that the power of the old relatively conservative labor wing of the party (the so-called *Kanalarbeiter*) had begun to fade and that a younger, more radical group led by such Bundestag members as Karsten Voight, Wolfgang Roth, and Heidemarie Wieczorek-Zeul, all active in the Young Socialist (Jung Sozialisten) movement were beginning to assert themselves. Given the U.S. involvement in Vietnam against which they were publicly inveighing, I felt some hesitation about inviting them for lunch at the residence but finally did. Somewhat to my surprise, they all accepted and turned up. The discussion proved to be animated. They made the expected criticisms of U.S. policy. I remember stressing the point that it was too restrictive to judge the United States solely on the basis of Vietnam, about which, as they knew, there were great differences of view in the United States. Moreover, by now it had become clear that we were getting out of Vietnam, having concluded that military victory could not be achieved. We covered many other topics, seldom agreeing totally on any. They were a bright and articulate lot. Drawing on experience, I had the consolation of knowing that, in all probability, service in the legislature would have a mellowing effect on sharp ideology and that they would gradually drift to the center. This proved to be the case for most of the Young Socialist leaders in the Bundestag.

I shall not bore the reader with further details of numerous similar contacts with CDU and FDP politicians or the frequent calls on or lunches with officials of the Foreign, Finance, and Interior Ministries. This was all bread-and-butter diplomacy. An ambassador who leaves this sort of work largely to his staff is simply not doing his job. I wish I could say it was pure prescience that led me to see Interior Minister Dietrich Genscher as often as I did. I found him an interesting commentator on German internal developments. I did not know, of course, that he would one day become the dean of European foreign ministers in terms of years in office, although his move to that position became more or less certain with the SPD/FDP decision to support Walter Scheel for the presidency to succeed Heinemann.

The diplomatic corps in Bonn had a goodly number of able ambassadors, some of whom had useful information to exchange. Perhaps most interesting was the Swedish ambassador, Swen Backlund, a close personal friend of the chancellor and other leading SPD politicians. A tall, thin, far from dour Swede, he seldom lacked one or two tidbits of intriguing information.

My Soviet colleague, Valentin Falin, later to become special political correspondent for *Izvestia* and to hold a number of senior official positions in Moscow, was obviously out of the top drawer of Soviet diplomacy.[4] We did not see each other often and then always at lunch. We spoke in German. As was generally the case in meetings with Soviet diplomats not involving actual negotiations, the conversation tended to remain in generalities with both of us stating known positions. Only sometimes toward the end of lunch would we descend to greater frankness. He seemed inordinately proud of his impressive faience collection displayed in a number of showcases. I could only guess its cumulative value, but it must have been considerable—somewhat out of place perhaps for the representative of a country whose ideology would seem to rule out such ostentatious wealth. I could appreciate the irony of the Soviet ambassador's having far more valuable personal possessions than the representative of capitalist America.

Any ambassador, however, who thinks he can do it all is a fool. Having an experienced and able staff is all-important. We had assembled a highly effective group of officers at the top of the various operating sections. My minister and deputy chief of mission, Frank Cash, was an experienced Foreign Service officer on whom I could totally rely to run the embassy well in my absence and to provide sound advice when I was there. My economics minister, Charles Wooton, led his large section with aplomb, bringing both good humor and wise counsel to my daily staff meeting of senior officers. My political counselor, Frank Meehan, knew much about German politics from previous service in the country and had an unusual gift of getting quickly to the essentials. He had served previously as my deputy chief of mission in Hungary and was destined to become ambassador to Czechoslovakia, Poland, and the GDR before his retirement. I could not have wished for a stronger team, a group supplemented by able people in charge of public and cultural affairs.

German Government Problems

The year 1973 did not prove to be an easy one for Willy Brandt and his government. With Barzel rejected, the CDU/CSU fought a hard rear-guard action against two legislative bills ratifying the Basic Relations Treaty with the GDR and authorizing the Federal Republic to apply for UN membership. The SPD/FDP coalition with its forty-six-seat majority would inevitably win out, but the opposition threatened to make more trouble in the Bundesrat (upper house). On the brighter side, Brandt had come through the SPD party congress held April 10–14 in Hannover with flying colors despite gloomy predictions that he would lose ground to the burgeoning left wing of the party. Although the Left did elect more of its representatives to the SPD's Executive Board, Brandt clearly dominated the programmatic discussion and the approval of resolutions.

The chancellor visited the United States for talks with President Nixon on May 1 and 2. It is customary, whenever the chief of state, head of government, or foreign minister visits the United States officially (except for the fall General Assembly UN session), that the ambassador also travel to Washington to participate in meetings. So I did on this occasion. Because of postwar military dependency and the continuing importance politically of a good and steady relationship with the United States, German chancellors and foreign ministers felt it necessary to visit Washington for *ernste Gespräche* (serious talks) at least once a year. Looking back in memory and after reviewing some of the now available declassified materials, I must conclude once again how general and substantively inconsequential so many of the discussions at the highest levels on such visits actually were. There were some exceptions, of course, when the principals made decisions that led to agreements (as when Chancellor Schmidt persuaded President Ford during his 1975 visit to end the U.S. demand for support costs for our troops in the Federal Republic), but the primary justification for socializing at the top is psychological. It can ideally lead to a sort of bonding in the face of common adversity and insoluble problems. It can also, of course, lead to seemingly irreparable mutual antipathy as in the case of Helmut Schmidt and Jimmy Carter.

A major subject of German concern, as we had anticipated, was the Federal Republic's representation of West Berlin in the United Nations as part of its representation of the Western sectors in international organizations. We did not expect any major problems with this, particularly since the Soviets were obviously eager to avoid delay in GDR membership in the United Nations. While in general the Quadripartite Agreement was to work quite well, the whole question of the Federal Republic's relationship to West Berlin, not a model of clarity in the agreement, continued for years to be a serious source of difficulty and exacerbation for Bonn. We also chimed in with protests whenever they seemed expedient.

During his early May visit, Brandt received the usual plaudits of the American media and public. He cut a fine figure of a statesman, his voice—perhaps a little hoarser than it had been—was still an instrument for moving oratory, and above all he spoke fluent English. Most Americans, as I have said before, automatically react more favorably to foreign leaders who do not require an interpreter.

What looked like a first-class scandal hit the SPD shortly after Brandt's return to Bonn. A former CDU Bundestag member, Julius Steiner, admitted in the June 4 issue of *Der Spiegel* that he had been a double agent working for the GDR while in the Bundestag and that he had cast one of the two abstaining votes on April 17, 1972, as a result of which Barzel had failed to become chancellor. At the same time CDU (formerly FDP) deputy Wilhelm Helms claimed that he was offered, presumably by the SPD whip, Karl Wienand, several hundred thousand marks not to vote for Barzel. Rumor had it that Wienand actually bribed Steiner to do the same.

One cannot say that this murky affair ever found a clear and satisfactory resolution. At a later point Wienand was forced to resign from the Bundestag and, in effect, from active political life, for other dubious financial transactions involving his party, but his precise role in the vote of no confidence other than as a forceful rallier of waverers remains unresolved.

Willy Brandt had never enjoyed much of a reputation as an administrator either as governing mayor of Berlin, as foreign minister, or as chancellor. By the fall of 1973 Bonn was full of complaints about the malfunctioning of the federal Chancellery. The SPD floor leader, Herbert Wehner, who had been feuding with Brandt for some time, was quoted as saying that the government was "headless." The problem seemed to be twofold: Brandt's own inability to make decisions expeditiously, encouraged by Minister without Portfolio Egon Bahr's tendency to fiddle around with complicated issues, and the absence of people on the Chancellery staff with coordinating skills and the ability to inform Brandt promptly of bad news. The inevitable outcome was a chancellor's office more and more isolated from the legislative process and administrative needs.[5] I made it a point to see Herbert Wehner on a regular basis; he was never one to withhold comment or to attempt glossing over what he considered weaknesses.

To an American observer, the government's situation in Bonn, despite all the electoral advantages that Brandt had gained in 1972, seemed to be unraveling. Not that Brandt appeared to be in any personal jeopardy as chancellor (or at least so it seemed as 1973 drew to a close), but in the hothouse of rumor that Bonn had become, few of the rumors seemed to be favorable to him.

The Yom Kippur War Reaches Germany

The Yom Kippur War of October 1973 provided one of the more personally embarrassing examples of American diplomacy that I have ever experienced. The facts were simple enough: Egypt launched a surprise attack on an Israel observing Yom Kippur (the Jewish Day of Atonement). At first the Egyptian forces made considerable advances, but the Israelis finally turned the situation around and were in a position to destroy a large part of the Egyptian armies when a cease-fire arranged with major U.S. and Soviet involvement ended hostilities. During the war the United States had alerted its forces worldwide on October 25, sent massive military aid to Israel mainly out of stockpiles and equipment in the Federal Republic, and complained vociferously about what it regarded as European lack of support. A more sensitive diplomacy that recognized the need for prior consultation, or at least prior provision of information in NATO, could have largely avoided the mutual carping and bitterness that resulted.

Henry Kissinger had taken over from William Rogers as secretary of state in August when the latter could no longer serve under a president enmired in the growing Watergate scandal. Our support for Israel had been a long-standing part of American Middle Eastern policy, and it was only natural that we would do what we could, short of sending troops, to help the Israelis avoid military defeat. Our NATO allies, especially the Germans, who could observe it at first hand, were aware that we had already stripped our forces in the Federal Republic down to the organizational bone to meet our requirements in Vietnam. They did not make a fuss over this regardless of any consequences it might have for the NATO strategy of flexible response. Properly handled, military aid could also have gone to Israel from Germany without major difficulty.

I had called on Foreign Minister Scheel on October 16. We did not dwell long on the Middle East except to note that the military situation still seemed unclear. Although the Germans knew in general that we were sending supplies to Israel from our troops in the Federal Republic, Scheel did not raise any objections, nor did I expect that he would. The German government had already made clear its neutrality in the Middle East. Needless to say, I was pretty much in the dark about what we were doing or intending to do and had received no instructions as to what line to take with the Germans about our sending supplies to Israel.

Then all hell broke loose. On October 24 a journalist telephoned State Secretary Paul Frank of the Foreign Ministry from Bremerhaven to ask what Foreign Minister Scheel had to say about the loading of war matériel on Israeli vessels in Bremerhaven. After discussing the development with Scheel and Brandt, Frank called me in to find out what I knew. Frank, a man of small stature but sharp intellect whom I had come to regard as a friend, could scarcely believe me when I said I had no information. Little did he understand the dearth of information provided American ambassadors when the great men of the Nixon administration were personally involved. Although when the whole affair had ended, my relations with Frank returned more or less to normal, I am sure he had lingering doubts about whether we had been perfectly honest with him then and during several more trips to the Foreign Ministry, one by my deputy Frank Cash while I was keeping a speaking engagement.

In the late evening of October 26 I received a troubled visit to my residence from Defense Minister Georg Leber, an honest and serious man out of the labor movement, admittedly a little lost in the strategic fastnesses of the Defense Ministry. He was alone and could only express his anxiety about the Israeli vessels visiting Bremerhaven without any prior notice to the German authorities. I could provide little consolation or information.

The official German protest handed to us was actually considerably milder in tone than a statement attributed to a foreign office official and published widely in the German and American press. According to Frank, this involved a mistake by an inexperienced German diplomat who had made a statement based on background guidance intended only for internal and not public use. In any event, the statement read: "Weapons deliveries using West German territory or installations from American depots in West Germany to one of the warring parties cannot be allowed. The West German government is relying on America to finally hold deliveries from and over West Germany."[6]

The statement went on to say that a third Israeli vessel was reported en route to Bremerhaven and that if it came into port, the United States had been asked not to load it; further: "and we assume it will not be loaded."

The inevitable happened. Although the third Israeli vessel turned around and war matériel for Israel was thereafter loaded on American vessels, the war of public words escalated. In a news conference on October 26 (Washington is six hours behind Bonn), President Nixon expressed discontent with the degree of European cooperation on helping us to work out a Middle East peace settlement and warned that without peace in that area Europe's supply of oil—80 percent of its needs—would be cut off. A few days later a congressional source quoted Kissinger as saying, "I don't care what happens to NATO I'm so disgusted."[7]

Cooler heads soon began the process of lowering the diplomatic temperature, although some Europeans expressed surprise at being criticized for not taking a common stand on the Middle East with the United States at the height of the crisis, since they were never asked to do that. Both we and they could make lawyers' cases for the different viewpoints that emerged. For the Europeans the overriding consideration was their dependency on Middle Eastern oil as a major source of energy. I do not contend that keeping the American embassy informed in advance together with adequate prior consultations in NATO would entirely have prevented the imbroglio of late October from developing. Such actions could, however, have avoided much of the acerbity, mutual suspicion, and loss of confidence in our diplomacy that the whole mess actually engendered.

Lack of humility is the curse of American diplomacy. It is perhaps not easy for the leaders of a superpower, or as the political scientists would have it, a hegemon, to develop a modest sense of limitations and the psychological acumen to judge the true reactions of foreign officials whose countries in one way or another have become dependent on us. The fact that we provided the essential deterrent of the Western alliance, enjoyed the most dynamic economy during the first twenty-five years or so after World War II, and played a natural leadership role in most of the great endeavors of the postwar era—all made it easy for us to seem demanding, impatient, and often downright patronizing to our allies. Most of the gaffes and miscalculations of our diplomacy, in my view, derived from this combination of factors and the inability of many of our leaders psychologically to rise above them.

A classic case in point was the speech of national security adviser Henry Kissinger on April 23, 1973, and its protracted aftermath. Addressing members of the Associated Press in New York, Kissinger announced that 1973 would be called the Year of Europe because of a dramatic change in the psychological climate of the West due to new problems and shifts in the strategic balance. The United States proposed to its Atlantic partners that before the end of the year we should work out "a new Atlantic charter setting the goals for the future" and that would, inter alia, create a new relationship for the Atlantic nations in which progress Japan could share. After noting that economic disputes with Europe had created some friction, Kissinger called on leaders to recognize the dimensions of the problem, to seek cooperative solutions to existing economic, military, and diplomatic problems, and to "articulate a clear set of common objectives with our allies."

The press, logically enough, concluded that President Nixon had approved the speech, and James Reston compared it historically to the Marshall Plan speech of Secretary of State George C. Marshall made in 1947.[8] Secretary of State Rogers, with whom the speech had apparently neither been cleared nor even discussed, got the word out that the speech did not really represent U.S. policy. In any event, Kissinger became secretary of state in August 1973 and was now set to carry out the implications of what he had said.

The trouble was the implications lacked clarity. The Bretton Woods system was obviously on the way to total demise by early 1973 as the dollar floated freely against other currencies. American descriptions of the crisis within the alliance had once again been hyperbolic as the Europeans perceived it. They did not see the need for a grandiose new Atlantic charter.

But Michel Jobert, the gamecock little French foreign minister, provided the real barrier to movement of a kind that most of our allies, including the Germans, might have been prepared to make reluctantly in response to American pressures. The diplomatic stalemate that took place focused on the American desire to enter at an earlier stage into the counsels and consultations of the European Economic Community—a privilege that the Europeans could only regard as equivalent to quasi membership on the cheap. Jobert would have none of it, of course, and I could only feel sorry for my successor as assistant secretary of state for European affairs, Walter Stoessel, who had to bear the brunt of negotiations to achieve the impossible. Although the Germans regarded our extreme position as unreasonable and derogatory to the whole purpose of having a developing European political and economic community, they were prepared to accept a greater degree of consultation with the United States by community governments and their officials meeting at community functions.

One of the signs of a good diplomat is to be able to retreat gracefully when one recognizes (better sooner than later, of course) that an original goal is unobtainable. At some point in early 1974 the secretary of state (now Kissinger) could only conclude that we must be satisfied with less than the full loaf as far as participation in EEC counsels was concerned and that any agreed NATO declaration would necessarily fall far short of the new charter that he had proposed.

The actual NATO declaration by the fifteen member foreign ministers in Ottawa on June 19, 1974, was therefore only a pale shadow of the basic new charter that we had originally envisaged. Its language reaffirmed the original NATO treaty signed in 1949, essentially endorsed what the alliance was doing, but also called for necessary adaptation to the process of change in Europe.[9]

It was not a particularly glorious outcome to a misconceived project. Sitting in Bonn, I could only wonder at Washington's inability to distinguish between the attainable and unattainable, to recognize that European reluctance might involve a different assessment of the alliance's condition and of the nature and goals of the European Economic Community. At least one could say that the United States had not persisted to the bitter end with clearly unacceptable demands but had finally demonstrated a commendable degree of flexibility in accepting the inevitable.

A visit to Washington of Foreign Minister Genscher in late July 1974 provided both a finish of sorts to the Year of Europe controversy and a pathetic opportunity to see President Nixon in San Clemente some days before his resignation. The talks in Washington between Kissinger and Genscher dealt, as seemed inevitable at such meetings, with Berlin and the German Democratic Republic. Old-timers would not rate the issues as of major importance. Despite all the differences of interpretation about what the Federal Republic would or could not do in the city, the Quadripartite Agreement on Berlin had effectively dispelled the automatic atmosphere of crisis that conflicts over Berlin had created in the past.

In remarks that he made during a reception for Genscher, Secretary Kissinger referred to the new quality of alliance consultations created by the Cyprus crisis and added, "This is the relationship as it should be, which means that the discussions of the last year have been transcended." This was interpreted—and rightly so—as drawing a line under the tensions and acrimonious exchanges that followed his announcement fifteen months earlier of the Year of Europe.[10]

I accompanied the foreign minister and his senior assistant, State Secretary Günther van Well, to San Clemente. We frankly did not know what to expect. A president under the pressures that Nixon had experienced for more than a year could hardly be interested in the kind of *tour d'horizon* that would be normal. When we were ushered in to see the president, we could see that he was obviously under great strain. He had visibly aged. Yet once the conversation started, he surprised us all by his up-to-date information about issues and ability to articulate his thoughts clearly and precisely. This was not a man who had plunged to the borders of irrationality. After an hour of lucid exchange an impressed Genscher and entourage made their farewells. Although he obviously knew me, I had never felt particularly close to Nixon, nor was I ever regarded as a confidant. On this occasion as I was leaving, he came up, put his hand on my shoulder, and said to State Secretary von Well, "He's a real pro." Van Well commented when we had left the room, "He really likes you." I could only interpret this as the action of a man, deserted by many of his former friends, reaching out in his loneliness and despair to someone familiar.

I have no judgment beyond the usual on Watergate. It all took place while I was out of the country. A White House atmosphere that I had earlier regarded as conspiratorial and unhealthy had led to a series of stupidities that, in any assessment of relative gains and losses, made absolutely no sense. The better qualities of Nixon that indubitably existed were engulfed by the miasmic forces around him to the growth of which he had contributed.

1974: A Year of Leadership Change

Nineteen seventy-four was destined to see the personally tragic demise from office of an American president and a German chancellor, but as the year began, in Germany at least, the position of Willy Brandt seemed secure. Truly enough, Brandt's government appeared to be adrift and his own office in a state of administrative shambles. His lack of rapport with Herbert Wehner, the parliamentary leader of his party, who felt that Brandt was simply not up to the job, was widely known. The chancellor's personal prestige, however, remained high within the SPD, and few seriously believed him to be in any real political jeopardy.

In the early spring of the year, Brandt was in one of his periodic blue funks. Several state elections had gone badly for the SPD, the 1973 oil shock had begun seriously to affect the German economy, the Young Socialists continued to be obstreperous in party counsels, and he was suffering from toothache caused by two infected wisdom teeth. To make matters worse a five-day trip to North Africa (April 19–26) provided him with a case of dysentery.

There occurs sometimes in the affairs of humankind an unexpected revelation that dramatically and irreversibly sets in motion a chain of causation leading to a totally unexpected conclusion. In the case of Willy Brandt this was to be the arrest on April 24 of Günther Guillaume, an official in the personal office of the chancellor, as an East German spy. By diligence and organizational skill, he had carved out an important role for himself and accompanied the chancellor to Norway on his holiday during the summer of 1973. Although the arrest of Guillaume obviously came as a shock, it could not have been a complete surprise. Hans Dietrich Genscher, the minister of the interior, had some nine months earlier transmitted to the chancellor a warning from Günther Nollau, head of the Federal Office for Protection of the Constitution, that Guillaume might be a security risk, but did nothing to prevent his going with Brandt to Norway or continuing to serve him in a close personal capacity.

The political scene in Bonn was obviously boiling. There could be little doubt that Guillaume must have had access to secret German documents of all sorts. This was particularly the case during the week in Norway, where the chancellor continued to receive sensitive messages including a personal letter from President Nixon.

The suspicions of Guillaume had been closely held to a few senior officials, but now that they were confirmed, there ensued the inevitable finger-pointing and denial of responsibility for giving the chancellor bad advice. The top security official, after all, had recommended that Guillaume be allowed to continue in office so that he could be more closely observed. Nollau denied, however, that he had concurred in letting Guillaume accompany Brandt as his personal aide during his 1973 holiday in Norway. In the ultimate analysis, however, the chancellor as head of government could not deny his own responsibility. From all the records of the period, including Brandt's own diary entries, it did seem as if he was determined to remain in office despite his mood of despondency, the obvious failures of his government, and the opposition to him, of which he was undoubtedly aware, within elements of his own party.[11]

Needless to say, we in the embassy followed these developments with fascination. Our political section and I tapped into our usual sources. Bonn was full of rumors, but there was also some hard information. I knew, for example, that Herbert Wehner was playing an important role in SPD party deliberations and had an appointment to see him. I had a feeling that events of some historical significance were unfolding that went far beyond the fact that an East German agent had infiltrated the inner circle of the chancellor's entourage, but at that point at least it seemed as if Brandt, while wounded, would survive politically.

Then came an additional shock. Information dug up by security officials investigating how much sensitive information had been compromised in the case indicated that Guillaume had also served, in effect, as the chancellor's procurer while accompanying him on campaign trips aboard a special train during various state elections earlier in the year. Brandt had never posed as a model of chastity, but the idea that the spy should also have recruited the women for his evenings added a stain to the whole affair that affected the chancellor himself as well as his harshest critics within the party. Wehner, a puritan at heart and a rigorous judge of what he considered inappropriate behavior, reacted to the point of now thinking that Brandt should resign and turn over the chancellorship to Helmut Schmidt.

Brandt received advice from all sides. Those personally closest to him argued that he should stay. The chancellor himself vacillated seemingly between what he regarded as the unfairness of having his private life dragged into public discussion and the continuing pull of office that most top officials find difficult to resist. His closest friends and advisers, some of them largely dependent on him for the positions they held, strongly opposed resignation, as one might have expected. In the end Herbert Wehner prevailed, and on the evening of May 6 the chancellor dispatched State Secretary Horst Grabert, the official in charge of Brandt's personal office, to travel to Hamburg and hand over his resignation to federal president Heinemann, who was visiting there.

When I saw Wehner the following day (somewhat to my surprise, given the uproar in Bonn, he did not cancel our appointment), he was obviously in a highly emotional state pacing up and down in his office. The immediate topic of conversation could only be Brandt's resignation. At some length he explained why reluctantly he had come to the conclusion that the chancellor had to go. Wehner had long been noted for his outbursts of temper in the Bundestag and elsewhere (some attributed this to his constant fight with diabetes), and at one point I thought he was going to take my head off as his emotional level and his voice rose to a near shout. "*Eine Schande*" (a disgrace), he exclaimed, presumably in reference to the use of Guillaume as procurer. Then he calmed down and more in sorrow than in anger referred to the inevitable resignation of Brandt the day before with sadness.

German commentators on the events that led to the resignation and the ascent to power of Helmut Schmidt stress various factors, but there seems to be a broad consensus that the role of Herbert Wehner was crucial. It was no secret in Bonn that the *Fraktion* chairman and the chancellor did not get along very well and that Wehner had made disparaging remarks about Brandt's inability to provide the effective leadership within the party that was needed. He knew that the chancellor wanted to replace him as the SPD parliamentary leader. From the first time I had met Herbert Wehner back in the early 1950s, I had found in him a strong puritan streak, an intolerance for behavior that he found reprehensible. As a former dedicated Communist who had come to accept as better the democratic institutions of the Federal Republic, he still believed that commitment to a cause and to a party should override selfish personal indulgence.

So the big *Machtwechsel* (change of power) of 1969 was followed by an internal *Machtwechsel* in 1974. I had little doubt that Helmut Schmidt would prove to be a more effective head of government than Brandt. He had greater basic intelligence and a deeper substantive knowledge of economic and military strategy added to an orderly mind and approach to governance. Like Brandt, he also spoke excellent English, ensuring a positive response in the United States. I had known him from my earlier period in Germany and respected his abilities. But at the same time one could not but feel sad at the demise of a charismatic politician who had dared to move beyond the frozen sterilities of the late sixties with his *Ostpolitik*. He was not to disappear completely from the German political scene, for he continued for many years as head of the SPD with his office now moved to *Die Barracken* (the barracks), as the rather ramshackle SPD party headquarters building on the Konrad Adenauer Allee was popularly called. He also continued to play an important role in the International Socialist movement and headed the special groups that produced the two Brandt Commission Reports on Third World needs and the related obligations of developed countries. The reports, I should note, had little impact on actual state behavior. His glory days were clearly over. His death in 1993 elicited much reminiscent praise around the world but related to someone whose basic achievements had taken place during a past historical era.

Helmut Schmidt the Chancellor

It quickly became obvious when Helmut Schmidt took over as chancellor from Willy Brandt that a more decisive and knowledgeable leader was now directing German policy. He early on acquired the sobriquet "der Macher" (the Doer). His sarcasm and harshness in parliamentary debates also meant that he continued to earn the sobriquet of "Schmidt-Schnauze" (Schmidt the Big Mouth). To ensure that his personal office ran more efficiently than that of his predecessor, he put his former state secretary in the Finance Ministry, Manfred Schüler, in charge. The latter kept it running like a well-oiled machine.

He was far from a simple man of action, however, but rather a complicated individual with a love for music (he played the organ) and a wide-ranging knowledge of economics and military strategy. His problems with a malfunctioning thyroid gland received wide coverage in the German media and were held accountable for occasional bouts of irritability. Given the fact that, apart from the normal domestic and foreign issues with which a chancellor had to deal, he also had to ride herd over a fractious left wing in his own political party, any fair assessment of his eight years in office must largely be positive. At the personal level, he simply could not get along with President Jimmy Carter, but that was after my time in Bonn.

By the spring of 1974 when Schmidt became chancellor, Nixon had for all practical purposes abandoned the presidency to try desperately to escape the enveloping Watergate octopus. His resignation in August and the succession to the presidency of Gerald Ford began a relationship of friendship and respect between the new German and American leaders that surprised those who might have felt that the sharp-tongued chancellor would have a low level of tolerance for a president who, from the start, had received rather poor marks from the press for his physical agility and mental quickness. On several occasions Schmidt expressed to me his personal respect and regard for Ford.

My own relationship with the chancellor, which went back many years, was good and friendly. I knew I could see him privately when necessary but understood that frivolous waste of his time served no purpose. I also came to recognize that direct communications from the secretary of state on a few subjects (without informing me) would be a continuing, if highly regrettable, fact of life. It was ironic that the American ambassador had to rely on his friends in the German Foreign Ministry (who were, of course, kept fully informed by the chancellor's office) for word about the content of such communications.

I was never completely sure of what Schmidt really thought about the United States. He was too much a realist not fully to appreciate the primary role in European security of the extended deterrence provided by our nuclear capability linked to our military presence in Europe. He accepted that NATO, heavily influenced, if not dominated, by the United States, was the necessary institutional embodiment of that reality. But he could also frankly criticize erratic or undependable American behavior, as in the case of the MNF (Multinational Nuclear Force), or question the wisdom or indeed the tolerability of certain aspects of American international economic behavior.[12] He enjoyed visiting the United States, where his fluent English made him a much-sought-after speaker both in and later out of office. He was not without his weaknesses, of course, but in an era in which high intelligence, depth of knowledge linked to extensive experience, and political astuteness were all too seldom found at the top, Helmut Schmidt stood out as an outstanding Western leader.

One thing we shared was attachment to the classical musical repertoire. During 1975–76 the Federal Republic experienced a wave of visits by leading American symphony orchestras. After their concerts in Bonn and sometimes in Berlin, the American ambassador would provide a massive reception (with plenty of food on a buffet for famished musicians) to which all members of the orchestra plus a medley of relevant guests would be invited. One could always count on a few gate-crashers from the so-called art world. We also quickly learned how much hungry musicians can eat at midnight.

One such performance in Bonn by the Los Angeles Philharmonic Orchestra under Zubin Mehta brought home to me how accidental even momentary fame can be. We had invited the chancellor and his wife, who sat next to Faith and me in our box at the Bonn Philharmonic Hall. There were a few other guests in the box. The orchestra played with unusual brilliance, and the applause would not stop. Finally Mehta put his orchestra together again for an encore. With dignified solemnity they played the majestic slow movement from Sir Edward Elgar's *Enigma Variations*. Schmidt along with all of us was impressed but obviously did not recognize the music. Nor did any of the other Germans in the box; I fear British composers have made little impression in music-drenched Germany. I was proud to rise to the occasion and identify the selection. This obviously impressed Schmidt, and I was glad that the American ambassador had been able to demonstrate musical literacy. The next morning's gossip column in one of the local papers noted that I had been the only one able to identify Mehta's encore for the chancellor. Thus by chance is at least fleeting fame achieved.

I attempt no catalog of the numerous visitors to Bonn, Berlin, or other parts of Germany during my more than four years as ambassador. A few, however, linger in memory.

William Casey became undersecretary of state for economic affairs in 1973; he had previously served as chairman of the Securities and Exchange Commission (SEC) and before that had made a fortune as a lawyer and through his publications on tax law. He brought with him on his first and only visit to the Federal Republic his later to become famous Casey mumble. I found him personable and friendly enough as a house guest not given to unreasonable demands. We had, of course, arranged relevant calls on senior government officials. These went off, we thought, without incident; he had brought with him no great new ventures to discuss, and it was not always easy to understand precisely what he was saying. After he had left Bonn, we received a frantic call from the Economics Ministry asking to see our memorandums of conversations with Casey, since they had failed to understand most of the points he had been trying to make.

Who would have predicted that this man of mumbles would later become campaign manager for President Reagan and then controversial director of the CIA? He did not last very long at State once Kissinger took over from Rogers; in 1974 he became director of the U.S. Export-Import Bank. His influence on high-level appointments in 1981 put him in a position to settle a few old scores.

Visits to foreign posts by Paul Volker, then undersecretary of the treasury for monetary affairs and later to become president of the Federal Reserve Board, always presented problems, not because he was personally difficult, which he was not, but because of his height (six feet seven inches or thereabouts). Few beds could hold him comfortably. In Bonn we had an extension made that fit at the bottom of a guest bed.

I particularly remember his visit to Bonn early in 1973. The remnants of the Bretton Woods Agreement were blowing away. The Smithsonian Agreement of December 1971, which in an outburst of hyperbole Nixon had called "the greatest monetary agreement in the history of the world," had proved to be a poor stopgap. By early 1973 Volker was doing the rounds in Europe after visiting Japan to inform other governments that the United States would have to devalue the dollar further—action that quickly led to the abandonment of all efforts to link currencies to gold and to the free floating of currencies against each other. To avoid returning to Tokyo, he attempted to communicate with the Japanese by telephone.

I recall sitting in our library while Volker finally got Tokyo and the Japanese finance minister on the phone. The undersecretary slowly and at times loudly made his points. I could not hear the response from Tokyo, but Volker finally seemed to feel he had clarified the U.S. position and received no thunderously negative response. I could not help but wonder how much direct and understandable communication had taken place in either direction, but so far as I am aware there were no subsequent recriminations. I would not have recommended the international telecommunications system of 1973 as the best way of making complicated points to a Japanese official whose English was weak and getting a knowledgeable response.

Another occasional visitor to Bonn was Secretary of Defense James Schlesinger. He would arrive in a converted KG-135 tanker shut off from the outside world. I had traveled in these flying coffins with no windows. They get you to your destination, but that is all one can say for them. I would be out at the airport as greeter along with my defense attaché. On the German side, Defense Minister Georg Leber would head a considerably larger group. The first arrival of the Schlesinger entourage brought an unforgettable introduction. When the plane came to a halt and the door swung open, the first person to appear was not the secretary of defense but a senior member of his group, who popped out dressed in a sweat suit and running shoes. An addicted jogger, he descended the staircase and sped off onto the runway to get the exercise the flight had denied him. The German greeters stood in bewilderment, but finally Dr. Schlesinger appeared and the usual rituals of an airport greeting could be observed.

Leber, a former Catholic trade union leader and a man of unimpeachable integrity, had to learn the jargon and the concepts of military strategy from scratch. He could hardly be anything other than in awe of the highly sophisticated and articulate secretary of defense with a background of many years in government and the Rand Corporation. Schlesinger delighted in explaining his frequently complicated thinking about nuclear strategy, counterforce targeting, and other subjects of frequent discourse in Washington. I could see that Leber and his advisers were frequently baffled by these intellectual gymnastics and would later require collective hand-holding and assurances that basic American strategy was not in the process of fundamental revision. It should theoretically not be the role of an American ambassador to explain after his departure what an American official really said or meant to say, but I found that some visitors made this a necessity if obvious misconceptions were not to linger on.

I liked Leber. He was a man of courage and honor. He knew his limitations, but among the politicians I have known he ranks high. He was not a smoothie able to hide his real feelings under a cloud of rhetoric and generalization. When he was agitated, he let you know.

After he became secretary of state, Henry Kissinger turned out to be by far the most frequent American visitor to Germany, even if only to attend the World Cup final soccer match in Munich between Bayern-München and the Netherlands. His trips to Bonn followed a fairly fixed routine. After the usual airport reception, he would be taken by helicopter to Schloss Gymnich, a castle in the countryside some twenty-five miles from the city used by the German foreign office as a VIP guest house. The secretary's party would be housed in the Schloss, and Chancellor Schmidt and Foreign Minister Genscher would also hold their talks in the castle as well as stage there the usual official lunches and dinners. It meant a lot of driving back and forth for the German officials involved and the American ambassador, but highly efficient German security for the visitor was thus ensured.

Some of the conversations were obviously interesting and occasionally got down to the nitty-gritty of problems. But as experience had long since taught me, when top officials converse, they very often do so in general terms equivalent to what the French call a *tour d'horizon* (a discussion of current issues). If staffs provide them with specific points to be made, they may oblige, but even the most experienced seem to prefer broad and sometimes superficial discussions of trends and situations. When there is a real crisis, one may believe, the degree of specificity increases.

One topic that did receive more detailed discussion was the situation in Portugal after the revolution of April 1974, when a military junta overthrew the Caetano dictatorship. There was a subsequent period of confusion as a struggle for control between left-wing elements in the military and those favoring democratic reforms worked itself out. One of the emerging democratic leaders was Dr. Mario Soares, later to become prime minister and then president of his country as leader of the Socialist Party. Early in 1975 he had visited Bonn and asked the German foreign minister to arrange a meeting with me. I agreed to receive him at my residence. In our conversation he obviously wanted to convey the assurances of those resisting a left-wing takeover that they would make every effort to prevent this, and to ask for such help as we could provide. There was not much that I could say in response except that I would report his points immediately to Washington. He impressed me as sincere and desperately anxious for the approval of the major Western democracies.

As I recall it, the silence from Washington reflected a generally negative attitude toward the process of change in Portugal—a negativism that Secretary Kissinger later brought with him during visits to the Federal Republic in conversations with Schmidt and Genscher. They, on the other hand, urged that the Western Allies give all the help they could to the democratic forces in Portugal, including direct assistance on the spot in setting up and maintaining functioning institutions. They were able to provide this through the major foundations funded by the federal budget and related to the political parties (the CDU Konrad Adenauer Stiftung, the SPD Friedrich Ebert Stiftung, and the FDP Friedrich Naumann Stiftung).

I remember how at one meeting in the German guest house, after a somewhat more optimistic evaluation by Schmidt and Genscher, Kissinger described the situation in Portugal as deteriorating to the point where the best possible outcome that we could expect would be an Algerian-type development. A year later the same cast of characters met in the same place. Democratic forces in Portugal were now seemingly in the ascendancy. Somewhat to my surprise (and I would surmise to that of Schmidt and Genscher) the secretary said the situation in the country was developing as he had predicted during his previous visit. It was clear that, despite the heroic efforts of our ambassador in Lisbon, Frank Carlucci, we had pretty much missed the boat on this one. The Germans and some of our other European allies deserved much credit for conducting a purposeful and effective policy with respect to Portugal in the years immediately after 1974. They obviously had better intelligence and political judgment about trends in the country than we did.

In early June 1974 the secretary was under attack from the press and congressional sources for allegedly having authorized the wiretapping in 1969–71 of some members of his staff who, he suspected, were leaking classified information to the press. Before he joined President Nixon on a trip to the Mideast, his schedule had him spending June 11 in Salzburg, Austria. Arrangements had been made for a late afternoon meeting near Berchtesgaden with Foreign Minister Genscher. As a dutiful ambassador I had proceeded to Salzburg to take the secretary to this session in my car and to sit in on his discussion with Genscher.

No one had expected Kissinger to call an unscheduled press conference in Salzburg. A goodly group of correspondents, American and European, showed up. I stood in the rear of the room with our ambassador to Austria. We had not the slightest idea what to expect. The secretary appeared to be in an emotionally wrought-up state, and his remarks fit his apparent mood. What he said in effect was that he would resign unless his name was cleared of the charges relating to wiretapping of some of his own staff members during the 1969–71 period. The atmosphere in the room became electric; this was obviously a big story. The *New York Times* published the entire text of the secretary's press conference, which dealt with no other subject.[13]

I make no attempt here to pass judgment on a complicated and typically Washington embroglio. Although I had, of course, been physically there during the years in question, my bureau had not been involved in any of the leaks or internal White House intrigues that had presumably precipitated the wiretaps. Certainly nothing that I knew about the Nixon White House would lead me to doubt that wiretapping ordered by it took place on a fairly extensive scale. Collective paranoia easily leads to paranoid behavior.

In any event, when Kissinger joined me for the half-hour drive to his meeting with Genscher, I expected him still to be in a highly emotional state. To my surprise he seemed to be completely calm and looking forward to his meeting with Genscher, which incidentally produced no surprises. I could only give him the highest marks for thespian ability. Nor did he subsequently resign.

One non-American visitor to Bonn worth noting was Leonid Brezhnev, general secretary of the Communist Party of the USSR. His first visit to Bonn in 1972 could have ended in disaster. The German government decided to house him and senior members of his party in the unused but still luxurious Petersburg Hotel perched on one of the seven hills on the other side of the Rhine from Bonn. (Refurbished, it was later to become a very exclusive guest quarters of the Foreign Ministry.)

The Germans were aware, of course, of Brezhnev's penchant for fast automobiles and had arranged a gift of a new silver Mercedes sports car. Brezhnev beamed, I was told, when he saw the vehicle parked in front of the hotel and immediately insisted on giving it a trial run. The German protocol types were hesitant, pointing out the steepness and the sharp turns of the road down from the top, but he would have none of it. So he got in and drove off with a roar.

I do not know where Brezhnev learned to drive. If the general secretary had flown off into space and down the mountainside with his new Mercedes, the German government would have faced an international crisis. All sorts of rumors about deliberate bad brakes or stuck accelerators would immediately have begun to circulate. Fortunately, he crashed into a tree, doing no harm to himself but considerable damage to the Mercedes. German efficiency produced an identical model in a few days that the Soviet leader could take back with him to Moscow.

German Domestic Politics: 1974–1976

Apart from the disarray within the Social Democratic Party, Helmut Schmidt inherited a generally difficult situation when he took over as chancellor in May 1974. The oil shock of 1973 with its quadrupling of crude oil prices had sown the seeds of what became known as stagflation, and all the major oil-importing industrialized countries saw economic growth turn into recession, which deepened in 1974 and 1975 into the sharpest of the postwar years. The synchronicity of the downturned business cycle in so many countries meant that no country could serve as the engine of growth that would help pull the others out of recession. Moreover, as far as the Federal Republic was concerned, the typical Keynesian approach of demand stimulation through fiscal policy could not suffice for a country within which every seventh worker was dependent on exports for his or her job.

Under these circumstances, despite the increased competence and determination that Schmidt obviously brought to his position, state elections that had begun in 1974 to show significant CDU gains continued, with one or two exceptions, to bring further SPD losses. While national campaigns in Germany are mercifully short compared with those in the United States, one should not make too much of this. The German voter is, of course, spared the prolonged series of primaries that stretch out for a year in the United States, but no ambitious German national politician can overlook the reality that he or she must campaign in the various state elections strewn throughout the calendar. Even in 1974 party activities were already clearly motivated by the prospect of federal elections in the early fall of 1976.

The nonsynchronicity of state and local elections was not specifically the intention of the postwar German founding fathers, but that is the way it has worked out. The result is that, between federal elections, there is an almost constant series of such elections in which national political leaders will be expected to participate. The wear and tear on politicians is thus as bad as, if not worse than, that on those American party leaders involved in our prolonged campaigns. A further consequence in the Federal Republic can be that the Bonn coalition in power, through a series of reverses in state elections, may see the opposition party in the Bundestag gain control of the Bundesrat even to the point of obtaining a two-thirds majority.

The other party in the coalition, the FDP, had also changed its leadership once Walter Scheel became president of the Federal Republic. Hans Dietrich Genscher took over as party chairman in October 1974. Some observers frequently made the point that on basic economic policy, the Free Democrats were really closer to the Christian Democrats than they were to the Social Democrats, but while there were periods of tension between Genscher and Schmidt, the latter was able to hold the intrinsically uneasy coalition together until 1982, when Genscher finally took a walk to join together with the CDU to oust Schmidt and make Helmut Kohl chancellor. Schmidt was able to achieve this largely because he waged a constant battle against the left wing of his party and espoused essentially a middle-of-the-road, if not conservative, economic policy.

Within the CDU, Kohl was able to strengthen his position as party chairman while remaining on as minister president of Rheinland-Pfalz. The big intraparty debate turned out to be over social policy. While the old Erhard formula of *soziale Marktwirtschaft* (social market economy) remained valid, some party leaders felt that there needed to be a clear recognition of the new social problems of the mid-1970s. Others argued that such concessions to a more socialist point of view would be unwise and damage the party. From Bavaria the powerful voice of the Christian Social Union Party boss, Franz Josef Strauss, gave the latter strong support. Kohl himself, though accepting the need for some rethinking of party positions, was not prepared to go all the way with the reformers. As the putative CDU chancellor candidate in 1976, he could only be aware that Strauss thought himself a fitter candidate for that position and that the loyalty of the CSU to the CDU/CSU coalition was essential to any victory in 1976. He was also aware, of course, that CDU state chairman Hans Filbinger in Baden-Würtemberg and state chairman Alfred Dregger in Hesse both favored the conservative position.

While all this was going on, the embassy reported regularly, and, I trust, with some discernment, the internal political developments in the Federal Republic. I continued to see Kohl in Mainz and a roster of SPD/FDP and CDU politicians in Bonn.

I met with Strauss only a few times either on visits to Munich or when he came to Bonn. He remained somewhat of a puzzle to me. Here was a man of enormous ability, linguistically gifted, the son of a butcher who had become a highly educated and eloquent politician, yet with some obvious flaws of character. Winning one state election after another, he had an impressive hold on the Bavarian electorate. He provided a natural target for German intellectuals and the liberal press and never seemed to appreciate that his unpopularity in northern Germany precluded his ever winning a national election. He was not to become the CDU/CSU candidate in 1976, but when he finally did in 1980, he suffered a defeat that effectively removed him from the national political scene. The course of history is strewn with the failed aspirations of politicians who, despite great natural talent, lacked either the luck or the ultimate capacity realistically to assess possibilities and probabilities.

It had become clear, even a year before the elections scheduled for October 3, 1976, that the SPD/FDP coalition would suffer serious losses. The best it could hope for was to retain power by a narrow margin. Schmidt was tireless in trying to organize his party to campaign effectively, but continuing stagflation and left-wing public restiveness within the SPD were a heavy burden to carry. The 1976 electoral results showed the CDU/CSU winning 48.6 percent of the votes cast and 243 seats in the Bundestag (up from 44.8 percent and 225 seats in 1972), while the SPD sank to 42.6 percent of the votes cast and 214 seats, compared with 45.9 percent and 230 seats in 1972. The FDP won 7.9 percent of the votes cast and 39 seats, compared with 8.4 percent and 41 seats in 1972. It did not require an Einstein to note that the coalition had barely survived with a margin of 10 seats in the Bundestag.[14] The election also provided an augury of the voter appeal of Helmut Kohl—something to be again demonstrated in the accelerated election of 1983 following the defection in 1982 of the FDP from its coalition with the SPD.

The Lie and the Reality in East Germany

A mystery to me over the years had been how a dictatorial regime so utterly lacking in merit as that of the German Democratic Republic could nevertheless be a continuing source of fascination, and in some cases even admiration, among left-wing intellectuals in Europe and the United States. Truly enough, the Communist leadership heavily subsidized the performing arts, which were frequently of high quality, and loyalist men and women of letters enjoyed the materially good life to which their special status entitled them. The total lack of political freedom, the pervasive presence of the secret police, and, after 1961, the enclosure psychology created by the Wall seemed to make little difference to intellectuals who accepted the verbal social commitments and slogans of the regime and in some cases actually claimed that the population of East Germany had developed a kind of patriotic loyalty to the institutions of the idealistic new order created by Walter Ulbricht and Erich Honecker.

Few politicians in Bonn believed any of this. They were the ones who had to provide the cash to ransom political prisoners held in East Germany and to pay the other subsidies and bounties by which the Federal Republic hoped to encourage better behavior, or at least less misbehavior, by the GDR regime. They were also aware of the massive intelligence effort of the East German regime targeted at West Germany (the Guillaume case had brought this very much home) and that any true relationship of trust and friendship was out of the question.

To an official observer of what was going on in the East, the idea that the Soviet Union had actually granted real and complete sovereignty to the GDR regime could only seem preposterous. Truly enough, it had restored a large measure of administrative autonomy to that regime, but when it came to the important decisions, Moscow still gave the orders. I was able to observe one little sign of who really ran things in East Berlin every time I called on the Soviet ambassador in his Unter den Linden palace. Normally the Eastern side of Checkpoint Charlie, through which all American visitors, official or otherwise, had to pass on their way into East Berlin, was completely under East German police control. No Russians were in evidence. However, whenever the American ambassador came to Checkpoint Charlie for a prearranged visit, every East German policeman would have vanished. A single Soviet military vehicle would be there waiting for my arrival. The driver would salute and lead my car unencumbered to the Soviet embassy. Likewise on my way out there would be no sign of any East German control. So much for GDR sovereignty!

A psychological parallel, if on a somewhat grander scale, was the persistent inability of some intellectuals in many Western countries to recognize Stalinism and the Soviet Union for what they really were. The only explanation, I suppose, is that wisdom and common sense are not the inevitable concomitants of even high intelligence that has become emotionally attached to what turns out to be a bad cause. In an age when religious faith no longer seems to be an option for many, the quest for some sort of certainty can lead to strange and blind allegiances.

Purely from a visual point of view, the contrast between West and East Berlin should have brought home the contrast in systems. Not that West Berlin was a city of beauty or inspired architecture. Unfortunately much of the rather frenzied postwar building showed little grace or sense of permanency. But it was a lively place with a thriving economy. The East Berlin regime had done a reasonably good job of reconstructing some of the historic buildings in the Unter den Linden area, but much of the Soviet sector seemed drab and in process of dissolution. There were some streets such as the Karl Marx Allee that had received a Moscow-type facade of tiled apartment buildings, but there was not much behind them, and after a few years the tiles began falling off to the peril of passing pedestrians. As the years went by, the East German regime made efforts to turn its part of the city into something of a showplace, but the lack of spirit and the poor service in hotels and restaurants could only remind one of the drabness and surliness of Moscow, and with a few exceptions like Budapest, of other cities in Communist Eastern Europe.

West Berlin was not without its ironies. Because the three occupying powers did not permit the extension of West German draft legislation to their sectors, the city quickly became a safe haven for draft dodgers. Anarchists and free-living radicals also found the atmosphere of the city congenial, even if some of that atmosphere was provided by liberal subsidies from the despised Bonn government. They became the core of the so-called *Chaoten* (chaotic ones) who demonstrated riotously or just plain rioted to show their rejection of the existing order and its institutions. Except on a few occasions that brought them all out for a major confrontation with the police, the city was generally large enough to swallow all of these elements of discordancy. I do not recall any personal encounters in Berlin with the undoubted hostility to the United States that our involvement in Vietnam had engendered. It was otherwise in the Federal Republic.

Life with Music

I have earlier noted the broad resuscitative effect that the revival of musical life had on German culture and society during the dismal early postwar years. As a listener during my adult years I had developed reasonably eclectic musical tastes but also some strong preferences and dislikes. Although I had played several instruments as a boy, I reached the correct conclusion in my teens that I simply lacked the manual and other skills required to become a really good musician and from that point on derived my pleasure listening to the performance of those more gifted than I.

Both West and East Berlin during my more than four years as ambassador were full of good music, but the most splendid of all was the Berlin Philharmonic Orchestra playing in its highly modern hall under the general direction of Herbert von Karajan. My close personal friendship with Wolfgang Stresemann, intendant (general manager) of the Philharmonic for many years (also son of the famous Weimar foreign minister and chancellor Gustav Stresemann), opened many doors that normally would have remained closed. Through him I met von Karajan occasionally, usually for a late postconcert dinner at the Tessiner Stube, his favorite Berlin restaurant, where he had a corner table on seemingly permanent reservation. The great conductor was a proud and impatient man who did not suffer fools or bad musicians gladly. He could be quite charming when he wanted to be and did not insist on talking about the performance of his orchestra or music in general. He suffered from a long-term back problem that grew worse with the years, particularly after a fall from the podium while conducting. I do not think he was the kind of person to whom Faith and I could ever have felt close, but in front of his orchestra and at his best he could extract breathtaking music from that magnificent ensemble.

He was greatly concerned about the need to provide for the *Nachwuchs* (succession) of young conductors. To help finance their training he and a group of German bankers and industrialists, most notably Jürgen Ponto (the head of the managing board of the Dresdener Bank, who was murdered in front of his home by terrorists some years later), founded the Karajan Stiftung (Karajan Foundation). Although I could not join this organization formally as American ambassador, Ponto and others invited Faith and me to attend social and other functions that it sponsored as well as to sit in on practice sessions of the Philharmonic. All of this was great fun and a welcome diversion from the exigencies and paper trails of official life.

An American ambassador to Germany with some attachment to music could hardly escape going to Bayreuth at least once for a portion of the Ring tetralogy. My reactions to Wagner have always been mixed. I could not deny the sheer power and magnificence of his music at its best. But his murky philosophy with its later appeal to the Nazis and the tediousness of the lengthy recitative portions of his operas left me cold. As I have said before, there was something febrile about nineteenth-century German romanticism, and Wagner suffered from a heavy dose.

Bayreuth was well prepared for the onslaught of devoted Wagnerites. Eating during long intermissions had become part of the ritual. I was surprised to note how many French were there. One old-timer told me that the Wagner cult was very strong in France, which sent many regulars to Bayreuth. I should not have expected that. The theater designed by Wagner to bring home to audiences the spirit of his works did not seem particularly inspired architecturally to me, but I could appreciate its acoustics and the quality of the performance. The mystique of cult music is indeed a peculiar thing. In a secular age it provides for some devotees a sort of poor substitute for religion. Their emotions can expand to the accompaniment of sound without commitment—a way of feeling good on the cheap.

Another place of musical pilgrimage reserved for the affluent was, and of course still is, Salzburg for the annual Music Festival. A lovely city taken over during the festival by such society as Europe provides (Snobsburg on the Salzach, as one wag called it), it has largely succumbed to the importunities of high-grade tourism. We went there twice as guests, and it would be impolite to knock it. The music was great. Particularly memorable was the premiere of Karajan's production of Verdi's *Don Carlos*. We had been lucky enough to see Salzburg at other than festival season by participating over the years in a number of Salzburg Seminar conferences, and of course we knew the other part of Austria well through frequent visits to Vienna, particularly during our time in Hungary. While never infected with the Vienna fever that seemed to grip so many American residents of the city, we found Austrian *Schlamperei* and the *Proporz* approach to political allocation problems a pleasant, if not particularly goal-obsessed, way of life. Having expected twice to go to Vienna as ambassador, my failure to get there left me with a mild feeling of disappointment and missed experience during visits to the capital.

My Last Year in Bonn

My last year in Bonn, 1976, was both a national election year for the Federal Republic and the year in which countless German cities and groups decided to help us celebrate the two hundredth anniversary of the Declaration of Independence. Despite the undoubted anti-Americanism of some intellectuals and the left wing of the SPD, the seemingly spontaneous outflow of goodwill and admiration that our anniversary elicited demonstrated that a large proportion of the German middle and working class still felt strong bonds of gratitude and affection for their American connection. Every town and institution seemed to want its day for a ceremonial observance at which the American ambassador would be invited to speak. My engagement book for the first six months of 1976 began to look like a traveling salesman's trip record. As already noted, between January 1 and June 30 I made roughly one hundred appearances and speeches around the country to help Germans commemorate our Declaration of Independence.

With the war in Vietnam now effectively over, with the two superpowers at a lower level of cold war intensity, and with the average West German relatively prosperous and hopeful about the economic future, the time was propitious for such a love feast. We no longer seemed to be involved in a tug-of-war (which had always been more of a diplomatic rather than a popular exercise) over our participation in European counsels, and the concerns caused by the oil shock of 1973 had somewhat abated as inflation and depreciation of the dollar reduced the real price of crude oil.

After more than four years in Bonn, I knew that I would soon be leaving. In August I received a visit in Bonn from John Loudon, chairman of the Board of Trustees of the Atlantic Institute for International Affairs in Paris. He wanted me to take over as director general of the institute at the beginning of 1977 to succeed Ambassador Jack Tuthill, an old Foreign Service friend, who likewise painted an attractive picture of what the institute offered. After some further telephone exchanges, I gave my tentative agreement. I saw nothing in the way the Foreign Service and Department of State were being run to indicate much hope of improvement in management or practice, or for that matter much of a role for myself under that management.

I knew that to leave the Foreign Service after more than thirty-five years would not be an easy experience without emotional wrench. The end of career must come to all of us, and I was among those retirees fortunate enough to be going on to a new position—a position, moreover, at somewhat higher pay, if without the pomp and circumstance associated with an ambassadorship at a major post. I had devoted what some people call the best years of one's life to the Foreign Service, and no matter what followed, I knew it could never involve the same combination of problems affecting the national interest, contact with the highest levels of decision making, and the personal authority that senior diplomatic positions brought with them.

I did hope to remain in Bonn until late in the year permitting a move directly to Paris. This was not to be. It seemed that our ambassador in Moscow, Walter Stoessel, had developed some sort of blood ailment. The Soviets had been bombarding his office in the embassy with sonic waves, as they had previous occupants of the position. I do not recall whether any causal link between Walt's blood problem and the bombardment of his office was ever established, but 1976 was a presidential election year, and both Ford and Kissinger wanted Stoessel out of Moscow (where he had served less than two years) and ensconced in Bonn as ambassador before the story broke in the press and became an issue in the Congress and possibly in the campaign itself. So our departure from Bonn for Washington took place in October after a brief visit to the Atlantic Institute in Paris.

When I left Germany, German-American relations, while still troubled in some respects, could hardly be called critical even by those commentators who tended to blow up every difference of view into a major confrontation. I have never had any illusions about the ability of an ambassador by himself to change the main course of history, but I had done as much as I could to improve the ties between our countries, to achieve better understanding of American policies and culture, and to show sympathetic understanding of continuing problems beyond the capacities of our governments and leaders to solve. Washington did not always help to strengthen my position by resorting to backchannel messages and by what at best could only be described as wrong judgments and advocacy of policies that were clearly unacceptable. But the parallelism of German and American interests in so many areas imposed by the cold war and any realistic analysis of our long-term relationship made any major break unlikely. Many German intellectuals and the left wing of the SPD did not, of course, accept such an analysis and advocated a more neutral position for the Federal Republic and ultimate dissociation from the American connection.

No one in 1976 to my knowledge had any real idea of what the years ahead would bring to Germany. Few, if any, even of those of us who still advocated it as an ultimate goal, thought that reunification would or could take place in the calculable future. German experts as much as American experts, relying on the doctored statistics and self-promotion of Communist regimes, vastly overestimated their strength and durability. It was a funny game we played, but at least one overriding reality that no one on the Western side could overlook was the destructive capability of Soviet nuclear weaponry.

10 Research Institute Director and Academic

. . . .

Retirement from the Foreign Service, to which I had devoted more than thirty-five years, was bound to be somewhat traumatic. The procedures involved were as graceless and bureaucratic as anonymous civil servants could concoct; they seemed to consist mainly of filling out and signing numerous forms. There was no golden watch. So I slipped away at the end of 1976. Fortunately, unlike so many of my retiring colleagues who went either into the job market or into rustication, I would be moving immediately into a new and potentially interesting position in Paris, where we would live. The pain of transition, we thought, would therefore be minimal and brief.

Once in Paris, Faith and I quickly came to realize how paternalistic the Foreign Service had become over the years compared with the frugal days of 1940 when I was sent off to Burma with a book of State Department drafts and told to submit regular accounts but little else. By 1976, at least for a senior officer, everything was laid on. In retirement one missed not so much the pomp and circumstance but the ministrations of the embassy's General Services officer and his bountiful staff ever ready to meet one's needs. The French staff at the Atlantic Institute for International Affairs were as helpful as they could be, but they obviously could not match the resources of a major embassy representing a superpower.

A first task was to obtain French work and residence permits. Françoise Lerch, my able administrative assistant, accompanied me to various offices, particularly the central police headquarters on the Île de la Cité, that issued the permits. It looked like 99 percent of all the applicants milling about in the overcrowded waiting room were out of Africa, north or west. For many of them, the waiting must have seemed endless. Françoise proved infinitely resourceful in expediting my progress, but it could not all be done in a single day. I started out with temporary permits, later to be converted into annual permits, but each year we had to go through the same rigmarole. The crowds at police headquarters never grew smaller.

After a month in my predecessor's apartment in the Rue Lota, which we found too dark and gloomy, we discovered a ground-floor apartment at 83 Avenue Foch with its own little enclosed garden. It was an address familiar to many, since, for nearly twenty years, Jean Monnet had used his brother's second-floor apartment above us as his Paris headquarters. We were close to the Porte Dauphine and the Bois de Boulogne as well as the terminus of the Porte Dauphine metro line. The former NATO headquarters building, now a branch of the University of Paris, provided a nearby reminder of de Gaulle's expulsion of the military part of the alliance from France. After dark the large traffic circle at the Porte Dauphine changed its coloration as large numbers of prostitutes, male and female, solicited business, each claiming a specific bit of turf as his or her own. If one did not bother them or insult them, they were all harmless enough to the permanent residents of the large apartment houses in the area.

For some five and a half years we were to lead interesting lives at 83 Avenue Foch, enjoying the countless amenities and aesthetic delights that Paris—the most beautiful of cities—had to offer. It was a happy time not devoid, of course, of the petty irritations and illnesses that inevitably intrude in life. Of all the concerns I had, the most onerous and troubling was trying to keep the Atlantic Institute financially afloat. I had not really inquired specifically enough about the balance sheet and income prospects of the institute, and no one had sufficiently warned me. I had made some general points about my not seeing my role as that of a fund-raiser, and as I looked back, these had never really received a direct response. In any event, there I was as director general of the Atlantic Institute for International Affairs, and it quickly became evident that we were heading for a financial crisis, particularly when almost the first letter I opened was from an American foundation reversing the substantial grant on which my predecessor had obviously counted.

So it was that I found it necessary, hat in hand, to enter the strange and wondrous world of the great foundations. Just as some White House staff members become arrogant as self-imagined reflectors of presidential power, foundation staff members all too often displayed the arrogance that the power to influence the dispensation of grant money brought with it. A quick trip to the United States during which I visited a number of foundation headquarters was a depressing experience. Some received me with minced mouth and clear impatience at my daring to be so importunate. Others were more polite but implied with gobbledygook that a grant was out of the question. A few actually listened patiently and sympathetically but ended the conversation by noting that their foundations were no longer in the business of providing the kind of support we needed. We were later to get some help from American foundations, but I never felt that we were able to break into the old-boy network, membership in which gave one an enormous advantage in tapping into foundation resources on a regular basis. Some organizations within the network seemed to come up year after year on the grantee list. The German foundations, on the other hand, and I confess my prejudice here, were much more objective and unconstrained by the patterns of the past. I also found that the paperwork requirements of the various foundations varied enormously. Some ran comparatively clean-cut and simple operations; others attempted to oversee everything, demanding frequent and detailed reports that undoubtedly justified bloated staffs at foundation headquarters but contributed little, if anything, to responsible safeguarding of grant money.

Some radical rethinking of the purposes and functions of the institute was clearly and urgently required. The Atlantic Institute, I could only conclude, was one of those postwar international organizations that had to find a new role or face extinction. It had originally been conceived as a forum for serious discussion (what the Germans would call *ernste Gespräche*) of current international problems by the founder generation of Europeans and Americans who, like Dean Acheson, had been present at, and in many cases had personally contributed to, the creation of successful Western institutions like NATO and the European Economic Community. Their continued association in the institute as members of the Board of Governors, it was thought, would lend support to those institutions. A few foundations, particularly the Ford Foundation, had provided start-up grants, and many members of the Board of Governors were personally generous in adding to the institute's resources.

But many of the governors were now aging as foundations gradually got out of the business of making grants to cover overhead. My predecessor had introduced the idea of so-called participating members—firms that paid an annual amount to attend special meetings arranged for them—but the plaguing problem of maintaining a balanced cash flow to pay staff salaries, stage meetings, cover travel costs, remained. The Germans, and somewhat surprisingly the Japanese, who created a special Atlantic Institute committee of the Keidanren, were particularly effective in coordinating the contributions of their participating member firms.

The solution at which my professional staff and I arrived after much discussion was that the research capability of the institute must be expanded so that we could attract foundation grants and enhance our reputation by producing a series of innovative and scholarly books on major themes of the day to add to the already existing Atlantic Papers published quarterly.

A distraction during my early months as director general was the active proposal that the Atlantic Institute and the Trilateral Commission merge. The idea was that the commission would continue to organize its regular meetings in Europe, the United States, and Japan, and we would provide the research arm of the new combined organization. After much discussion, the project, which I personally favored, collapsed mainly but not entirely because of opposition within the Trilateral Commission. Given the failure of the merger proposal, it was sadly ironic that the French terrorist group Action Direct, years later during the time of my successor as director general, blew up the headquarters building of the Atlantic Institute charging that it was a front for the Trilateral Commission.

Once it became clear that we had to remain on our own, we moved ahead quickly with our new emphasis on research. We obtained substantial grants from the German Thyssen and Volkswagen Foundations as well as smaller amounts from other sources. That relieved the immediate pressure, and though in the subsequent years we never piled up any significant surpluses, we did manage to balance our accounts at the end of each calendar year. I had learned quickly, once out of the government, how important it was to be able to meet a payroll.

Without listing all the numerous books and monographs that the institute produced in the next five years, I note here a few that were in one way or another noteworthy: *Japanese Direct Foreign Investment*; *National Industrial Strategies and the World Economy*; *The Future of Berlin*; *The Internal Fabric of Western Security*; *Global Insecurity: A Strategy for Energy and Economic Renewal*. I had a hand in steering all of these. Some I edited and in one case partly wrote.

Apart from this outpouring of books and monographs, we continued to mount conferences for our governors and participating members as well as those smaller meetings connected specifically with research projects. Our big conferences reverberated with eloquent defenses of Western values, and the orators were worthy of respect. Some of our governors, however, had an overriding attachment to the past and the belief that anything good in the future must be largely a repetition of the past. It was difficult for them to think ahead into a different kind of world.

Perhaps the most spectacular of our conferences, at least in its public impact, was our twentieth anniversary meeting held in Brussels in 1980, cosponsored by the Center for Strategic Studies in Washington. Among the invited participants was Henry Kissinger. In his opening statement, fully reported by the European and American journalists present, he described the strategic situation in lugubrious terms, claiming that the Europeans would be fools to believe they could count on the strategic forces of the United States to come to the defense of the NATO alliance, since use of those forces would inevitably involve the destruction of the United States. Doubts about the ultimate reliability of the American nuclear deterrent had been expressed before, but usually in low key and in private. To have a former secretary of state declare this publicly was bound to stir up a storm. Kissinger realized that he might have said too much and tried to correct his statement for release to the press. But it was too late. The reporters present at the open session had heard him and taken careful notes. Many Europeans reacted with dismay, even though Kissinger no longer spoke for the government and other officials tried to provide reassurances.[1] There are some truths, or apparent truths, that are better publicly unexpressed. The whole problem of deterrence was too complex and wrapped in ambiguities to be captured in sweeping generalizations by a well-known public figure.

Into Academia

So the Atlantic Institute, though never flush with money, prospered in its work. Itinerant scholars from the United States, Germany, and Japan would use our facilities, and our library became a good general research tool. After more than five years of this, I was psychologically ready to leave, although I knew that departure from Paris would be a wrench for Faith and myself. On the other hand, we did not want to fall into the category of permanent expatriates, as so many of our elderly American friends had become, yearning to return to their roots in the United States but psychologically unable to manage the tearing move from Paris.

At this point, in the late spring of 1982, I received several phone calls from the University of Georgia, including one from Dean Rusk, who asked if I might be interested in being the first occupant of the newly created Rusk Chair in International Relations. Almost the last place in the world I could have imagined coming to was Athens, Georgia, but Faith had been raised in Georgia after some six years in Japan, and I had no particular desire or motive to return to either Washington or Chicago. I was not really ready to retire, and this might provide the opportunity to prolong my active life for some additional years. In any event Faith and I made a quick trip to Athens to look over the place and the university and to let the university look me over. We liked most of what we saw, and after I had made several presentations and met with the Political Science Department faculty, a firm offer was made, which I accepted beginning with the fall quarter of 1982. That gave me a few months in Paris to liquidate my work at the institute and to prepare for departure. I had already alerted John Loudon, chairman of the Board of Governors, and the staff that I might well be leaving and that John and the governors should think about finding a successor as director general. It was to be Richard Vine, also a retiring Foreign Service officer, who had just served as ambassador to Switzerland. I agreed to stay on as a member of the Board of Governors.

The prospect of leaving Paris, of course, saddened us, but there comes a time in one's life when a new opportunity must be grasped or lost forever. Carpe diem. The institute was in reasonably good shape, and I had no feeling of abandoning ship. We were confident that we would be returning to Paris on personal visits and as a consultant to International Advisory Associates of New York, with which I already had a strong relationship. We used those last months in the city to see and to do some of the things we had put off for the future. It was hard to give up our apartment on the Avenue Foch and to take off for the United States.

So many people have written so many eloquent things about the magic of Paris that to avoid triteness is not easy. One leaves with regret for the opportunities missed, the experiences postponed and now lost, but one is consoled by the kaleidoscope of good memories, aesthetic, social, and gustatory. It had been truly Hemingway's *Moveable Feast* for us. We knew that revisiting Paris would never be the same as living there, but one could always engage in a more active, if still Proustian, *recherche du temps perdu*. At the time, I did not know, of course, that during my years as professor at the University of Georgia, I would be back in Paris at least twice a year and sometimes more frequently.

Paris—a place of light but also of darkness. What Victor Hugo called "the heavy burden of history" hangs over the city. There is much blood as well as glory in that history. Every night close to our apartment at the Porte Dauphine we could witness a seamier side of Parisian life, and in the metros, under bridges, and in the Bois de Boulogne what seemed like an ever growing number of clochards displayed their poverty and their homelessness—though never in such oppressive numbers and misery as we were to see in the great American cities.

We said goodbys to the concierge, the waiters in our favorite restaurants, the green grocer, the cheese merchant, the butcher, and the baker in the Rue des Belles Feuilles and left for the United States—no longer by comfortable passenger ship but by jet plane—after the usual awful experience with the packers of our effects. How many times had we done this as diplomats, and how often did we lose cherished possessions to breakage, water seepage, or theft? It was to be no different this time. Of one thing we would be sure based on sad experience: no matter how costly, the insurance would not, and in some cases could not, cover our losses. We learned early and often that too close attachment to possessions could only lead to grief.

We were no longer a relatively young couple with three children leaving Paris, as we had been in 1956. Our later years there had been more staid and less exciting as befits the aging and the experienced. But it was a good time, and it helped both to round out our life abroad and to prepare us for the next phase to come.

I did not approach the role of Dean Rusk Professor of International Relations with much trepidation. I had the requisite Ph.D. degree, had once at Columbia seriously thought of an academic career, and was reasonably certain that I had kept up with the field and knew the jargon. It was not presumptuous to think that my experience as a diplomat might provide some insights into the real world of policy making that a pure academic might lack.

Faith had stayed on for a week in Athens after my return to Paris and demonstrated commendable initiative in finding and buying a house that turned out to be ideal for us both in terms of location, comfort, and beautiful surroundings, including an impressive stand of oak, hickory, and pine trees. It was to provide us for more years than we would have thought possible with the kind of real home that life in the Foreign Service had made impossible to achieve. Athens is a city in the Georgia Piedmont built literally in the midst of a forest, and walking my dogs—first Canute, our shepherd who died in 1984, and then Othello, our black labrador retriever—has provided a continuing nonurban type of experience and exercise. We have always had dogs: four generations of shepherds, a Scotty, a terrier, and now a labrador. They have been an integral part of our lives, friends on whose loyalty and affection you could always count. The sad part about dogs is their relatively short life spans. When a pet dog dies, a part of his master dies along with him. One must have a sense of proportion, I know. A dog's life is not a human life, but attachments between humans and animals can run deep.

I had few illusions about academic life as I came to the University of Georgia. My own background and continuing exposure to professors of all varieties while a government official and international institute director had amply demonstrated that they shared all the conceits and foibles to which flesh is heir. I understood that knowledge alone—and no one would deny that professors should be more knowledgeable than run-of-the-mill humans—does not automatically equate with wisdom, character, moderation, or common sense. Vanity, fecklessness, and pettiness are as common in academia as elsewhere in society. Superior knowledge does, however, enhance one's ability to rationalize and to indulge in outrageous speculation that a dose of common sense would exclude from the outset. Yet I also knew and could quickly observe at Georgia many academics with character and wisdom, as well as knowledge, who deserved highest admiration.

It was a pleasure to find that the University of Georgia—a megauniversity of some twenty-five thousand students at the time (now some thirty thousand)—had preserved many of the older traditions and gentilities and that most of the professors did not run madly off in pursuit of the latest academic fads, often imported from France after they had become more or less passé there. The Political Science Department, of which I would be a member, struck me as particularly strong.

On the whole, our university years have proved a happy and peaceful time for us. The cycle of the academic year has a peculiar rhythm of its own, and year after year passes almost imperceptibly. Suddenly one finds that a whole decade and more has gone by. Student faces come and go; some impress with their eagerness, brightness, and ambition, but they quickly pass from the scene to be replaced by a new crop. I always found the opening of the fall term a stimulating time before the academic routine takes hold. There is a recurrent sense of a new beginning and even a fresh vitality as the young students assemble, most of them at least eager for the new experiences that lie ahead. It is easy to understand why lifetime academics sometimes find that the transition from youth to maturity to retirement seems woefully rapid.

As someone who had previously been involved in conferences of all sorts, the academic penchant for national meetings within each discipline as well as regional and subdisciplinary meetings did not leave me aghast, if somewhat surprised. Participants frequently spout much nonsense at the superabundance of panels that these sessions feature, but one can sometimes also learn about the useful research of others, and there is always the pleasure of meeting old colleagues. David Lodge, the English novelist, has spoofed the "learned" meetings of English and comparative literature professors, and one can legitimately conclude from other supporting evidence that the level of absurdity in these fields sometimes exceeds that of the less faddish and more sober field of political science.

What I had not anticipated, however, was the countless intradepartmental, interdepartmental, and special meetings of all sorts that help to fill one's days as an academic. I had assumed that government was the worst offender in this regard, but the bureaucratization of universities has almost reached a point comparable to Washington. The more complicated the hierarchical structure, the more prolific will be the creation of paper and demands for paper from others. I wish it were possible to say that the progressively more generalized use of computers has streamlined the paper flow. The word processor, the fax machine, and E-mail just add to the flow of paper or of requests, although they admittedly make the production process more expeditious. I fail to note any real improvement in content, however.

Apart from the courses that I gave either regularly or occasionally—Introduction to Global Policy Studies and the Politics of International Economics at the undergraduate level, and International Political Economy, International Security, and Advanced Political Systems at the graduate level—I took over in 1983 the directorship of the Center for Global Policy Studies, a center primarily devoted to the encouragement of interdisciplinary studies in the university, with its own certificate program. I gave this up in 1991, having in 1987 also become codirector of the Center for East-West Trade Policy (later the Center for International Trade and Security). Off the campus I accepted numerous speaking engagements and served on a number of boards and committees and as a consultant. General student counseling and direction of M.A. theses and Ph.D. dissertations consumed additional time, as did the writing of many chapters of edited books and sporadic work on the present memoir. It was, all in all, a busy life, and I was glad as I moved into my seventies to still have the energy to do all these things. Thought of ultimate and complete retirement I put off from year to year.

The life of a senior diplomat may touch frequently on the fringes and sometimes on the core of events that shape history. The academic out of government is obviously not in the same position—a source of regret and frustration for some professors who would be movers and shakers. To attempt a chronology of my years as Dean Rusk Professor of International Relations at the University of Georgia would serve little purpose, but a few general comments from someone with my background may be of interest.

One traumatic experience for university officials came in 1985 with the lawsuit of Jan Kemp against the University of Georgia—a case that received national publicity and damaged the reputation of the university in a way typical of sloppy and one-sided media reporting. College football is a subject that can arouse deep emotions. Its critics view it as a modern-day version of the Roman circus calculated to distract the masses from more serious things such as, in this case, the abuse of college athletes. Its fans, including the vast majority of the alumni, think of it as a way both of recapturing their youth and of providing a basis for enthusiasm and dedication to a cause in the course of lives that provide all too few such opportunities. As it happens, many of the best football players, including running backs and pass receivers, are blacks. At many big football schools only a relatively small percentage of football players were ever graduated, only a much smaller percentage of these because professional teams entice them away before they complete their course work. There is obviously much human wastage involved. Some of the players are simply not capable of doing college-level work and eventually flunk or drop out. Prodded by the majority of university presidents, the NCAA (National Collegiate Athletic Association) has several times raised minimum entrance requirements for athletes on scholarship, eliciting the inevitable criticism from some that such actions were racially biased. One need not look for much logic when contrary arguments arouse the same emotional bias.

In any event, Jan Kemp won her suit against the university. A jury awarded her more than a million dollars in damages as well as restoration of the position in developmental studies from which she had been fired, she claimed, for having resisted exiting of athletes from developmental studies who had not met the requirements for such action. The case was lost when, in his initial salvo, the defense lawyer said something to the effect that football players were better off even with only a few years in college, since they would then no longer be condemned to be garbage collectors but could aspire to work for the post office. In the aftermath, Fred Davison, president of the university, and Virginia Trotter, vice president for academic affairs, resigned from their positions, and Jan Kemp became a national heroine. From the mountain of publicity the case received one detail emerged clearly: whatever the merit or lack of merit of the university's case, its legal representation in court had been completely outmaneuvered by Kemp's lawyer.

Before his resignation, Davison had already put into effect much tighter entrance criteria for athletes than the NCAA required, but media criticism of the university continued. Although I was not personally involved in any of this, I could not help regretting the continuing emotional bias of the media against a major institution like the university. Balanced reporting, any attempt to evaluate arguments and counterarguments in an objective way, was completely lacking. Sports and editorial writers for the *Atlanta Constitution* were among the worst in their display of animosity. The whole business confirmed what I already knew from sad experience: once the media has taken sides, fair and impartial reporting goes out the window.

College football has changed considerably over the years. It remains, as do basketball and other major sports, an exciting spectacle requiring strength, speed, and a high degree of skill. Entrance and retention standards are now higher at the University of Georgia and many similar institutions, although there are obviously some cheaters. Hand-tailored curricula for athletes continue to exist at some schools, but a greater percentage of athletes are at least getting college degrees than ten years ago. Much hypocrisy remains on both sides of the argument, which is really a subcase of the broader issue of the role of higher education in our society. Should possession of a college degree have become so important a part of the search for a job? Does it really provide the best kind of training for the positions in life that many will necessarily be fated to fill? Professional educators will generally provide affirmative answers by reflex to such questions. I confess I am not so sure, but I recognize that that is the way it is and that, at the very least, most professors contrive to ensure that the majority of those who leave with a B.A. or B.S. degree know at least a little more than when they entered and that the brightest and most promising students can still find the kind of stimulation, guidance, and exposure to the best of human knowledge that faculty can provide.

The possibility that the really athletically gifted may look forward to a professional career, particularly now that salaries and bonuses may run into the millions, has produced an efflorescence of so-called agents who represent the interests of athletes but also contribute to the process of corrupting them. Most coaches and athletic directors inveigh against the easy money promising athletes may be provided (as sort of retainers) as well as the money overly enthusiastic alumni may slip to star athletes, but they and the NCAA seem relatively powerless to do anything effective about such abuses. In a few spectacular cases the NCAA has had no other option but to intervene punitively; its general policy seems more or less random.

The Best of Human Knowledge

The verbal battles that have raged in academia over political correctness and multiculturalism provide a good example of what Aristotle called logomachy. Some officials and professors of some universities have spouted enough nonsense to confuse a whole generation of their students. Who in his right mind can deny that a truly educated person should know something about the major cultures that exist in the world today or have played a significant historical role? Yet who in his right mind can deny that the prevailing culture in which we find ourselves and which provides the constitutive elements of our sciences, art, music, and the achievements that make up our civilization requires the special attention and concentrated study of the truly educated person? The latter is precisely what some in academia deny today, whether it be repudiated as the work of dead white European males or the product of a historically dominant and repressive system. One could write, and some have done so, whole books on the subject pro and con. I fear that many students are being misled at some institutions of learning. From a purely pragmatic point of view, it makes little sense to waste those few years in a university by filling the heads of the young with subject matter that will not give them the substantive foundational knowledge, insights, and ability to find additional information to supplement what they already know. Unless they hope to teach the same subjects in a university or college setting, they will find themselves seriously handicapped in taking advantage of such opportunities as our competitive society provides.

It does not require the skills of a dowser to identify the best of human knowledge that should be the heart of what a truly educated person has learned. Despite all the howling from the wings, there is still a broad consensus among the professoriat about what students need to know, even though each teacher will perhaps weight the content somewhat in favor of his or her own area of specialization. That is why undergraduate catalogs contain such a multiplicity of courses. Most will still accept the need for a core curriculum to provide, preferably at an early point in college careers, the foundation upon which to build further learning.

More than fifty years ago the Columbia University Press published in book form a version of my Ph.D. dissertation entitled *Power and Morals*.[2] In it I attacked some social scientists for not understanding the logical implications of the broader epistemological and metaphysical systems that they personally endorsed or at least passively accepted. My thesis remains valid today. With a few exceptions, only those deeply conversant with political or sociological theory seem to have any inkling of the broad philosophic assumptions they implicitly make and of their implications. In arriving at a more precise breakdown of the best of human knowledge, I would include a strong dose of philosophy, its history, its great figures, and its continuing quest for answers to the fundamental issues of human existence.

We all owe a certain deference to the sincere sensitivities of others. Abstention from gratuitous insult or slander is a universal obligation. To this extent I find nothing wrong with the emphasis on so-called political correctness that has swept so many university campuses in recent years, if it is defined essentially as a code of polite behavior. When, however, this reaches the point of absurdity, when elaborate codes emanate from university authorities proscribing freedom of speech and practically any kind of behavior that someone might find objectionable on some ground, the whole thing becomes an exercise in the grotesque. I could only be thankful that the stupidities perpetrated on a few northern and western campuses have not caught hold at the University of Georgia.

I would not want to give the impression that I spend much time sitting in my office or at home fulminating in the void about the inanities of academia. On the whole I have found my time as a professor stimulating and a fitting end passage to an active life. Most of my colleagues are men and women of sincere dedication to their disciplines, and if they sometimes stress methodology at the expense of substance, this is the price they pay for being social scientists. The mathematization of economics, political science, and to a lesser degree even sociology, in the view of some who have watched the process, took place partly at least because of inferiority feelings with respect to the so-called hard sciences. Academic economics, as taught in many departments of economics, has become more and more remote from real life, and unfortunately the same is true to a lesser extent of political science. The stuff that the editors regularly accept for publication in the *American Economic Review* and the *American Political Science Review* makes the working government official wince at its irrelevance to the real problems with which he must deal. I found it thus as a diplomat at a time when the so-called behavioralists dominated the study of political science, and while their active influence has diminished, much of their heritage lingers on.

As an official I criticized research that was not operationally or policy relevant, but I am willing to admit that in the quest for knowledge such a seemingly utilitarian standard is too extreme. Certainly in the pure sciences, the arts, literature, and linguistics, as well as in the social sciences, adding to the sum total of human knowledge is a good thing even if such knowledge has no apparent value for the understanding of why we are here or the living of the good life. What one can object to is the reaching of conclusions, sometimes by the use of elaborate methodologies, that are clearly contrary to fact, or so obvious that it is a waste of time and labor to attain them so circuitously.

In an ahistorical era during which the popular culture stresses the immediate sensation, the immediate gratification of desire, and almost compulsive narcissism, the sense of history dwindles and for many vanishes. I have found many students, even some bright ones, historically illiterate, young men and women who cannot really understand where we are because they have only the vaguest idea of how we got here. I have therefore found it necessary to interlard all my courses with a great deal of historical background. In a more general sense, no one with any pretense to being educated can be disinterested in the broad historical forces that have shaped the world and our country during this troubled century. Henry Ford's oft-quoted remark that "history is bunk" was the comment of an uneducated man, no matter how ingenious he was in adapting the assembly line process to the mass manufacture of automobiles.

I do not deny, of course, that profound epistemological and methodological questions arise in the study of history. One in particular has troubled me in the light of my own experience: when the actual participants in important events depart from the scene, perhaps leaving at most memoirs or some other record of their experience, can future historians reconstruct the past accurately, purely on the basis of such written materials and artifacts as may survive? This is not just a problem of writing a history of Assyria or some other civilization long dead. The revisionists of the sixties and seventies who tried to reinterpret the origins of the cold war lacked insight into the way decision makers and those who influenced them actually felt about the Soviet threat. The documentary record seldom provides this kind of information. The result was lopsided history. Today we have an enormous proliferation of sources: oral history projects, systematic collections of official documents, books galore—but will they suffice? As time goes on, will the absence of recorded sentiments, beliefs, and reactions on the part of some decision makers so dilute or distort the recording of events and their causes that a definitive appraisal becomes impossible?

In the final analysis, however, I believe, one can reconstruct the main course of events with reasonable accuracy. Insofar as there are written contemporary records, we can convey what those records say and draw logical conclusions. The imputation of motives obviously presents more difficulty, particularly in the absence of any available statements by those making decisions or by those in a position to know what the motives of decision makers might have been. However, even here one can make logical deductions provided one accepts that such deductions are at best only probable and not certain. The arrogant historian aflush with his own prejudices and preconceived notions, who is prepared to go beyond the evidence or to impose on the evidence his own preconceptions, gives the writing of history a bad name. The more modest historian, who recognizes both his own limitations and those imposed by the considerations I have noted, will come much closer to the truth. Needless to say, the denial of any possibility of objective history now so fashionable is clearly professionally suicidal.

The Pressures and Pleasures of Academe

The popular image of academic life usually does not involve a harassed professor constantly pressured by students, administrators, and the demands of his own personal life and scholarship. In some ways the academic does indeed seem to have a relatively easy life. The physical demands are not heavy, but I found along with many of my colleagues that there was frequently not enough time to do the teaching, the reading, the research, and, perish the thought, the thinking that one would have liked. A conscientious professor will devote a great deal of time to his or her students. Those working for higher degrees need considerable supervision as they write their research papers, theses, and dissertations. The amount of bad prose that one must plough through is deadly; perhaps only the professor of law condemned to the casebook method of instruction is exposed to more. But there are the compensatory intermittent new insights, the startling bit of inspired research, and occasionally even some reasonably elegant prose.

One experience I was spared was the need to strive for tenure shared by young assistant professors. The pressure for them to publish in so-called refereed journals overshadows their first years. Some, often excellent teachers, do not achieve tenure because they lacked the necessary number of published articles. Books seem to have somewhat inferior status, even though the effort and scholarship that go into writing a book clearly exceeds that of an article, or even a series of articles.

I have been around long enough and in enough different settings to know that one should never underestimate the role of old-boy networks in awarding scholarships, endowment grants, and acceptances for publication in refereed journals. Pure merit will sometimes shine out, but in the world of journal decision making, previous contacts and associations make a big difference. Academe cannot rise above this harsh reality, but it will in most cases recognize true merit in the long run. Good people who don't quite fit will fall by the wayside, but those who make it and achieve tenure will move into the heights of status. They will be secure in their jobs barring egregious bad behavior, and allowing for the possible effects of moves to force through periodic reviews of tenured professors.

Certainly one of the great pleasures of my time at the University of Georgia was the opportunity for many years before his death to have frequent contact with former secretary of state Dean Rusk. He was still actively teaching in the law school when I arrived in 1982, but some years later ill health led to his becoming professor emeritus but still a regular attendee at his office in the Rusk Center for Comparative and International Law. I found his mind not only lucid but the source of many sage observations about both past and current events. This was a man whom some historians have not treated well, dismissing him as sort of an owlish enigma. My conviction is that the final judgment of history will be much more positive.

Academic Foibles

The tolerance of some academics for the patently absurd, particularly when it has a foreign label of origin, is seemingly unlimited. Over the postwar years I have watched a whole succession of European existentialists, structuralists, semioticians, and most recently postmodernists (especially deconstructionists), many of them French, become the latest fashion in academia—particularly in the humanities, comparative literature, and indeed some of the social sciences—usually long after they have gone out of style in Europe. The long line of Sartre, Beauvoir, Lévi-Strauss, Adorno, Eco, Althuser, Lacan, Barthes, Foucault, Derrida, and DeMan—and who shall be next we know not—has passed by, or in the case of Derrida still currently presides. When I return to Paris, I find them passé, but in the United States the combination of congenial ideology, the academic compulsion to publish, and the repudiation of common sense spawns endless articles and books. What effect all of this has on malleable young minds, impressed by jargon and impervious to the bad prose that seems almost standard for the so-called learned journals, I do not know—but it cannot be good.

Why devotees of Derrida or DeMan should think they can support any cause at all within the context of the kind of epistemology they espouse escapes me. They don't recognize a solipsist when they see one or the logical implications of solipsism in undermining any cause or generalization including the basic claim to be correct or indeed to have anything worthwhile saying at all. Reading the stuff put out by deconstructionists is both intellectually nauseating and a sad reminder of the jargon to which some can sink.

I have seen much in a fairly long life spent in many parts of the world, but I take my hat off to the self-conceived cognoscenti when it comes to the invention and defense of nonsense. There seems to be no limit to the absurdities to which an aberrational logic rigidly pursued can lead. What is lacking, I suppose, is that modicum of common sense that prevents most people, faced with ridiculous conclusions, from pursuing them to the end.

I have made a serious effort during recent years to read some of this stuff on the unlikely possibility that golden nuggets of wisdom lie hidden somewhere in all the verbiage. I have not found them. Without indulging too much in wishful thinking, one can indeed see the beginnings of a counterattack within the academy. The battle will be verbally bloody for reputations are on the line; the outcome may well be mutual exhaustion.

When I was a State Department official, as I have noted before, I was impressed over the years by the irrelevance to the conduct of foreign policy of much academic research in the social sciences. This was particularly true of the so-called behavioralist school that dominated political science for many years and sought wisdom in the quantification of the irrelevant. There were some notable exceptions, of course, that I found provided new ways of understanding complicated political phenomena, and there were many historians as well who did not try to compress the record of the past into a preconceived mold of theory. But the genuine nuggets among the debris were all too scarce.

This leads inevitably to some possibly unconventional thoughts about the role that academic research has come to play in general. I do not speak here primarily of the hard sciences that impose a prescription of their own in the search for truth, except to note that even here the compulsion to do research has led to some conspicuous recent examples of doctored evidence and outright falsification. What, however, does worthwhile research mean in the social sciences and the humanities? Obviously the quest for new knowledge or the review of established knowledge to verify its accuracy requires research within a reasonable definition of the term, that is, study of available documents, previous literature, and the weight of the evidence. That is how we add to the sum total of human learning. Whatever contribution this memoir might make will derive in part, at least, from the research behind it as well as the memories of actual experiences that I alone can recall.

An essential problem, however, arises out of the sheer multiplicity of putative researchers. The logical result of the demand for at least some measure of originality is an ever thinner slice of subject matter for M.A. theses and Ph.D. dissertations, especially in the more popular areas of the humanities and social sciences. Established experts also need to publish or perish if they do not have tenure, and those who do have it need to publish to maintain scholarly reputations. According to Professor Michael Shenefelt, in 1987 academic journals published more than five hundred articles on Shakespeare. This sort of thing has led to the description of the modern scholar as knowing more and more about less and less. Renaissance men have been scarce in every generation, but the broad-gauged scholar interested in many subjects apart from his or her own field of specialization, particularly those profound issues that determine the ultimate meaning of human endeavor, is a relative rarity among academic careerists seeking only their personal advancement. Fortunately, I have found, both at the University of Georgia and at other universities and colleges, enough men and women of high intellectual stature to make one think that personal participation in the academic enterprise can be essentially worthwhile.

According to Professor Shenefelt, much of the stuff published by academic journals falls into the category of what he calls "disposable scholarship" intended not so much to be read but rather to be cited as published products in résumés. The end result has been "a wonderful profusion of humbug."[3]

Much of what he has to say is admittedly true, particularly in those areas that are enjoying a golden age of gibberish and execrable prose reinforced by the process of peer review. In the social sciences, as well as in the physical and biological sciences, peer review can serve a useful purpose. It can also serve as an excuse for not reading the article itself on the part of these passing judgment on the author, since his peers have presumably already done that in evaluating it for printing. Despite all this, articles do appear (some even reasonably well written) that make a net contribution to the sum total of human knowledge. There are many able and conscientious professors teaching and writing, including many in the Political Science Department of the University of Georgia, who avoid to the extent humanly possible the constraints and pretensions of academe and bring to their duties redeeming senses of humor and proportion.

I recognize that little of what I have said about university life is new or profound, but it does reflect, I believe, conclusions drawn from reasonably objective observation of the passing academic scene and shared by many of my colleagues.

Can Economists Add and Subtract?

As someone who had done a postdoctoral year studying economics at Harvard and who had been deeply interested in economic developments as a diplomat, I could not help becoming bemused in 1981, while still in Paris, by the so-called supply-side economics adopted by the new Reagan administration. It struck me then that the Laffer curve was a frivolity that unfortunately fit into the predispositions of the president and his economic advisers. The tax legislation of 1981 appeared to be the ultimate folly, destructive, in the words of James Schlesinger, of the fiscal basis of the U.S. government.

When I came to the University of Georgia the following year and prepared to teach International Political Economy, I was appalled to find how many economists seemed to be comfortable with what had happened in Washington. From my admittedly sporadic exposure to American and British economic journals during my diplomatic days, and more regular exposure at the Atlantic Institute, I had been aware how more and more detached from reality a great portion of economic theory had become. Econometrics, microeconomic theorizing about the market, a sizable segment of macroeconomics—the whole business—had little relevance to the actual processes of government or economic behavior.

Then came the revelations of David Stockman, Reagan's director of the Office of Budget and Management—which, depending on what one emphasized, could lead to the conclusion either that the administration had simply stumbled into economic and statistical quicksand from which it could not extricate itself or that the whole thing was a surreptitious attempt to whittle down the size and responsibilities of government by denying it adequate funding. The latter would have required a degree of Machiavellianism that seemed beyond the capacity of the president, and in more recent statements on the subject Stockman seems to have come out in favor of the morass explanation.[4]

As the Reagan years went on and economic growth returned with zooming budgetary and current account deficits, I was again surprised at how few economists attributed this growth to the obvious cause. As any good neo-Keynesian knew, if a country had budget deficits of the size that we were running in the United States, demand would be sufficiently stimulated to cause economic growth, even at a time when overvaluation of the dollar due to high U.S. interest rates was destroying the competitiveness of our old-line industrial base. The supply-siders had faded away, along with the increased government revenues that they had predicted but that never came. The monetarists who took over from the supply-siders and dominated the Reagan administration espoused a doctrine that contained some truths about the relationship of money supply to economic growth and inflation, but they never quite caught on to the overriding reality that debt accumulation was pumping enormous amounts of money into our economy to stimulate demand in a number of crucial sectors, not least that part dedicated to the production of military equipment and the maintenance of a huge military establishment. Eventually, of course, even Reagan's and Bush's unacknowledged Keynesianism on a grand scale could not withstand the causal pressures of the business cycle.

As a political scientist teaching international economics, I could not help but wonder why more economists did not worry about whether the whole structure of debt and debt-stimulated growth would come crashing down. A minority did express concern, of course, about the ever increasing burden that accumulating debt would impose on our economy. Their voices were seldom heeded or dismissed as overly alarmist. The Bush presidency fell victim to the poor economic advice that its own experts provided. Within a few years, of course, the emphasis has dramatically shifted. Ultimate budget balancing as a goal of policy has become the vogue regardless of possible economic consequences.

Another economic phenomenon about which I could only wonder was the relative insouciance of many economists about the growing international debt of the United States. Some argued that it didn't really matter, others that it mattered but that we couldn't do much about it until we restored our lost international competitiveness. Some tried to make it vanish with mathematical wizardry by pointing out that the net international indebtedness put out by the Department of Commerce took American foreign direct investment at book value rather than current value and thus greatly understated our assets abroad. The point was well taken, and the Department of Commerce obliged by dropping its annual table disclosing our total net foreign indebtedness. The President's Council of Economic Advisers also obliged by not substituting its own estimate for the new missing Commerce table. Yet anyone who watched this statistical manipulation could, of course, arrive at the growing indebtedness figures by putting together other Commerce data.

Many years ago, Baron Alexandre Lamfalussy, recently head of the Interim Agency of the European Union, declared American international imbalances to be "unsustainable," and Lester Thurow compared the situation to an economic black hole. They were wrong, of course, at least in the short term. Foreign capital continued to flow into the United States to finance further international deficits, and the higher profits of American multinationals operating abroad permitted greater annual transfers back to the United States than the remitted profits of foreign firms operating in the United States. But with some exceptions, the degree of equanimity maintained by most academic economists, and many government economists as well, could not but leave this political economist perplexed. International indebtedness plus ever mounting domestic budgetary deficits partly financed by foreign capital were bound to have some negative effects on our capacity to conduct an effective foreign policy. Our mounting international indebtedness, of course, had to be serviced. Poor Peter Tarnov, former president of the New York Council on Foreign Relations appointed as undersecretary of state for political affairs in the Clinton administration! He had the misfortune to state early in 1993 that our economic weaknesses meant that we could not play as important a role internationally as in the past! The reaction to the truth so uttered silenced him for some time.[5]

Extracurricular Activities

One of the pleasures of academe is the opportunity that it provides to engage in activities off the campus not directly connected with the university. Shortly after arriving in Athens I became associated with the Southern Center for International Studies in Atlanta, first as a senior fellow, then as a member of the Board of Governors, chairman of the Board of Governors for a two-year term, and then again a member of the board. Peter White, the president, and his wife, Julia White, vice president and legal counsel, were full of ideas and energy. Before I came, the former board chairman,

Ann Cox Chambers, had resigned over differences of policy between her, the Whites, and the majority of the board. Her successor, Sam Ayoub, also resigned. Some unfortunate negative publicity for the center followed, including a hatchet job on the Whites in the *Atlanta Constitution*. This was the inauspicious setting when I took over as board chairman in 1988. My heritage when I left the chairmanship two years later was a still functioning center with improved financial prospects, a Board of Trustees pretty much free of internal dissension, better general morale, and an ambitious program for the future. The Whites and the center's vice president for educational activities, Cedric Suzman, have shown much imagination in devising activities that won a Peabody Award and put the center at the forefront of public television and the production of educational videos.

Like most nonprofit organizations without a significant endowment, the Southern Center lived from one annual budget to the next. Maintaining a balanced cash flow of revenues and expenses remained an elusive goal. In recent years, however, some substantial foundation grants have eased the situation, but ensuring adequate financial resources will continue to be a problem. Fortunately, the center has never depended on U.S. government funding. With the partial drying up of U.S. government research funding in the post–cold war era, even the so-called Beltway bandits in the Washington, D.C., area have faced harder times, and some will inevitably have to close down. The comings and goings of nonprofit organizations have almost a biological regularity. Their closure can be traumatic for officers and staff, and the quality of their work may be inversely proportional to their viability. Some people are born to be natural fundraisers, just as some turn out to be consummate salespersons.

Since coming to the University of Georgia and until 1995, Faith and I were able to make a minimum of two trips a year to Europe, and frequently more. My association as consultant to International Advisory Associates, a New York educational firm with many clients spread across the country in the community of institutional investors, provided the context for semiannual visits usually to Paris, Frankfurt or Bonn, and London but sometimes also to Rome, Madrid, Berlin, Vienna, Brussels, Budapest, and Prague. Since we met at each stop with senior officials including central bankers, these trips provided a valuable means of keeping current with political and economic developments frequently not available in the press. There have also been numerous other trips to conferences and meetings on economic and political subjects that, I trust, are less frivolous than those of the itinerant professors of English and comparative literature so amusingly described by David Lodge in several of his novels.

I might add that for three and a half years (1990–93) I served as member of the Board of Directors of Mercedes Benz North America—a period of declining sales for a quality product caused by the combination of appreciated deutschemark, luxury car tax, gas guzzler tax, American recession, high production costs, and Japanese competition. I would put it under the heading of useful and pleasant experience, though I would be the first to admit that I brought little to my board membership in the way of specific knowledge of the American car market. I was able, however, to make presentations at board meetings about the American political and economic scene. In 1992 German members had a hard time believing that Clinton would ever beat Bush, and my remarks to that effect in July were greeted with much skepticism. I fear German business leaders were as capable of wishful thinking as their American counterparts.

. . . .

On July 1, 1997, I retired as the Dean Rusk Professor of International Relations at the conclusion of fifteen academic years at the University of Georgia. Effective the same date the State Board of Regents approved my emeritus status. I shall, of course, greatly miss the daily contact with students and the vitality and aspiration they bring to life, but I hope to continue to be available for such individual consultation as they may find helpful. Apart from pursuing intellectual and religious interests for which there has been insufficient time in the past for either reading or thought, I also look forward to continuing relevant activity on campus and as a member of some outside boards and organizations. What this will add up to only time will tell.

11 Reflections

....

Who can deny the advantages of hindsight? Those reflecting on the past in the aftermath of the tumultuous events of 1989 and the years that followed in Eastern Europe and the former Soviet Union now have the advantage of a perspective that would have been impossible a few years ago. All the expertise in the world did not lead anyone, within my knowledge, to predict the complete collapse of Communist regimes within such a short period of time and with so little effort to maintain themselves in power by the use of force. It is easy now to say that what happened was preordained, that the structural and operational weaknesses of those systems, whether in the German Democratic Republic, Poland, or the Soviet Union itself guaranteed their inevitable collapse. The chain of causation is relatively simple to trace when we can observe it as past history. In a peculiarly ironic exemplification of the classical Marxist doctrine that economics determines politics, the gradual disintegration of the Soviet economy first brought Gorbachev to power and then destroyed him and the Soviet Union as a coherent state.

The fact is, of course, that we in the West did not really know how intrinsically weak the malfunctioning Communist economies really were. We now are aware of how doctored, how essentially phony, their official statistics that measured economic performance and the productivity of individual enterprises actually turned out to be. Our intelligence services, our governments, all regurgitated these falsified data as if they were gospel and inevitably drew faulty conclusions about the strength and durability of individual countries and of the Soviet bloc as a whole. I was no better than the rest in distinguishing the false from the true, although the arguments of Professor Franklin Holtzman of Tufts University that the CIA was systematically overestimating Soviet military expenditures impressed me.[1] In any event, that is all behind us. Whether we have learned any real lessons about the collection and trustworthiness of economic data remains to be seen. In any event, a situation directly parallel to the confrontation of the two nuclear superpowers in the cold war period seems unlikely to recur.

Another reality was that we in the West were only dimly aware of the psychological readiness for change in Eastern Europe. We knew, of course, that the prevailing Communist regimes oppressed their populations with varying degrees of harshness while providing all sorts of privileges for the party elites (although we were generally unaware of the deep degree of their personal corruption). We had come to accept that populations massively bombarded with state-directed propaganda and subjected to controlled education were so intellectually regimented that they would scarcely know how to demand fundamental political and economic change—this despite the Hungarian uprising of 1956 and the Prague Spring of 1968 as well as the general availability of Western radio and even television in border areas and the environs of West Berlin.

A puzzling question is why, when confronted with massive street demonstrations and other signs of popular discontent, Communist regimes (with the exception of Ceauşescu's in Romania) collapsed without any real attempt to use the security and military forces under their control to break up these demonstrations by violence. I know of no complete answer, but I would scarcely attribute the relative moderation of response to the humane instincts of Communist leaders. Ever since my period in Hungary in the late 1960s, I have been referring to a phenomenon that I labeled "the waning of ideological fervor in Communist systems." There was a time when Marxism or Marxism-Leninism provided a sort of ersatz religion for which its devotees were willing to make extreme personal sacrifices and in some cases even to give up their lives. I found little such fervor in Hungary or the rest of Eastern Europe and concluded that these regimes were run by leaders primarily interested in the privileges and perquisites that the exercise of power brought with it, but largely bereft of any idealistic or visionary motivation. Mr. Kádár probably believed that the goulash Communist way of organizing society was the best way, but in my view he knew too much about the leadership of the Soviet Union to have any profound ideological commitment to Marxism as a philosophy. It is easy for such a leader to confuse personal interest with the welfare of the people. The *nomenklatura* (to use that now popular term to describe those who ran the party, the government, and the economy in Communist systems) obviously had much to lose if it gave up power, but since its motives were essentially selfish, its top members lacked the firm sense of purpose and the enduring will to stand up against the populace. So ensued the surprising collapse of regimes seemingly firmly in power.

The Limits of Intelligence

Critics of American intelligence operations have pointed to the failure of the CIA and other branches of the U.S. government intelligence establishment to predict the events of the post-1989 period and, in fact, their seeming effort to hang on to increasingly obsolete claims in the face of clearly emerging trends. It is argued that the prevailing analysis of the Mikhail Gorbachev period, and the weaknesses it revealed, fell short of what was necessary to adequate understanding of the internal situation in the Soviet Union. The nongovernmental community of Soviet experts itself was, of course, split down the middle on the meaning and the durability of the Gorbachev phenomenon.[2]

At least some of this criticism derives from unrealistic assumptions about how the CIA operates and what its capacity actually is. A plethora of spy thrillers abetted by Hollywood movies have created an image of intelligence that has little relationship to the real thing. As an ambassador who had certain general supervisory responsibilities for intelligence operations in the country of his assignment (though obviously not involved in the details), I could observe in a general way what was taking place. Over the long years, in Washington and in the field, I learned to evaluate both the strengths and weaknesses of the CIA.

One should not expect miracles from the organization. The James Bonds do not exist, and there are clear limits to what any intelligence-gathering organization can produce. The CIA has an enormous bureaucracy back in Arlington, Virginia, doing essentially what is called "research and analysis." Much of the raw material does not come from agency sources at all but from the standard political and economic reporting of State Department missions around the world. I can recall how irritated Secretary Rogers and I would become when, at National Security Council meetings during Nixon's first term, each session would begin with a rather laborious reading by CIA director Richard Helms of the so-called intelligence situation for the day. Most of it seemed to Rogers and me to be little more than a regurgitation of telegrams from our diplomatic posts that we had read earlier in the morning. I doubt that the situation has changed much over the years. The hot political and economic information from major or minor posts will in all probability have been reported in embassy transmissions over the names of the ambassador or chargé d'affaires.

If there was a failure of analysis and of forecasting with reference to the Communist East, it was, of course, partly an intelligence failure. But the failure must be shared much more broadly than to blame it all on the CIA, which, in the future, will have an important, if somewhat more limited, mission.

I do not speak here, of course, of CIA so-called covert operations such as the Bay of Pigs, the overthrow of President Allende of Chile, the support of insurgents in Nicaragua and Angola—all of which have suffered criticism on various grounds. Neither do I refer to the signal and electronic intelligence-gathering operations of the National Security Agency or to the kind of military-related intelligence gathered by various service attachés in our embassies around the world. Judgment of their value must be made on the basis of different criteria, but few of these produce political or economic intelligence of a kind likely to be of major use to American diplomacy.

The Unification of Germany

To someone like myself, who for a goodly portion of his life has been concerned about things German, the unification of that country in the autumn of 1990 came as a climactic event in a period of great change. When the opportunity rose after the collapse of Communism in East Germany, Chancellor Helmut Kohl acted with decisiveness in the face of opposition party flabbiness to push through the process. Without the concurrence of Mr. Gorbachev and a strong American supportive position, as well as British and French acquiescence to reality, the whole thing might have been unduly delayed. There was a certain inevitability in the chain of events, but Mr. Kohl will ultimately deserve well, I believe, in the historical judgment of his performance.

The behavior of some German intellectuals in both the West and the East proved to be disgracefully wrongheaded. Presumably on the assumption that the system in the GDR was somehow superior to that in the Federal Republic, writers like Günter Grass, Christa Wolf, and others argued against unification. They found a ready audience among fellow intellectuals, and even such a German politician as the SPD chancellor candidate Oskar Lafontaine had to eat his expressed early hesitations. The Communist leadership of the GDR had successfully managed to conceal the degree of its own corruption and the intrinsic rottenness of the economic and political structure it had created. One could only wonder once again at the depths of illogic, if not moral dishonesty, to which some intellectuals can sink in the face of obvious reality. This having been said, the persistence of the so-called *Mauer im Kopf* (wall in the head) between many East and West Germans is a psychological problem that may require a generation to erase.

The aftermath so far has, of course, proved deeply disappointing in both monetary and human cost, only partly because doctored GDR statistics concealed how near collapse the whole economic system had come. Disillusionment in both East and West was inevitable, but the process of amalgamation goes on, and after a further period of trial, I am confident, a united Germany will emerge with moderate prosperity in the East. To expect economic homogeneity is to expect the impossible. In all countries one will find more prosperous and less prosperous regions. We certainly have such disparities in the United States, as did the Federal Republic of Germany prior to unification. There will always be the discontented and those who rebel against the inequalities and injustices that the institutions of humankind impose or allow. In the final analysis, I suppose, it is the system that creates the most overall wealth through superior efficiency and productivity, and distributes that wealth with greater relative equality, that can morally be justified, despite all the imperfections that inevitably must inhere in any system run by men and women. We have now become aware that the degree of environmental friendliness involved must also be introduced into the moral equation.

Thinking back into those long cold war years when the achievement of German unification seemed like an idle dream, dependent as its realization was on the willingness of the Soviet Union to redefine its basic security interests in Europe, one can now pose some new and perplexing questions. A puzzlement that thoughtful diplomats and historians must face is to what extent the tumultuous changes that took place in the Soviet bloc and the former Soviet Union itself in 1989 and thereafter were inextricably linked to an internal chain of events that would have worked itself out largely without regard to external factors. Was, for example, the *Ostpolitik* of Willy Brandt actually an important part of the chain of causation that led to German reunification, and what, if anything, did the period of Nixonian détente really contribute to the process of change in the USSR? For those to whom the Eastern policy of the Brandt government came as a welcome relief from a seemingly stale and exhausted formula, it is difficult now to admit that it may only have served as a historical blip that, if anything, merely helped to shore up a bankrupt regime in East Germany. I suppose the same could be said about the entire West German program of aid (starting with the Adenauer government) provided in various generous forms to the GDR. The pretext, of course, was that all this aid ultimately contributed to some improvement in the lives of fellow Germans living in the GDR, and no one can doubt the West German sincerity or generosity of motives that went into this over the years.

In his book *In Europe's Name: Germany and the Divided Continent*, Timothy Garton Ash seems at times to argue that *Ostpolitik* had more bad consequences than good.[3] It was obviously based on the assumption that any fundamental change in the East would have a much longer time horizon than it actually required. Reunification as a goal of policy, precisely because it seemed so far in the future, tended to be submerged in the more urgent limited goals of *Ostpolitik*. The great tectonic movements of history have their own momentum and complicated chain of causality that frequently catch the politicians and the experts by surprise.

After the euphoria of 1990–91, the problem of absorbing the former East Germany into the Federal Republic was magnified by a major downturn of the business cycle in the European Community. Europeans and particularly Germans expressed concern that their economic problem was not only cyclical but structural, that decades of ever more expensive social programs, costly wage settlements, and a diminution of the work ethic had destroyed the basic competitiveness of core industries in an emerging industrial world of lower-cost countries and the omnipresent Japanese drive to export. Imitating large American multinationals, major German and European firms tried during 1993–94 to cut costs by large-scale reductions in force around the world but particularly in the European mother countries.

As I write this, the mood in Germany and the rest of Europe is still relatively gloomy as unemployment remains high and economic growth low. German money has continued to flow into the five states of the former GDR, some have said into a seeming black hole, while the public finances of the Federal Republic have gone into heavy deficit.[4] Although improvements of infrastructure have become evident, more general signs of economic progress in the East have come with disappointing slowness. With some bemusement I remember the concerns expressed by some commentators that this new united Germany would prove to be an economic powerhouse that would sweep all aside as it economically dominated Europe. Such views were exaggerated then and seem even more unrealistic now. The strength of the deutschemark, partly due to capital flows induced by the high interest rate policy of the Bundesbank itself, justified by the central bank as an anti-inflationary necessity, gave a false impression of overall economic strength.

The seeming inability of the German government a few years ago effectively to control the antidemocratic and criminal activities of skinheads and other neo-Nazi groups was bound to precipitate alarmist commentary about the political future of the country. The reasons for the violence were clear enough: they were perhaps an inevitable reaction on the part of a small, discontented minority looking for a cause, against the flood of refugees, mainly from Eastern Europe, that ended up in the Federal Republic. Given our own historical experience, we Americans should be the last not to recognize the antagonisms that foreigners can arouse in what had been a largely ethnically homogeneous country.

To my mind, the danger of a significant neo-Nazi, fascist, extreme right-wing—call it what you will—revival in Germany is likely to arise only against a background similar to that in the Weimar Republic of domestic economic chaos, hyperinflation, destruction of the middle class, deep worldwide depression, and a breakdown of effective government partly because of constitutional weaknesses. All of these occurred in the 1920s and early 1930s, but only the blackest pessimist can envisage a repetition in the years ahead.

One can see some difficult years before the world as we move beyond the end of this century, but I do not see looming catastrophe caused by a Germany again gone haywire. Demography alone assures a diminishing, aging population in the years ahead.

The Cold War Ends but Our Problems Remain

The cold war brought many uncertainties, but it also brought to the Western alliance and the governments that formed it a clarity of purpose and a sense of rectitude over an extended period that is unusual in human affairs. It also involved the assurance that official behavior patterns in Eastern Europe and the former Soviet Union would follow certain predictable paths. One could, moreover, assume that Soviet dominance over its so-called satellites left them little room for individual initiatives or behavior that Moscow would consider deviant.

If the cold war gave us a fixed frame of reference and a seemingly clear sense of what was right and what was wrong, even our deviations from principle could be excused as cases of the end justifying the means. It also helped us to shove under the rug, or at least to subordinate, other pressing problems such as growing Third World poverty and environmental degradation. The revisionists who argued that the United States bore equal, or perhaps even more than equal, responsibility for the cold war could be dismissed as academic no-accounts detached on their campuses from the harsh realities of life—a judgment that I largely shared and still believe to have been essentially correct, despite the admitted need to revise our assessment of some decisions on both sides and the thinking behind them.

I can accept, therefore, that we are still far from having completely definitive answers to all of the conundrums of postwar history. I would essentially agree, however, with the judgments, incorporating much new material from Soviet archives, of John Lewis Gaddis in his latest book, *We Now Know: Rethinking Cold War History.*[5] As has been generally the case, Gaddis's views are the most scholarly and balanced on this whole issue of cold war responsibility.

Is the claim in the West to have won the cold war justified? I should think we can honestly answer in the affirmative by any reasonable definition of victory. We have witnessed the complete collapse of Marxist-Leninist systems in Eastern Europe and the former Soviet Union, if not so much through our efforts as the inherent weaknesses of those systems. We are still, however, in an uncertain period of transition with perhaps more upheaval in prospect. Perhaps it is better not to speak in terms of victory or defeat but of the end of an era—the era of the gulag, of purges, of crushed revolutions as in Hungary and Czechoslovakia—and of the opening to new opportunities that may or may not be realized.

An error of assessment that many of us made in both the West and the East during those early heady days of 1989–90 was to imagine that the transition from centrally planned to market-oriented economies would be relatively easy and self-reinforcing once the will to do so was present. There was almost a talismanic belief that, if one repeated "market orientation" frequently enough, everything would fall in place. We now know how difficult the process of economic transformation has actually proved to be. The weaknesses of the old system did not simply disappear but became an inherent and sometimes intractable deterrent to real reform. Ironically enough, some of the old *nomenklatura*, knowing their way around better than anyone else, turned out to be the most successful entrepreneurs, often operating in that shadowland between the newly legal and the old black markets. As I write this, one can only withhold judgment on how it will all end without losing hope that the new democratic or partially democratic institutions of Eastern Europe will survive the inevitable and continuing economic stresses and strains. Some, like Poland, the Czech Republic, and Hungary, seem at this point to have the best chances, but, of course, the future of Russia will in a real sense be historically determining.

Cutting across the cold war period and the confrontation between the two alliance systems was the grim reality of nuclear weaponry. We do not know how the postwar world would have developed without it, either with respect to the direct intercontinental confrontation of the two super-powers or with respect to extended deterrence within the Western alliance as its strategy of flexible response gradually evolved. I have written else-where about the nature and problems of deterrence as they seemed at the time, but I do not think that my major conclusions require significant modification in the light of hindsight.[6] We are unlikely ever to know what the Soviet leadership, and particularly the venturesome Nikita Khru-shchev, believed the actual correlation of forces to be at any specific time, but it is likely to have been a realistic assessment—perhaps more realistic than our own. In any event, the Soviets in practice were deterred suffi-ciently from carrying out threatened unilateral actions, whether in Berlin or in Cuba, that might have led to a nuclear confrontation.

Some have argued that, while Western deterrence sufficed to prevent execution of the ultimate Soviet threat against Berlin, it did not prevent the politico-diplomatic crisis that consumed so much of our and their en-ergies over an extended period. This is true enough, but then in reality the Soviets knew that the ultimate decision as to how far to go was theirs to make. If Khrushchev really feared that the United States might make a preemptive nuclear strike against the Soviet Union, some recent evidence for which exists, his seeming confidence and bluster had a considerable hollow ring to it. One theory that I do not find unreasonable is that he was basically a high-stakes gambler who thought he could bluff the three Allied powers out of Berlin and was prepared to take some serious polit-ical risks to achieve his purpose. He consistently backed away, however, from actions that would lead to major confrontation. This, as I have pre-viously noted, was essentially de Gaulle's view.

Whatever the terrible logic of deterrence in practice, there is also the overwhelming moral repulsiveness of nuclear weapons and the destruc-tion they can cause if used. As the American Catholic bishops found when they tried to grapple with the problem in a pastoral letter, the traditional requirements for a just war have to be stretched to the breaking point to justify a system of deterrence that predicates the threat of an ultimate nu-clear use. The inherent paradox of deterrence: its credibility rests on the possibility of nuclear use, yet such use is unthinkable, itself both raising and blurring the moral issue.

A harsh reality with which the perplexed moralist must deal is that the technology for the building of nuclear weapons cannot be stuffed back into the minds of a few nuclear physicists. Ever broader nuclear prolifera-tion must be our concern. When the Soviet nuclear superpower disinte-grated, the disposition of its nuclear weapons and the knowledge and skills of the thousands of scientists and engineers working on them became a matter of immediate concern to the United States and its allies as well as to the leaders of Russia and the Ukraine. The realist may argue that the prospects for containment over the years seem grim. It is a historical irony that absence of effective export control systems in the states of the former Soviet Union has greatly contributed to the problem.

The more I think about it, the less do I believe that a nuclear war, realistically conceived, can ever be morally justified. However, in the context of the situation just described, American policy makers will ask what the irreducible minimum of nuclear warheads and delivery systems is to which we can go down from present levels in future arms reduction agreements.

When the East-West confrontation ended a few years ago, perceptive observers quickly became aware that a whole new set of problems would arise as those to which we had all become accustomed in the West vanished or radically changed. Some, like then deputy secretary of state Lawrence Eagleburger, almost expressed a yearning for the ancient certainties, as did the experts in Washington think tanks, the Pentagon, and the CIA. Some tried desperately to cling to old assumptions, budgetary and operational, but the State Department—to its credit—moved with reasonable quickness along with the White House to draw logical conclusions from the process of change going on before its collective eyes and to assist, where possible, the movement toward German reunification and to proceed with the arms reduction agreements that Gorbachev and then Boris Yeltsin made it possible to achieve.

There has been considerable groping around to find new and meaningful missions for NATO, but the economic weakness of the United States has made any really effective American leadership along the lines of the post–World War II era difficult to exercise. One reality that emerges from the confusion of our times is the continuing need for a vigorous, imaginative, and intelligent American diplomacy conducted by the very best talent we can muster.

Diplomacy

It is difficult to write about modern diplomacy without resorting to truisms. Every country wants its diplomacy to be effective in protecting national interests and achieving goals consonant with that purpose. Whether the enormous proliferation of diplomats that decolonization and the creation of so many new countries have brought about serves a purpose commensurate with the expense is an open question. A good case can be made that a consolidation of diplomatic establishments by poor countries in those capitals where they really have some business to perform would bring clear economic benefits, and I am inclined to think regional embassies in some parts of the world rather than embassies in every small country, with perhaps a consular presence in each, would be most consonant with the interests of even the so-called major powers. I know this is wishful thinking. The vested interests in the status quo are both strong and enduring.

Granted that there are too many diplomats in the world, those who deal with the important relations of governments with each other will continue to perform an indispensable function. The role of the modern diplomat has obviously changed in this era of the mass media, jet travel, and almost instantaneous communications around the world by E-mail, fax, telephone, and computerized cryptography. No longer can an American ambassador enunciate policy on important matters of state based merely on general guidance he may have received weeks earlier. If he is located in a pleasant capital on the main air routes, he can count on a constant flow of visitors from Washington, from the congressional or executive branch, as his residence becomes a hotel and his dining room a restaurant. The overblown American bureaucracy engaged in one way or another in foreign affairs assures a never ending stream of requests and instructions, some trivial and a few important, involving issues that, if they persist, inevitably mean visitors from Washington and the helping and sometimes heavy hand of the frequently inexperienced and insensitive.

Despite all these changes linked inexorably to modern technology, certain basic verities remain valid in determining the effectiveness of a diplomat whether of middle or senior rank. The slick operator, the glad-hander without sincerity, the pompous obscurantist—all quickly acquire a reputation among colleagues for what they are. Even more so the chronic deceiver who simply cannot be trusted. This does not mean, of course, that diplomats must reveal all they know about a given subject or their country's ultimate fallback position at the outset of negotiations. Selective choice of information to buttress an argument is the essence of human discourse. What must be avoided is the distortion of alleged facts, or even worse their invention, the claim to have foreseen a development when it is clear on the record or in the memory of interlocutors that one did not— in other words the deliberate lie. As Harold Nicolson pointed out more than fifty years ago in his classic treatise, no matter how brilliant the presentation, how clearly intelligent the presenter, if a diplomat does not enjoy a reputation for honesty, his or her best efforts at persuasion will be in vain.[7] Once credibility is lost, regaining it becomes almost impossible.

Looking ahead, I can see a continuing need for intelligent, knowledgeable, and honorable American diplomats of the very highest quality.

Washington cannot conduct diplomacy from within the Beltway no matter how sophisticated the communications equipment, any more than it can effectively govern the United States completely out of the capital. If this be true, then we need to give high priority to maximizing the quality of our diplomats and ensuring a Foreign Service with strong morale and the dedication that comes with it. I fear we are currently failing to accomplish either of these aims.

I would be the first to admit that, since leaving the Foreign Service, I have not followed every tergiversation or pronouncement from on high affecting our diplomacy, but I still have enough friends within the organization and contacts with its operations to venture some generalizations. Morale is currently bad in the Foreign Service for a variety of reasons. One is certainly the continuing multiplicity of political appointees. No other country tolerates the practice of rewarding political supporters in large numbers with ambassadorial appointments, presumably because they believe it would lower the overall quality of their diplomacy. In my experience, they are clearly right. Any veteran Foreign Service officer, particularly when he or she has served as a regional assistant secretary of state, knows of the many turkeys forced on American diplomacy by a succession of presidents. The negative effect on staff morale apart, a principal concern must be the lowering of professional standards, sometimes down to the level of the absurd, and the small regard for the conduct of U.S. foreign policy that the practice reflects. Observers have also noted a growing tendency to politicize the so-called subcabinet levels of the State Department—positions that, in the past, senior Foreign Service officers could have expected to fill while on Washington assignment.

It would be foolish to deny that presidents have appointed some excellent individuals as ambassadors over the years. Names like David Bruce, Averill Harriman, Ellsworth Bunker, and some others quickly come to mind. They have served their country well in difficult times and places, but their numbers are relatively small compared with the mediocrities and sometimes downright disasters that we have inflicted on countries the capitals of which are known as "cushy posts." Even when political appointees do a presentable, if not outstanding, job, the fact remains that they do it at the expense of some career officer who could also have done a presentable, and perhaps better, job. If there is merit in having a highly trained and experienced career diplomatic service, as I believe only the ignorant and the obtuse would deny, it would be better for the United States to adopt the standard appointment practices of other countries with which we must primarily compete, or at least negotiate, in the real world.

The realist must accept that this is not going to change. The spoils mentality is too deeply engraved in American political practice, and those big embassies in London, Paris, Tokyo, Rome, and Bonn, and numerous smaller embassies in pleasant capitals beckon too invitingly to the political worthy. We will continue to pay a price, but we shall as a country be paying many other and more serious prices for the governmental foibles of our times.

Economics and Power

During the cold war nuclear weapons were the highest manifestation of power, and the prospect of their proliferation remains highly troubling today. We and the Soviet Union, as the major possessors of nuclear strength, with enormous overkill capability on both sides, were clearly the two superpowers. The United States, so powerful both in weaponry and in economic productivity, became the natural leader of the industrialized non-Communist world. What the cold war concealed, at least in part, was the gradual erosion of our international economic strength, accentuated during the 1980s and the early 1990s by our mounting domestic and foreign debt and the loss of competitiveness in many branches of industry where we had once been dominant. A whole bevy of books appeared less than ten years ago arguing either that the United States is in serious decline, largely for economic reasons, or that despite deceptive appearances we are still great and condemned to provide leadership in the world.[8]

As so often occurs when competing advocates make their cases, the truth gets mangled between the arguments. It seems to me beyond question that the position of the United States in the world economy is far weaker than it was in the earlier postwar era. Despite all the brave talk about our continuing creativity in high tech (which is true enough), the fact is that we seem unable to achieve much in bringing down the lopsided deficits in our trade and current accounts with the countries of Asia. Such deficits are statistically unsustainable in the long run, and at what point we shall reach the long run is difficult to predict. On the other hand our international accounts with Europe are in much better balance and should in all probability remain so. Loose talk about shifting national priorities away from Europe to Asia reflects a basic ignorance of both economic and political realities. We need to keep our priorities both in Europe and in Asia.

Globalization has become the favorite word these days to describe trends in the international economy, generally in a positive sense that this is a sound and productive process bound to improve the conditions of life for all. I wish I could be as sure. Globalization may also mean globalization of pollution on an ascending scale. Can the world really endure the intensive industrialization of China, India, and other major countries in Asia, Latin America, the Middle East, and even the relatively undeveloped parts of Europe?

I recognize that my sense of limitations runs counter to the mood of what has been called "irrational exuberance" prevailing on Wall Street in early 1998 and the generally favorable economic outlook for growth, high employment levels, and low inflation. It has yet to be proved that we have eliminated the business cycle or the mounting consequences of foreign and private debts.

Superimposed on shifting economic realities are some overriding military facts. We remain the sole superpower in the sense that we still have a coherent military structure, command system, and organized forces—not to speak of our nuclear capability. Russia as the largest remaining segment of the former Soviet Union retains, of course, a formidable nuclear potential, but its economy and society are in such a general mess that for the time being at least it cannot compete with us on the world stage. Indeed, a primary concern has been that the absence of an effective export control system could make it a primary factor in the further proliferation of nuclear weapons.

Thus we seem to be left with political, economic, and military obligations that we can no longer afford. Or so it would seem if one accepts the historical perspective of Professor Paul Kennedy in his *The Rise and Fall of the Great Powers*.[9] His argument is essentially that great historical military powers such as Spain, France, and England (and, by implication, the United States) spend so much on arms as to unbalance their economies and bring about an inevitable decline of strength in all areas. He has been a careful and deliberate, if controversial, scholar, unimpressed by those who seek quick and easy solutions to problems that are highly complex and bear a heavy burden of history.

On the other hand, I am reminded of my own dismal first impressions when I first came to war-torn Germany, impressions sustained by eminent economists and administrators. Germany was a physical and psychological wreck, its cities destroyed and its remaining population demoralized. It could never recover economically, at least not within generations. We know how wrong we all were. People are capable of great achievements when greatly challenged.

Looking Ahead

The past record of attempts to predict the future is a mixed one. A few have been remarkably prophetic on one point or another, but much of the stuff ground out by so-called futurologists seems either obvious or at best educated guessing. Two dominant schools have emerged, as has always been the case in looking at the future, one basically optimistic, the other basically pessimistic. In today's context, we have the prophets of gloom like Professor Kennedy in his *Preparing for the Twenty-First Century*.[10] On the other side stand those whose overwhelming confidence in technology makes them see limitless vistas for an ever advancing humankind.

In my life I have seen many confident predictions about technology fail to materialize, and some of the choice fruits of technology, such as nuclear weapons, threaten human existence. I cannot say that as yet the computer has made any real improvement in the intellectual or writing skills of my students despite the undoubted contribution it has made to the physical appearance, if not the content, of term papers, theses, and dissertations. The educative process surely involves more than the mastery of technical gadgetry.

Computer literacy is becoming more and more an operational requirement in the workplace and should be one of the goals of education. By itself it will never solve the problem of making the most of individual human minds through meaningful education. I note a rash of recent books by proponents and opponents of the cyberspace revolution. Their emotional level and the breadth of the generalizations made seem more indicative of basic puzzlement and uncertainty about the kind of world we shall have in the twenty-first century than of the deep conviction that needs no hyperbole.

As a man of the twentieth century I cannot forget that the weapons of war have also benefited in the vast increase of their destructiveness from the applications of modern science, including the computer. The peril remains that proliferation of nuclear, bacteriological, and chemical weapons may take place despite all the serious contemporary efforts to prevent this. The logic of deterrence could escape the terrorist or leader of a rogue state intent on inflicting maximum damage without regard for any consequences.

I find it hard on bad days, however, not to believe that there is something radically askew in this world of ours. Members of the upper middle class have their problems of health and personal relationships along with the rest of humankind, but they are spared the grinding hopelessness of the impoverished and usually the oppressive boredom of uninteresting work to which many are condemned for life. The yuppie phenomenon of the 1980s reflected in its worst exponents a yawning impoverishment of concern about those not so fortunate and a need to gratify every consumer want. Many of that now aging generation are discovering that consumerism is not the road to happiness and does not bring the kind of deep and abiding satisfaction with our way of life that we desire—this despite current American economic euphoria partly stimulated by the Wall Street bull market of recent years. Imperfection is the way of the world and utopia for groups or individuals never within reach.

One can, of course, sink into a sea of fatalism, but as has been noted, humankind sometimes responds most effectively to major challenges that demand major changes. The hope for the twenty-first century must, in my view, be for some revival of traditional sources of American strength including a broader acceptance of Judeo-Christian values.

Notes

· ·

Chapter 2. Entry into the Foreign Service: Switzerland, the China-Burma-India Theater, Mozambique

1. A book with that title about the old Department of State actually came out in 1978. See Martin Weil, *A Pretty Good Club* (New York: W. W. Norton, 1978).

2. See Cordell Hull, *The Memoirs of Cordell Hull*, 2 vols. (New York: Macmillan, 1948), 1:822–29, for a detailed account of the Havana Conference; 2:1227–31, for an account of the secretary's differences with Welles leading finally to the latter's forced resignation in 1943.

3. Louis Allen, *Burma, the Longest War, 1941–1945* (New York: St. Martin's Press, 1984); Raymond Callahan, *Burma, 1942–1945* (London: Davis-Poynter, 1978).

4. Barbara W. Tuchman, *Stilwell and the American Experience in China, 1911–1945* (New York: Macmillan, 1970), 300.

5. See Callahan, *Burma*, 42; Allen, *Burma*, 71–72. See also Jack Belden, *Retreat with Stilwell* (New York: Alfred A. Knopf, 1943), for a journalist's account of Stilwell's flight through the jungle.

6. Callahan, *Burma*, 41.

7. Michael Edwardes, *The Last Years of British India* (London: Cassell, 1963), 71. For a good discussion of political developments in India from a moderate Indian viewpoint, see B. Shiva Rao, "India, 1935–1947," in *The Partition of India Policies and Perspectives, 1935–1947*, ed. C. H. Philips and Mary Doreen Wainwright (London: George Allen and Unwin, 1970), 415–67.

8. See Allen, *Burma*, 167–70.

9. Percival Spear, *India: A Modern History*, 2d ed. (Ann Arbor: University of Michigan Press, 1972), 405.

10. Press interview dated July 14, 1942, included in *The Collected Works of Mahatma Gandhi, LXXVI (April 1, 1942–December 17, 1942)* (New Delhi: Government of India: Ministry of Information and Broadcasting, 1979), 295.

11. Martin J. Hillenbrand, *Power and Morals* (New York: Columbia University Press, 1949), 110.

12. For Slim's own account of the war in Burma, see Field Marshall Sir William

Slim, *Defeat into Victory* (New York: David McKay, 1961). See also Callahan, *Burma*, and Allen, *Burma*.

13. E. J. Kahn Jr., *The China Hands: America's Foreign Service Officers and What Befell Them* (New York: Viking Press, 1975). See also John Paton Davies Jr., *Dragon by the Tail: American, British, Japanese, and Russian Encounters with China and One Another* (New York: W. W. Norton, 1972).

14. B. M. Bhatia, *Famines in India, 1860–1965*, 2d ed. (Bombay: Asia Publishing House, 1967), 334. This book provides the best description of the 1943 Bengal famine that I have come across.

15. See Allen, *Burma*, 149–50, 156, and passim; Callahan, *Burma*, 138–39.

16. Callahan, *Burma*, 137.

17. A cynic might quote, as does Allen from Southey (*Burma*, 630):

> "But what good came of it at last?"
> Quote little Peterkin:—
> "Why, that I cannot tell," said he,
> "But 'twas a famous victory."

18. Davies, *Dragon*, 372.

19. For a generally unfavorable assessment of Portuguese colonial rule in Mozambique, see Thomas H. Henriksen, *Mozambique: A History* (London: Rex Collings, 1978), esp. 99–183. See also Hugh Kay, *Salazar and Modern Portugal* (London: Eyre & Spottiswoode, 1970), esp. 203–19; Malyn Newitt, *Portugal in Africa: The Last Hundred Years* (London: Longman, 1981), 7–19, 57–63, 94–147.

Chapter 3. Postwar Germany

1. The full text of the directive may be found in *Germany, 1947–1949: The Story in Documents* (Washington, D.C.: Department of State Publication 3556, 1950), 21–33.

2. See Henry Morgenthau Jr., *Germany Is Our Problem* (New York: Harper & Brothers, 1945). The text of the memorandum summarizing "The Morgenthau Plan" that President Roosevelt took with him to the Quebec Conference in September 1944 is reproduced in the front of the book.

3. See Lucius D. Clay, *Decision in Germany* (Garden City: Doubleday, 1950), 77. On pp. 73–78, Clay reprints most of his cable of May 26, 1946, in which he expresses such a view.

4. See John Gimbel, *The American Occupation of Germany: Politics and the Military, 1945–1949* (Stanford: Stanford University Press, 1968), 54–91.

5. The complete text of Byrnes's speech may be found in *Germany, 1947–1949*, 3–8.

6. Two full and scholarly discussions of the Nuremberg Trials are Bradley P. Smith, *The Road to Nuremberg* (New York: Basic Books, 1981), and Ann Tusa and John Tusa, *The Nuremberg Trial* (New York: Atheneum, 1984). A good earlier book is Eugene Davidson, *The Trial of the Germans* (New York: Macmillan, 1967).

7. See Gimbel, *American Occupation*, 174.

8. Hannah Arendt, *Eichmann in Jerusalem: A Report on the Banality of Evil* (New York: Viking Press, 1963); see esp. 231.

9. Alfred Grosser, *Germany in Our Time* (New York: Praeger, 1971), 53.

10. See *Germany, 1947–1949*, 66. The full text of Marshall's report at the London session of the Council of Foreign Ministers (November 25–December 16, 1947, is contained on pp. 63–67.

11. For a detailed description of the West German constitution-making process, see my chapter "America and Establishment of the Bundestag," in *The Congress and the Bundestag*, ed. Gerald Livingston, Jane Thaysen, and Roger Davidson (Boulder: Westview Press, 1987).

12. See, for example, Theodor Eschenburg, *Jahre der Besatzung 1945–1949*, Band 1 of, *Geschichte der Bundesrepublik Deutschland* (Stuttgart: Deutsche Verlags-Anstalt, 1983), 424–34. See also Clay, *Decision in Germany*, 208–15, for his account of currency reform, and Edwin Hartrich, *The Fourth and Richest Reich* (New York: Macmillan, 1980), 126–50, for a knowledgeable American journalist's version.

13. Eschenburg, *Geschichte der Bundes-Republik Deutschland*, 434–41.

14. Quoted in ibid., 433.

15. See my chapters "Berlin: Politics, Symbolism, and Security" and "The Legal Background of the Berlin Situation," in *The Future of Berlin*, ed. Martin J. Hillenbrand (Montclair, N.J.: Allanheld, Osmum & Co., 1980), esp. 6–8, and 48–49, for an account of the blockade from both a political and legal point of view.

16. Hillenbrand, *Future of Berlin*, 7.

17. Daniel Yergin, *Shattered Peace* (Boston: Houghton Mifflin, 1977), 385.

18. This is particularly true, of course, of revisionist books on the subject.

19. Clay alludes to General Tunner only in passing in his *Decision in Germany*.

20. See Martin J. Hillenbrand, "America and Establishment of the Bundestag," in Livingston, Thaysen, and Davidson, *Congress and the Bundestag*. I have drawn on this source for the details that follow.

21. See Terry H. Anderson, *The United States, Great Britain, and the Cold War, 1944–1947* (Columbia: University of Missouri Press, 1981), 85–91, 106–8, 110–17.

Chapter 4. Cambridge, Washington, Paris

1. Carl J. Friedrich, *The Age of the Baroque, 1650–1660* (New York: Harper & Brothers, 1952).

2. John Lewis Gaddis, *Strategies of Containment: A Critical Appraisal of Postwar American National Security Policy* (New York: Oxford University Press, 1982).

3. X [George F. Kennan], "The Sources of Soviet Conduct," *Foreign Affairs* 25 (July 1947): 566–82.

4. George F. Kennan, *Memoirs, 1925–1950* (Boston: Little, Brown, 1967), 442–44.

5. Jean Monnet, *Memoirs*, trans. by Richard Mayne (Garden City: Doubleday & Co., 1978), 288–370.

6. Dean Acheson, *Present at the Creation: My Years in the State Department* (New York: W. W. Norton, 1969), 458.

7. The text of the EDC Treaty may be found in *American Foreign Policy, 1950–1955: Basic Documents*, vols. 1 and 2 (Washington, D.C.: Department of State Publication 6446, 1957), 1107–50.

8. For the texts of the various notes exchanged, see *Documents on Germany, 1944–1985* (Washington, D.C.: Department of State Publication 9446, n.d.), 361–71, 374–78, 385–93, 395–97.

9. For the text of the Convention on Relations, see *Message from the President of the United States Transmitting the Convention on Relations between the Three Powers and the Federal Republic of Germany, Signed at Bonn on May 26, 1952* (Washington, D.C.: U.S. Government Printing Office, 1952). For the text of this convention, as amended by Schedule II to the Protocol on the Termination of the Occupation Regime in the Federal Republic of Germany, October 23, 1954, see *American Foreign Policy, 1950–1955*, 486–98.

10. Sebastian Haffner, *Der Selbstmord des Deutschen Reiches* (Bern: Scherz, 1970).

11. Rolf Steiniger, *Eine vertane Chance: Die Stalin-Note vom 10. Marz 1952 und die Wiedervereinigung* (Berlin: J. H. W. Dietz Nachf., 1986).

12. I am here largely drawing on my own recollection of events.

13. Haffner, *Der Selbstmord*, 133.

14. See E. J. Kahn Jr., *The China Hands: America's Foreign Service Officers and What Befell Them* (New York: Viking Press, 1975), and John Paton Davies Jr., *Dragon by the Tail: American, British, Japanese, and Russian Encounters with China and One Another* (New York: W. W. Norton, 1972), esp. 365 and passim.

15. Raymond Aron, "Historical Sketch of the Great Debate," in *France Defeats EDC*, ed. Daniel Lerner and Raymond Aron (New York: Frederick A. Praeger, 1957), 8.

16. The text of Bidault's speech, as well as the complete text of the proposed treaty, is contained in *Draft Treaty Embodying the Statute of the European Community: Information and Official Documents of the Constitutional Committee of the Ad Hoc Assembly* (Paris: Secretariat of the Constitutional Committee, 1953).

17. See *Foreign Relations of the United States, 1952–1954*, vol. 5, pt. 1 (Washington: Department of State Publication 9288, 1983), 702–1092.

18. Ibid., 461–68, for text of Secretary Dulles's speech.

19. For text of the Eden Plan, see *Foreign Ministers Meeting: Berlin Discussions, January 25–February 18, 1954* (Washington: Department of State Publication 5399, 1954), 223–25.

20. See Aron, "Historical Sketch," 17.

21. *Foreign Relations*, 1092–93.

22. Ibid., 1094–1113.

23. Anthony Eden, *Full Circle: The Memoirs of Anthony Eden* (Boston: Houghton Mifflin, 1960), 171–81.

24. Ibid., 169.

25. Ibid., 182–88. See also *Foreign Relations of the United States, 1952–1954*, vol. 5, pt. 2 (Washington: Department of State Publication 9289, 1983), 1192–97, 1209–28, 1263–78.

26. *Foreign Relations*, pt. 2, 1294–1370.

27. All of the pertinent four-power, six-power, nine-power, and fourteen-power documents for this intensive period of negotiations can be found in *American Foreign Policy, 1950–1955*, 483–612, 968–91, 1458–70.

28. See *Die Auswärtige Politik der Bundesrepublic Deutschland: Herausgegeben vom Auswärtigen Amt* (Köln: Verlag Wissenschaft und Politik, 1972), 31–34 for narrative, and attached Documents 75, 79, and 87.

29. *Foreign Relations*, pt. 2, 1225.

30. See, for example, George W. Ball, *The Past Has Another Pattern: Memoirs* (New York: W. W. Norton, 1982), 92–94. Monnet, *Memoirs*, 397–98. See also Richard Mayne, *Post-War: The Dawn of Today's Europe* (New York: Schocken Books, 1983), 316.

Chapter 5. Berlin, Washington, and the Eisenhower Years of the Berlin Crisis

1. See my chapter "The Legal Background of the Berlin Situation," in *The Future of Berlin*, ed. Martin J. Hillenbrand (Montclair, N.J.: Allanheld, Osmum & Co., 1980), 41–80.

2. I have reconstructed this extended imbroglio largely from personal recollections and journals. Our reporting to Washington was fairly detailed, but the U.S. mission, and specifically the American political adviser, were allowed considerable discretionary authority in negotiating with the Soviets.

3. See, for example, Robert M. Slusser, *The Berlin Crisis of 1961* (Baltimore: Johns Hopkins University Press, 1973). The very title of his book suggests such a bifurcation. See also his "The Berlin Crises of 1958–1959 and 1961," in *Force without War: U.S. Armed Forces as a Political Instrument*, ed. Barry M. Blechman and Stephen S. Kaplan (Washington: Brookings Institution, 1978), 343–439. The book by Jack M. Schick, *The Berlin Crisis, 1958–1962* (Philadelphia: University of Pennsylvania Press, 1971), is well crafted and sees the crisis as a continuum. Unfortunately, he was forced to rely almost entirely on press sources and other published materials.

4. Both extracts from the Khrushchev speech of November 10 and the Soviet note of November 27 are contained in *Documents on Germany, 1944–1985* (Washington, D.C.: Department of State Publication 9446, n.d.), 542–46, 552–59.

5. Ibid., 346–52, for pertinent extracts from Secretary Dulles's news conference remarks. For memorandum of conversation between Dulles and German ambassador Grewe, see *Foreign Relations of the United States, 1959–1960*, vol. 8, *Berlin Crisis, 1958–1959* (Washington: U.S. Government Printing Office, 1993), 76–80. The four volumes on the Berlin crisis included in the State Department's

Foreign Relations series, although it omits some materials, are about as complete a collection of Berlin documents as one is likely to get. The full text of Dulles's press conference remarks may be found on pp. 121–27 of vol. 8 noted above.

6. Alexander L. George and Richard Smoke, *Deterrence in American Foreign Policy: Theory and Practice* (New York: Columbia University Press, 1974), 405.

7. Strobe Talbot, ed., *Khrushchev Remembers* (Boston: Little, Brown, 1970), 452–58.

8. Adam B. Ulam, *Expansion and Coexistence: The History of Soviet Foreign Policy, 1917–1967* (New York: Frederick A. Praeger, 1968), 620.

9. George and Smoke, *Deterrence*, 396.

10. *NATO Final Communiques, 1949–1970* (Brussels: NATO Information Office, n.d.), 105.

11. In 1960 and the years following, American continuing support of the proposal for a multilateral nuclear force (MLF) of seaborne Polaris missiles, with warheads still under American control but with a European finger on the trigger, was largely motivated by such psychological considerations.

12. Richard Ned Lebow, "Provocative Deterrence: A New Look at the Cuban Missile Crisis," in *Arms Control Today* (July–August 1988): 15–16.

13. Slusser, "Berlin Crises of 1958–1959 and 1961," 366.

14. See *Documents on Germany*, 560–73, for the full text of the department's legal study.

15. See Hillenbrand, *Future of Berlin*, 51–52, for a discussion of the change in Soviet legal argumentation between the November 27 note and the Geneva Conference of Foreign Ministers.

16. *Documents on Germany*, 573–76. I should note that, apart from the citations from published collections of documents, much of what follows describing the handling of the Berlin crisis derives either from personal recollections and journals or from State Department materials declassified at my request under the Freedom of Information Act.

17. Ibid., 585–606.

18. Telegram from the Department of State to U.S. Embassy Bonn, January 29, text in *Foreign Relations*, 196–299. *Documents on Germany*, 607–8. Whenever materials are available in both the single-volume *Documents on Germany* and the four volumes of the Foreign Relations series, I have preferred to use the reference to the more easily available *Documents* volume.

19. *Documents on Germany*, 607–8.

20. Ibid., 609–10.

21. Harold Macmillan, *Riding the Storm, 1956–1959* (New York: Harper & Row, 1971), 583.

22. *Documents on Germany*, 615–16.

23. Strangely enough, the text of the Soviet response of March 30 does not appear in the State Department collection of documents cited above, or for that matter in the comparable British collection of documents published in 1961. Such are the vagaries of editors of document collections.

24. Slusser, "Berlin Crises of 1958–1959 and 1961," 373.

25. *Foreign Ministers Meeting, May–August 1959, Geneva* (Washington: Department of State Publication 6882, September 1959).

26. The text of the final communiqué, as well as of all other nonclassified documents noted in my discussion of the Geneva conference, can be found in the State Department collection cited in the previous note. This includes the full text of the Western Peace Plan.

27. Dwight D. Eisenhower, *Waging Peace, 1956–1961* (Garden City: Doubleday & Co., 1965), 390.

28. *Documents on Germany*, 683–84.

29. The Eisenhower memoirs, *Waging Peace, 1956–1961*, esp. 434–49, remain the best source for the private exchanges between the president and Khrushchev. His impressions of the Soviet leader are shrewd.

30. *Foreign Relations of the United States, 1958–1960*, vol. 9, *Berlin Crisis, 1959–1960* (Washington: U.S. Government Printing Office, 1993), 46.

31. *Documents on Germany*, 683–86.

32. He was obviously highly literate. The five volumes of his gracefully composed memoirs show all the signs of having been largely written by himself, with some research assistance of course.

33. This memorandum has not been published. Reference to it is made in Arthur Kogan's compilation "The Berlin Crisis," originally Top Secret but now declassified though also unpublished. Kogan's work was undertaken at my request to the historian of the Department of State. It has generally proved to be a valuable source.

34. The text of Khrushchev's May 5 speech to the Supreme Soviet may be found in *American Foreign Policy: Current Documents, 1960* (Washington, D.C.: Department of State Publication 7624, n.d.), 408–12.

35. See *Waging Peace, 1956–1961*, 543–47, 550–53. His description of the abortive summit provides a colorful summary (553–57).

36. *Documents on Germany*, 707, contains a pertinent extract.

Chapter 6. Kennedy and the Berlin Crisis

1. Thomas V. Schoenbaum, *Waging Peace and War: Dean Rusk in the Truman, Kennedy, and Johnson Years* (New York: Simon and Schuster, 1988). Dean Rusk, *As I Saw It* (New York: W. W. Norton, 1990).

2. Examples of such books are Arthur M. Schlesinger Jr., *A Thousand Days: John F. Kennedy in the White House* (Boston: Houghton Mifflin, 1965); Roger Hilsman, *To Move a Nation: The Politics of Foreign Policy in the Administration of John F. Kennedy* (Garden City: Doubleday & Co., 1967); Theodore Sorensen, *Kennedy* (New York: Harper & Row, 1965).

3. See *Documents on Germany, 1944–1985* (Washington, D.C.: Department of State Publication 9446, n.d.), 723–27, for pertinent extracts. The narrative that follows in this chapter, as in the preceding chapter, is based on public documents

when available, on personal recollections and journals, and on State Department materials declassified under the Freedom of Information Act. The publication by the Department of State of several volumes of documents on the Berlin crisis in the Foreign Relations series, cited individually below, has provided a whole new range of documentation, although there are still a few gaps. The study of the Berlin crisis by Arthur Kogan of the Historian's Staff, formerly classified Top Secret but now declassified, also provides a detailed chronological account that I have found valuable.

4. Moscow's telegram 2147, March 10, 1901. Text in *Foreign Relations of the United States, 1961–1963*, vol. 14, *Berlin Crisis, 1961–1962* (Washington, D.C.: U.S. Government Printing Office, 1993), 18–20.

5. For summary of my memorandum, see ibid., 33–34.

6. For report of meeting, see ibid., 36–40.

7. Ibid.

8. Ibid., 64–65, for report of quadripartite meeting of foreign ministers.

9. Ibid., 80–86, for report of de Gaulle–Kennedy talks.

10. Ibid., 87–96, 96–98, for reports of Khrushchev-Kennedy talks.

11. For the text of the aide-mémoire, see *Documents on Germany*, 728–82.

12. Ibid., 732–33, for the pertinent portion of Kennedy's report.

13. Schoenbaum, *Waging Peace and War*, 339; Rusk, *As I Saw It*, 222.

14. See *Documents on Germany*, 734–36.

15. See *Foreign Relations*, 107–9.

16. See *Documents on Germany*, 753–62, for the text of the U.S. note, and Kennedy's statement.

17. See, for example, Honoré M. Catudal, *Kennedy and the Berlin Wall Crisis: A Case Study in U.S. Decision Making* (Berlin: Berlin Verlag, 1980), 143–47. The complete text of a late version of the Acheson report may be found in *Foreign Relations*, 138–59.

18. For text of NSAM No. 58, see *Foreign Relations*, 163–65.

19. For text of NSAM No. 59, see ibid., 197–98.

20. For text dated July 17, 1961, see ibid., 207–9.

21. *Documents on Germany*, 573–76.

22. Ibid., 762–65, for pertinent extracts from Kennedy's speech.

23. See *Foreign Relations*, 223–24.

24. For the text of the long telegram, see ibid., 269–80.

25. See ibid. for other coverage of Paris talks.

26. See *Documents on Germany* for essential extracts, 766–69.

27. Bundesministerium für Gesamtdeutsche Fragen, *Die Flucht aus der Sowjet zone und die Sperrmassnahmen des kommunistischen Regimes vom 13 August in Berlin* (Bonn: Federal Ministry for All-German Questions, 1961), 15–18.

28. See *Documents on Germany*, 776–78, for all of these texts.

29. *Foreign Relations*, 333–34.

30. See ibid., 532–62, for exchanges with regard to the Checkpoint Charlie tank confrontation.

31. Ibid., for text of the president's memorandum.

32. Ibid., for texts relating to Rusk-Gromyko talks, 431–33, 439–41, 456–60, 468–80.

33. See ibid., 709–800, 846–52, 859–62, for texts of instructions sent to Thompson and his cable reporting conversations with Gromyko.

34. *Documents on Germany*, 804–5.

35. The restriction of Western flights in the three Berlin air corridors to altitudes below ten thousand feet had a long history; by 1962, it had become accepted practice.

36. See *Foreign Relations of the United States, 1961–1963*, vol. 15, *Berlin Crisis, 1962–1963* (Washington, D.C.: U.S. Government Printing Office, 1993), 48–94, for relevant texts bearing on the Principles nonpaper. See ibid., 69–71, for version handed to Gromyko.

37. See *Documents on Germany*, 807–12, for extracts from Gromyko's and Rusk's statements.

38. For text of April 3, 1962, version see *Foreign Relations*, vol. 15, 95–98. As noted, this revised paper was never given to Ambassador Dobrynin.

39. Ibid., 105 and passim, for materials bearing on German reaction and exchanges with the United States. For text of Department of State statement proposing an International Access Authority to Control Ground and Air Routes to Berlin, see *Documents on Germany*, 806–7.

40. Reports on Rusk's talks with Ambassador Dobrynin may be found in *Foreign Relations*, vol. 15, 114–19.

41. For report of Rusk's October 6, 1962, meeting with Gromyko in New York, see *Foreign Relations*, vol. 15, 348–51.

42. Reference is made to this memorandum in Kogan, "The Berlin Crisis."

43. See *Foreign Relations*, vol. 15, 395 and passim, for reference to what became known as the Berlin-NATO Subcommittee.

44. James Blight and David Welch, *On the Brink: Americans and Soviets Reexamine the Cuban Missile Crisis* (New York: Hill and Wang, 1989).

45. *Khrushchev Remembers* (Boston: Little, Brown, 1970), 494.

46. Blight and Welch, *On the Brink*, 116–17.

47. See *Foreign Relations*, vol. 15, 370–76, for text of Akalovsky's (our interpreter) memorandum on that portion of conversation dealing with Germany and Berlin.

48. Quoted in Blight and Welch, *On the Brink*, 304.

49. Khrushchev's message of October 28.

50. See *Documents on Germany*, 830–33, for extracts from the Khrushchev speeches.

51. Blight and Welch, *On the Brink*, 296–97.

52. Quoted in Bernard Ledwidge, *De Gaulle* (New York: St. Martin's Press, 1982), 269.

53. Martin J. Hillenbrand, "NATO and Western Security in an Era of Transition," *International Security* 2 (Fall 1977): 18–19.

54. McGeorge Bundy, *Danger and Survival: Choices about the Bomb in the First Fifty Years* (New York: Random House, 1988), 379.

1. This description of the "tailgate" crisis has been based largely on my own notes and recollections. See also George McGhee, *At the Creation of a New Germany: From Adenauer to Brandt, an Ambassador's Account* (New Haven: Yale University Press, 1989), 106–8; *Foreign Relations of the United States, 1961–1963*, vol. 15, *Berlin Crisis, 1962–1963* (Washington: U.S. Government Printing Office, 1994), 591 and passim.

2. See, for example, Osterheld's lengthy section in Horst Osterheld, Terence Prittie, and François Seydoux, *Konrad Adenauer Leben und Politik* (Stuttgart: Verlag Bonn Aktuell, 1975), 67–118. See also Horst Osterheld, *Konrad Adenauer: Ein Charakterbild* (Bonn: Eichholz Verlag, 1993).

3. Bernard Ledwidge, *De Gaulle* (New York: St. Martin's Press, 1982), 275–88. See also George W. Ball, *The Past Has Another Pattern: Memoirs* (New York: W. W. Norton, 1982), 268–71; Wolfram F. Hanrieder, *Germany, America, Europe: Forty Years of German Foreign Policy* (New Haven: Yale University Press, 1989), 170–77; Maurice Couve de Murville, *Une Politique Etrangère* (Paris: Editions Plon, 1971), 106.

4. Hans Peter Schwarz, *Die Ära Adenauer 1957–1963*, Band 2 of *Geschichte der Bundesrepublik Deutschland* (Stuttgart: Deutsche Verlags-Anstalt, 1983), 228–46. Professor Schwarz provides the best general account of the German political scene during the later Adenauer years as chancellor. But see also Dennis L. Bark and David R. Gress, *A History of West Germany*, vol. 1, *From Shadow to Substance, 1945–1963* (Oxford: Basil Blackwell, 1989), 491–525.

5. For text of speech, see *Public Papers of the Presidents of the United States* (Washington, D.C.: U.S. Government Printing Office, 1963), 337–39.

6. See Martin J. Hillenbrand, "The Future of the European Community as a Problem of American-European Relations," in *America and Western Europe: Problems and Prospects*, ed. Karl Kaiser and Hans-Peter Schwarz (Lexington, Mass.: Lexington Books, 1977), 316–30.

7. Ball, *Past Has Another Pattern*, 274.

8. See note 3 to chapter 11 below for a citation raising a basic question for the discussion in that chapter of the role of *Ostpolitik* in the achievement of German unification. An extensive account of the development and thinking behind *Ostpolitik* may be found in William E. Griffith, *The Ostpolitik of the Federal Republic of Germany* (Cambridge: MIT Press, 1978).

9. For the full text of the Deutschland Vertrag, see *Die Auswärtige Politik der Bundesrepublik Deutschland*, published by the German Foreign Ministry (Köln: Verlag Wissenschaft und Politik, 1972), 262–66.

10. Dean Rusk, *As I Saw It* (New York: W. W. Norton, 1990), 263–66, esp. 264.

11. See Ball, *Past Has Another Pattern*, 174.

12. Helmut Schmidt, *Men and Powers: A Political Retrospective*, trans. Ruth Hein (New York: Random House, 1989), 142.

13. U.S. Embassy Bonn telegrams 1430 (October 18, 1963) and 1438 (October 19, 1963) to secretary of state.

14. Schmidt, *Men and Powers*, 143.

15. McGhee, *Creation of a New Germany*, 202–3, 212–17, and passim.

16. For the most complete and interesting account of the internal German political scene during the Erhard and Kiesinger chancellorships, I can only recommend Klaus Hildebrand, *Von Erhard zur Grossen Coalition 1963–1969*, Band 4 of *Geschichte der Bundesrepublik Deutschland* (Stuttgart: Deutsche Verlags-Anstalt, 1986). Unfortunately, the five mammoth volumes of this major contribution to postwar German history are probably too voluminous ever to be translated into English for those who do not read German. The book by Ambassador George McGhee, *At the Creation of a New Germany*, provides many useful and interesting insights into the period.

17. *New York Times*, October 18, 1967. See also *Newsweek*, October 30, 1967, 37–38.

18. We often joked that, because of the cardinal, we were undoubtedly the best-guarded embassy in Budapest.

19. U.S. Embassy Budapest telegram 539 (October 23, 1967) reported my conversation with the cardinal and later developments of the day.

20. See U.S. Embassy Budapest telegram 626 (November 20, 1967).

21. U.S. Embassy Budapest telegram 622 (November 17, 1967).

22. U.S. Embassy Budapest telegram 663 (November 30, 1967) reported my conversation with Kádár.

23. U.S. Embassy Budapest telegram 1012 (March 8, 1968).

24. Jozsef Mindszenty, *Memoirs*, trans. Richard and Clara Winston (New York: Macmillan, 1974).

Chapter 8. Washington: The First Nixon Years

1. *U.S. Foreign Policy for the 1970's: A New Strategy for Peace*, A Report to the Congress by Richard Nixon President of the United States, February 18, 1970, 29.

2. Henry Kissinger, *White House Years* (Boston: Little, Brown, 1979), 83.

3. This essentially describes Italian politics prior to the political upheavals of 1993–94. Some cynics, however, would question whether Italian politics have really changed all that much other than a new cast of characters and new party labels.

4. Kissinger, *White House Years*, 386.

5. Pertinent portions of the various texts cited may be found in *Documents on Germany, 1944–1985* (Washington, D.C.: Department of State Publication 9446, n.d.).

6. James S. Sutterlin and David Klein, *Berlin: From Symbol of Confrontation to Keystone of Stability* (New York: Praeger, 1989).

7. Martin J. Hillenbrand, ed., *The Future of Berlin* (Montclair, N.J.: Allanheld, Osmun & Co., 1980), chaps. 1 and 2, esp. 25–31, 55–76.

8. The best single account of *Ostpolitik*, although dated in spots, remains William E. Griffith's *The Ostpolitik of the Federal Republic of Germany* (Cambridge: MIT Press, 1978).

9. Such as that provided by Sutterlin and Klein, *Berlin*, and the now declassified account of the negotiations in Arthur G. Kogan, "The Quadripartite Berlin Negotiations, 1970–1971," Department of State research project no. 1035, Office of the Historian, Washington, D.C. This latter project was undertaken by Kogan at my specific request.

10. Kissinger, *White House Years*, 411.

11. Sutterlin and Klein, *Berlin*, 114–20.

12. All the pertinent German documentation, including the texts of the Moscow and Warsaw Treaties, can be found in *Dokumentation zur Entspannungspolitik der Bundesregierung*, Herausgegeben von Presse und Informations Amt der Bundesregierung (Hamburg: Hanseatische Druckanstalt, 1981).

13. For example, Willy Brandt, *Erinnerungen* (Frankfurt am Main: Propyläen Verlag, 1984).

14. Kissinger, *White House Years*, 400–402.

15. The prolonged exchanges with Mintoff were fairly accurately reported in the *New York Times* and *Washington Post* over the relevant period. The voluminous cable traffic has not yet been published in the Foreign Affairs of the United States series.

16. *Washington Post*, May 26, 1973.

17. Martin J. Hillenbrand, "NATO and Western Security in an Era of Transition," *International Security* 2 (Fall 1977): 3.

18. *New York Times*, March 5, 9, 26, 1969.

19. This article of the German constitution was largely drafted on German initiative to strengthen one of the weaknesses of the Weimar constitution.

20. A good account may be found in Karl Dietrich Bracher, Wolfgang Jaeger, and Werner Link, *Republik in Wandel, 1969–1974: Die Ära Brandt*, Band 5/1 of *Geschichte der Bundesrepublik Deutschland* (Stuttgart: Deutsche Verlags-Anstalt, 1986), 68–74.

21. Kissinger, *White House Years*, 1191–92.

22. For example, ibid., 1202–57.

23. Gerard Smith, *Doubletalk: The Story of the First Strategic Arms Limitation Talks* (New York: Doubleday & Co., 1980), 407–45.

Chapter 9. Ambassador in Bonn

1. For a good account of political events before and after the elections of 1972, see Arnulf Baring, *Machtwechsel: Die Ära Brandt-Scheel* (Stuttgart: Deutsche Verlags-Anstalt, 1982), 361–73. See also Karl Dietrich Bracher, Wolfgang Jäger, and Werner Link, *Republik in Wandel 1969–1974: Die Ära Brandt*, Band 5/1 of *Geschichte der Bundesrepublik Deutschland* (Stuttgart: Deutsche Verlags-Anstalt, 1986), 15–116.

2. Text of Kissinger-Gromyko draft may be found in James S. Sutterlin and David Klein, *Berlin: From Symbol of Confrontation to Keystone of Stability* (New York: Praeger, 1989), 174.

3. For text, see *Die Bundesrepublik Deutschland Mitglied der Vereinten Nationen* (Bonn: Federal Republic of Germany Press and Information, 1973), 191.

4. He was one of those senior officials who until the collapse of the Soviet Union seemed able to survive various changes of leadership. The German version of his memoirs, Valentin Falin, *Politische Erinnerungen*, trans. from Russian by Heddy Press-Veerth (München: Dreemer Knaur, 1993), is disappointing. It lacks documentation and seems to be largely a personal apologia. If he took some of the positions that he claims, his influence on actual Soviet policy was minimal.

5. This was the consensus of political observers in Bonn.

6. See Paul Frank, *Entschlüsselte Botschaft: Ein Diplomat Macht Inventur* (Stuttgart: Deutsche Verlags-Anstalt, 1981), 266–68.

7. Ibid., esp. 269–73.

8. See *New York Times*, April 24, 1973, for both the text of the Kissinger speech and the Reston commentary.

9. *NATO Final Communiques: 1970–1975* (Brussels: NATO Information Service, n.d.).

10. *New York Times* and *Washington Post* of June 7, 1974.

11. See Baring, *Machtwechsel*, 733–63. For an account of the whole Guillaume episode written by an experienced American journalist who knew Brandt well personally, see David Binder, *The Other German: Willy Brandt's Life and Times* (Washington, D.C.: New Republic Book Co., 1975), 307–53. See also Bracher, Jäger, and Link, *Geschichte der Bundesrepublik Deutschland*, 118–126.

12. In Helmut Schmidt's *Men and Powers: A Political Retrospective*, trans. Ruth Hein (New York: Random House, 1989), the author devotes an entire chapter entitled "The Temptation of Economic Dominance" (263–74) to criticism of American economic policy.

13. See *New York Times*, June 12, 1974, for full text of press conference and long descriptive article.

14. Martin J. Hillenbrand, *Germany in an Era of Transition* (Paris: Atlantic Institute for International Affairs, 1983), 17.

Chapter 10. Research Institute Director and Academic

1. Although fully covered by the European media, the former secretary of state's remarks did not draw much attention in the American press.

2. Martin J. Hillenbrand, *Power and Morals* (New York: Columbia University Press, 1949).

3. Michael Shenefelt, "Disposable Scholarship," *Washington Post*, September 12, 1989.

4. David Stockman, *The Triumph of Politics: Why the Reagan Revolution Failed* (New York: Harper & Row, 1986).

5. He had made the mistake of talking to the Overseas Writers Club without apparently understanding that "for background only" applied only to the members present and not to the rest of the Washington press corps.

Chapter 11. Reflections

1. In conversations with Professor Franklin Holtzman during the months he spent doing research at the Atlantic Institute for International Affairs in Paris. See his *Financial Checks on Soviet Defense Expenditures* (Lexington, Mass.: Lexington Books, 1975) and "Soviet Military Expenditures—Assessing the Numbers Game," *International Security* 4 (Spring 1982): 78–101.

2. However, as Dr. Loch Johnson has recently pointed out, the record of the CIA's Office of Soviet Analysis was considerably further ahead in its appraisal of the weakening situation in the USSR than the Bush administration and top CIA administration wanted to hear. He also argues for a strong continuing CIA role in the interpretation of a broad range of technical intelligence such as photographic imagery.

3. Timothy Garton Ash, *In Europe's Name: Germany and the Divided Continent* (New York: Random House, 1993).

4. The figure usually given out for the transfer of governmental capital in various forms to the five new Eastern states of the Federal Republic comes to more than U.S. $100 billion per year.

5. John Lewis Gaddis, *We Now Know: Rethinking Cold War History* (New York: Oxford University Press, 1997).

6. See, for example, Martin J. Hillenbrand, "Strategic Forces and Deterrence," in *Through the Straits of Armageddon*, ed. Paul F. Diehl and Loch K. Johnson (Athens: University of Georgia Press, 1987), 49–73, and "NATO and Western Security in an Era of Transition," *International Security* 2 (Fall 1977): 3–24.

7. First published in 1939 and revised in 1963, Sir Harold George Nicolson's *Diplomacy* (London: Oxford University Press, 1965) remains a fount of wisdom about the practice of diplomacy and the necessary qualities of the successful practitioner. See esp. 55–67.

8. For example, on the negative side, Paul M. Kennedy, *The Rise and Fall of the Great Powers* (New York: Random House, 1987), and Benjamin M. Friedman, *Day of Reckoning: The Consequences of American Economic Policy* (New York: Random House, 1988); on the positive side, Joseph S. Nye, *Bound to Lead: The Changing Nature of American Power* (New York: Basic Books, 1990), and Henry R. Nau, *The Myth of America's Decline: Leading the World Economy into the 1990s* (New York: Oxford University Press, 1990).

9. Kennedy, *Rise and Fall*.

10. Paul M. Kennedy, *Preparing for the Twenty-first Century* (New York: Random House, 1993).

Index

Berlin, 49, 316; airlift from, 67, 68; Allied occupation of, 109; crisis, 115, 120, 121, 143, 163, 168, 207, 208, 220, 243; tank confrontation in, 195; and air traffic dispute, 199; media interest in, 321
Berlin Air Safety Center (BASC), 118
Berlin Task Force, 181
Berlin Wall, 13, 187, 189
Bettencourt, José Tristao de, 43
Bevin, Ernest, 71
Bhutan, 35
Bidault, Georges, 93, 96, 101
Biedenkopf, Kurt, 323
Bizonal Economic Administration, 63, 65
Bizonia, 51
Black market, 53, 57, 58, 64, 66, 67, 75
Boeckler, Hans, 62
Boers, 46
Böll, Heinrich, 73
Bonn, 46, 76
Bose, Subhas, 36
Bowie, Robert, 228
Brady, Austin C., 20
Brandin, Bob, 180
Brandt, Willy, 59, 111, 115, 270, 279, 283, 285, 303, 311; and United States, 116; on Western response to Berlin Wall, 190; and Ostpolitik, 280; and Kosygin, 289; and electoral fraud scandal, 327; resignation of, 334
Bravo, Lopez, 298
Bremen, 49
Brentano, Heinrich von, 94, 171, 186; on German settlement, 139; and Herter, 141
Bressier, Raymond, 110
Bretton Woods, 330
Brezhnev, Leonid, 258, 260, 283, 303, 306, 308, 309, 342
Brezhnev Doctrine, 258
British class structure, 269
British imperialism, 22
British Overseas Airways Corporation, 29
Bruce, David, 90, 91, 115, 385
Bruce Mission, 90, 91, 94, 96, 99, 100, 101

Brussels Treaty, 102, 103
Budapest, 265
Buell, Bob, 26
Bundestag, 304, 305
Bundy, McGeorge, 170, 184
Bunker, Ellsworth, 385
Burlatsky, Fyodor, 208
Burma, 17, 18, 30; society in, 21; fall of, 27; government in exile of, 38
Burma Road, 24, 28, 29, 33, 40
Byrnes, James, 56
Byroade, Henry, 81

Caetano, Marcello, 299, 340
Calcutta, 31, 32, 36, 37
Camp David, 143, 149
Canada, 302, 303
Capone, Al, 296
Carlucci, Frank, 341
Carrington, 295
Carstens, Karl, 231, 319
Carter, Jimmy, 326, 336
Casey, R. G., 39
Casey, William, 338
Cash, Frank, 325
Castiella, Fernando, 298, 300
Castle, Barbara, 269
Catholic Worker movement, 8
Ceaușescu, Nicolae, 276
Center for Strategic Studies, 355
Central Intelligence Agency (CIA), 112, 374, 376, 377
Chambers, Ann Cox, 372
Chayes, Abe, 179, 185
Checkpoint Charlie, 195
Chennault, Claire L., 25, 26
Chiang Kai-shek, 24, 40, 41
China-Burma-India Theater (CBI), 17, 24, 33
China Hands, The (Kahn), 38
China National Aviation Corporation (CNAC), 30, 31, 34
Chinese Defense Supplies, Inc., 25
Christian Democratic Party, 51
Christian Democratic Union, 62, 89, 222, 223, 236, 237, 240, 279, 283, 303–5, 317–19, 323, 325, 343, 344
Christian Social Union, 89, 236, 317, 318, 325

Churchill, Winston, 33, 35, 100, 102, 106

Clay, Lucius, 54, 55, 56, 65, 66, 71, 175, 193; resignation of, 74; in Berlin, 192; and U.S. military command, 194

Coal Steel Community (CSC), 90

Cold war, 69, 81, 82

Cold warrior syndrome, 116

Columbia University, 5, 7, 9

Committee on the Challenges of Modern Society (CCMS), 275

Communist Party, 62, 98, 105, 255

Conant, James Bryant, 115

Conventional Armed Forces in Europe (CFE), 291

Cripps, Sir Stafford, 35

Crosland, Anthony, 269

Crossman, Richard, 269

Cuban missile crisis, 178, 187, 202, 203, 204, 206

Czech Republic, 381

Darjeeling, 35

Davison, Fred, 361

Debré, Michel, 95

De Gasperi, Alcide, 85

De Gaulle, Charles, 133, 159, 172, 173, 175, 184, 271; and negotiations with Soviets, 186; and NATO, 238; and Algerian policy, 242; involvement of, in Quebec problem, 303

De Murville, Couve, 133, 173, 186

Denazification of Germany, 50, 60

De-Stalinization of the Soviet Union, 69, 107

Deterrence, 382

Deutschland Plan, 86

Diplomacy, 383–86

Dirks, Walter, 73

Dobrynin, Anatoly, 287, 305, 308

Dorman-Smith, Sir Reginald, 29

Doubletalk (Smith), 310

Douglas-Home, Sir Alec, 176, 310

Dregger, Alfred, 344

Dubček, 258, 260

Dulles, John Foster, 92, 96, 102, 122, 127, 129–34, 139, 170

Dungan, Ralph, 177

Eagleburger, Lawrence, 383

East Berlin, 346

East Germany. *See* German Democratic Republic

East-West summit, 161

Eckhardt, Felix von, 146

Eden, Anthony, 96, 102

Eden Plan, 140

Egypt, 327

Eisenhower, Dwight, 131, 139, 150, 175; on U.S.-Soviet strategic disparity, 151; and Adenauer, 154; and Khrushchev, 156; and suggested East-West summit, 159

Elbrick, C. Burke, 92

Enigma Variations (Elgar), 337

Erhard, Ludwig, 65, 68, 238, 239; and Adenauer, 222, 224; and German economic miracle, 223; and German-U.S. relations, 235; as Chancellor, 236

Erler, Fritz, 237

Eurocommunism, 255

European Coal and Steel community, 84, 94

European Community, 379

European Defense Community (EDC), 84, 86, 88, 91, 93, 94, 95, 100, 101, 106; and France, 92; collapse of, 99; failure of, 106

European Economic Community (EEC), 100, 106, 226, 228, 239, 331, 354

European Political Community, 94

Falin, Valentin, 306, 324

Farrell, William, 19

Federal Republic of Germany, 72; creation of, 65; and East Germany, 131, 171, 282, 288, 379; and Interzonal Trade Agreement, 167; after World War II, 213; political scene of, 223, 317–20; and Soviet Union, 288; and United Nations, 318, 320; and West Berlin, 326

Filbinger, Hans, 344

Finletter, Thomas, 228

Flag orders, 115

Flying Tigers, The, 25, 27, 28

Fock, Jeno, 251, 258

Ford, Gerald, 326, 336
Fordham University, 8
Four-Power Working Group, 128, 133, 138, 140, 141–44, 146, 154, 161–64, 185, 187, 188, 193
France, 13, 16, 98, 238
Franco, Francisco, 298–99
Franco-German rapprochement, 225
Franco-German Treaty of Friendship and Cooperation, 225, 226
Frank, Paul, 328
Frankfurt, 48
Frankfurter Hefte, 73
Free Democratic Party (FDP), 59, 223, 236, 239, 240, 279, 303, 304, 324, 343, 344
Freedom of the press, 273
Freeman, Paul, 34, 231
Freers, Ed, 128
Free University of Berlin, 119, 120
French National Assembly, 91
Friedrich, Carl, 79
Furtwaengler, Wilhelm, 111

Gandhi, Mahatma, 35, 36, 37
Gaullism, 95
Gaullist Rally of the French People, 95
Geneva Conference of Foreign Ministers, 144
Genscher, Hans Dietrich, 324, 331, 333, 340, 341, 343
George, Alexander, 124
German-American relations, 201
German armies, 16
German Democratic Republic (GDR), 13, 87, 88, 89, 110, 112, 121, 280, 282, 374; development of, 73; and West Germany, 171, 285; refugee flow from, 172
German Trade Union Federation, 62
German Trizonal Administration, 66
German unification, 377–80; possibility of, 73, 86, 87, 89, 109; Eden Plan for, 96; and Western proposal for, 140; in 1960s and 1970s, 233; Soviet opposition to, 234
Germany, 70, 71, 74, 342–45

Globalization, 386, 387
Gorbachev, Mikhail, 107, 148, 264, 374, 376, 377
Goulash Communism, 250, 266
Grabert, Horst, 334
Grass, Günther, 318, 377
Great Rift Valley, 44
Grewe, Wilhelm, 122, 128
Gromyko, Andrei, 85, 126, 130, 136, 145, 150, 288; and Gorbachev, 148; anti-American attitude of, 148; and Rusk, 198; and Cuban missile crisis, 204; and West Berlin negotiations, 282
Grosser, Alfred, 61
Groth, Edward, 53, 67
Gufler, Bernard, 107, 111
Guillaume, Günther, 333
Guisan, Henry, 13

Haffner, Sebastian, 86, 87
Haiphong Harbor, 306
Hall, H. Fielding, 31
Hallstein Doctrine, 285, 286
Hancock, Patrick, 137
Hanoi, 306
Harriman, Averill, 252, 385
Hartman, Arthur, 237
Harvey, Mose, 206
Hassel, Kai-Uwe von, 239
Healey, Dennis, 269
Heinemann, Gustav, 314, 317, 324, 334
Helms, Richard, 376
Helms, Wilhelm, 327
Helsinki agreement, 283
Hemingway, Ernest, 25
Henderson, Loy, 135
Henderson, Sir Nicholas, 320, 321, 322
Herter, Christian, 135, 138, 140, 164
Herz, Martin, 100
Hess, Rudolf, 117, 118
Heuss, Theodor, 78
Hillenbrand, Martin: youth of, 1–9; in Switzerland, 11; in Officers Training School, 15; in Burma, 18; marriage of, 24; in India, 31; in Mozambique, 41; in Bonn, 46, 207, 313–16; in Bremen, 49; in Paris, 90, 357; on

Andrei Gromyko, 126, 148; on
Wilhelm Greve, 140; on Couve de
Murville, 148; on Selwyn Lloyd, 149;
on Heinrich von Brentano, 149; on
Christian Herter, 149; on Dwight
Eisenhower, 153, 211; on Nikita
Khrushchev, 158; on Charles de
Gaulle, 160; on Harold Macmillan,
161; on John F. Kennedy, 211; on
George McGhee, 218; on Ludwig
Erhard, 231; on Kurt-Georg
Kiesinger, 240; in Budapest, 243–
44; and Lyndon Johnson, 245; and
Cardinal Mindszenty, 247; and Jeno
Fock, 251; and János Kádár, 251;
on Cardinal Mindszenty, 256; on
Richard Nixon, 267, 277; on
William Rogers, 277; on Henry
Kissinger, 277; on Pat Moynihan,
277; on Willy Brandt, 283; on Egon
Bahr, 283; and Lopez Bravo, 298;
and Portugal, 301; on Rainer Barzel,
319; on Jean Sauvagnargues, 321;
on Sir Nicholas Henderson, 321;
on Yuri Yefremov, 321; on Helmut
Kohl, 323; and Richard Nixon,
332; on Herbert Wehner, 335;
on Helmut Schmidt, 335, 336; on
Franz Josef Strauss, 344; and end
of ambassadorial appointment,
349; retirement of, from the Foreign
Service, 352; academic position of,
360
Hilsman, Roger, 179
Hinduism, 34
Hitler, Adolf, 8
Holocaust, 60, 61
Holtzman, Franklin, 374
Home, lord, 186
Honecker, Erich, 345
Hubertus, Prince zu und von
Loewenstein, 59
Huebner-Malinin Agreement, 117
Hull, Cordell, 16, 17
Hungarian Revolution, 112
Hungary, 381; and Vatican, 248;
government structure of, 249;
economic reform in, 256; and
crashing of Prague Spring, 259;

U.S. property claims against, 260;
reaction of, to Vietnam War, 262;
early economic reforms in, 264

India, 17, 31, 35
Indian Civil Service, 22, 32
Indian National Army, 36
Indochina, 97, 99
*In Europe's Name: Germany and the
Divided Continent* (Ash), 379
International conference of Communist
and workers' parties, 254
International Military Tribunal, 59
Interzonal Trade Agreement, 167
Iraq, 17
Iron Curtain, 112, 266
Israel, 327, 329
Istanbul, 163

Jackle, Kurt, 52
Japan, 40
Jenkins, Roy, 269
Jessup, Philip, 74
Jessup-Malik Agreement, 74
Jinnah, Mohammed Ali, 36
Jobert, Michel, 331
Johnson, Lyndon, 191, 240, 241, 242,
246, 271
Johnson, U. Alexis, 299
Judeo-Christian values, 389

Kádár, János, 249, 251, 253, 256,
258, 375
Kahn, Herman, 181
Kaisen, Wilhelm, 52, 319
Kali, 36
Karajan, Herbert von, 347
Kashmir, 34, 35
Kemp, Jan, 360, 361
Kennan, George, 82
Kennedy, John F., 168, 170, 171,
172, 174, 175, 179, 190; and
Khrushchev, 173; attitude of,
toward the State Department, 178;
and Cuban missile crisis, 205; in
West Germany, 215; and Germans,
216, 224
Kennedy administration, 169, 191
Keynesianism, 370

Khrushchev, Nikita, 88, 107, 124,
139, 142, 143, 149, 150, 169, 171–
75, 180, 252, 382; advent to power
of, 69; on Western influence in
Berlin, 115, 117; and Berlin crisis,
121, 125, 126; in United States,
155; and Eisenhower, 156; and
Paris summit, 165; and Kennedy,
170, 173; after Berlin crisis, 209
Kiesinger, Kurt-Georg, 240, 270, 278
Kipling, Rudyard, 32
Kissinger, Henry, 268, 275, 277, 286,
287, 292, 303, 306, 307, 308, 322,
355; on NATO, 269, 290; and
Nixon, 273; and State Department,
276; as Secretary of State, 328; and
EEC, 330; and Genscher, 331; in
West Germany, 339
Koblo, Martin, 54
Koenig, cardinal, 246
Koenig, Marie-Pierre-Joseph-François,
71
Kohl, Helmut, 318, 319, 323, 343,
345, 377
Kohler, Foy, 169, 179, 180, 181
Korea, 81
Korean War, 81
Kosygin, Aleksey, 281, 289, 308
Kozlov, Frol, 126, 150
Krekeler, Hans, 83
Kroll, Hans, 51
Krueger National Park, 44
Kuznetsov, Wassili, 308

Lafontaine, Oskar, 377
Laloy, Jean, 128, 138
Lamfalussy, Baron Alexandre, 371
Lampson Ted, 137
Laukhuff, Perry, 85
League of Nations, 144
Leber, Georg, 323, 329, 339
Leddy, John, 240, 244
Ledwidge, Bernard, 110
Legal realists, 7
Lemmer, Ernst, 188
Lend-lease legislation, 24, 25
Lerch, Françoise, 352
Libya, 294
Linlithgow, lord, 39
Lloyd, Selwyn, 123, 133, 137

Lodge, David, 359, 372
London Six-Power Conference, 64
Loudon, John, 349, 356
Lourenço Marques, 42
Luns, Joseph, 295

Machiavellianism, 370
Macmillan, Harold, 123, 133, 136,
139, 159, 170, 176, 184
Madras, 37
Malenkov, Georgi, 89
Malik, Jacob, 74
Malta, 294–95
Mansfield, Mike, 290
Mansfield Amendments, 290
Marshall, George C., 64, 330
Marshall Plan, 83, 330
Marx, Karl, 144
Marxism, 264
Marxism-Leninism, 263, 375
Mautner, Karl, 111
Mayer, René, 93, 101
Maymyo, 29
McCloy, John J., 74, 81
McGhee, George, 179, 207, 215,
245
McNamara, Robert, 230, 239
Meehan, Frank, 325
Mehta, Zubin, 337
Mende, Erich, 240
Menderes, Adnan, 163
Mendes-France, Pierre, 99
Menuhin, Yehudi, 272
Merchant, Livingston, 89, 92, 127,
133, 135, 169, 228
Merrill, Frank, 28, 29, 39
Merrill's Marauders, 39
Mikoyan, Anastas, 131
Mindszenty, cardinal, 246, 247, 256,
257
Mintoff, Dom, 294
Mitchell, John, 285, 287
Molotov, Vyacheslav, 64, 85, 96
Monnet, Jean, 83, 84
Morgenthau, Henry, 55
Morgenthau, Robert M., 296
Morris, Brewster, 214
Moscow Summit, 307–10
Moscow Treaty, 285, 289, 292, 293,
303, 305

Mouvement Républicain Populaire (MRP), 93
Moynihan, Pat, 275, 277
Mozambique, 41, 42, 44
Multilateral force (MLF), 225, 227, 228, 229, 237, 238
Multinational Nuclear Force (MNF), 337
Murphy, Robert, 49, 54, 67, 71, 127, 135, 262
Mutaguchi, Renya, 40
Mutual and balanced force reductions (MBFR), 289, 291

National Assembly of France, 93, 105
National Collegiate Athletic Association (NCAA), 361, 362
NATO. *See* North Atlantic Treaty Organization
NATO Council, 89
Naval intelligence, 42
Nehru, Javaharlal, 36
Nepal, 35
Nicolson, Harold, 384
Nine-Power Conference, 102, 103
Nixon, Richard, 262, 267, 271, 275, 282, 285, 287, 303, 306, 308, 309, 330, 332, 341; address to NATO by, 268; in West Berlin, 270; and Kissinger, 273; in Romania, 275; and Berlin, 281, 291; and Soviet Union, 310
Nollau, Günther, 333
Nomenklatura, 218, 375
Norstad, Lauris, 162, 227
Norstad Plan, 162
North Atlantic Treaty Organization (NATO), 90, 103, 106, 226, 274, 275, 295, 297, 328, 329, 331, 337, 354, 383; and Western security, 81; and Europe, 125; and Social Democratic Party, 126; and United States, 183; plans of, to transform into a nuclear power, 227; expulsion of, from France, 238; address to, by Nixon, 268; assessment of, by Kissinger, 269, 290; ministerial meetings of, 297
Nuclear Nonproliferation Treaty, 230, 243

Nuclear weapons, 196, 210, 382, 383, 387
Nuremberg Trials, 50, 59

Office of European Economic Cooperation (OEEC), 83
Office of Military Government United States (OMGUS), 49, 77
Officers Training School, 15
Ollenhauer, Erich, 82
Organization for Economic Cooperation and Development (OECD), 275
Orwell, George, 22
Osterheld, Horst, 224
Ostpolitik, 116, 288, 303, 317, 319, 335, 378, 379; origins of, 233; and Willy Brandt, 280
Owen, Henry, 228

Pact of Madrid, 299
Page, Edward, 103
Palais Rose negotiations, 88
Paris Agreements, 104–6
Parker, Leonard, 20
Parsons, Talcott, 80
Patman, Wright, 296
Paul VI, 271
Pearl Harbor, 22–26, 45
Pentagon, 132
People's Republic of China, 254, 288
Peter, János, 249
Phony war, 13
Pickett, Wascom J., 37
Pinay, M. Antoine, 93
Pleasure of Ruins, The (Macaulay), 54
Pleven, René, 84, 93
Pleven Plan, 84
Podgorny, Nikolai, 308
Poland, 13, 374, 381
Politburo, 87, 259, 303
Political correctness, 362
Ponto, Jürgen, 347
Portugal, 299, 300, 340
Potsdam Agreement, 56, 121, 130
Power and Morals (Hillenbrabd), 37, 76, 363
Prague Declaration, 88
Prague Spring, 253, 258, 259, 281, 375